BERTOLT BRECHT
COLLECTED PLAYS

Volume 5

BERTOLT

Bertolt Brecht: Plays, Poetry, & Prose

Edited by
Ralph Manheim and John Willett
Wolfgang Sauerländer, Associate Editor

BRECHT

COLLECTED PLAYS

VOLUME 5

Life of Galileo

The Trial of Lucullus

Mother Courage and Her Children

Pantheon Books, A Division of Random House, New York

Library of Congress Catalog Card Number: 71-113718
ISBN: 0-394-47107-5

Contents

Introduction

The crisis years 1938–39 and
their aftermath

1

The three works in this volume were of particular importance
in Brecht's development, and they occupied him longer and
more intensively than anything else he wrote. Dating from just
after he turned forty, they are in every sense crucial, for not
only did they originate in a crisis of human history but their
later evolution spanned much the same years as that crisis took
to work itself out. In Brecht's own life they cover three very
different periods: his Scandinavian exile, his years on the fringe
of Hollywood, then his return after the Second World War to
an honored position in the Communist half of Germany. Two
of them, *Galileo* and *Mother Courage*, were in 1947 and 1949 given
productions which struck him, quite rightly, as among the chief
events in his theatrical career; all three were subjected to textual
changes which have drawn much critical comment and attention, notably those made to *Lucullus* in 1951; finally it has become
common, if questionable, practice to take the figure of Galileo
as in every way a spokesman for the author's own opinions.
Hence the wealth of notes and variant material relating to these
plays. Hence also the inclusion of so much of it in the present
edition.

For Brecht 1938 seems to have been a general turning-point,
marking a new detachment from immediate political tasks,
whether anti-Nazi like the sketches making up *Fear and Misery
of the Third Reich* (whose wartime version was called *The Private
Life of the Master Race*) or pro-Soviet like the "Lenin Cantata"
which he wrote with Hanns Eisler the previous year. The

change affected his esthetic outlook, not only his willingness to tackle contemporary themes, and it came at a time when Brecht on his Danish island was finding himself in sharp disagreement with the concept of Socialist Realism advocated by Georg Lukács and the more influential Moscow-based exiled intellectuals. What made this extra painful was that Lukács's views were being set out in *Das Wort*, a Moscow monthly magazine of which Brecht was an editor and in which his anti-Nazi sketches and his short poems for the German Freedom Radio were then appearing. When in June, a month after a group of the *Fear and Misery* sketches had been performed in Paris under the title *99%*, Lukács wrote approvingly about one of them, Brecht commented in his diary that "Lukács has welcomed 'The Informer' as if I were a sinner who had entered the bosom of the Salvation Army." Evidently this was something that he was by no means keen to do.

There was something much more serious at stake here than a mere literary debate, and Brecht was made fully aware of this fact by his knowledge of the Soviet scene. Of the three Russian friends whom he had approached in March 1937 with a view to forming an international "Diderot Society" of like-minded theater people, within a matter of weeks Eisenstein had been denounced in *Pravda* and stopped working on *Bezhin Meadow*, Okhlopkhov had lost his theater, and Tretiakov had been arrested and shot. This was only part of a much more widespread cultural reaction which also involved measures against Meyerhold and Tairov, the other two Soviet theater directors of that time who can be linked with Brecht, and which coincided unmistakeably with the political terror under Stalin's notorious Commissar for Internal Affairs, Yezhov. By the middle of 1937 Kun and Knorin, the two Comintern members who had shown themselves friendly to him in Moscow in 1935, had been arrested and tortured, while one of his leading actresses, Carola Neher, had been arrested with her Russian husband and sentenced to ten years' hard labor on an espionage charge; all three were later killed. Such horrifying developments within Brecht's own camp combined with the unchecked progress of the Nazi enemy (e.g., the swallowing of Austria in the spring of 1938), to bring a new element of sadness and solitude into his work. Thus

Walter Benjamin, who arrived in Brecht's village at the end of June 1938 when Tretiakov's probable fate had become clear, and stayed till after the Munich Agreement, found that his friend seemed to have got much less prickly and provocative, and interpreted this in a letter to Theodor Adorno as a sign of his growing isolation.

It was what Brecht in his verse of 1938–39 calls "the dark times," a "bad time for poetry": a kind of paralyzed horror fills the poems which he then wrote about Neher and Tretiakov and which remained unpublished until after his death. Though the émigré press continued to publish his earlier and more topical writings, the satires, songs, and playlets now fell off, nor after 1937 did he make any further public statements or speeches in the anti-Fascist cause. He did however write a number of essays in refutation of the "arbiter of art" Lukács, all of which likewise remained unpublished even though the two best known were clearly intended for *Das Wort;* after March 1939 that magazine itself ceased to appear. Also during 1938 Brecht began writing the still more private *Me-Ti* aphorisms (or *Book of Changes*), with their half-camouflaged criticisms of Stalin and evident doubts about the Soviet show trials. Elsewhere he had begun to turn increasingly to remoter peoples and periods: to Roman history in his unfinished Julius Caesar novel, to the Chinese poets in a group of translations from Arthur Waley, to the German classics in the literary sonnets of that summer. At the same time he was bringing out a new selection of his poems, originally as part of the Malik-Verlag edition of his work, whose first two volumes had appeared in the spring, then when the Nazis seized the sheets at the binders' in the Sudetenland, as a new book of *Svendborger Gedichte* to be printed in Copenhagen.

He wrote *Galileo* during the first three weeks of November 1938, though he must have carried the idea around in his head much longer than that and got through a good deal of preliminary reading. It was his first big play for four years, and from the outset it was a statement of faith in the "new age," irrespective of setbacks, and also in the power of the human reason in face of authoritarian systems of thought. The principal figure had long interested him, for Galileo's had been one of the cases considered for the series of trial scenes which he had planned to write before 1933, and (as Professor Schumacher has suggested in his valuable book on the play; see p. 265) it could indeed have been brought to mind again by the tricentenary in that year. Among the books which he used in his researches, according to Schumacher, were the standard German biography by Emil Wohlwill, nineteenth-century translations of the *Discorsi* and of Bacon's *Novum Organum*, and German versions of Jeans's *The Mysterious Universe* and Eddington's *The Nature of the Physical World*; he also had discussions with the Danish physicist Professor C. Møller, then one of Niels Bohr's assistants. He stuck quite closely to the historical facts, apart from altering Galileo's family circumstances (he actually had three children, of whom Virginia disappeared into a convent at the age of sixteen); the smuggling out of the *Discorsi* in 1636 did indeed take place. Since other left-wing German novelists and playwrights had already begun using comparable historical settings—Feuchtwanger and Heinrich Mann for instance, and Friedrich Wolf in his Beaumarchais play—Brecht was far from being unorthodox in this (for him) new venture. And, satisfactory as it must have been to have Aristotle as the ideological villain of the piece, he almost at once began worrying about the conventionality of its form.

Early in 1939 he revised it, but without making any drastic changes; inspired by the *Dialogues Concerning the Two Chief World Systems*, he also began working on *The Messingkauf Dialogues*, which were to set out his theoretical ideas of theater. In March he looked out his old project for *The Good Woman of Szechwan*, then on April 23 he left Denmark for Lindingö in Sweden, where he was to stay a bare year. It was here that he wrote the other two plays in this volume, both of which were finished by early November and seem to have been written more rapidly and with greater ease than *Szechwan*, on which he worked incon-clusively during the summer. *Lucullus* was commissioned by Stockholm radio and completed in a fortnight; Hilding Rosen-berg was due to write the music, but it never got done and the broadcast did not take place. The play itself can be seen as a by-product of the Caesar novel, or at least of Brecht's reading for it, which had included Plutarch, Dio Cassius, Suetonius and Sallust, now reviewed in the light of the Nazi invasion of Po-

land and the Anglo-French mobilization. *Mother Courage*, with
its theme of the devastating effects of a European war and the
blindness of anyone hoping to profit by it, is said to have been
written in a month; judging by the almost complete absence of
drafts or any other evidence of preliminary studies it must have
been an exceptionally direct piece of inspiration. The obvious
precedents here, though we do not know how Brecht actually
used them, were Schiller's *Wallensteins Lager*, with its mongrel
army milling round the canteen tents and Grimmelshausen's
picaresque seventeenth-century novel *Die Landstörzerin Coura-
sche*, which must have given him the name. But if Grimmelshausen's Amazonian adventuress shared certain turns of
speech with Brecht's canteen woman, she none the less sprang
from a higher social class and followed a career more like that
of his Yvette. Nor, contrary to what some critics have suggested, can he have been much influenced by the sutler Lotte
Svärd of Johan Ludvig Runeberg's early nineteenth-century
ballads about the Russian-Swedish war, for she (in C. B. Shaw's
translation) was "a pearl on the pathway of war," always up
with the troops; "And the dear young soldiers' heroic mood/
She loved in its full display." Brecht's Courage was more like
a blend of Widow Begbick in his *A Man's a Man* with that
favourite military character, Jaroslav Hašek's Good Soldier
Schweyk.

The first of the three plays to be performed was *Lucullus*,
which was broadcast by the Bern studio of the Swiss-German
radio on May 12, 1940, while Norway and Holland were falling
to Hitler and the blitzkrieg on France was impending; alas, no
recording has survived. Brecht himself at that time had just
arrived in Finland, where he now began work with the opera
conductor Simon Parmet on the setting of the *Courage* songs.
According to Parmet's recollections of some seventeen years
after, Brecht was hoping for a counterpart to the *Threepenny
Opera*, in which the songs would play a similar role and lead to
a comparable success. Though he appeared satisfied with the
result, the music for the first production at the Zurich Schauspielhaus a year later was written by the Swiss composer Paul
Burkhard, seemingly without the benefit of any personal contact with Brecht. *Galileo* too was under consideration by the

same theater, which by then must have been the one professional German-language theater left outside the Nazi orbit; but unfortunately the swift Nazi victory in the west seems to have made it too dangerous to stage any successor to *Mother Courage* until the whole tide of the war had turned. Not that the timing of these three Swiss productions can in fact have been all that important from Brecht's point of view, since under wartime conditions he could neither attend them nor have any effective say. Nor indeed were they what he had originally planned to do with the plays, for *Galileo* had been meant for production in New York, while the part of the object of putting a dumb character in *Mother Courage* is said to have been to give his wife Helene Weigel a role which she could act in any non-German theatre (e.g., in the first place, Stockholm). As for their results, he could only judge them by such hearsay as he could pick up, which was to the effect that despite fine settings by Teo Otto and a magnificent performance by Therese Giehse as Courage the point of both plays had somehow been missed, Courage impressing the audience above all as the irrepressible mother, Galileo three and a half years later as the cunning intellectual who shows that in the end reason must prevail and the truth get out.

2

Within a month of the *Courage* premiere—hence before he could take the play up again—Brecht left Finland and traveled via Moscow and the Trans-Siberian railway to California, where he found a house in Santa Monica. Living in what the actor Fritz Kortner called "a kind of penurious comfort," he seems at first to have been quite disorientated and unable to work, then in the course of 1942 to have embarked on various more or less mediocre film projects, of which the most important and lucrative was a script for Fritz Lang's *Hangmen Also Die*. Though he himself moved almost entirely among the exiled German community who had sponsored his entry into the United States, even then the first steps were being taken to introduce his work to American readers, for in 1941 New Directions published a

translation of *Mother Courage* by H. R. Hays, to whom Eisler had
given a script, while two years later a translation of *Lucullus*
followed. Brecht's own first serious return to these two plays
dates from his meeting with Paul Dessau in New York early in
1943, in connection with a Brecht recital at the New School in
which Peter Lorre and Elisabeth Bergner were to take part.
Dessau, who was then working on a New Jersey chicken farm,
had written the music for the Paris *99%*, and a song of his was
on the program; when the lady soloist dropped out Brecht made
Dessau sing it himself. Pleased with the result, Brecht gave him
a number of texts with a view to possible setting, then invited
him to Hollywood, where at some undefined date he handed
him the *Mother Courage* songs, specifying the melody for the
opening song as he had previously done with Parmet; these
were actually completed in 1946. He also gave him the script of
Lucullus, leading Dessau to conclude that he "wanted to see
Lucullus turned into an opera." However, by asking Dessau if
he could not interest Stravinsky in writing the music for this
work he seems to have effectively discouraged the one composer
without getting any response from the other, who in the event
told Dessau that he was booked up for the next two years. Later,
after the end of the war, the director Henry Schnitzler got
Brecht's agreement to let Roger Sessions make an opera, which
was performed at Los Angeles on April 18, 1947, but has remained surprisingly little known. It does not seem that Brecht
took any very close interest in this undertaking, which was of
course based on Hays's translation rather than on his own text.
It was otherwise with the American *Galileo*, which for Brecht
was certainly the most important achievement of his whole
six-year stay in the United States, and of all productions of his
plays the one to which he devoted the most thought. He had
looked at the play briefly in the winter of 1941–42, when Oskar
Homolka was thinking of a production, but when nothing came
of this he put it aside first for film work, then to concentrate on
the writing of *Simone Machard*, *Schweyk*, and *The Duchess of Malfi*
adaptation (his first venture into English). In the winter of
1943–44—that is, after the Zurich première had at last taken
place—he spent some four months in New York, where he
managed to interest the producer Jed Harris, who had put on

Wilder's *Our Town* in 1938. When he got back to Santa Monica (and to concentrated work on *The Caucasian Chalk Circle*) he began thinking how to amend *Galileo* so as to make the smuggling of the *Discorsi* seem less heroic and more in tune with the real fate of the truth in Nazi Germany and the conformist attitude of scientists at war. The Harris project somehow fizzled out, but he was now seeing a certain amount of Charles Laughton, who invited him to one-man readings of *Measure for Measure* and *The Tempest*, and for whom he wrote the long poem "Garden in Progress" that summer. Stimulated possibly by Orson Welles, at some point Laughton got and read a translation of Brecht's play.

Two factors seem to have influenced Laughton in his preoccupation with *Galileo*, which lasted on and off for the next three years. The first was his discontent with the kind of supporting parts and second-rate scripts which he had been getting after his brilliant start in such films as Korda's *Rembrandt* (for which Brecht's old colleague Carl Zuckmayer had written the script). As his biographer Kurt Singer put it,

How could he escape this treadmill? He thought he saw his great opportunity in a play by the German dramatist Berthold Brecht.

The second, also according to Singer, was his organization of a small Shakespeare reading group with a discharged GI called Bill Cottrell who heard one of his solo readings in Californian army hospitals and became the inquisitor in the Hollywood production. That autumn he agreed with Brecht that they would set aside the existing translations (which included one by Desmond Vesey and one by Welles's nominees Brainerd Duffield and Emerson Crocker) in order to adapt the play into English together. Brecht's diary shows that they had started by December 10, 1944, but in the first half of the new year there were long interruptions, first between February and April, (when Laughton was acting in the pirate film *Captain Kidd* and Brecht consoled himself by starting to put the Communist Manifesto into hexameters), then in June and July when Brecht was in New York for the production of Eric Bentley's translation of *The Private Life of the Master Race* and further work on

The Duchess of Malfi. During this year he also wrote some more film treatments. Otherwise the collaboration seems to have gone much as he describes it in "Building up a part," (see p. 230) with Laughton proposing the elimination of Doppone, the "positive appearance" of the iron founder in scene 2, the argument between Ludovico and Galileo in the sunspot scene, and the transposition of the handing-over of the *Discorsi* in scene 14, while Brecht worked to make the latter more of a piece with Galileo's concern for his own comforts, of which thinking now became one. In this, as in the new emphasis on Galileo's sensuality, he was aided by Laughton's character, of which Professor Bentley has said that

> It is unlikely that anyone again will combine as he did every appearance of intellectual brilliance with every appearance of physical self-indulgence.

An added topicality was given by the dropping of the first atomic bomb on August 6, but about the only significant change to which this led was the addition of the passage about a "universal cry of fear" in that same scene. The concept of a Hippocratic oath for scientists was not yet included, though Brecht drafted the relevant passage, (the idea itself having already been put forward by Lancelot Law Whyte in *Nature* in 1938 and discussed in an editorial in the *New York Times*).

With the exception of the ballad-singer's song the American version of the play was finished by December 1, 1945, when Laughton read the result to the Brechts, Eisler, Berthold Viertel, Feuchtwanger, and friends. A little later he read it also to Orson Welles, who agreed to direct it in the following spring, when the impresario Paul Czinner hoped to finance a production. Laughton thought this too early, while a subsequent discussion between Brecht, Mike Todd, and Joseph Losey (whom Brecht had met in Moscow in 1935) broke down, according to Losey, when Todd offered to "dress the production in Renaissance furniture from the Hollywood warehouses." This occurred some time in the middle of 1946, and left Laughton himself holding the baby, with Losey as director. Abe Burrows, part author of *Guys and Dolls*, was brought in to translate the missing songs, but his work was not accepted, so that in the end

the job was done by Brecht himself and Laughton, with some
help from Losey and from Hanns Eisler who composed the
music; (Albert Brush was named in the New York program as
adaptor of the "lyrics"). The production finally materialized on
July 30, 1947, in the little Coronet Theater in Beverly Hills, with
simple sets by Robert Davison. A New York production was
then to follow, presented by T. Edward Hambleton with an
entirely different cast apart from Laughton himself, but by the
time this opened on December 7 Brecht and Eisler had been
heard before the Un-American Activities Committee and had
left the country. A week later it closed abruptly, for the reasons
given thus in Laughton's biography:

> At first it seemed destined for success. The New York
> drama critics hailed Laughton's performance and admired
> the skill with which he had adapted the original text, which
> was rather ponderous and wordy, into a fast-moving and
> stirring drama. However, the production soon ran into
> snags.
>
> The trouble lay in the political affiliations of the play-
> wright. Berthold Brecht was a dyed-in-the-wool Commu-
> nist. On the point of being deported from the United States
> for his Communist activities, he escaped and turned up in
> East Germany, where he became the Soviet's pet author,
> supervising the literary life of the Soviet-controlled zone
> and turning out odes to Stalin on the various state holidays.
> The musical score for the play on Galileo had been com-
> posed by Hanns Eisler, another convinced Communist who
> had composed many propaganda songs, including *The Co-
> mintern March*. Several actors in the cast turned out to be
> Communists, too. [. . .]
>
> When the facts of the matter were put before Laughton
> by his manager, Charles saw that he was playing into Com-
> munists' hands. He had fallen into bad company. There was
> nothing left for him to do but withdraw from the produc-
> tion . . .

3

None the less on arriving in Zurich Brecht set down his experiences of the collaboration in what was in effect the first of the "Model" books, "Building up a part," with its accompanying photographs of the two performances by Ruth Berlau; it also forms the subject of section 63 of the *Short Organum for the Theater*, which he was writing about the same time. A year later, on October 22, 1948, he went to East Berlin to join Erich Engel, the original director of *In the Jungle* in 1923, in staging *Mother Courage* at Max Reinhardt's old Deutsches Theater, now being managed by Wolfgang Langhoff, the Eilif of the Zurich première. This production too, with Helene Weigel in the title part, was decisive for him not only in leading to the formation of the Berliner Ensemble but, at the Paris International Theater Festival six years later, in securing his long-delayed recognition as the greatest theater man of our day. In the changes which he made to its text he was certainly influenced by what he understood to be the faults of the Zurich production, but, as our notes show, they were not in fact very extensive and they were supplemented by further small amendments before his Munich production with Therese Giehse in 1950. These alterations have been much discussed by Brecht's interpreters, as evidence that he was unable to make his characters as inhuman as his ideology required them to be, but they seem slight by comparison with his wholesale rewriting of his earlier plays, and more like safeguards against any misunderstanding by actors and director than revisions of the original conception.

The fact perhaps is that in this case Brecht's relentless itch to alter his own work was transferred to the (alas unrealized) film version, whose making was decided on as early as September 1949. Quite apart from the introduction of a love interest for dumb Kattrin and the changes (of nationality and prominence) resulting from the choice of Simone Signoret as Yvette and Bernard Blier as the cook, the basic conception of the play was in some measure altered to reflect the problems of occupied Germany after the war. With his old collaborator Emil Burri he now stressed the division of the country, the "Babylonian confusion of languages," and the role of the camp prostitutes, of whom Yvette was just the most socially successful. As in his adaptation of *Coriolanus* in the same years, the defenders of the sleeping city in the drum scene became armed peasants, driving off the attacking Croats, with whom Courage finally decided her best interests lay. He also however included a devastating blow at those whom many German audiences liked to see as the play's true heroes, the "little people." "Nonsense," says a peasant in the take after Eilif's death. "The little people are the worst of the lot. Why? The big shots plan it, and the little people carry it out."

During the play's rehearsals he and Dessau met a Hamburg director who asked if *Lucullus* could be made into a radio opera for the North-West German Radio. No contract followed, but the suggestion again stimulated Dessau, who set to work on an opera version in the course of 1949 and to that end persuaded Brecht to make many of the textual changes described in our editorial note. It was he who insisted that this should be described as an opera, whereas Hermann Scherchen, the designated conductor, wanted it rather to be a "musical play." Unfortunately in February 1948 the Soviet Central Committee, with Zhdanov as its chief spokesman, had strongly condemned the "formalism" of such composers as Prokofieff and Shostakovitch, and in all the arts the old standards of Socialist Realism were now being reinforced, in East Germany no less dutifully than elsewhere. Thus the discordant score and the undifferentiating pacifism of the new work disturbed the cultural politicians, who only agreed to let it be performed at first to a closed audience of party people and Free German Youth on the very day (March 17, 1951) when the Central Committee passed a resolution "Against Formalism in Art and Literature." The ensuing reviews were predictably hostile, objecting alike to the Stravinskian flavor of the music and to the cool detachment of Brecht's text, which in the current state of international tension failed to come down explicitly on the Russian side. As a result the directors of the State Opera proposed to drop the planned production, and were threatened with legal action by Brecht, who had a contract and was not subject to any party discipline. This situation was only resolved by a meeting be-

tween Brecht and Dessau and members of the government led
by the prime minister, who persuaded them to add the passages
exempting a defensive war (which many intelligent East Germans then feared they might have to fight) from the general
condemnation. A good deal of outside criticism of Brecht followed, much of it coming from the western propaganda services
and the organs of the Congress for Cultural Freedom. Brecht
himself however was not at all averse to telling the story or, as
in his notes, spelling out the additions (though not the quite
equally drastic changes involved in making an opera of the play
in the first place). And certainly *Lucullus* as subsequently
played, starting with the public première on October 12 and
continuing through further productions and more revisions by
the composer, remains a serious work of art and very remote
from the kind of tuneful party-line optimism which its critics
would have best liked to see.

In 1953 Brecht also had a new version made of *Galileo*, which
kept the changed gist of the American version while re-intro-
ducing a number of passages, and even entire scenes or sub-
scenes, from the prewar version, of which the most vital was the
long opening speech about the "new times." This had its première at Cologne on April 15, 1955, after which Brecht began
preparing to stage it himself with the Berliner Ensemble. As
Galileo he now cast Ernst Busch, who was playing Azdak in
The Caucasian Chalk Circle and the cook in the revival of *Mother
Courage*, an old Communist friend who had sung to the troops
in Spain, been interned in 1939 by the French, then handed over
to the Gestapo and wounded in the bombing of Berlin: in short
a somewhat different proposition from Laughton. From mid-
December to the end of March 1956 he conducted rehearsals,
which were recorded on tape and have been extensively
analyzed by his assistant Käthe Rülicke (in *Materialien zu Brecht's
"Leben des Galilei,"* Suhrkamp-Verlag, 1963). They were brought
to an end by his illness, so that the production was only completed under Engel's direction and after Brecht's death, when
Busch, who had all along disagreed with him about the need
to "condemn" Galileo in scene 14, was unable to make the
handing-over of the *Discorsi* seem anything but a piece of justified foxiness. The best clue to Brecht's own intentions lies

perhaps in his repeated insistence to the actors that Galileo's "My aim is not to prove that I've been right but to find out whether or not I have been" was the most important sentence in the play.

The marks of all these vicissitudes lie buried in the texts as we now have them; they will, we hope, become visible from a study of the notes. Their background is what gives Brecht's works their particular depth, as well as those elements of inconsistency which were so characteristic of him. Yet these three plays' surface seems firm enough, and it has not really altered all that much since their origins at the beginning of the war. *Lucullus* may have been more economical in its original form, but it is still an antimilitarist work, not an apology for the People's Army and the People's Police. *Mother Courage* still argues that war is a continuation of business by other means and that those who make it so are being fatally short-sighted, often against their own better instincts. *Galileo* is still a hymn to reason and a stubborn proclamation of faith in the "new age," however delayed it may be, besides being an attack on rigid official dogmas—of which there is only one in Eastern Europe today, as its East German audiences cannot but know. The two latter plays overlap significantly in their coverage of the first third of the seventeenth century, a period which specially interested Brecht because it led to scientific humanism as he understood it (as well as to the late Shakespeare plays), yet at the same time did such lasting damage to his own country. The Thirty Years' War, he told Parmet, should really be known as the Three Hundred Years' War.

The most obvious thing about these works is that they mark the start of a new stage in Brecht's writing, the period (in most critics' opinion) of his greatest plays. They represent a decisive break from the more short-term and (on the whole) short-winded political works which preceded them, whether it be interpreted as a development away from propagandist Communism to a more broadly human outlook or, as nowadays in Eastern Europe, as a reaction against such sectarian methods as montage and agit-prop and a reconciliation with the spirit of the Popular Front against Fascism and with Socialist Realism as it is now conceived to be. Which of these views one in fact favors scarcely matters so long as nothing is done to falsify the attitudes of mind adopted by Brecht himself and others at the time. Either way it is clear that these are critical plays, arising from a critical situation, and that for Brecht, as for the wider world, the crisis lay not only in the policies of the Nazis and their helpers but also inside Stalin's USSR. Here, as so often, he proved to be a writer geared to his age, which was at once a new one and a dark one. As that crisis erupted in war, with all its consequences, many of the old polarities which had stimulated him were blurred or altered. The world itself was changing, as well as his own sometimes precarious circumstances, and in these three plays, for the rest of his life, he was working the implications out.

THE EDITORS

Life of Galileo

Play

Collaborator: M. Steffin

Translators: Wolfgang Sauerlander and Ralph Manheim

CHARACTERS

GALILEO GALILEI

ANDREA SARTI

MRS. SARTI, Galileo's
housekeeper, Andrea's
mother

LUDOVICO MARSILI, a rich
young man

MR. PRIULI, procurator of the
university of Padua

SAGREDO, Galileo's friend

VIRGINIA, Galileo's daughter

FEDERZONI, a lens grinder,
Galileo's collaborator

THE DOGE

SENATORS

COSMO DE' MEDICI, Grand
Duke of Florence

THE LORD CHAMBERLAIN

THE THEOLOGIAN

THE PHILOSOPHER

THE MATHEMATICIAN

THE OLDER LADY-IN-WAITING

THE YOUNGER
LADY-IN-WAITING

A LACKEY at the Grand
Duke's court

TWO NUNS

TWO SOLDIERS

THE OLD WOMAN

A FAT PRELATE

TWO SCHOLARS

TWO MONKS

TWO ASTRONOMERS

A VERY THIN MONK

THE VERY OLD CARDINAL

FATHER CHRISTOPHER CLAVIUS,
an astronomer

THE LITTLE MONK

THE CARDINAL INQUISITOR

CARDINAL BARBERINI, later
Pope Urban VIII

CARDINAL BELLARMINE

TWO ECCLESIASTICAL
SECRETARIES

TWO YOUNG LADIES

FILIPPO MUCIUS, a scholar

MR. GAFFONE, rector of the
university of Pisa

THE BALLAD SINGER

HIS WIFE

VANNI, an iron founder

AN ATTENDANT

A HIGH OFFICIAL

A SHADY INDIVIDUAL

A MONK

A PEASANT

A BORDER GUARD

A CLERK

MEN, WOMEN, CHILDREN

1

Galileo Galilei, teacher of mathematics in Padua, sets out to demonstrate the new Copernican system.

> In the year sixteen hundred and nine
> Science' light began to shine.
> At Padua city, in a modest house
> Galileo Galilei set out to prove
> The sun is still, the earth is on the move.

Galileo's modest study in Padua. It is morning. A boy, Andrea, the housekeeper's son, brings in a glass of milk and a roll.

GALILEO (*washing his torso, puffing and happy*)   Put the milk on the table, but don't shut any books.

ANDREA   Mother says we've got to pay the milkman. Or he'll make a circle around our house, Mr. Galilei.

GALILEO   You must say, "describe a circle," Andrea.

ANDREA   Of course. If we don't pay he'll describe a circle around us, Mr. Galilei.

GALILEO   And Mr. Cambione, the bailiff, will head for us in a straight line, covering what sort of distance between two points?

ANDREA (*grinning*)   The shortest.

GALILEO   Good. I've got something for you. Look behind the star charts.

(*Andrea fishes a large wooden model of the Ptolemaic system from behind the star charts*)

ANDREA   What is it?

GALILEO   An armillary sphere. It shows how the stars move around the earth, in the opinion of the ancients.

ANDREA How?

GALILEO Let's examine it. First of all: description.

ANDREA There's a little stone in the middle.

GALILEO That's the earth.

ANDREA There are rings around it, one inside another.

GALILEO How many?

ANDREA Eight.

GALILEO Those are the crystal spheres.

ANDREA There are balls fastened to the rings . . .

GALILEO The stars.

ANDREA There are tags with words painted on them.

GALILEO What kind of words?

ANDREA Names of stars.

GALILEO Such as?

ANDREA The bottommost ball is the moon, it says. The one above it is the sun.

GALILEO Now spin the sun around.

ANDREA (*sets the rings in motion*) That's pretty. But we're so shut in.

GALILEO (*drying himself*) Yes, that's just what I felt when I saw the thing for the first time. Some people feel that way. (*Throws Andrea the towel, meaning that he should rub his back*) Walls and rings and immobility. For two thousand years men believed that the sun and all the stars of heaven were circling around them. The pope, the cardinals, princes and scholars, the captains, merchants, fishwives and schoolchildren, all thought they were sitting motionless inside this crystal sphere. But now we'll get out of it, Andrea, we're in full sail. Because the old times are gone, and this is a new age. For the last hundred years mankind has seemed to be expecting something.

Cities are narrow, and so are minds. Superstition and plague. But now we say: Since things are thus and so, they will not remain thus and so. Because, my friend, everything is in motion.

I like to think that it all started with ships. From time immemorial ships had hugged the shores, but suddenly they abandoned the shores, and sailed out upon the oceans.

A rumor has sprung up on our old continent—that there are new continents. And now that our ships have been going

there, people on all the laughing continents are saying that
the big dreaded ocean is nothing but a small lake. And a great
desire has arisen to find the causes of all things: Why a stone
falls when it's released and how it goes up when it's thrown
into the air. Every day something new is being discovered.
Even men a hundred years old let youngsters shout in their
ears to tell them about the latest discoveries.

A great deal has been discovered, but there's much more to
be discovered. Plenty of work for future generations.

When I was a young man in Siena I saw some masons, after
arguing for five minutes, discard an age-old method of moving granite blocks in favor of a new and more practical arrangement of the ropes. Then and there I realized that the old
times are over and that this is a new day. Some men will know
all about their habitat, this heavenly body they live on.
They're no longer satisfied with what it says in the ancient
books.

Because where faith had ruled for a thousand years, doubt
has now set in. Today everybody is saying: Yes, that's what
the books tell us, but we want to see for ourselves. The most
sacred truths are being looked into. Things that were never
held in doubt are being doubted now.

All this has stirred up a breeze that lifts even the gold-
braided coats of princes and prelates, revealing stout or
spindly legs, legs just the same as ours. The heavens, we know
now, are empty. And that has given rise to joyous laughter.

The waters of the earth supply power to the new spinning
wheels, and in shipyards and the workshops of ropers and
sailmakers new methods enable five hundred hands to work
together.

I foresee that in our lifetime people will talk astronomy in
the market place. Even the sons of fishwives will go to school.
The people of our cities are always eager for novelty, they
will be glad to hear that in our new astronomy the earth
moves too. It has always been taught that the stars are pinned
to a crystal vault, which prevents them from falling down.
Now we've mustered the courage to let them float free, with
nothing to hold them; they're in full sail, just as our ships are
in full sail.

And the earth rolls merrily around the sun, and all the fishwives, merchants, princes and cardinals, and even the pope, roll with it.

Overnight, the universe has lost its center and now in the morning it has any number of centers. Now any point in the universe may be taken as a center. Because, suddenly, there's plenty of room.

Our ships sail far out into the ocean, our planets revolve far out in space, and even in chess nowadays the rooks range over many fields.

What does the poet say? "Oh, early morning . . ."

ANDREA

"Oh, early morning of beginning!
Oh, breath of wind that
Comes from new-found shores!"

And you'd better drink your milk. There'll be people coming in a minute.

GALILEO   Did you figure out what I told you yesterday?

ANDREA   What? You mean Kippernick and all that turning business?

GALILEO   Yes.

ANDREA   No. Why do you want me to figure it out? It's too hard for me, I'll only be eleven in October.

GALILEO   I want you to understand it, you in particular. To make everybody understand, that's why I work and buy expensive books instead of paying the milkman.

ANDREA   But I can see that the sun's not in the same place in the evening and morning. So it can't stand still. It just can't.

GALILEO   You "see"! What do you see? You see nothing at all. You're just gaping. Gaping isn't seeing. (*He places the iron washstand in the center of the room*) Now, that's the sun. Sit down. (*Andrea sits down in the only chair. Galileo stands behind him*) Where is the sun, right or left?

ANDREA   Left.

GALILEO   And how does it get to the right?

ANDREA   When you carry it over to the right. Naturally.

GALILEO   Only then? (*He picks up the chair with him in it and turns it halfway around*) Where's the sun now?

ANDREA   On the right.

GALILEO   Has it moved?

ANDREA   I guess it hasn't.

GALILEO   What moved?

ANDREA   Me.

GALILEO (*roars*)   Wrong! Stupid! the chair!

ANDREA   But me with it!

GALILEO   Obviously. The chair is the earth. You're sitting on it.

MRS. SARTI (*has come in to make the bed. She has watched the scene*)
Mr. Galilei, what on earth are you doing with my boy?

GALILEO   I'm teaching him how to see, Mrs. Sarti.

MRS. SARTI   By carrying him around the room?

ANDREA   Never mind, mother. You don't understand.

MRS. SARTI   Is that so? But of course you understand. A young
gentleman is here, he wants to take lessons. Very well
dressed, and he has a letter of recommendation. (*Hands over
the letter*) When you get through with my Andrea, he'll be
saying that two times two make five. You've got him all mixed
up. Last night he tried to prove to me that the earth moves
around the sun. He says some fellow by the name of Kippernick figured it out.

ANDREA   Didn't that Kippernick figure it out, Mr. Galilei? You
tell her.

MRS. SARTI   Do you really tell him such nonsense? He blabs it
out in school and the priests come running to me because of
all the sinful stuff he says. You should be ashamed of yourself,
Mr. Galilei.

GALILEO (*eating his breakfast*)   Mrs. Sarti, as a result of our investigations, and after heated arguments, Andrea and I have
made discoveries which we can no longer keep secret from
the world. A new age has dawned, a great age, and it's a joy
to be alive.

MRS. SARTI   I see. I hope we'll able to pay the milkman in the
new age, Mr. Galilei. (*Pointing at the letter*) Just do me a favor
and don't turn this one away. I'm thinking of the milk bill.
(*Out*)

GALILEO (*laughing*)   Just give me time to finish my milk!—(*To
Andrea*) Well, you seem to have understood something yesterday after all.

ANDREA   I only told her to get a rise out of her. But it's not true. You only turned the chair with me in it around sideways, but not like this. (*He moves his arm in a circle to the front*) Because I'd have fallen off the chair, and that's a fact. Why didn't you turn the chair over? Because that would prove I'd fall off the earth if it moved that way. There.

GALILEO   But I proved to you . . .

ANDREA   But last night I figured out that if the earth turned that way I'd hang down head first at night, and that's a fact.

GALILEO   (*takes an apple from the table*)   Look here. This is the earth.

ANDREA   Don't always use that kind of example, Mr. Galilei. That way you can prove anything.

GALILEO   (*putting the apple back*)   Very well.

ANDREA   You can do anything with examples if you're clever. But I can't carry my mother around in a chair like that. So you see, it was a bad example. And what would happen if the apple were the earth? Nothing would happen.

GALILEO   (*laughs*)   I thought you weren't interested.

ANDREA   All right, take the apple. What would keep me from hanging head down at night?

GALILEO   Well, here's the earth, and you're standing here. (*He sticks a splinter from a log into the apple*) And now the earth turns.

ANDREA   And now I'm hanging head down.

GALILEO   What do you mean? Look closely! Where's the head?

ANDREA   (*shows on the apple*)   There. Below.

GALILEO   Sure? (*Turns the apple back*) Isn't the head still in the same place? Aren't the feet still below it? When I turn it, do you stand like this? (*He takes the splinter out and turns it upside down*)

ANDREA   No. Then, why don't I notice the turning?

GALILEO   Because you're turning too. You and the air above you and everything else on the globe.

ANDREA   But why does it look as if the sun were moving?

GALILEO   (*again turns the apple with the splinter*)   Look, you see the earth underneath, it stays that way, it's always underneath and as far as you're concerned it doesn't move. Now look up. The lamp is over your head. But now that I've turned it, what's over your head, in other words, above?

ANDREA (*making the same turn*)   The stove.

GALILEO   And where's the lamp?

ANDREA   Below.

GALILEO   Aha!

ANDREA   That's great. That'll get a rise out of her.

(*Ludovico Marsili, a rich young man, enters*)

GALILEO   This place is as busy as a pigeon house.

LUDOVICO   Good morning, sir. My name is Ludovico Marsili.

GALILEO (*examining his letter of recommendation*)   You've been in Holland?

LUDOVICO   Where I heard a great deal about you, Mr. Galilei.

GALILEO   Your family owns property in the Campagna?

LUDOVICO   My mother wanted me to look around and see what's going on in the world. That kind of thing.

GALILEO   And in Holland they told you that in Italy, for instance, I was going on?

LUDOVICO   And since mother also wanted me to take a look at the sciences . . .

GALILEO   Private lessons: Ten scudi a month.

LUDOVICO   Very well, sir.

GALILEO   What are your interests?

LUDOVICO   Horses.

GALILEO   I see.

LUDOVICO   I have no head for science, Mr. Galilei.

GALILEO   I see. In that case it'll be fifteen scudi a month.

LUDIVICO   Very well, Mr. Galilei.

GALILEO   I'll have to take you first thing in the morning. You'll be the loser, Andrea. Naturally I'll have to drop you. You understand, you don't pay.

ANDREA   All right, I'm going. Can I take the apple?

GALILEO   Yes.

(*Andrea leaves*)

LUDOVICO   You'll have to be patient with me. Mostly because in science everything's the opposite of common sense. Take that crazy tube they're selling in Amsterdam. I've examined it carefully. A green leather casing and two lenses, one like this (*he indicates a concave lens*) and one like this (*indicates a convex lens*). As far as I know, one magnifies and the other reduces.

Any sensible person would expect them to cancel each other out. But they don't. When you look through the thing everything's five times as big. That's science for you.

GALILEO   What do you see five times as big?

LUDOVICO   Steeples, pigeons, anything far away.

GALILEO   Have you seen these magnified steeples?

LUDOVICO   Certainly, sir.

GALILEO   You say the tube has two lenses? (*He makes a sketch on a sheet of paper*) Like this? (*Ludovico nods*) How old is this invention?

LUDOVICO   I believe it wasn't much more than a few days old when I left Holland, at least it hadn't been on the market any longer than that.

GALILEO (*almost friendly*)   Why do you insist on physics? Why not horse breeding?

(*Enter Mrs. Sarti, unnoticed by Galileo*)

LUDOVICO   Mother thinks a little science won't hurt me. Everybody's eating and drinking science nowadays, you know.

GALILEO   Why not try a dead language or theology? They're easier. (*Sees Mrs. Sarti*) All right, come Tuesday morning. (*Ludovico leaves*)

GALILEO   Don't look at me like that. I've accepted him.

MRS. SARTI   Because you saw me in the nick of time. The procurator of the university is here.

GALILEO   Bring him in. He's important. It might mean five hundred scudi. Then I wouldn't have to take pupils. (*Mrs. Sarti shows the procurator in. Galileo has completed dressing while scribbling figures on a slip of paper*)

GALILEO   Good morning, lend me half a scudo. (*Gives the coin the procurator has fished out of his purse to Mrs. Sarti*) Sarti, would you send Andrea to the spectacle maker for some lenses? Here are the measurements.

(*Mrs. Sarti goes out with the slip of paper*)

THE PROCURATOR   I've come in regard to your request for a raise of salary. You have asked for a thousand scudi. Unfortunately I cannot recommend such an increase to the university. You are aware, I am sure, that courses in mathematics don't attract students to the university. Mathematics doesn't pay. Not that

the republic doesn't value it highly. It may not be as important as philosophy or as useful as theology; still, it gives endless pleasure to the connoisseur.

GALILEO (*immersed in his papers*)   My dear man, I can't get along
on five hundred scudi.

THE PROCURATOR   But, Mr. Galilei, all you do is give a two-hour
lecture twice a week. Surely your extraordinary reputation
must attract any number of students who can afford private
lessons. Haven't you got private pupils?

GALILEO   Sir, I have too many! I'm teaching all the time. When
am I to learn? Good God, man, I'm not as clever as the gentlemen of the philosophical faculty. I'm stupid. I don't understand a thing. I've got to plug the holes in my knowledge. And
where am I to find time for that? When am I to study and
experiment? My knowledge, sir, is thirsty for more knowledge. In all the biggest problems we still have nothing but
hypotheses to go by. What we need is proofs. How can I get
anywhere if, to keep my household going, I have to drum it
into the head of every idiot who can pay that parallel lines
meet in infinity?

THE PROCURATOR   The republic may not pay as much as certain
princes, but don't forget, it guarantees freedom of inquiry.
We in Padua even admit Protestants as students. And we
grant them doctor's degrees. Did we hand Mr. Cremonini
over to the Inquisition when we had proof—proof, Mr. Galilei!—that he had made sacrilegious statements? No, we even
granted him an increase in salary. As far away as Holland
Venice is known as the republic where the Inquisition has
nothing to say. That ought to be worth something to an
astronomer like you, working in a field where the doctrines
of the church have not been held in due respect of late.

GALILEO   You handed Giordano Bruno over to Rome. Because
he professed the teachings of Copernicus.

THE PROCURATOR   Not because he professed the teachings of
Mr. Copernicus which, incidentally, are wrong, but because
he was not a citizen of Venice and was not employed here.
You can leave him out of it, even if they did burn him. And
by the by, for all our liberties I shouldn't advise you to make
too free with a name that has been expressly anathematized

by the church, not even here, no, not even here.

GALILEO   Your protection of freedom of thought is rather good business, isn't it? You get good teachers for low pay by pointing out that other towns are run by the Inquisition, which burns people. In return for protection from the Inquisition, your professors work for next to nothing.

THE PROCURATOR   You're being unfair. What good would it do you to have all the time you want for research if any witless monk of the Inquisition could simply suppress your ideas? No rose without thorns, Mr. Galilei, no prince without monks!

GALILEO   And what's the use of free investigation without free time to investigate? What happens to the results? Why don't you submit my work on the laws of falling bodies (*He points at a sheaf of manuscript*) to the gentlemen of the signoria and ask them if it's not worth a few scudi more.

THE PROCURATOR   It's worth infinitely more, Mr. Galilei.

GALILEO   Not infinitely more, sir, but five hundred scudi more.

THE PROCURATOR   Only what brings in scudi is worth scudi. If you want money, you'll have to come up with something different. If you have knowledge to sell, you can ask only as much as it earns the purchaser. For instance, the philosophy Mr. Colombe is selling in Florence brings the prince at least ten thousand scudi a year. Granted, your laws of falling bodies raised some dust. They're applauding you in Paris and Prague. But the gentlemen who applaud don't pay the university of Padua what you cost it. Your misfortune, Mr. Galilei, is your field.

GALILEO   I get it: free trade, free research. Free trade in research, is that it?

THE PROCURATOR   But Mr. Galilei! How can you say such a thing? Permit me to observe that I don't fully appreciate your witticism. The flourishing trade of the republic is hardly to be sneered at. Much less can I, as long-time procurator of the university, countenance the, I must say, frivolous tone in which you speak of research. (*While Galileo sends longing glances toward his worktable*) Think of the world around us! The whip of slavery under which science is groaning at certain universities—where old leather-bound tomes have been cut into

whips. Where no one cares how the pebble falls, but only
what Aristotle writes about it. The eyes have only one purpose: reading. What use are the new laws of gravity when the
law of suavity is all that matters? And then think of the
immense joy with which our republic accepts your ideas.
Here you can do research! Here you can work! Nobody spies
on you, nobody oppresses you. Our merchants, who know the
importance of better linen in their competition with Florence, listen with interest to your cry for "Better physics!"
And don't forget how much physics owes to the campaign for
better looms! Our most eminent citizens—men for whom
time is money—take an interest in your work, they come to
see you and watch demonstrations of your discoveries. Don't
despise trade, Mr. Galilei! None of us here would ever allow
your work to be interfered with or permit outsiders to create
difficulties for you. You've got to admit, Mr. Galilei, that this
is the ideal place for your work!
GALILEO (*in despair*)   Yes.
THE PROCURATOR   Then the financial aspect: All you have to do
is come up with another invention as clever as that splendid
proportional compass of yours which a person ignorant of
mathematics can use to (*He counts on his fingers*) trace a line,
compute compound interest, reproduce a land survey in enlarged or reduced scale, and determine the weight of cannon
balls.
GALILEO   Flimflam.
THE PROCURATOR   An invention that delighted and amazed our
leading citizens and brought in money—you call that flimflam. I'm told that even General Stefano Gritti can do square
roots with it.
GALILEO   Quite a gadget—all the same, Priuli, you've given me
an idea. Priuli, I may have something along those lines for
you. (*He picks up the sheet with his sketch*)
THE PROCURATOR   Really? That would be the solution. (*Gets
up*) Mr. Galilei, we know you are a great man. A great but
dissatisfied man, if I may say so.
GALILEO   Yes, I am dissatisfied and that's what you should be
paying me for if you had any sense. Because I'm dissatisfied
with myself. But you do everything to make me dissatisfied

with you. I admit it amuses me to do my bit for my Venetian friends, working in your great arsenal with its shipyards and armories. But you leave me no time to follow up the speculations which result from this work. You muzzle the ox that does your threshing. I'm forty-six years old and I've accomplished nothing that satisfies me.

THE PROCURATOR   In that case I won't disturb you any longer.

GALILEO   Thank you.

(*The procurator leaves. Galileo remains alone for a few moments and begins to work. Then Andrea comes running in*)

GALILEO (*at work*)   Why didn't you eat the apple?

ANDREA   I need it to show her that the earth turns.

GALILEO   I must tell you something, Andrea. Don't mention our ideas to other people.

ANDREA   Why not?

GALILEO   Our rulers have forbidden it.

ANDREA   But it's the truth.

GALILEO   Even so, they forbid it.—And there's another reason. We still have no proofs for what we know to be right. Even the doctrine of the great Copernicus is not yet proven. It's only a hypothesis. Give me the lenses.

ANDREA   Half a scudo wasn't enough. I had to leave him my jacket. As a pledge.

GALILEO   How will you get through the winter without a jacket?

(*Pause. Galileo arranges the lenses on the sheet with the sketch*)

ANDREA   What's a hypothesis?

GALILEO   It's when we consider something probable but have no facts. We assume that Felice, nursing her baby down there outside the basket weaver's shop, is giving milk to the baby and not getting milk from it. That's a hypothesis as long as we can't go and see for ourselves and prove it. In the face of the heavenly bodies we're like worms with dim eyes that see very little. The ancient doctrines that have been accepted for a thousand years are rickety. There's less solid timber in those immense edifices than in the props needed to keep them from collapsing. Too many laws that explain too little, whereas our new hypothesis has few laws that explain a great deal.

ANDREA   But you've proved it all to me.

GALILEO Only that it's possible. You see, the hypothesis is a
very elegant one and there's no evidence to the contrary.

ANDREA I want to be a physicist too, Mr. Galilei.

GALILEO Very sensible in view of all the problems remaining
to be solved in our field. (*He has gone to the window and looked
through the lenses. Mildly interested*) Take a look, Andrea.

ANDREA Holy Mary! Everything comes close. The bells of the
campanile are right here. I can even read the copper letters:
GRACIA DEI.

GALILEO It'll get us five hundred scudi.

2

Galileo presents a new invention to the republic of Venice.

No one's virtue is complete:
Great Galileo liked to eat.
You will not resent, we hope
The truth about his telescope.

*The great arsenal of Venice near the harbor. Senators, headed by the
doge. On one side Galileo's friend Sagredo and Virginia Galilei, fifteen;
she is holding a velvet cushion on which lies a telescope about two feet
long, encased in red leather. Galileo is standing on a dais. Behind
him the tripod for the telescope; the lens grinder Federzoni is in charge
of it.*

GALILEO Your Excellency, august signoria! As professor of
mathematics at your university in Padua and director of the
great arsenal here in Venice, I have always felt it incumbent
upon me not only to fulfill my duties as a teacher but also to
procure special advantages to the republic of Venice by
means of useful inventions. With great satisfaction and in all

due humility, I shall demonstrate and present to you today an entirely new instrument, my spyglass or telescope, manufactured in your world-famous great arsenal in accordance with the highest scientific and Christian principles, the fruit of seventeen years of your obedient servant's patient labors. (*Galileo leaves the dais and stands next to Sagredo*) (*Applause, Galileo takes a bow*)

GALILEO (*softly to Sagredo*)   What a waste of time!

SAGREDO (*softly*)   You'll be able to pay the butcher, old friend.

GALILEO   Yes, they'll make money on it. (*Makes another bow*)

THE PROCURATOR (*steps up on the dais*)   Your Excellency, august signoria! Once again a glorious page in the great book of human accomplishments is being written in Venetian characters. (*Polite applause*) A scholar of world renown is presenting to you, and to you alone, a highly salable tube for you to manufacture and market at your pleasure. (*Stronger applause*) Has it occurred to you that in the event of war this instrument will enable us to recognize the nature and number of the enemy's ships at least two hours before they have a clear view of ours and, in full cognizance of his strength, decide whether to pursue, engage or withdraw? (*Loud applause*) And now, Your Excellency, august signoria, Mr. Galilei bids you accept this instrument of his invention, this evidence of his genius, from the hands of his charming daughter.

(*Music. Virginia steps forward, bows, hands the telescope to the procurator who passes it on to Federzoni. Federzoni places it on the tripod and adjusts it. The doge and the senators mount the dais and look through the tube*)

GALILEO (*softly*)   I can't promise to go through with this farce. They think they're getting a profitable gadget, but it's much more than that. Last night I turned the tube on the moon.

SAGREDO   What did you see?

GALILEO   It has no light of its own.

SAGREDO   What?

SENATORS   Mr. Galilei, I can see the fortifications of Santa Rosita.—Over there on that boat they're having lunch. Fried fish. I'm getting hungry.

GALILEO   I tell you, astronomy has been marking time for a thousand years for lack of a telescope.

SENATOR   Mr. Galilei!

SAGREDO   You're wanted.

SENATOR   One sees too well with that thing. I'll have to warn my ladies to stop bathing on the roof.

GALILEO   Do you know what the Milky Way consists of?

SAGREDO   No.

GALILEO   I do.

SENATOR   A thing like that is worth its ten scudi, Mr. Galilei. (*Galileo bows*)

VIRGINIA (*takes Ludovico to her father*)   Ludovico wants to congratulate you, father.

LUDOVICO (*embarrassed*)   Congratulations, sir.

GALILEO   I've improved on it.

LUDOVICO   So I see, sir. You made the casing red. In Holland it was green.

GALILEO (*turns to Sagredo*)   I wonder if I couldn't prove a certain doctrine with that thing.

SAGREDO   Watch your step!

THE PROCURATOR   Your five hundred scudi are in the bag, Mr. Galilei.

GALILEO (*paying no attention to him*)   Of course, I'm always wary of rash conclusions.
(*The doge, a fat, modest man, has approached Galileo and is attempting, with clumsy dignity, to address him*)

THE PROCURATOR   Mr. Galilei, His Excellency the doge.
(*The doge shakes Galileo's hand*)

GALILEO   Oh yes, the five hundred! Are you satisfied, Your Excellency?

DOGE   Unfortunately our city fathers always need some sort of pretext before they can do anything for our scholars.

THE PROCURATOR   Otherwise, where would the incentive be, Mr. Galilei?

DOGE (*smiling*)   This is our pretext.
(*The doge and the procurator lead Galileo to the senators, who surround him. Virginia and Ludovico slowly go away*)

VIRGINIA   Did I do it all right?

LUDOVICO   It seemed all right to me.

VIRGINIA   What's the matter?

LUDOVICO   Oh, nothing. A green casing might have done just as well.

VIRGINIA   I think they're all very pleased with father.
LUDOVICO   And I think I'm beginning to understand something
about science.

3

January 10, 1610: By means of the telescope Galileo
discovers celestial phenomena which prove the
Copernican system. Warned by his friend of the possible consequences of his investigations, Galileo
affirms his faith in reason.

> January ten, sixteen ten:
> Galileo Galilei abolishes heaven.

*Galileo's study in Padua. Night. Galileo and Sagredo, both in heavy
overcoats, at the telescope.*

SAGREDO (*looking through the telescope, in an undertone*)   The edge
of the crescent is quite irregular, rough and serrated. In the
dark part near the luminous edge there are luminous points.
They are emerging, one after another. From these points the
light spreads out over wider and wider areas and finally
merges with the larger luminous part.
GALILEO   How do you account for those luminous points?
SAGREDO   It can't be.
GALILEO   But it is. They're mountains.
SAGREDO   On a star?
GALILEO   Gigantic mountains. Their peaks are gilded by the
rising sun while the surrounding slopes are still deep in darkness. You can see the light descending from the highest peaks
into the valleys.

SAGREDO   But that contradicts all the astronomy of two thousand years.

GALILEO   True. No mortal has ever seen what you are seeing, except me. You're the second.

SAGREDO   But the moon can't be another earth with mountains and valleys, any more than the earth can be a planet.

GALILEO   The moon can be an earth with mountains and valleys, and the earth can be a planet. Simply another heavenly body, one among thousands. Take another look. Is the dark part of the moon entirely dark?

SAGREDO   No. When I look closely, I see a feeble gray light on it.

GALILEO   What can that light be?

SACREDO   ?

GALILEO   It's from the earth.

SAGREDO   Nonsense. How can the earth with its mountains and forests and oceans—a cold body—give light?

GALILEO   The same way the moon sheds light. Because both bodies are illuminated by the sun, that's why they shed light. What the moon is to us we are to the moon. The moon sees us by turns as a crescent, as a half-circle, as full, and then not at all.

SAGREDO   Then there's no difference between moon and earth?

GALILEO   Apparently not.

SAGREDO   Less than ten years ago a man was burned in Rome. His name was Giordano Bruno and he had said the same thing.

GALILEO   I know. But we can see it. Keep your eyes to the tube. What you see is that there's no difference between heaven and earth. This is the tenth of January, 1610. Humanity notes in its diary: Heaven abolished.

SAGREDO   It's terrifying.

GALILEO   I've discovered something else. Perhaps something even more amazing.

MRS. SARTI (*comes in*)   The procurator.

(*The procurator rushes in*)

THE PROCURATOR   I apologize for the late hour. I'd be much obliged if we could talk privately.

GALILEO   Mr. Sagredo can hear anything I can hear, Mr. Priuli.

THE PROCURATOR   It might embarrass you to have the gentleman hear what has happened. Unfortunately, it's something quite incredible.

GALILEO   Mr. Sagredo is used to hearing incredible things in my presence.

THE PROCURATOR   I wonder. (*Pointing at the telescope*) There it is, your splendid gadget. You might as well throw it away. It's worthless, absolutely worthless.

SAGREDO (*who has been restlessly pacing the floor*)   What do you mean?

THE PROCURATOR   Do you realize that this invention of yours, "the fruit of seventeen years of patient labor," is for sale on every street corner in Italy for a couple of scudi? Made in Holland, I might add. At this very moment a Dutch freighter is unloading five hundred telescopes in the harbor.

GALILEO   You don't say.

THE PROCURATOR   Your equanimity, sir, is beyond me.

SAGREDO   I fail to see what's troubling you. Let me tell you that just in these last few days Mr. Galilei—with this very instrument—has made the most revolutionary discoveries concerning heavenly bodies.

GALILEO (*laughing*)   Have a look for yourself, Priuli.

THE PROCURATOR   Let me tell you that after having Mr. Galilei's salary doubled on the strength of this worthless gadget I'm quite satisfied with the discovery I've already made. It's sheer accident that when the gentlemen of the signoria first looked through your tube, confident of having acquired something for the republic that could be manufactured only here, they failed to see—seven times magnified—a common peddler on the next corner hawking that same tube for a song.

(*Galileo roars with laughter*)

SAGREDO   Dear Mr. Priuli, I may not be able to judge the instrument's value to the economy, but its value to philosophy is so enormous that . . .

THE PROCURATOR   To philosophy! What business has Mr. Galilei, a mathematician, meddling with philosophy? Mr. Galilei, you once invented a very respectable pump for the city; your irrigation system functions. The weavers, too, are very pleased with your machine. How on earth could I have anticipated anything like this?

GALILEO   Not so fast, Priuli. Sea routes are still long, unsafe and
expensive. We lack a dependable clock in the sky. A guide to
navigation. I have reason to believe that with the telescope we
can very clearly perceive certain stars with very regular motions. New star charts, Mr. Priuli, could save the shipping
interests millions of scudi.

THE PROCURATOR   Forget it. I've heard more than enough. In
return for my kindness you've made me the laughingstock of
the city. I'll be remembered as the procurator who fell for a
worthless telescope. You have every reason to laugh. You've
got your five hundred scudi. But I'm telling you, and I speak
as an honest man: This world makes me sick! (*He leaves, bang-
ing the door behind him*)

GALILEO   He's rather likable when he gets angry. Did you hear
what he said: A world where you can't do business makes him
sick.

SAGREDO   Did you know about the Dutch instruments?

GALILEO   Of course. From hearsay. But the one I made for those
skinflints in the signoria is twice as good. How can I do my
work with the bailiff at the door? And Virginia will need her
trousseau soon, she's not bright. Besides, I like to buy books,
and not only about physics, and I like to eat well. I get my
best ideas over a good meal. A rotten time to live in! They
weren't paying me as much as the teamster who carts their
wine barrels. Four cords of firewood for two courses in mathematics. I've wormed five hundred scudi out of them, but I've
got debts, some of them twenty years old. Give me five years
of leisure and I'll prove everything. Let me show you something else.

SAGREDO (*hesitates to go to the telescope*)   I almost think I'm afraid,
Galileo.

GALILEO   I want to show you a milky-white patch of luminous
mist in the galaxy. Tell me what it's made of.

SAGREDO   Why, stars, countless stars.

GALILEO   In the constellation of Orion alone there are five hundred fixed stars. Those are the many worlds, the countless
other worlds, the stars beyond stars that the man they burned
talked about. He didn't see them, but he knew they would be
there.

SAGREDO   Even if our earth is a star, it's still a long way to

Copernicus' contention that the earth revolves around the sun. There isn't any star in the heavens with another revolving around it. And the earth, you'll have to admit, has the moon revolving around it.

GALILEO   Sagredo, I wonder. I've been wondering for two days. There's Jupiter. (*He adjusts the telescope*) Now, near it there are four smaller stars that you can only make out through the tube. I saw them on Monday but I didn't pay too much attention to their positions. Yesterday I looked again. I could have sworn that all four had moved. I recorded their positions. Now they're different again. What's that now? There were four of them. (*Getting excited*) You look!

SAGREDO   I see three.

GALILEO   Where's the fourth? Here are the tables. We must compute the movements they can have made.

(*Agitated, they sit down to work. The stage turns dark, but on a cyclorama Jupiter and its satellites remain visible. When it grows light again, they are still sitting there in their winter coats*)

GALILEO   Now we have proof. The fourth must have moved behind Jupiter where we can't see it. There you have a star with another revolving around it.

SAGREDO   But the crystal sphere that Jupiter is fastened to?

GALILEO   Where is it indeed? How can Jupiter be fastened to anything if other stars revolve around it? There is no scaffolding in the sky, there's nothing holding the universe up! There you have another sun!

SAGREDO   Calm down. You're thinking too fast.

GALILEO   Fast, hell! Man, get excited! You're seeing something that nobody ever saw before. They were right!

SAGREDO   Who? The Copernicans?

GALILEO   Yes, and you know who. The whole world was against them, and yet they were right. That's something for Andrea! (*Beside himself, he runs to the door and shouts*) Mrs. Sarti! Mrs. Sarti!

SAGREDO   Galileo, please calm yourself!

GALILEO   Sagredo, please get excited! Mrs. Sarti!

SAGREDO (*turning the telescope aside*)   Will you stop yelling like a fool?

GALILEO Will you stop standing there like a stockfish when we've discovered the truth?

SAGREDO I'm not standing here like a stockfish, I'm trembling for fear it's the truth.

GALILEO What?

SAGREDO Have you taken leave of your senses? Don't you realize what you're getting into if what you see is really true? And if you go shouting all over town that the earth is a planet and not the center of the universe?

GALILEO Yes, and that the whole enormous cosmos with all its stars doesn't revolve around our tiny earth, as anyone could have guessed anyway.

SAGREDO So that there's nothing but stars!—But where does that put God?

GALILEO What do you mean?

SAGREDO God! Where's God?

GALILEO (*furious*) Not out there! Any more than He'd be on earth if somebody out there started looking for Him here.

SAGREDO Where is God then?

GALILEO Am I a theologian? I'm a mathematician.

SAGREDO First of all you're a human being. And I ask you: Where is God in your world system?

GALILEO Inside us or nowhere!

SAGREDO (*shouting*) As the man who was burned said?

GALILEO As the man who was burned said!

SAGREDO That's why he was burned! Less than ten years ago!

GALILEO Because he couldn't prove it! Because all he could do was say so! Mrs. Sarti!

SAGREDO Galileo, I know you're a clever man. For three years in Pisa and seventeen here in Padua you've patiently instructed hundreds of students in the Ptolemaic system as advocated by the church and confirmed by the scriptures on which the church is grounded. Like Copernicus you thought it was wrong, but you taught it.

GALILEO Because I couldn't prove anything.

SAGREDO (*incredulous*) You think that makes a difference?

GALILEO All the difference in the world! Look here, Sagredo! I believe in man and that means I believe in reason. Without that belief I wouldn't have the strength to get out of bed in the morning.

SAGREDO   Then let me tell you this: I don't believe in reason. Forty years' experience has taught me that human beings are not accessible to reason. Show them a comet with a red tail, put dark fear into them, and they'll rush out of their houses and break their legs. But make a reasonable statement, prove it with seven good reasons, and they'll just laugh at you.

GALILEO   That's all wrong and it's slander. I don't see how you can love science if you believe that. Only the dead are impervious to argument.

SAGREDO   How can you mistake their contemptible cunning for reason?

GALILEO   I'm not talking about their cunning. I know they call a donkey a horse when they're selling and a horse a donkey when they're buying. That's their cunning. But the old woman with calloused hands who gives her mule an extra bunch of hay the night before setting out on a trip; the sea captain who allows for storms and doldrums when he lays in his stores; the child who puts on his cap when he realizes that it may rain—these people are my hope, they accept the law of cause and effect. Yes, I believe in the gentle force of reason, in the long run no one can resist it. Nobody can watch me drop (*He lets a pebble fall from his hand to the floor*) a pebble and say: It doesn't fall. Nobody can do that. The seduction of proof is too strong. Most people will succumb to it and in time they all will. Thinking is one of the greatest pleasures of the human race.

MRS. SARTI (*comes in*)   Did you want something, Mr. Galilei?

GALILEO (*back at the telescope, scribbling notes, very kindly*)   Yes, I want Andrea.

MRS. SARTI   Andrea? But he's in bed, he's sound asleep.

GALILEO   Can't you wake him?

MRS. SARTI   What do you want him for, may I ask?

GALILEO   I want to show him something that'll please him. He's going to see something that no one but us has ever seen since the earth began.

MRS. SARTI   Something through your tube?

GALILEO   Something through my tube, Mrs. Sarti.

MRS. SARTI   And for that you want me to wake him in the middle of the night? Are you out of your mind? He needs his sleep. I wouldn't think of waking him.

GALILEO   Not a chance?

MRS. SARTI   Not a chance.

GALILEO   Mrs. Sarti, in that case maybe you can help me. You see, a question has come up that we can't agree on, perhaps because we've read too many books. It's a question about the sky, involving the stars. Here it is: Which seems more likely, that large bodies turn around small bodies or small bodies around large ones?

MRS. SARTI (*suspiciously*)   I never know what you're up to, Mr. Galilei. Is this a serious question or are you pulling my leg again?

GALILEO   A serious question.

MRS. SARTI   Then I can give you a quick answer. Do I serve your dinner or do you serve mine?

GALILEO   You serve mine. Yesterday it was burned.

MRS. SARTI   And why was it burned? Because you made me get your shoes while I was cooking it. Didn't I bring you your shoes?

GALILEO   I presume you did.

MRS. SARTI   Because it's you who went to school and can pay.

GALILEO   I see. I see there's no difficulty. Good morning, Mrs. Sarti.

(*Mrs. Sarti, amused, goes out*)

GALILEO   And such people are supposed not to be able to grasp the truth? They snatch at it.

(*The matins bell has begun to peal. In comes Virginia in a cloak, carrying a shaded candle*)

VIRGINIA   Good morning, father.

GALILEO   Up so early?

VIRGINIA   I'm going to matins with Mrs. Sarti. Ludovico will be there too. How was the night, father?

GALILEO   Clear.

VIRGINIA   May I look through it?

GALILEO   What for? (*Virginia has no answer*) It's not a toy.

VIRGINIA   I know, father.

GALILEO   By the way, the tube's a big flop. You'll hear all about it soon. It's being sold on the street for three scudi, it was invented in Holland.

VIRGINIA   Didn't you find anything new in the sky with it?

GALILEO   Nothing for you. Only a few dim specks on the left side of a big star, I'll have to find a way of calling attention to them. (*Speaking to Sagredo over his daughter's head*) Maybe I'll call them the "Medicean Stars" to please the grand duke of Florence. (*Again to Virginia*) It may interest you, Virginia, to know that we'll probably move to Florence. I've written to ask if the grand duke can use me as court mathematician.

VIRGINIA (*radiant*)   At court?

SAGREDO   Galileo!

GALILEO   I need leisure, old friend. I need proofs. And I want the fleshpots. With a position like that I won't have to ram the Ptolemaic system down the throats of private students, I'll have time—time, time, time, time!—to work out my proofs. What I've got now isn't enough. It's nothing, it's just bits and pieces. I can't stand up to the whole world with that. There's still no proof that any heavenly body revolves around the sun. But I'm going to find the proofs, proofs for everybody from Mrs. Sarti to the pope. The only thing that worries me is that the court may not want me.

VIRGINIA   Oh, I'm sure they'll take you, father, with your new stars and all.

GALILEO   Go to your mass.

(*Virginia leaves*)

GALILEO   I'm not used to writing letters to important people. (*He hands Sagredo a letter*) Do you think this will do?

SAGREDO (*reading aloud the end of the letter which Galileo has handed him*)   "Withal I am yearning for nothing so much as to be nearer to Your Highness, the rising sun which will illuminate this age." The grand duke of Florence is nine years old.

GALILEO   I know. I see, you think my letter is too servile. I wonder if it's servile enough, not too formal, as if I were lacking in genuine devotion. A more restrained letter might be all right for someone with the distinction of having proved the truth of Aristotle; not for me. A man like me can only get a halfway decent position by crawling on his belly. And you know I despise men whose brains are incapable of filling their stomachs.

(*Mrs. Sarti and Virginia walk past the two men on their way to mass*)

SAGREDO   Don't go to Florence, Galileo.

GALILEO   Why not?

SAGREDO   Because it's ruled by monks.

GALILEO   There are distinguished scholars at the Florentine court.

SAGREDO   Toadies.

GALILEO   I'll take them by the scruff of their necks and drag them to my tube. Even monks are human beings, Sagredo. Even monks can be seduced by proofs. Copernicus—don't forget that—wanted them to trust his figures, I'm only asking them to trust the evidence of their eyes. When truth is too weak to defend itself, it has to attack. I'll take them by the scruff of their necks and make them look through the tube.

SAGREDO   Galileo, you're on a dangerous path. It's bad luck when a man sees the truth. And delusion when he believes in the rationality of the human race. Who do we say walks with open eyes? The man who's headed for perdition. How can the mighty leave a man at large who knows the truth, even if it's only about the remotest stars? Do you think the pope will hear your truth when you tell him he's wrong? No, he'll hear only one thing, that you've said he's wrong. Do you think he will calmly write in his diary: January 10, 1610, Heaven abolished? How can you want to leave the republic with the truth in your pocket and walk straight into the trap of the monks and princes with your tube in your hands? You may be very skeptical in your science, but you're as gullible as a child about anything that looks like a help in pursuing it. You may not believe in Aristotle, but you believe in the grand duke of Florence. A moment ago when I saw you at your tube looking at the new stars I thought I saw you on a flaming pyre and when you said you believed in proofs I smelled burnt flesh. I love science, but I love you more, my friend. Galileo, don't go to Florence!

GALILEO   If they'll have me I'll go.

(*On a curtain appears the last page of the letter*)

In assigning the sublime name of the Medicean line to these stars newly discovered by me I am fully aware that

when gods and heroes were elevated to the starry skies
they were thereby glorified, but that in the present case it
is the stars that will be glorified by receiving the name of
the Medici. With this I recommend myself as one among
the number of your most faithful and obedient servants,
who holds it the highest honor to have been born your
subject.

Withal I yearn for nothing so much as to be nearer to
Your Highness, the rising sun which will illuminate this
age.

Galileo Galilei

4

Galileo has exchanged the Venetian republic for the
court of Florence. The discoveries he has made with
the help of the telescope are met with disbelief by the
court scholars.

> The old says: What I've always done I'll always do.
> The new says: If you're useless you must go.

*Galileo's house in Florence. Mrs. Sarti is getting Galileo's study ready
to receive guests. Her son Andrea is seated, putting celestial charts
away.*

MRS. SARTI   Ever since we arrived in this marvelous Florence
I've seen nothing but bowing and scraping. The whole town
files past this tube and I can scrub the floor afterwards. But
it won't do us a bit of good. If these discoveries amounted to
anything, the reverend fathers would know it, wouldn't they?
For four years I was in service with Monsignor Filippo, I
never managed to dust the whole of his library. Leather-

bound volumes up to the ceiling and no love poems either. And the good monsignor had two pounds of boils on his behind from poring over all that learning. Wouldn't a man like that know what's what? The big demonstration today will be another flop and tomorrow I won't be able to look the milkman in the face. I knew what I was saying when I told him to give the gentlemen a good dinner first, a nice piece of lamb, before they start in on his tube. Oh no! (*She imitates Galileo*) "I've got something better for them."
(*Knocking downstairs*)

MRS. SARTI (*looks in the window-mirror*)   Goodness, there's the grand duke already. And Galileo still at the university! (*She runs downstairs and admits Cosmo de' Medici, grand duke of Tuscany, accompanied by the lord chamberlain and two ladies-in-waiting*)

COSMO   I want to see the tube.

THE LORD CHAMBERLAIN   Perhaps Your Highness would prefer to wait until Mr. Galilei and the other gentlemen have returned from the university. (*To Mrs. Sarti*) Mr. Galilei wanted the professors of astronomy to examine the newly discovered stars which he calls the Medicean stars.

COSMO   They don't believe in the tube, far from it. Where is it?

MRS. SARTI   Upstairs, in his workroom.
(*The boy nods, points to the staircase, and upon a nod from Mrs. Sarti dashes up the stairs*)

THE LORD CHAMBERLAIN (*a very old man*)   Your Highness! (*To Mrs. Sarti*) Must we go up there? I only came because the tutor is ill.

MRS. SARTI   Nothing can happen to the young gentleman. My boy's upstairs.

COSMO (*entering above*)   Good evening.
(*The two boys ceremoniously bow to each other. Pause. Then Andrea goes back to his work*)

ANDREA (*much like his teacher*)   This place is as busy as a pigeon house.

COSMO   Lots of visitors?

ANDREA   Stumble about and gape and don't know beans.

COSMO   I see. Is that . . . ? (*Points at the tube*)

ANDREA   Yes, that's it. But don't touch it. It's not allowed.

COSMO   And what's that? (*He indicates the wooden model of the Ptolemaic system*)

ANDREA   That's the Ptolemaic system.

COSMO   It shows how the sun moves, doesn't it?

ANDREA   Yes, so they say.

COSMO (*sitting down in a chair, he takes the model on his knees*)   My tutor has a cold. So I was able to get away early. It's nice here.

ANDREA (*is restless, ambles about irresolutely, throwing suspicious glances at the strange boy, and at last, unable to resist the temptation any longer, takes from behind the star charts another wooden model representing the Copernican system*)   But of course it's really like this.

COSMO   What's like this?

ANDREA (*pointing at the model on Cosmo's knees*)   That's the way people think it is and that's (*Pointing at his model*) the way it really is. The earth turns around the sun. See?

COSMO   You really think so?

ANDREA   Of course. It's been proven.

COSMO   You don't say!—I wish I knew why they didn't let me go in to see the old man. Last night he was at dinner as usual.

ANDREA   You don't seem to believe it, or do you?

COSMO   Why certainly, I do.

ANDREA (*pointing at the model on Cosmo's knees*)   Give it back, you don't even understand that one!

COSMO   But you don't need two.

ANDREA   Give it back this minute. It's not a toy for little boys.

COSMO   I don't mind giving it back but you ought to be a little more polite, you know.

ANDREA   You're stupid and I don't care about being polite. Give it back or you'll see.

COSMO   Hands off, do you hear.

(*They start fighting and are soon rolling on the floor*)

ANDREA   I'll show you how to treat a model. Give up!

COSMO   You've broken it. You're twisting my hand.

ANDREA   We'll see who's right and who isn't. Say it turns or I'll box your ears.

COSMO   I won't. Ouch, you redhead. I'll teach you good manners.

ANDREA Redhead? Am I a redhead?

(*They continue to fight in silence. Below, Galileo and several university professors enter. Behind them Federzoni*)

THE LORD CHAMBERLAIN Gentlemen, a slight illness has prevented Mr. Suri, His Highness' tutor, from accompanying His Highness.

THE THEOLOGIAN Nothing serious, I hope.

THE LORD CHAMBERLAIN No, no, by no means.

GALILEO (*disappointed*) Isn't His Highness here?

THE LORD CHAMBERLAIN His Highness is upstairs. May I ask you gentlemen to proceed. The court is so very anxious to hear the opinion of our illustrious university about Mr. Galilei's extraordinary instrument and those marvelous new stars.

(*They go upstairs*)

(*The boys lie still. They have heard sounds downstairs*)

COSMO Here they come. Let me up.

(*They quickly get up*)

THE GENTLEMEN (*as they file upstairs*) No. No, there's nothing to worry about.—The faculty of medicine has declared that the cases in the inner city can't possibly be plague. The miasma would freeze at the present temperature.—The worst danger in these situations is panic.—We can always expect an epidemic of colds at this time of year.—No ground for suspicion. —Nothing to worry about.

(*Salutations upstairs*)

GALILEO Your Highness, I am extremely pleased that you should be present while I communicate our new discoveries to the gentlemen of your university.

(*Cosmo makes formal bows to all, including Andrea*)

THE THEOLOGIAN (*seeing the broken Ptolemaic model on the floor*) There seems to have been some breakage here.

(*Cosmo stoops quickly and hands the model politely to Andrea. At the same time Galileo slyly puts away the other model*)

GALILEO (*at the telescope*) As Your Highness no doubt knows, we astronomers have for some time been encountering great difficulties in our calculations. We are using a very old system which seems to be in agreement with philosophy but unfortunately not with the facts. According to this old system, the Ptolemaic system, the movements of the planets are extremely complicated. Venus, for instance, is supposed to move something like this. (*He sketches on a blackboard the epicyclic course of Venus according to Ptolemy*) But if we predicate these complicated movements, we are unable to calculate the position of any star accurately in advance. We do not find it in the place where it should be. Furthermore there are stellar motions for which the Ptolemaic system has no explanation at all. According to my observations, certain small stars I have discovered describe motions of this kind around the planet Jupiter. If you gentlemen are agreeable, we shall begin with the inspection of the satellites of Jupiter, the Medicean stars.

ANDREA (*pointing to the stool in front of the telescope*)   Kindly sit here.

THE PHILOSOPHER   Thank you, my child. I'm afraid it will not be so simple. Mr. Galilei, before we apply ourselves to your famous tube, we should like to request the pleasure of a disputation: Can such planets exist?

THE MATHEMATICIAN   A formal disputation.

GALILEO   I thought you'd just look through the telescope and see for yourselves.

ANDREA   Here, if you please.

THE MATHEMATICIAN   Yes, yes.—You are aware, of course, that in the view of the ancients no star can revolve around any center other than the earth and that there can be no stars without firm support in the sky.

GALILEO   Yes.

THE PHILOSOPHER   And, regardless of whether such stars are possible, a proposition which the mathematician (*He bows to the mathematician*) seems to doubt, I as a philosopher should like with all due modesty to raise this question: Are such stars necessary? Aristotelis divini universum . . .

GALILEO   Oughtn't we to continue in the vernacular? My colleague, Mr. Federzoni, doesn't understand Latin.

THE PHILOSOPHER   Does it matter whether he understands us?

GALILEO   Yes.

THE PHILOSOPHER   I beg your pardon. I thought he was your lens grinder.

ANDREA   Mr. Federzoni is a lens grinder and a scholar.

THE PHILOSOPHER   Thank you, my child. If Mr. Federzoni insists . . .

GALILEO   I insist.

THE PHILOSOPHER   The debate will lose in brilliance, but this is your house.—The cosmos of the divine Aristotle with its spheres and their mystical music, with its crystal vaults and the circular courses of its heavenly bodies, with the oblique angle of the sun's course and the mysteries of its tables of satellites and the wealth of stars in the catalog of the southern hemisphere and the inspired construction of the celestial globe is an edifice of such order and beauty that we shall be well advised not to disturb its harmony.

GALILEO   Your Highness, would you care to observe those impossible and unnecessary stars through the telescope?

THE MATHEMATICIAN   One might be tempted to reply that if your tube shows something that cannot exist it must be a rather unreliable tube.

GALILEO   What do you mean by that?

THE MATHEMATICIAN   It certainly would be much more to the point, Mr. Galilei, if you were to tell us your reasons for supposing that there can be free-floating stars moving about in the highest sphere of the immutable heavens.

THE PHILOSOPHER   Reasons, Mr. Galilei, reasons!

GALILEO   My reasons? When a look at these stars and my calculations demonstrate the phenomenon? This debate is getting absurd, sir.

THE MATHEMATICIAN   If it were not to be feared that you would get even more excited than you are, one might suggest that what is in your tube and what is in the sky might be two different things.

THE PHILOSOPHER   It would be difficult to put it more politely.

FEDERZONI   They think we painted the Medicean stars on the lens!

GALILEO   You accuse me of fraud?

THE PHILOSOPHER   We wouldn't dream of it! In the presence of His Highness!

THE MATHEMATICIAN   Your instrument, whether we call it your own or your adoptive child, has doubtless been very cleverly constructed.

THE PHILOSOPHER   And we are convinced, Mr. Galilei, that neither you nor anyone else would ever dare to grace stars with
the illustrious name of the ruling house if there were the
slightest doubt of their existence.
(*All bow deeply to the grand duke*)
COSMO (*turning to the ladies-in-waiting*)   Is there something
wrong with my stars?
THE OLDER LADY-IN-WAITING (*to the grand duke*)   Your Highness'
stars are fine. The gentlemen are only wondering whether
they really and truly exist.
(*Pause*)
THE YOUNGER LADY-IN-WAITING   They say you can see the scales
of the Dragon with this instrument.
FEDERZONI   Yes, and you can see all sorts of things on the Bull.
GALILEO   Are you gentlemen going to look through it, or not?
THE PHILOSOPHER   Certainly, certainly.
THE MATHEMATICIAN   Certainly.
(*Pause. Suddenly Andrea turns around and walks stiffly out through
the length of the room. His mother intercepts him*)
MRS. SARTI   What's got into you?
ANDREA   They're stupid. (*Tears himself loose and runs away*)
THE PHILOSOPHER   A deplorable child.
THE LORD CHAMBERLAIN   Your Highness, gentlemen, may I re-
mind you that the state ball is due to start in forty-five min-
utes?
THE MATHEMATICIAN   Why beat about the bush? Sooner or later
Mr. Galilei will have to face up to the facts. His moons of
Jupiter would pierce the crystal sphere. That's all there is to
it.
FEDERZONI   You'll be surprised, but there is no crystal sphere.
THE PHILOSOPHER   Any textbook will tell you there is, my good
man.
FEDERZONI   Then we need new textbooks.
THE PHILOSOPHER   Your Highness, my esteemed colleague and
I are supported by no less an authority than the divine Aris-
totle.
GALILEO (*almost abjectly*)   Gentlemen, belief in the authority of
Aristotle is one thing, observable facts are another. You say
that according to Aristotle there are crystal spheres up there

and that certain motions are impossible because the stars would have to pierce the spheres. But what if you observed these motions? Wouldn't that suggest to you that the spheres do not exist? Gentlemen, I humbly beseech you to trust your own eyes.

THE MATHEMATICIAN My dear Galilei, though it may seem dreadfully old-fashioned to you, I'm in the habit of reading Aristotle now and then, and I can assure you that when I read Aristotle I do trust my eyes.

GALILEO I'm used to seeing the gentlemen of all faculties close their eyes to all facts and act as if nothing had happened. I show them my calculations, and they smile; I make my telescope available to help them see for themselves, and they quote Aristotle.

FEDERZONI The man had no telescope!

THE MATHEMATICIAN Exactly!

THE PHILOSOPHER (*grandly*) If Aristotle, an authority acknowledged not only by all the scientists of antiquity but by the church fathers themselves, is to be dragged through the mire, a continuation of this discussion seems superfluous, at least to me. I refuse to take part in irrelevant arguments. Basta.

GALILEO Truth is the child of time, not of authority. Our ignorance is infinite, let's whittle away just one cubic millimeter. Why should we still want to be so clever when at long last we have a chance of being a little less stupid? I've had the good fortune to lay hands on a new instrument with which we can observe a tiny corner of the universe a little more closely, not much though. Make use of it.

THE PHILOSOPHER Your Highness, ladies and gentlemen, I can only wonder what all this will lead to.

GALILEO I submit that as scientists we have no business asking what the truth may lead to.

THE PHILOSOPHER (*in wild alarm*) Mr. Galilei, the truth can lead to all sorts of things!

GALILEO Your Highness. In these nights telescopes are being directed at the sky all over Italy. The moons of Jupiter don't lower the price of milk. But they have never been seen before, and yet they exist. The man in the street will conclude that a good many things may exist if only he opens his eyes. And you ought to back him up. It's not the motions of some remote stars that make Italy sit up and take notice, but the news that doctrines believed to be unshakeable are beginning to totter, and we all know that of these there are far too many. Gentlemen, we oughtn't to be defending shaky doctrines!

FEDERZONI   You are teachers, you ought to be doing the shaking.

THE PHILOSOPHER   I wish your man there would keep out of a scientific debate.

GALILEO   Your Highness! My work in the great arsenal of Venice brought me into daily contact with draftsmen, architects and instrument makers. Those people taught me many new ways of doing things. They don't read books but they trust the testimony of their five senses, most of them without fear as to where it will lead them . . .

THE PHILOSOPHER   Fancy that!

GALILEO   Very much like our seamen who left our shores a hundred years ago, without the slightest idea of what other shores, if any, they might reach. It looks as if we had to go to the shipyards nowadays to find the high curiosity that was the glory of ancient Greece.

THE PHILOSOPHER   After what we have heard here today, I have no doubt that Mr. Galilei will find admirers in the shipyards.

THE LORD CHAMBERLAIN   Your Highness, I note to my great dismay that this exceedingly instructive conversation has taken a little longer than foreseen. Your Highness must rest a while before the court ball.

(*At a signal, the grand duke bows to Galileo. The court quickly prepares to leave*)

MRS. SARTI (*stepping in the way of the grand duke and offering him a plate of pastry*)   A bun, Your Highness?

(*The older lady-in-waiting leads the grand duke away*)

GALILEO (*running after them*)   But all you gentlemen need do is look through the instrument.

THE LORD CHAMBERLAIN   His Highness will not fail to obtain an expert opinion on your statements by consulting our greatest living astronomer, Father Christopher Clavius, astronomer-in-chief at the papal college in Rome.

5

Undaunted even by the plague, Galileo continues his investigations.

a)

Early morning. Galileo bending over his notes at the telescope. Virginia comes in with a traveling bag.

GALILEO Virginia! Is anything wrong?
VIRGINIA The convent is closed. They sent us home. There are five cases of plague in Arcetri.
GALILEO (*calls out*) Sarti!
VIRGINIA And last night our market was roped off. They say two people have died in the old city, and there are three more dying in the hospital.
GALILEO As usual, they've hushed it up until the last minute.
MRS. SARTI (*comes in*) What are you doing here?
VIRGINIA The plague.
MRS. SARTI My God! I'd better pack. (*Sits down*)
GALILEO No need to pack. Take Virginia and Andrea. I'll go get my notes.
(*He hurries back to the table and gathers his papers in great haste. Mrs. Sarti puts a coat on Andrea as he runs in, and goes to get some food and bedding. One of the grand duke's lackeys enters*)
LACKEY His Highness has left the city for Bologna because of the raging disease. Before leaving he insisted that Mr. Galilei should be given an opportunity to escape. The coach will be here in two minutes.
MRS. SARTI (*to Virginia and Andrea*) Go right outside, you two. Here, take this.
ANDREA Why? If you don't tell me why, I won't go.

MRS. SARTI   It's the plague, my child.

VIRGINIA   We'll wait for father.

MRS. SARTI   Mr. Galilei, are you ready?

GALILEO (*wrapping the telescope in a tablecloth*)   Put Virginia and Andrea in the coach. I'll join you in a minute.

VIRGINIA   No, we won't leave without you. You'll never be ready if you start packing your books.

MRS. SARTI   The carriage is here.

GALILEO   Be reasonable, Virginia. If no one gets in, the coachman will just drive away. The plague is no joke.

VIRGINIA (*protesting as Mrs. Sarti leads her and Andrea out*)   Help him with his books or he won't come.

MRS. SARTI (*calls out from the house door*)   Mr. Galilei! The coachman says he won't wait.

GALILEO   Mrs. Sarti, I don't think I should leave. Everything is in such a muddle here, you know, all my notes of the last three months, I might as well throw them away if I don't go on with them for a night or two. And anyway the plague is everywhere.

MRS. SARTI   Mr. Galilei! Come this minute! You're out of your mind.

GALILEO   You go with Virginia and Andrea. I'll come later.

MRS. SARTI   In another hour they won't let anyone leave the city. You must come! (*Listens*) He's driving off! I've got to stop him. (*Out*)

(*Galileo walks back and forth. Mrs. Sarti returns, very pale, without her bundle*)

GALILEO   Don't stand around like that! The coach with the children will leave without you.

MRS. SARTI   They've left. They had to hold Virginia down. The children will be taken care of in Bologna. But who'd get you your meals?

GALILEO   You're crazy. Staying in the city to cook! . . . (*Takes up his papers*) You mustn't take me for a fool, Mrs. Sarti. I can't interrupt my observations. I have powerful enemies, I've got to supply proofs for certain propositions.

MRS. SARTI   You needn't apologize. But it's not reasonable.

b)

*Outside Galileo's house in Florence. Galileo comes out of the door and
looks down the street. Two nuns are passing by.*

GALILEO (*addresses them*)   Sisters, could you tell me where I can
buy milk? This morning the milk woman didn't come, and
my housekeeper is away.

THE FIRST NUN   Only the shops in the lower city are open.

THE OTHER NUN   Did you come out of this house? (*Galileo nods*)
This is the street!
(*The two nuns cross themselves, mumble an Ave Maria and run. A
man passes*)

GALILEO (*addresses him*)   Aren't you the baker who brings us our
bread? (*The man nods*) Have you seen my housekeeper? She
must have gone out last night. She hasn't been here all morning.
(*The man shakes his head. A window across the street is opened and
a woman looks out*)

THE WOMAN (*screams*)   Run! Quick! They've got the plague!
(*Frightened, the man runs away*)

GALILEO   Do you know anything about my housekeeper?

THE WOMAN   Your housekeeper collapsed in the street. Up
there. She must have known. That's why she left you. How
can people be so inconsiderate? (*She bangs the window shut*)
(*Children come down the street. When they see Galileo they run away
screaming. As Galileo turns around, two soldiers in full armor come
rushing in*)

THE SOLDIERS   Get back in that house! (*With their long lances they
push Galileo back into his house. They bolt the door behind him*)

GALILEO (*at a window*)   Can you tell me what's happened to the
woman?

THE SOLDIERS   They take 'em to potter's field.

THE WOMAN (*appears at her window again*)   The whole street back
there's infected. Why don't you close it off?
(*The soldiers stretch a rope across the street*)

THE WOMAN   But now nobody can get into our house! Don't
put your rope there. We're all well here. Stop! Stop! Can't
you hear? My husband's gone to the city, he won't be able

to get back. You beasts! You beasts!

(*Her sobbing and screaming are heard from inside. The soldiers leave. An old woman appears at another window*)

GALILEO   There seems to be a fire back there.

THE OLD WOMAN   The firemen won't touch it if there's any suspicion of plague. All they can think about is the plague.

GALILEO   Just like them! Their whole system of government is like that. They cut us off like a withered fig branch that's stopped bearing fruit.

THE OLD WOMAN   You mustn't say that. They're helpless, that's all.

GALILEO   Are you alone in your house?

THE OLD WOMAN   Yes. My son sent me a note. Thank God he heard last night that someone had died around here, so he didn't come home. There've been eleven cases in the neighborhood during the night.

GALILEO   I can't forgive myself for not sending my housekeeper away in time. I had urgent work to finish, but she had no reason to stay.

THE OLD WOMAN   We can't go away either. Who would take us in? You mustn't reproach yourself. I saw her. She left this morning, at about seven o'clock. She was sick, because when she saw me step out to bring in the bread she circled around me. I suppose she didn't want your house to be sealed off. But they get wise to everything.

(*A rattling sound is heard*)

GALILEO   What's that?

THE OLD WOMAN   They're making noise to drive away the clouds that carry the seeds of the plague.

(*Galileo roars with laughter*)

THE OLD WOMAN   How can you laugh?

(*A man comes down the street and finds it roped off*)

GALILEO   Hey, you! The street's closed and there's nothing to eat in the house.

(*The man has already run away*)

GALILEO   You can't just let us starve here! Hey! Hey!

THE OLD WOMAN   Maybe they'll bring us something. If they don't, I can put a pitcher of milk on your doorstep, if you're not afraid, but not until after dark.

GALILEO   Hey! Hey! Somebody ought to hear us.

(*Suddenly Andrea stands at the rope. His face is stained with tears*)

GALILEO   Andrea! How did you get here?

ANDREA   I was here this morning. I knocked, but you didn't open. People told me . . .

GALILEO   Didn't you go away?

ANDREA   I did. But I managed to jump out. Virginia went on. Can I come in?

THE OLD WOMAN   No, you can not. You must go to the Ursulines. Maybe your mother is there too.

ANDREA   I've been there. But they wouldn't let me see her. She's too sick.

GALILEO   Did you walk the whole way back? You've been gone for three days.

ANDREA   That's how long it took, don't be angry. And once they caught me.

GALILEO (*helplessly*)   Don't cry, Andrea. You know, I've found out a few things in the meantime. Shall I tell you? (*Andrea nods, sobbing*) But listen carefully, or you won't understand. Remember when I showed you the planet Venus? Don't listen to that noise, it's nothing. Remember? You know what I saw? It's like the moon. I saw it as a half-circle and I saw it as a crescent. What do you think of that? I can show you the whole thing with a little ball and a lamp. It proves that Venus has no light of its own either. And it describes a simple circle around the sun, isn't that marvelous?

ANDREA (*sobbing*)   Yes, and that's a fact.

GALILEO (*softly*)   I didn't stop her from leaving.

(*Andrea is silent*)

GALILEO   But of course if I hadn't stayed it wouldn't have happened.

ANDREA   Will they have to believe you now?

GALILEO   I've got all the proofs I need. You know what? When all this is over, I'll go to Rome and show them.

(*Two muffled men with long poles and buckets come down the street. With the poles they hold out bread to Galileo and the old woman in their windows*)

THE OLD WOMAN   There's a woman with three children over there. Give her some too.

GALILEO   I've nothing to drink. There's no water in the house. (*The two shrug their shoulders*) Will you be back tomorrow?

THE MAN (*with muffled voice, his mouth covered by a cloth*)   Who knows what tomorrow will bring?

GALILEO   If you do come, could you reach up to me a little book that I need for my work?

THE MAN (*with a muffled laugh*)   A book won't do you any good now. Lucky if you get bread.

GALILEO   This boy, my pupil, will be here to give it to you. It's a table showing the period of Mercury, Andrea. I've mislaid mine. Will you find me one at school?

(*The men have already moved on*)

ANDREA   Sure. I'll get it for you, Mr. Galilei. (*Out*)

(*Galileo retires. The old woman steps out of the house opposite and places a pitcher at Galileo's door*)

6

1616: The Collegium Romanum, the research institute of the Vatican, confirms Galileo's discoveries.

> Things take indeed a wondrous turn
> When learned men do stoop to learn.
> Clavius, we are pleased to say
> Upheld Galileo Galilei.

Large hall in the Collegium Romanum, Rome. It is night. High ecclesiastics, monks, scholars, in groups. Galileo on one side, alone. Great merriment. Before the scene opens, boisterous laughter is heard.

A FAT PRELATE (*holds his belly for laughter*)   Oh stupidity! Oh stupidity! Can anyone tell me of a proposition that has *not* been believed?

A SCHOLAR   What about the proposition that you have an inconquerable aversion to food, monsignor!

THE FAT PRELATE   Will be believed, never fear. Only reasonable statements are not believed. The existence of the devil is being doubted. But that the earth spins around like a marble in a gutter, that's being believed. Sancta simplicitas!

A MONK (*acting out a comedy*)   I'm dizzy. The earth is turning too fast. Permit me to hold on to you, professor. (*He pretends to stagger and holds on to a scholar*)

THE SCHOLAR (*joining in the fun*)   Yes, she's dead drunk again, the old hag.

THE MONK   Stop, stop! We're sliding off! Stop, I say!

ANOTHER SCHOLAR   Venus is listing badly. I can only see half of her behind. Help!

(*A cluster of monks is forming who with much laughter pretend to be on a storm-tossed ship, struggling to avoid being thrown overboard*)

ANOTHER MONK   If only we don't get thrown on the moon. Brothers, they say it bristles with sharp mountain peaks!

THE FIRST SCHOLAR   Plant your foot against it.

THE FIRST MONK   And don't look down. I feel as sick as a monkey.

THE FAT PRELATE (*pointedly loud in Galileo's direction*)   What! Monkey business in the Collegium Romanum?

(*Loud laughter. Two astronomers of the Collegium come out of a door. Quiet sets in*)

A MONK   Still investigating? That's a scandal!

THE FIRST ASTRONOMER (*angrily*)   Not us!

THE SECOND ASTRONOMER   Where's this going to end? I can't understand Clavius ... Are all the claims made in the last fifty years to be taken at face value? In 1572 a new star appeared in the highest sphere, the eighth, the sphere of the fixed stars. It was rather larger and brighter than its neighbors and a year and a half later it was gone, overtaken by perdition. Is that any reason to question the eternal immutability of the heavens?

THE PHILOSOPHER   If we let them, they'd smash up the whole universe.

THE FIRST ASTRONOMER   Yes, what's the world coming to! Five years later, Tycho Brahe, a Dane, determined the trajectory of a comet. It started above the moon and broke through all the spheres, the material carriers of all movable celestial bodies. It met with no resistance, its light was not deflected. Is that any reason to doubt the existence of the spheres?

THE PHILOSOPHER   Out of the question! How can Christopher Clavius, the greatest astronomer of Italy and of the church, lower himself to investigating such stuff!

THE FAT PRELATE   Scandalous!

THE FIRST ASTRONOMER   But there he is, investigating. There he sits, gaping through that devil's tube.

THE SECOND ASTRONOMER   Principiis obsta! The whole trouble began years ago when we started using the tables of Copernicus—a heretic—for calculating such things as the length of the solar year, the dates of solar and lunar eclipses, the positions of the celestial bodies.

A MONK   I ask you: What is better, to get a lunar eclipse three days behind schedule or to miss out on eternal salvation altogether?

A VERY THIN MONK (*steps forward with an open Bible, fanatically stabbing his finger at a passage*)   What does the Book say? "Sun, stand thou still upon Gibeon; and thou, moon, in the valley of Ajalon." How can the sun stand still if it never moves as these heretics claim? Does the Book lie?

THE FIRST ASTRONOMER   No, and that's why we're leaving.

THE SECOND ASTRONOMER   Yes, there *are* phenomena that perplex us astronomers, but must man understand everything? (*Both go out*)

THE VERY THIN MONK   They degrade the home of mankind, a planet they call it. They load man, animal, plant and soil on a cart and chase it in circles through the empty sky. Heaven and earth, they claim, have ceased to exist. The earth because it's a star in the sky, and the sky because it consists of many earths. There's no longer any difference between above and below, between eternal and transient. That we are transient, that we know. But now they tell us that heaven itself is transient. There are sun, moon and stars, but we live on this earth, that's what we've learned and what the Book says; but now, according to them, the earth is just another star. One day they'll be saying there's no difference between man and beast, that man himself is an animal and only animals exist.

THE FIRST SCHOLAR (*to Galileo*) Mr. Galilei, you've dropped something.

GALILEO (*who had taken his pebble out of his pocket during the preceding speech and dropped it on the floor, as he stoops to pick it up*) It didn't drop, monsignor, it rose.

THE FAT PRELATE (*turns his back on him*) The insolence of the man!

(*A very old cardinal comes in, supported by a monk. The others reverentially make room for him*)

THE VERY OLD CARDINAL Are they still in there? Can't they get this foolishness over with? Surely Clavius knows his astronomy. I hear this Mr. Galilei has moved man from the center of the universe to somewhere on the edge. Obviously he's an enemy of mankind. And ought to be treated as such. Man is the crown of creation, every child knows that, he's God's highest and most beloved creature. Would God have put his most marvelous work, his supreme effort on a little far-away star that's constantly on the move? Would he have sent His Son to such a place? How can there be men so perverse as to believe these slaves of their mathematical tables? How can one of God's creatures put up with such a thing?

THE FAT PRELATE (*in an undertone*) The gentleman is present.

THE VERY OLD CARDINAL (*to Galileo*) Oh, you're the man? You know, I don't see too well any more, but I can see that you look remarkably like the man—what was his name again?—whom we burned a few years ago.

THE MONK Your Eminence, you mustn't excite yourself. The doctor . . .

THE VERY OLD CARDINAL (*brushing him off, to Galileo*) You want to degrade our earth, though you live on it and receive everything from it. You're fouling your own nest! But I for one will not stand for it. (*He pushes the monk out of the way and struts proudly back and forth*) I'm not some nondescript being on some little star that briefly circles around somewhere. I walk with assurance on a firm earth, it stands still, it is the center of the universe, I am in the center, and the Creator's eye rests on me, on me alone. Around me, fixed to eight crystal spheres, revolve the fixed stars and the mighty sun, which was created

to illumine my surroundings. And myself as well, in order
that God may see me. Hence obviously and irrefutably, everything depends on me, man, the supreme work of God,
the creature in the center, the image of God, imperishable
and . . . (*He collapses*)

THE MONK   Your Eminence, you have overtaxed yourself!
(*At this moment the door in the rear is opened and the great Clavius
comes in at the head of his astronomers. Quickly, without a word or
a glance aside, he traverses the hall and, near the exit, says to a monk*)

CLAVIUS   He's right.
(*He goes out, followed by the astronomers. The door in the rear
remains open. Deadly silence. The very old cardinal revives*)

THE VERY OLD CARDINAL   What happened? Has there been a decision?
(*No one dares to tell him*)

THE MONK   Your Eminence, you must let them take you home.
(*The old man is helped out. All leave the hall, perturbed. A little
monk, a member of Clavius' investigating commission, stops at Galileo's side*)

THE LITTLE MONK (*furtively*)   Mr. Galilei, before he left Father
Clavius said: Now the theologians can see about setting the
heavenly spheres right again. You have prevailed. (*Out*)

GALILEO (*trying to hold him back*)   It has prevailed. Not I, reason
has prevailed!
(*The little monk has gone. Galileo is leaving too. In the doorway he
meets a tall cleric, the cardinal inquisitor, accompanied by an astronomer. Galileo bows. Before going out, he whispers a question to a
doorkeeper*)

DOORKEEPER (*whispering back*)   His Eminence the cardinal inquisitor.
(*The astronomer leads the cardinal inquisitor to the telescope*)

7

But the Inquisition places the Copernican doctrine on the Index (March 5, 1616).

> When Galileo was in Rome
> A cardinal asked him to his home.
> He wined and dined him as his guest
> And only made one small request.

The house of Cardinal Bellarmine in Rome. A ball is in progress. In the vestibule, where two ecclesiastical secretaries are playing chess and exchanging observations about the guests, Galileo is received by an applauding group of masked ladies and gentlemen. He is accompanied by his daughter Virginia and her fiancé Ludovico Marsili.

VIRGINIA   I won't dance with anyone else, Ludovico.

LUDOVICO   Your shoulder clasp is loose.

GALILEO
"Your tucker, Thaïs, is askew. Don't
Set it straight, for preciously it shows me
And others too some deeper disorder.
In the candlelight of the swirling ballroom
It makes them dream of
Darker coigns in the expectant park."

VIRGINIA   Feel my heart.

GALILEO (*places his hand on her heart*)   It's beating.

VIRGINIA   I want to look beautiful.

GALILEO   You'd better, or else they'll start doubting again that the earth revolves.

LUDOVICO   It doesn't revolve at all. (*Galileo laughs*) All Rome is talking of nothing but you, sir. After tonight Rome will be talking about your daughter.

GALILEO   Everybody agrees that it's easy to look beautiful in the Roman spring. I myself probably look like a paunchy Adonis.

(*To the secretaries*) I'm to wait here for the cardinal. (*To the couple*) Run along and enjoy yourselves!
(*Before they reach the ballroom in the rear Virginia skips back once more*)

VIRGINIA   Father, the hairdresser on Via del Trionfo took me first and made four ladies wait. He knew your name right away. (*Out*)

GALILEO (*to the secretaries playing chess*)   How can you go on playing chess the old way? Too confined. As it's played now, the larger pieces can range over many fields. The rook goes like this (*He demonstrates it*) and the bishop like this, and the queen like this and this. That gives you plenty of room and you can plan ahead.

THE FIRST SECRETARY   It doesn't fit in with our small salaries. We can only afford to move like this. (*He makes a short move*)

GALILEO   It's the other way round, my friend. If you live grandly, you can get away with anything. You must go with the times, gentlemen. You mustn't keep hugging the shore, one fine day you must venture out on the high seas.
(*The very old cardinal of the previous scene crosses the stage, steered by his monk. He notices Galileo, passes him by, then turns uncertainly and greets him. Galileo sits down. The beginning of Lorenzo de' Medici's famous poem about the transience of the world is heard from the ballroom, sung by boys*)

"I who have seen the summer's roses die
And all their petals pale and shriveled lie
Upon the chilly ground, I know the truth:
How evanescent is the flower of youth."

GALILEO   Rome.—Big party?

THE FIRST SECRETARY   The first carnival after the years of plague. All the great families of Italy are represented here tonight. The Orsinis, the Villanis, the Nuccolis, the Soldanieris, the Canes, the Lecchis, the Estensis, the Colombinis . . .

THE SECOND SECRETARY (*interrupts*)   Their Eminences, Cardinals Bellarmine and Barberini.
(*Enter Cardinal Bellarmine and Cardinal Barberini. They hold,*

respectively, a lamb's and a dove's mask mounted on sticks before their faces)

BARBERINI (*pointing his index finger at Galileo*) "The sun also ariseth, and the sun goeth down, and hasteth to his place where he arose." So says Solomon, and what does Galileo say?

GALILEO When I was this big (*He shows with his hand*), Your Eminence, I was on a ship, and I cried out: The shore's moving away.—Today I know that the shore stood still and the ship was moving.

BARBERINI Clever, clever. What we see, Bellarmine, to wit, that the stars in heaven are turning, need not be so, witness ship and shore. And what is true, to wit, that the earth turns, cannot be observed! Very clever. On the other hand, his satellites of Jupiter are hard nuts for our astronomers. Unfortunately, I too once read a little astronomy, Bellarmine. It clings to you like the itch.

BELLARMINE We must go with the times, Barberini. If star charts based on a new hypothesis make navigation easier for our seamen, let's use them. We disapprove only of doctrines that put scripture in the wrong. (*He waves a greeting to the ballroom*)

GALILEO Scripture.—"He that withholdeth corn, the people shall curse him." Proverbs of Solomon.

BARBERINI "A prudent man concealeth knowledge." Proverbs of Solomon.

GALILEO "Where no oxen are, the crib is clean: but much increase is by the strength of the ox."

BARBERINI "He that ruleth his spirit is better than he that taketh a city."

GALILEO "But a broken spirit drieth the bones." (*Pause*) "Doth not wisdom cry?"

BARBERINI "Can one go upon hot coals, and his feet not be burned?"—Welcome to Rome, my dear Galileo. You remember the founding of Rome? Two little boys, the story goes, received milk and shelter from a she-wolf. Ever since then all the she-wolf's children have had to pay for their milk. In return, the she-wolf provides all manner of pleasures, spiritual and worldly, from conversations with my learned

friend Bellarmine to three or four ladies of international re-
pute, would you like to see them? (*He leads Galileo toward the
rear to show him the ballroom. Galileo follows reluctantly*) No? He
prefers a serious discussion. Very well. Are you sure, friend
Galilei, that you astronomers aren't just trying to make astronomy a little easier for yourselves? (*He leads him back to the
front*) You like to think in circles or ellipses and in uniform
velocities, in simple motions commensurate with your minds.
But what if God had been pleased to make His stars move like
this? (*He moves his finger through the air in a very complicated course
with varying velocity in the air*) What would become of your
calculations?

GALILEO   Your Eminence, if God had created the world like this
(*He retraces Barberini's course*) He would have constructed our
minds like this too (*He repeats the same course*) to enable them
to recognize these courses as the simplest. I believe in reason.

BARBERINI   I consider reason inadequate. No answer. He's too
polite to say he considers mine inadequate. (*Laughs and returns
to the balustrade*)

BELLARMINE   Reason, my friend, doesn't go very far. All around
us we see nothing but falsehood, crime and weakness. Where
is the truth?

GALILEO (*angrily*)   I believe in reason.

BARBERINI (*to the secretaries*)   Don't take anything down. This is
a scientific discussion among friends.

BELLARMINE   Consider for a moment the intellectual effort it
cost the church fathers and many after them to make some
sense out of this world (abominable, isn't it?). Consider the
cruelty of those who have their peasants whipped half-naked
around their estates in the Campagna and the stupidity of the
wretches who kiss their feet in return.

GALILEO   Shameful! On my way here I saw . . .

BELLARMINE   We've transferred the responsibility for such conditions (the very stuff of life) which we cannot understand to
a higher being, we say that certain purposes are served
thereby, that a master plan is being followed. Not that our
minds are set entirely at ease. But now you come along and
accuse this supreme being of not knowing how the planets
move, when it's perfectly clear to you. Is that wise?

GALILEO (*launching into an explanation*)   I'm a faithful son of the church . . .

BARBERINI   He's really dreadful. In all innocence he accuses God of the juiciest boners in astronomy! I suppose God didn't work hard enough at His astronomy before He wrote Holy Scripture? My *dear* friend!

BELLARMINE   Don't you think it likely that the Creator knows more about His creation than any of His creatures?

GALILEO   But, gentlemen, after all we can misinterpret not only the movements of the heavenly bodies, but the Bible as well.

BELLARMINE   But wouldn't you say that after all the interpretation of the Bible is the business of the Holy Church?
(*Galileo is silent*)

BELLARMINE   You see, you don't answer. (*He makes a sign to the secretaries*) Mr. Galilei, the Holy Office has decided tonight that the doctrine of Copernicus, according to which the sun is the center of the cosmos and motionless, whereas the earth moves and is not the center of the cosmos, is inane, absurd, and heretical. I have been charged to admonish you to relinquish this opinion. (*To the first secretary*) Please repeat.

FIRST SECRETARY   His Eminence, Cardinal Bellarmine, to the aforementioned Galileo Galilei: The Holy Office has decided that the doctrine of Copernicus, according to which the sun is the center of the cosmos and motionless, whereas the earth moves and is not the center of the cosmos, is inane, absurd and heretical. I have been charged to admonish you to relinquish this opinion.

GALILEO   What does this mean?
(*From the ballroom another verse of the poem is heard, sung by boys*)

"I said, the seasons do not stay
Pluck the roses while it's May."

(*Barberini motions Galileo to keep quiet while the singing continues. They all listen*)

GALILEO   What about the facts? I understand that the astronomers of the Collegium Romanum have confirmed my observations.

BELLARMINE   And expressed their profound satisfaction, in a manner most complimentary to you.

GALILEO   But the satellites of Jupiter, the phases of Venus . . .

BELLARMINE   The Holy Congregation has arrived at its decision without taking these particulars into account.

GALILEO   In other words, all further scientific research . . .

BELLARMINE   Is guaranteed, Mr. Galilei. In keeping with the church tenet that we cannot know but may investigate. (*Again he salutes a guest in the ballroom*) You are at liberty to deal with this doctrine as a mathematical hypothesis. Science is the legitimate and most beloved daughter of the church, Mr. Galilei. None of us seriously believes that you wish to undermine man's trust in the church.

GALILEO (*angrily*)   To invoke trust is to exhaust it.

BARBERINI   Really? (*Laughing heartily, he slaps his shoulder. Then with a sharp look he says, not unkindly*) Don't throw the baby out with the bath water, my friend. Nor shall we. We need you more than you need us.

BELLARMINE   I can't wait to introduce Italy's greatest mathematician to the commissioner of the Holy Office who has the highest regard for you.

BARBERINI (*taking Galileo's other arm*)   Whereupon he changes back into a lamb. You too, my friend, should have come here in disguise—as a respectable doctor of scholastic philosophy. It's my mask that allows me a little freedom tonight. When I wear it, you may even hear me murmuring: If God did not exist, we should have to invent Him. Well, let's put our masks on again. Poor Galilei hasn't got one.

(*They take Galileo between them and lead him into the ballroom*)

FIRST SECRETARY   Have you got the last sentence?

SECOND SECRETARY   Putting it down. (*They write eagerly*) What was that about his believing in reason?

(*Enter the cardinal inquisitor*)

THE INQUISITOR   Has the interview taken place?

FIRST SECRETARY (*mechanically*)   First Mr. Galilei arrived with his daughter. She was betrothed today to Mr. . . . . (*The inquisitor motions him to skip it*) Mr. Galilei went on to tell us about the new method of playing chess in which, contrary to the rules, the pieces are moved over many squares.

THE INQUISITOR (*again beckons "no"*)   The minutes.

(*A secretary hands him the minutes and the cardinal sits down to skim through them. Two young ladies in masks cross the stage and curtsy to the cardinal*)

THE FIRST LADY   Who's that?

THE SECOND LADY   The cardinal inquisitor.

(*They giggle and leave. Enter Virginia, looking around for someone*)

THE INQUISITOR (*from his corner*)   Well, my daughter?

VIRGINIA (*with a little start as she has not seen him*)   Oh, Your Eminence!

(*The inquisitor, without looking up, tenders his right hand. She approaches, kneels down, and kisses his ring*)

THE INQUISITOR   Glorious night! Allow me to congratulate you on your engagement. Your fiancé comes of a distinguished family. Will you stay in Rome?

VIRGINIA   Not for the present, Your Eminence. There's so much to be done for a wedding.

THE INQUISITOR   Then you'll go back to Florence with your father. I'm glad to hear it. I imagine your father needs you. Mathematics is a cold housewife, I should say. A woman of flesh and blood in such surroundings makes all the difference. It's so easy to lose oneself in the universe which is so very immense if one happens to be a great man.

VIRGINIA (*breathless*)   You're very kind, Your Eminence. I really know practically nothing about these things.

THE INQUISITOR   Indeed? (*He laughs*) Well, I suppose they don't eat fish in the fisherman's house. It will amuse your father to hear that, come right down to it, you learned what you know about the heavenly bodies from me. (*Leafing through the minutes*) I read here that our innovators, whose acknowledged leader is your father—a great man, one of the greatest—regard our present ideas about the importance of our good earth as somewhat exaggerated. Well then, from the age of Ptolemy, a sage of antiquity, to the present day, the whole of creation, that is, the entire crystal globe with the earth at its center, has been computed to measure approximately two thousand earth diameters. Quite a lot of space, but not enough, not nearly enough, for the innovators. They maintain, so I hear, that the universe extends further than we can imagine, that the distance between earth and sun—a rather considerable distance, we always thought—is so negligibly

small when compared with the distance between our poor
earth and the fixed stars on the outermost crystal sphere, that
there is no need whatever to consider it in our calculations.
Yes, our innovators live on a very grand scale.
(*Virginia laughs. The inquisitor, too, laughs*)

THE INQUISITOR   And indeed, certain gentlemen of the Holy
Office, not so long ago, came very close to taking offence at
such a picture of the world, compared to which our old picture is a mere miniature that might well be hanging from the
charming neck of a certain young lady. The gentlemen of the
Holy Office are worried that a prelate or even a cardinal
might get lost in such enormous spaces. The Almighty might
even lose sight of the pope himself. Yes, it's all very amusing.
But even so, my dear child, I'm glad that you'll be staying
with your eminent father, whom we all hold in the highest
esteem. I wonder if I know your father confessor . . .

VIRGINIA   Father Christopher of St. Ursula.

THE INQUISITOR   Well then, I'm glad you'll be going with your
father. He will need you, perhaps you can't conceive of such
a thing, but the time will come. You're very young and very
much alive and greatness is not always an easy thing to bear
for those to whom God has given it, no, not always. No
mortal is too great to be included in a prayer. But I'm keeping
you, dear child, and I'm making your fiancé jealous and perhaps your father too by telling you something about the heavenly bodies—which may, to be sure, be quite obsolete. Hurry
back to the ball, but don't forget to give Father Christopher
my regards.
(*Virginia, after a deep curtsy, leaves quickly*)

8

A Conversation

> Galileo, feeling grim
> A young monk came to visit him.
> The monk was born of common folk.
> It was of science that they spoke.

In the palace of the Florentine ambassador to Rome, Galileo listens to the little monk, who after the session of the Collegium Romanum repeated Father Clavius' remark to him in a whisper.

GALILEO Speak up, speak up! The cloth you wear entitles you to say what you please.

THE LITTLE MONK I've studied mathematics, Mr. Galilei.

GALILEO That might be a good thing if it led you to admit that two times two is sometimes four.

THE LITTLE MONK For three nights I haven't been able to sleep, Mr. Galilei. I can't figure out how to reconcile the decree which I've read with the satellites of Jupiter which I've seen. So I decided to read mass this morning and come and see you.

GALILEO To tell me that Jupiter has no satellites?

THE LITTLE MONK No. I recognized the wisdom of the decree. It showed me how dangerous unrestricted inquiry can be to mankind, and I've decided to give up astronomy. Still, I felt I had to acquaint you with the motives which compel me, even though I'm an astronomer, to desist from pursuing a certain doctrine.

GALILEO I can assure you that such motives are well known to me.

THE LITTLE MONK I understand your bitterness. You're thinking of certain exceptional means of pressure exerted by the church.

GALILEO Don't beat about the bush: instruments of torture.

THE LITTLE MONK   Yes, but I'd like to speak of other motives. Forgive me if I talk about myself. I grew up in the Campagna. My parents are peasants, simple folk. They know all about olive trees, but very little else. As I observe the phases of Venus, I can see my parents sitting by the stove with my sister, eating lasagna. I see the beams over their heads, blackened by the smoke of centuries, I see distinctly their work-worn old hands and the little spoons they hold in them. They're very poor, but even in their misery there is a certain order. There are cyclic rhythms, scrubbing the floor, tending the olive trees in their seasons, paying taxes. There's a regularity in the calamities that descend on them. My father's back wasn't bowed all at once, no, a little more with every spring in the olive grove, just as the child-bearing that has made my mother more and more sexless occurred at regular intervals. What gives them the strength to sweat their way up stony paths with heavy baskets, to bear children, even to eat, is the feeling of stability and necessity they get from the sight of the soil, of the trees turning green every year, of their little church standing there, and from hearing Bible verses read every Sunday. They have been assured that the eye of God is upon them, searching and almost anxious, that the whole world-wide stage is built around them in order that they, the players, may prove themselves in their great or small roles. What would my people say if I were to tell them they were living on a small chunk of stone that moves around another star, turning incessantly in empty space, one among many and more or less significant? What would be the good or necessity of their patience, of their acquiescence in their misery? What would be the good of the Holy Scripture which explains everything and demonstrates the necessity of all their sweat, patience, hunger and submission, if it turns out to be full of errors? No, I can see their eyes waver, I can see them rest their spoons on the table, I can see how cheated and betrayed they feel. In that case, they will say, no one is watching over us. Must we, untaught, old and exhausted as we are, look out for ourselves? No one has given us a part to play, only this wretched role on a tiny star which is wholly dependent, around which nothing turns? There is no sense in our misery, hunger means no more than going without food, it is no longer a test of strength; effort means no more than bending and carrying, there is no virtue in it. Can you understand now that in the decree of the Holy Congregation I discern a noble motherly compassion, a great goodness of soul?

GALILEO   Goodness of soul! Don't you simply mean that there's nothing left, the wine's been drunk, their lips are parched, so let them kiss the cassock. But why is nothing left? Why is there no order in this country but the order in an empty drawer, and no necessity but the necessity of working oneself to death? Amid overflowing vineyards and wheat fields? Your peasants in the Campagna are paying for the wars which the vicar of gentle Jesus is waging in Spain and Germany. Why does he put the earth at the center of the universe? Because he wants the See of St. Peter to be in the center of the world! That's the crux of the matter. You're right; the question is not the planets, but the peasants of the Campagna. And don't talk to me about the beauty of phenomena in the golden glow of old age. Do you know how the Margaritifera oyster produces pearls? By contracting a near-fatal disease, by enveloping an unassimilable foreign body, a grain of sand, for instance, in a ball of mucus. It almost dies in the process. To hell with the pearl, give me the healthy oyster. Virtue is not bound up with misery, my friend. If your people were prosperous and happy, they could develop the virtues of prosperity and happiness. But today the virtues of exhausted people derive from exhausted fields, and I reject those virtues. Yes, sir, my new water pumps can work more miracles than your preposterous superhuman toil.—"Be fruitful and multiply," because your fields are barren and you are decimated by wars. You want me to lie to your people?

THE LITTLE MONK (*in great agitation*)   The very highest motives bid us keep silent: the peace of mind of the wretched and lowly!

GALILEO   Would you care to see a Cellini clock that Cardinal Bellarmine's coachman left here this morning? You see, my friend, as a reward for my letting your good parents have their peace of mind, the government offers me the wine which they press in the sweat of their countenance, which as you know was fashioned in the image of God. If I agreed to keep silent, my motives would undoubtedly be rather sordid: an easy life, no persecution, and so on.

THE LITTLE MONK   Mr. Galilei, I'm a priest.

GALILEO   You're also a physicist. And you can see that Venus has phases. Look out there. (*He points out the window*) Can you see the little Priapus by the laurel tree at the well? The god of gardens, birds, and thieves, rustic, obscene, two thousand years old. He wasn't so much of a liar. All right, we'll skip that, I too am a son of the church. But do you know the *Eighth Satire* of Horace? I've been rereading him lately, he gives me a certain balance. (*He reaches for a small book*) He puts words in the mouth of this same Priapus, a little statue that used to stand in the Esquiline Gardens. Here's how it starts:

"I was a figtree stump, wood of little use
When once a carpenter, pondering whether
To fashion a Priapus or a footstool
Decided on the god . . ."

Do you think Horace would have let anyone forbid him the footstool and put a table in the poem instead? Sir, a cosmology in which Venus has no phases violates my esthetic sense! We can't invent machines for pumping river water if we're forbidden to study the greatest machine before our eyes, the mechanism of the heavenly bodies. The sum total of the angles in a triangle can't be changed to suit the requirements of the curia. Nor can I calculate the courses of flying bodies in such a way as to account for witches riding on broomsticks.

THE LITTLE MONK   Don't you think the truth will prevail, even without us, if it is the truth?

GALILEO   No, no, no. Truth prevails only when we make it prevail. The triumph of reason can only be the triumph of reasoning men. You describe your peasants in the Campagna as if they were moss on their huts. How can anyone imagine that the sum of the angles of a triangle runs counter to *their* needs! But if they don't rouse themselves and learn how to think, the best irrigation systems in the world won't do them any good. Damn it, I see the divine patience of your people, but where is their divine wrath?

THE LITTLE MONK   They're tired.

GALILEO (*throws a bundle of manuscripts in front of him*)   Are you a physicist, my son? Here you'll find the reasons for the ocean's tides. But don't read it, do you hear. Ah, reading already? I see you're a physicist.

(*The little monk has immersed himself in the papers*)

GALILEO   An apple from the tree of knowledge. He gobbles it up. He'll be damned for all eternity, but he's got to bolt it down, the hapless glutton. Sometimes I think I'd gladly be locked up in a dungeon ten fathoms below ground, if in return I could find out one thing: What is light? And the worst of it is: What I know I must tell others. Like a lover, a drunkard, a traitor. It's a vice, I know, and leads to ruin. But how long can I go on shouting into empty air—that is the question.

THE LITTLE MONK (*points at a passage in the papers*)   I don't understand this sentence.

GALILEO   I'll explain it to you, I'll explain it to you.

9

After a silence of eight years Galileo feels encouraged by the enthronement of a new pope, himself a scientist, to resume his research in the forbidden field. The sunspots.

> Eight long years with tongue in cheek
> Of what he knew he did not speak.
> The temptations grew too great
> And Galileo challenged fate.

Galileo's house in Florence. Galileo's pupils, Federzoni, the little monk and Andrea Sarti, now a young man, are gathered for an experiment. Galileo, standing, is reading a book.—Virginia and Mrs. Sarti are sewing bridal linen.

VIRGINIA   Sewing a trousseau is fun. This is for the long dining table, Ludovico loves to have company. But it has got to be right, his mother notices every stitch. She isn't happy about father's books. Any more than Father Christopher.

MRS. SARTI   He hasn't written a book in years.

VIRGINIA   I think he saw he was mistaken. In Rome, a very high ecclesiastic told me a lot of things about astronomy. The distances are too great.

ANDREA (*writes the program for the day on a blackboard and reads aloud*) "Thursday afternoon: Floating bodies."—That means ice again; bucket of water; scales; iron needle; Aristotle. (*He fetches the objects*)
(*The others are looking up things in books. Enter Filippo Mucius, a scholar in his middle years. He appears to be upset*)

MUCIUS   Would you tell Mr. Galilei he must see me? He has condemned me without a hearing.

MRS. SARTI   I've told you he doesn't wish to see you.

MUCIUS   God will reward you if you ask him again. I must speak to him.

VIRGINIA (*goes to the staircase*)   Father!

GALILEO   What is it?

VIRGINIA   Mr. Mucius!

GALILEO (*looks up brusquely, goes to the head of the stairs, his pupils trailing behind him*)   What do you want?

MUCIUS   Mr. Galilei, I request permission to explain the passages in my book which seem to indicate a condemnation of the Copernican doctrine that the earth revolves. I've . . .

GALILEO   What is there to explain? You are in full agreement with the Holy Congregation's decree of 1616. You are perfectly within your rights. It's true, you studied mathematics with us, but we have no authority to make you say that two times two is four. You have every right to say that this stone (*He takes the pebble from his pocket and throws it down to the ground floor*) has just flown up to the ceiling.

MUCIUS   Mr. Galilei, I . . .

GALILEO   Don't talk about difficulties! The plague didn't prevent me from going on with my observations.

MUCIUS   Mr. Galilei, the plague is not the worst.

GALILEO   Let me tell you this: Not to know the truth is just stupid. To know the truth and call it a lie is criminal! Leave my house at once!

MUCIUS (*tonelessly*) You are right. (*He goes out*)

(*Galileo returns to his study*)

FEDERZONI That's how it is, I'm afraid. He doesn't amount to much and no one could pay any attention to him if he hadn't been your pupil. But now of course they all say: He's heard everything Galileo had to say and is forced to admit that it's all wrong.

MRS. SARTI I feel sorry for the gentleman.

VIRGINIA Father was very fond of him.

MRS. SARTI I wanted to talk to you about your marriage, Virginia. You're such a young thing, and you have no mother, and your father just puts little pieces of ice in water. Anyway, I wouldn't ask him questions about your marriage if I were you. He would say the most dreadful things for a week, naturally at meals when the young people are there, because he hasn't half a scudo's worth of shame in him, never did have. That's not what I had in mind, I'm thinking of what the future has in store. Not that I know anything, I'm only an ignorant woman. But this is a very serious thing, you mustn't go into it blindly. I do think you should go to a real astronomer at the university and consult him about your horoscope. Then you'll know what to expect. Why are you laughing?

VIRGINIA Because I've been.

MRS. SARTI (*very curious*) What did he say?

VIRGINIA For three months I must be careful because the sun will be in Aries, but then I get a very good ascendant and the clouds will part. As long as I don't lose sight of Jupiter, I can go on any journey I please, because I'm an Aries.

MRS. SARTI And Ludovico?

VIRGINIA He's a Leo. (*After a little pause*) That means sensual, I think.

(*Pause*)

VIRGINIA I know that step. It's Mr. Gaffone, the rector.

(*Enter Mr. Gaffone, the rector of the university*)

GAFFONE Just thought I'd bring you a book that might be of interest to your father. For heaven's sake don't disturb Mr. Galilei. I can't help feeling that every minute taken from that great man is a minute taken from Italy. I'll just put the book in your little hands, and disappear, on tiptoe.

(*He goes out. Virginia hands the book to Federzoni*)

GALILEO   What's it about?

FEDERZONI   I don't know. (*Spelling it out*) "De maculis in sole."

ANDREA   On the sunspots. Another one!

(*Federzoni angrily hands it to him*)

ANDREA   Listen to this dedication! "To the greatest living authority on physics, Galileo Galilei."

(*Galileo has immersed himself once more in his book*)

ANDREA   I've read the treatise by Fabricius in Holland. He believes the spots are clusters of stars passing between the earth and the sun.

THE LITTLE MONK   Isn't that doubtful, Mr. Galilei?

(*Galileo does not answer*)

ANDREA   In Paris and Prague they think they're vapors from the sun.

FEDERZONI   Hm.

ANDREA   Federzoni has his doubts.

FEDERZONI   Kindly leave me out of it. I said "Hm," that's all. I'm the lens grinder, I grind lenses, you people look through them and observe the sky, and what you see is not spots, but "maculis." How can I doubt anything? How many times do I have to tell you I can't read these books, they're in Latin. (*In his anger he gesticulates with the scales. A pan falls to the floor. Galileo walks over and silently picks it up*)

THE LITTLE MONK   It's blissful to doubt; I wonder why.

ANDREA   Every sunny day in the last two weeks I've climbed up to the attic, right under the roof. A thin beam of light comes down through a tiny crack in the tiles. With that beam you can catch the reverse image of the sun on a sheet of paper. I saw a spot as big as a fly and blurred like a small cloud. It moved. Why don't we investigate those spots, Mr. Galilei?

GALILEO   Because we're working on floating bodies.

ANDREA   Mother has whole baskets full of letters. All Europe wants your opinion. With the reputation you've built up, you can't be silent.

GALILEO   Rome has allowed me to build up a reputation because I've kept silent.

FEDERZONI   But you can't afford to be silent any more.

GALILEO   Nor can I afford to be roasted over a wood fire like a ham.

ANDREA   Do you think the spots come into it?

(*Galileo does not answer*)

ANDREA   All right, let's stick to our little pieces of ice. They can't hurt you.

GALILEO   Exactly.—Our proposition, Andrea!

ANDREA   We assume that whether a body floats or not depends essentially not on its shape, but on whether it is lighter or heavier than water.

GALILEO   What does Aristotle say?

THE LITTLE MONK   "Discus latus platique . . ."

GALILEO   Translate, translate!

THE LITTLE MONK   "A broad, flat disk of ice floats in water, whereas an iron needle sinks."

GALILEO   Why then, according to Aristotle, doesn't ice sink?

THE LITTLE MONK   Because, being broad and flat, it cannot divide the water.

GALILEO   Very well. (*A piece of ice is handed to him and he puts it into the bucket*) Now I press the ice firmly down to the bottom of the bucket. I remove the pressure of my hands. What happens?

THE LITTLE MONK   It rises to the surface.

GALILEO   Correct. In rising it seems to be able to divide the water. Fulganzio!

THE LITTLE MONK   But why then does it float at all? Ice is heavier than water, because it is condensed water.

GALILEO   What if it were diluted water?

ANDREA   It must be lighter than water, or it wouldn't float.

GALILEO   Aha!

ANDREA   Just as an iron needle can't float. Everything lighter than water floats, everything heavier sinks. Which was to be proved.

GALILEO   Andrea, you must learn to think carefully. Give me the iron needle. A sheet of paper. Is iron heavier than water?

ANDREA   Yes.

(*Galileo places the needle on a sheet of paper and floats it in the water. Pause*)

GALILEO What happens?

FEDERZONI The needle floats! Holy Aristotle, they never checked up on him!

(*They laugh*)

GALILEO One of the main reasons for the poverty of science is that it is supposed to be so rich. The aim of science is not to open the door to everlasting wisdom, but to set a limit to everlasting error. Take that down.

VIRGINIA What's the matter?

MRS. SARTI Every time they laugh, a fright comes over me. I wonder what they're laughing about.

VIRGINIA Father says theologians have their church bells and physicists have their laughter.

MRS. SARTI At least I'm glad he doesn't look through his tube so much any more. That was much worse.

VIRGINIA No, he only puts pieces of ice in water. No harm can come of that.

MRS. SARTI Who knows?

(*Enter Ludovico Marsili in traveling garb, followed by a manservant with luggage. Virginia runs toward him and embraces him*)

VIRGINIA Why didn't you let us know you were coming?

LUDOVICO I was near here inspecting our vineyards, and I just couldn't stay away.

GALILEO (*as though nearsighted*) Who's that?

VIRGINIA Ludovico.

THE LITTLE MONK Can't you see him?

GALILEO Oh yes, Ludovico. (*Goes toward him*) How are the horses?

LUDOVICO They're fine, sir.

GALILEO Sarti, let's celebrate. Bring us a jug of that old Sicilian wine!

(*Mrs. Sarti goes out with Andrea*)

LUDOVICO (*to Virginia*) You look pale. Country life will do you good. Mother is expecting you in September.

VIRGINIA Wait, I want to show you my wedding dress. (*Runs out*)

GALILEO Sit down.

LUDOVICO I hear you have more than a thousand students in

your lectures at the university, sir. What are you working on at the moment?

GALILEO   Routine stuff. Did you come through Rome?

LUDOVICO   Yes.—Before I forget, mother congratulates you on your admirable tact in connection with all that fuss over the sunspots in Holland.

GALILEO (*dryly*)   That's kind of her.

(*Mrs. Sarti and Andrea bring wine and glasses. All gather around the table*)

LUDOVICO   Rome has found a topic of conversation for February. Christopher Clavius said he was afraid the whole earth-around-the-sun circus would flare up again because of those sunspots.

ANDREA   Don't let it worry you.

GALILEO   Any other news from the Holy City, apart from hopes for new sins on my part?

LUDOVICO   You heard, of course, that the Holy Father is dying?

THE LITTLE MONK   Oh.

GALILEO   Who's mentioned as successor?

LUDOVICO   Mostly Barberini.

GALILEO   Barberini.

ANDREA   Mr. Galilei knows Barberini personally.

THE LITTLE MONK   Cardinal Barberini is a mathematician.

FEDERZONI   A scientist in the chair of St. Peter!

(*Pause*)

GALILEO   I see, now they need men like Barberini who've read a little mathematics. Things will start moving, Federzoni, we may live to see the day when we won't have to glance over our shoulders like criminals every time we say that two times two is four. (*To Ludovico*) I like this wine, Ludovico. What do you think of it?

LUDOVICO   It's good.

GALILEO   I know the vineyard. The slope is steep and stony, the grapes are almost blue. I love this wine.

LUDOVICO   Yes, sir.

GALILEO   There are little shadows in it. And it's almost sweet, but stops at the "almost."—Andrea, put the stuff away, the ice and bucket and needle.—I value the consolations of the flesh.

I have no patience with cowardly souls who speak of weakness. I say: To enjoy yourself is an achievement.

THE LITTLE MONK   What are you taking up next?

FEDERZONI   We're starting in again on the earth-around-the-sun circus.

ANDREA (*singing in an undertone*)
The Book says it stands still. And so
Each learned doctor proves.
The Holy Father takes it by the ears
And holds it fast. And yet it moves.

(*Andrea, Federzoni and the little monk hurry to the workbench and clear it*)

ANDREA   We might even find out that the sun revolves too. How would you like that, Marsili?

LUDOVICO   What's the excitement about?

MRS. SARTI   You're not going back to those abominations, Mr. Galilei?

GALILEO   Now I know why your mother sent you here. Barberini is on the rise. Knowledge will be a passion and research a delight. Clavius is right, these sunspots do interest me. You like my wine, Ludovico?

LUDOVICO   I said I did, sir.

GALILEO   You really like it?

LUDOVICO (*stiffly*)   I like it.

GALILEO   Would you go so far as to accept a man's wine or his daughter without asking him to give up his profession? What has my astronomy got to do with my daughter? The phases of Venus don't affect my daughter's rear end.

MRS. SARTI   Don't be vulgar. I'll go get Virginia.

LUDOVICO (*holds her back*)   In families like mine marriages are not decided by sexual considerations alone.

GALILEO   Did they prevent you from marrying my daughter for the last eight years because I was on probation?

LUDOVICO   My wife will also have to cut a figure in our village church.

GALILEO   You mean, your peasants won't pay their rent if the lady of the manor is insufficiently saintly?

LUDOVICO   In a way.

GALILEO   Andrea, Fulganzio, get the brass mirror and the

screen! We'll project the sun's image on it to protect our eyes. That's your method, Andrea.

(*Andrea and the little monk get mirror and screen*)

LUDOVICO   Years ago in Rome, sir, you signed a pledge to stay away from this earth-around-the-sun business.

GALILEO   Oh well. We had a reactionary pope in those days.

MRS. SARTI   Had! His Holiness isn't even dead yet!

GALILEO   Pretty near, pretty near!—Put a grid over the screen. We'll proceed methodically. And we'll be able to answer all those letters, won't we, Andrea?

MRS. SARTI   "Pretty near!" Fifty times that man weighs his pieces of ice, but when something happens that suits his purposes he believes it blindly!

(*The screen is put up*)

LUDOVICO   Mr. Galilei, if His Holiness should die, the next pope—no matter who he is or how much he loves science—will have to take account of how much the country's leading families love him.

THE LITTLE MONK   God made the physical world, Ludovico; God made the human brain; God will allow physics.

MRS. SARTI   Galileo, let me tell you something. I've watched my son fall into sin for the sake of these "experiments" and "theories" and "observations," and I haven't been able to do anything about it. You set yourself against the authorities and they gave you a warning. The greatest cardinals spoke to you the way you'd speak to a sick horse. It worked for a while, but two months ago, right after the Immaculate Conception, I caught you sneaking back to your "observations." In the attic! I didn't say anything, but I knew. I ran out and lit a candle for St. Joseph. It's more than I can bear. When we're alone you show some sense, you say you've got to behave because it's dangerous, but two days of "experiments" and you're as bad as ever. If I lose my eternal salvation because I stand by a heretic, that's my business, but you have no right to trample your daughter's happiness with your big feet!

GALILEO (*gruffly*)   Get the telescope!

LUDOVICO   Giuseppe, put the luggage back in the coach.

(*The manservant goes out*)

MRS. SARTI   She'll never get over this. You can tell her yourself.

(*She runs out, still holding the pitcher*)

LUDOVICO   I see you've made up your mind. Mr. Galilei, three quarters of the year mother and I live on our estate in the Campagna and I can assure you that our peasants lose no sleep over your treatises on the moons of Jupiter. They work too hard in the fields. It might upset them, though, if they heard that attacks on the holy doctrine of the church were going unpunished. Don't forget that those poor brutalized wretches get everything mixed up. They really are brutes, you have no idea. A rumor that somebody's seen a pear growing on an apple tree makes them run away from their work to gab about it.

GALILEO (*with interest*)   Really?

LUDOVICO   Animals. When they come to the manor with a trifling complaint, mother has to have a dog whipped in front of them to remind them of discipline and order and good manners. You, Mr. Galilei, you may occasionally see flowering corn fields from your traveling coach, or absent-mindedly eat our olives and our cheese, but you have no idea how much effort it takes to raise all these things—all the supervision!

GALILEO   Young man, I never eat my olives absent-mindedly. (*Rudely*) You're wasting my time. (*Calls toward outside*) Is the screen ready?

ANDREA   Yes. Are you coming?

GALILEO   You whip more than dogs to keep discipline, don't you, Marsili?

LUDOVICO   Mr. Galilei, you have a marvelous brain. Too bad.

THE LITTLE MONK (*amazed*)   He's threatening you.

GALILEO   Yes, I might stir up his peasants to think new thoughts. And his servants and his overseers.

FEDERZONI   How? They don't know Latin.

GALILEO   I could write in the vernacular for the many instead of in Latin for the few. For our new ideas we need people who work with their hands. Who else wants to know the causes of everything? People who never see bread except on their tables have no desire to know how it's baked; those bastards would rather thank God than the baker. But the men who make the bread will understand that nothing can move unless something moves it. Fulganzio, your sister at the olive press won't be much surprised—she'll probably laugh—when she hears that the sun is not a gold escutcheon, but a lever: The earth moves because the sun moves it.

LUDOVICO   You'll always be a slave to your passions. Convey my apologies to Virginia. It's better, I think, if I don't see her now.

GALILEO   The dowry is at your disposal. At any time.

LUDOVICO   Good day. (*He goes*)

ANDREA   Our regards to all the Marsilis!

FEDERZONI   Who tell the earth to stand still so their castles won't fall off.

ANDREA   And to the Cencis and Villanis!

FEDERZONI   The Cervillis!

ANDREA   The Lecchis!

FEDERZONI   The Pierleonis!

ANDREA   Who'll only kiss the pope's foot as long as he tramples the people with it.

THE LITTLE MONK (*also at the instruments*)   The new pope will be an enlightened man.

GALILEO   And now let's start observing these spots in the sun which interest us—at our own risk, not counting too much on the protection of a new pope . . .

ANDREA (*interrupting*)   But fully confident of dispelling Mr. Fabricius' star shadows and the solar vapors of Prague and Paris, and proving that the sun rotates.

GALILEO   Reasonably confident that the sun rotates. My aim is not to prove that I've been right, but to find out whether or not I have been. I say: Abandon hope, all ye who enter upon observation. Maybe it's vapors, maybe it's spots, but before we assume that they're spots, though it would suit us if they were, we'd do better to assume they're fishtails. Yes, we shall start all over again from scratch. And we won't rush ahead with seven-league boots, but crawl at a snail's pace. And what we find today we'll wipe from the blackboard tomorrow, and not write it down again until we find it a second time. And if there's something we hope to find, we'll regard it with particular distrust when we do find it. Accordingly let us approach our observation of the sun with the inexorable resolve to prove that the earth *stands still!* Only after we have failed, after we have been totally and hopelessly defeated and are licking our wounds in utter dejection, only then shall we begin to ask whether the earth does not indeed move! (*With a twinkle*) But then, when every other hypothesis has gone up in smoke, then no mercy for those who have never observed anything, yet go on talking. Take the cloth off the tube and focus it on the sun! (*He adjusts the brass mirror*)

THE LITTLE MONK   I knew you had taken up your work again. I knew it when you didn't recognize Mr. Marsili.

(*In silence they begin their examinations. When the flaming image of the sun appears on the screen Virginia in her bridal gown runs in*)

VIRGINIA   You've sent him away! (*She faints. Andrea and the little monk rush to her aid*)

GALILEO   I've got to know.

10

In the course of the next ten years Galileo's doctrine is disseminated among the common people. Pamphleteers and ballad singers everywhere seize upon the new ideas. In the carnival of 1632 the guilds in many Italian cities take astronomy as the theme for their carnival processions.

A half-starved couple of show people with a five-year-old girl and an infant enter a market place where many people, some with masks, are awaiting the carnival procession. They carry bundles, a drum and other props.

THE BALLAD SINGER (*drumming*)   Citizens, ladies and gentlemen! Before the great carnival procession of the guilds arrives we bring you the latest Florentine song which is being sung all over northern Italy. We've imported it at great expense. The title is: The horrendous doctrine and teaching of Mr. Galileo Galilei, court physicist, or, A Foretaste of the Future. (*He sings*)

When the Almighty made the universe
He made the earth and then he made the sun.
Then round the earth he bade the sun to turn—
That's in the Bible, Genesis, Chapter One.
And from that time all beings here below
Were in obedient circles meant to go.

They all began to turn around
The little fellows round the big shots
And the hindmost round the foremost
On earth as it is in heaven.
Around the popes the cardinals
Around the cardinals the bishops
Around the bishops the secretaries
Around the secretaries the aldermen
Around the aldermen the craftsmen
Around the craftsmen the servants
Around the servants the dogs, the chickens and the
  beggars.

That, my friends, is the great order, ordo ordinum, as the
theologians call it, regula aeternis, the rule of rules. And then,
my friends, what happened then? (*He sings*)

  Up stood the learned Galileo
  (Chucked the Bible, pulled out his telescope, and took a
    look at the universe)
  And told the sun: Stand still!
  From this time on, the wheels
  Shall turn the other way.
  Henceforth the mistress, ho!
  Shall turn around the maid.
Now that was rash, my friends, it is no matter small:
For heresy will spread today like foul diseases.
Change Holy Writ, forsooth? What will be left at all?
Why: each of us would say and do just what he pleases!

Esteemed citizens, such doctrines are utterly impossible. (*He
sings*)

Good people, what will come to pass
If Galileo's teachings spread?
The server will not serve at mass
No servant girl will make the bed.
Now that is grave, my friends, it is no matter small:
For independent spirit spreads like foul diseases!
Yet life is sweet and man is weak and after all—
How nice it is, for once, to do just as one pleases!

Now, my good friends, here, look to the future and see what
the most learned doctor Galileo Galilei predicts. (*He sings*)

Two ladies at a fishwife's stall
Are in for quite a shock
The fishwife takes a loaf of bread
And gobbles up all her stock.
The carpenters take wood and build
Houses for themselves, not pews
And members of the cobblers' guild
Now walk around in shoes!
Is this permitted? No, it is no matter small:
For independent spirit spreads like foul diseases!
Yet life is sweet and man is weak and after all—
How nice it is, for once, to do just as one pleases!

The tenant kicks his noble master
Smack in the ass like that
The tenant's wife now gives her children
Milk that made the parson fat.
No, no my friends, for the Bible is no matter small:
For independent spirit spreads like foul diseases!
Yet life is sweet and man is weak and after all—
How nice it is for once to do just as one pleases!

THE SINGER'S WIFE

The other day I tried it too
And did my husband frankly tell
Let's see now if what you can do
Other stars can do as well.

BALLAD SINGER

No, no, no, no, no, no, stop, Galileo, stop!
For independent spirit spreads like foul diseases.
People must keep their place, some down and some on top!
Though it is nice for once to do just as one pleases.

BOTH

Good people who have trouble here below
In serving cruel lords and gentle Jesus
Who bids you turn the other cheek just so
While they prepare to strike the second blow:
Obedience will never cure your woe
So each of you wake up and do just as he pleases!

THE BALLAD SINGER   Esteemed citizens, behold Galileo Galilei's phenomenal discovery: The earth revolving around the sun! (*He belabors the drum violently. His wife and child step forward. The wife holds a crude replica of the sun, and the child, holding a gourd, image of the earth, over her head, circles around the woman. The singer excitedly points at the little girl as if she were performing a dangerous acrobatic feat in jerkily taking step after step in rhythm with the drumbeats. Then drumming from the rear*)
A DEEP VOICE (*calls out*)   The procession!
(*Enter two men in rags drawing a little cart. The "Grand Duke of Florence," a figure in sackcloth with a cardboard crown, sits on a ridiculous throne and peers through a telescope. Over the throne a painted sign "Looking for trouble." Next, four masked men march in carrying a huge tarpaulin. They stop and bounce a large doll representing a cardinal. A dwarf has posted himself to one side with a sign "The New Age." Among the crowd a beggar raises himself by his crutches and stomps the ground in a dance until he collapses. Enter a stuffed figure, more than life-size, Galileo Galilei, which bows to the audience. In front of it a child displays a giant open Bible with crossed-out pages.*)
THE BALLAD SINGER   Galileo Galilei, the Bible-smasher!
(*An outburst of laughter among the crowd*)

11

1633. The inquisition summons the world-famous scholar to Rome.

> The depths are hot, the heights are chill
> The streets are loud, the court is still.

Antechamber and staircase of the Medici Palace, Florence. Galileo and his daughter are waiting to be admitted to the grand duke.

VIRGINIA   It's been a long wait.

GALILEO   Yes.

VIRGINIA   There's that man again who's been following us. (*She points at a shady individual who passes by without paying attention to them*)

GALILEO (*whose eyesight is impaired*)   I don't know him.

VIRGINIA   I've seen him several times lately. He gives me the shivers.

GALILEO   Nonsense. We're in Florence, not among Corsican robbers.

VIRGINIA   There's Rector Gaffone.

GALILEO   *He* frightens *me*. The blockhead will draw me into another interminable conversation.

(*Mr. Gaffone, the rector of the university, descends the stairs. He is visibly startled when he sees Galileo and walks stiffly past the two, with rigidly averted head and barely nodding.*)

GALILEO   What's got into him? My eyes are bad again. Did he greet us at all?

VIRGINIA   Just barely.—What have you said in your book? Can they think it's heretical?

GALILEO   You hang around church too much. Getting up before dawn and running to mass is ruining your complexion. You pray for me, don't you?

VIRGINIA   There's Mr. Vanni, the iron founder. The one you designed the smelting furnace for. Don't forget to thank him for the quails.

(*A man has come down the stairs*)

VANNI   How did you like the quails I sent you, Mr. Galileo?

GALILEO   Maestro Vanni, the quails were excellent. Again many thanks.

VANNI   They're talking about you upstairs. They claim you're responsible for those pamphlets against the Bible that are being sold all over.

GALILEO   I know nothing about pamphlets. My favorite books are the Bible and Homer.

VANNI   Even if that were not the case: Let me take this opportunity of assuring you that we manufacturers are on your side. I don't know much about the movement of stars, but the way I look at it, you're the man who is fighting for the freedom to teach new knowledge. Just take that mechanical cultivator from Germany that you described to me. Last year alone five works on agriculture were published in London. Here we'd be grateful for one book about the Dutch canals. It's the same people who are making trouble for you and preventing the physicians in Bologna from dissecting corpses for research.

GALILEO   Your vote counts, Vanni.

VANNI   I hope so. Do you know that in Amsterdam and London they have money markets? And trade schools too. And newspapers that appear regularly. Here we're not even free to make money. They're against iron foundries because they claim too many workers in one place promote immorality. I swim or sink with men like you, Mr. Galilei! If ever they try to harm you, please remember that you have friends in every branch of industry. The cities of northern Italy are behind you, sir.

GALILEO   As far as I know no one has any intention of harming me.

VANNI   Really?

GALILEO   Really.

VANNI   I believe you'd be better off in Venice. Not so many cassocks. You'd be free to carry on the fight. I have a coach and horses, Mr. Galilei.

GALILEO   I can't see myself as a refugee. I love comfort.

VANNI   I understand. But to judge by what I heard up there, there's no time to be lost. I got the impression that right now they'd prefer not to have you in Florence.

GALILEO   Nonsense. The grand duke is a pupil of mine, not to mention the fact that if anyone tries to trip me up the pope himself will tell him where to get off.

VANNI   You don't seem able to distinguish your friends from your enemies, Mr. Galilei.

GALILEO   I'm able to distinguish power from lack of power. (*He brusquely steps away*)

VANNI   Well, I wish you luck. (*Goes out*)

GALILEO   (*back at Virginia's side*)   Every Tom, Dick and Harry with a grievance picks me as his spokesman, especially in places where it doesn't exactly help me. I've written a book on the mechanism of the universe, that's all. What people make or don't make of it is no concern of mine.

VIRGINIA   (*in a loud voice*)   If people only knew how you condemned the goings-on at last year's carnival.

GALILEO   Yes. Give a bear honey if it's hungry and you'll lose your arm.

VIRGINIA   (*in an undertone*)   Did the grand duke send for you today?

GALILEO   No, but I've sent in my name. He wants the book, he's paid for it. Ask somebody, complain about the long wait.

VIRGINIA   (*goes to talk to an attendant, followed by the individual*)   Mr. Mincio, has His Highness been informed that my father wishes to speak to him?

THE ATTENDANT   How should I know?

VIRGINIA   That's no answer.

THE ATTENDANT   Really?

VIRGINIA   You ought to be polite.

(*The attendant half turns his back on her and yawns while looking at the shady individual*)

VIRGINIA   (*has come back*)   He says the grand duke is still busy.

GALILEO   I heard you say something about "polite." What was it?

VIRGINIA   I thanked him for his polite answer, that's all. Can't you just leave the book for him? You're wasting your time.

GALILEO   I'm beginning to wonder what my time is worth. Maybe I should accept Sagredo's invitation to go to Padua for a few weeks. My health hasn't been up to snuff.

VIRGINIA   You couldn't live without your books.

GALILEO   We could take some of the Sicilian wine, one, two cases.

VIRGINIA   You always say it doesn't travel. And the court owes you three months' salary. They won't forward it.

GALILEO   That's true.

VIRGINIA (*whispers*)   The cardinal inquisitor!

(*The cardinal inquisitor descends the stairs. Passing them, he bows low to Galileo*)

VIRGINIA   What's the cardinal inquisitor doing in Florence, father?

GALILEO   I don't know. His attitude was respectful, I think. I knew what I was doing when I came to Florence and held my peace all these years. Their praises have raised me so high that they have to take me as I am.

THE ATTENDANT (*announces*)   His Highness, the grand duke!

(*Cosmo de' Medici comes down the stairs. Galileo approaches him. Cosmo, slightly embarrassed, stops*)

GALILEO   May I present Your Highness with my *Dialogues on the Two Chief Syst* . . .

COSMO   I see, I see. How are your eyes?

GALILEO   Not too good, Your Highness. With Your Highness' permission, I should like to present my . . .

COSMO   The state of your eyes alarms me. Yes, it alarms me a good deal. Haven't you been using your splendid tube a little too much? (*He walks off without accepting the book*)

GALILEO   He didn't take the book, did he?

VIRGINIA   Father, I'm afraid.

GALILEO (*subdued, but firmly*)   Don't show your feelings. We are not going home, but to Volpi, the glass cutter's. I've arranged with him to have a cart with empty wine casks ready in the tavern yard next door, to take me away at any time.

VIRGINIA   Then you knew . . .

GALILEO   Don't look back.

(*They start to leave*)

A HIGH OFFICIAL (*descending the stairs*)   Mr. Galilei, I have orders to inform you that the court of Florence is no longer in a position to oppose the request of the Holy Inquisition for your interrogation in Rome. Mr. Galilei, the coach of the Holy Inquisition is waiting for you.

12

The pope.

A room in the Vatican. Pope Urban VIII (formerly Cardinal Barberini) has received the cardinal inquisitor. During the audience the pope is being dressed. From outside the shuffling of many feet is heard.

THE POPE (*very loud*)   No! No! No!

THE INQUISITOR   Then Your Holiness really means to tell the doctors of all the faculties, the representatives of all the religious orders and of the entire clergy, who have come here guided by their childlike faith in the word of God as recorded in scripture to hear Your Holiness confirm them in their faith —you mean to inform them that scripture can no longer be considered true?

THE POPE   I won't permit the multiplication tables to be broken. No!

THE INQUISITOR   Yes, these people say it is only a matter of the multiplication tables, not of the spirit of rebellion and doubt. But it is not the multiplication tables. It is an alarming unrest that has come over the world. It is the unrest of their own minds, which they transfer to the immovable earth. They cry out: The figures force our hands! But where do these figures come from? Everyone knows they come from doubt. These people doubt everything. Is our human community to be built on doubt and no longer on faith? "You are my master, but I doubt whether that is a good arrangement." "This is your house and your wife, but I doubt whether they should not be mine." On the other hand, as we can read on the house walls of Rome, disgraceful interpretations are being put on Your Holiness' great love for art, to which we owe such marvelous collections: "The Barberinis are stripping Rome of what the barbarians failed to take." And abroad? It has pleased God to visit heavy tribulation upon the Holy See. Your Holiness' policy in Spain is misunderstood by persons lacking in insight, your rift with the emperor is deplored. For fifteen years Germany has been a shambles, people have been slaughtering one another with Bible quotations on their lips. And at a time when under the onslaught of plague, war and reformation, Christianity is being reduced to a few disorganized bands, a rumor is spreading through Europe that you are in secret league with Lutheran Sweden to weaken the Catholic emperor. This is the moment these mathematicians, these worms, choose to turn their tubes to the sky and inform the world that even here, the one place where your authority is not yet contested, Your Holiness is on shaky ground. Why, one is tempted to ask, this sudden interest in so recondite a science as astronomy? Does it make any difference how these bodies move? Yet, thanks to the bad example of that Florentine, all Italy, down to the last stableboy, is prattling about the phases of Venus and thinking at the same time of many irksome things which are held in our schools and elsewhere to be immutable. Where will it end, if all these people, weak in the flesh and inclined to excess, come to rely exclusively on their own reason, which this madman declares to be the ultimate authority? They begin by doubting whether the sun stood still at Gibeon and end up directing their unclean doubts at the church collections. Since they began sailing the high seas—to which I have no objection—they have been putting their trust in a brass sphere that they call a compass, and no longer in God. Even as a young man this Galileo wrote about machines. With machines they expect to work miracles. What kind of miracles? Of course they have no more use for God, but what is to be the nature of these miracles? For one thing, they expect to do away with Above and Below. They don't need it any more. Aristotle, whom in other respects they regard as a dead dog, said—and this they quote—: If the shuttle were to weave by itself and the plectron to pluck by itself, masters would no longer need apprentices nor lords servants. They believe that this time has come. This evil man knows what he is doing when he writes his astronomical works not in Latin but in the idiom of fishwives and wool merchants.

THE POPE   It's certainly in bad taste. I'll tell him.

THE INQUISITOR   Some he incites, others he bribes. The north Italian ship owners keep clamoring for Mr. Galilei's star charts. We shall have to yield to them, since material interests are involved.

THE POPE   But these star charts are based on his heretical statements, on the movements of certain heavenly bodies which become impossible if his doctrine is rejected. You can't reject the doctrine and accept the star charts.

THE INQUISITOR   Why not? It's the only solution.

THE POPE   This shuffling makes me nervous. Forgive me if I seem distracted.

THE INQUISITOR   Perhaps it speaks to you more clearly than I can, Your Holiness. Are all these people to go home with doubts in their hearts?

THE POPE   After all the man is the greatest physicist of our time, a beacon for Italy, and not some good-for-nothing crank. He has friends. There's Versailles. There's the court in Vienna. They will call the church a cesspool of rotten prejudices. Hands off!

THE INQUISITOR   Actually, we wouldn't have to go very far in his case. He is a man of the flesh. He would cave in very quickly.

THE POPE   He gets pleasure out of more things than any man I ever met. Even his thinking is sensual. He can never say no to an old wine or a new idea. I will not stand for any condemning of physical facts, any battle cry of "church" against "reason." I gave him leave to write his book provided it ended with a statement that the last word is not with science but with faith. He has complied.

THE INQUISITOR   But how did he comply? His book is an argument between a simpleton who—naturally—propounds the opinions of Aristotle, and an intelligent man, just as naturally voicing Mr. Galilei's opinions; and the concluding remark, Your Holiness, is made by whom?

THE POPE   What was that again? Who states our opinion?

THE INQUISITOR   Not the intelligent one.

THE POPE   That is impudence. This stamping in the halls is insufferable. Is the whole world coming here?

THE INQUISITOR   Not the whole world, but the best part of it. (*Pause. The pope is now fully robed*)

THE POPE   At the very most the instruments may be shown to him.

THE INQUISITOR   That will suffice, Your Holiness. Mr. Galilei is well versed in instruments.

13

On June 22, 1633, Galileo Galilei abjures his doctrine of the motion of the earth before the Inquisition.

> June twenty-second, sixteen thirty-three
> A momentous day for you and me.
> Of all the days that was the one
> An age of reason could have begun.

Palace of the Florentine ambassador in Rome. Galileo's pupils are waiting for news. The little monk and Federzoni are playing the new chess with its sweeping movements. Virginia kneels in a corner saying an Ave Maria.

THE LITTLE MONK   The pope refused to see him. No more scientific debates.

FEDERZONI   The pope was his last hope. I guess Cardinal Barberini was right when he said to him years ago: We need you. Now they've got him.

ANDREA   They'll kill him. The *Discorsi* will never be finished.

FEDERZONI (*with a furtive glance at him*)   You think so?

ANDREA   Because he'll never recant.

(*Pause*)

THE LITTLE MONK   When you lie awake at night you chew on the most useless ideas. Last night I couldn't get rid of the thought that he should never have left the republic of Venice.

ANDREA   He couldn't write his book there.

FEDERZONI   And in Florence he couldn't publish it.
(*Pause*)

THE LITTLE MONK   I also kept wondering whether they'd let him keep the stone he always carries in his pocket. His touchstone.

FEDERZONI   Where they're taking him people don't wear pockets.

ANDREA (*screaming*)   They won't dare! And even if they do, he'll never recant. "Not to know the truth is just stupid. To know the truth and call it a lie is criminal."

FEDERZONI   I don't think so either, and I wouldn't want to go on living if he did, but they have the power.

ANDREA   Power isn't everything.

FEDERZONI   Maybe not.

THE LITTLE MONK (*softly*)   He's been in prison for twenty-three days. Yesterday was the great interrogation. Today the judges are in session. (*As Andrea is listening, he raises his voice*) When I came to see him here two days after the decree, we were sitting over there; he showed me the little Priapus by the sundial in the garden—you can see it from here—and compared his own work with a poem by Horace, in which it is also impossible to change anything. He spoke of his esthetic sense, which compels him to look for the truth. And he told me his motto: Hieme et aestate, et prope et procul, usque dum vivam et ultra. He was referring to the truth.

ANDREA (*to the little monk*)   Did you tell him what he did in the Collegium Romanum while they were examining his tube? Tell him! (*The little monk shakes his head*) He acted the same as always. He put his hands on his hams, stuck out his belly and said: Gentlemen, I beg for reason! (*Laughingly he imitates Galileo*)
(*Pause*)

ANDREA (*referring to Virginia*)   She's praying for him to recant.

FEDERZONI   Let her pray. She's all mixed up since they talked to her. They brought her confessor down from Florence.
(*Enter the shady individual from the grand ducal palace in Florence*)

THE SHADY INDIVIDUAL   Mr. Galilei will be here soon. He may
want a bed.

FEDERZONI   Has he been released?

THE SHADY INDIVIDUAL   Mr. Galilei is expected to recant at five
o'clock before the plenary session of the Inquisition. The big
bell of St. Mark's will be rung and the wording of the abjura-
tion will be proclaimed publicly.

ANDREA   I don't believe it.

THE SHADY INDIVIDUAL   Because of the crowds in the streets, Mr.
Galilei will be conducted to the postern on this side of the
palace. (*Out*)

ANDREA (*suddenly in a loud voice*)   The moon is an earth and has
no light of its own. And Venus has no light of its own either
and is like the earth and moves around the sun. And four
moons revolve around the planet Jupiter which is as far away
as the fixed stars and not fastened to any sphere. And the sun
is the center of the universe and immovable in its place, and
the earth is not the center and not immovable. And he was
the man who proved it.

THE LITTLE MONK   No force can make what has been seen unseen.

(*Silence*)

FEDERZONI (*looks at the sundial in the garden*)   Five o'clock.

(*Virginia prays louder*)

ANDREA   I can't stand it! They're beheading the truth! (*He holds
his hands to his ears, so does the little monk. The bell is not rung. After
a pause filled with Virginia's murmured prayers Federzoni shakes his
head in the negative. The others drop their hands*)

FEDERZONI (*hoarsely*)   Nothing. It's three minutes past five.

ANDREA   He's resisting.

THE LITTLE MONK   He hasn't recanted!

FEDERZONI   No. Oh, my friends!

(*They embrace. They are wildly happy*)

ANDREA   You see: They can't do it with force! Force isn't everything! Hence: Stupidity is defeated, it's not invulnerable!
Hence: Man is not afraid of death!

FEDERZONI   Now the age of knowledge will begin in earnest.
This is the hour of its birth. Just think! If he had recanted!

THE LITTLE MONK   I didn't say anything but I was very worried.

I was faint of heart.

ANDREA   I knew it.

FEDERZONI   It would have been as if morning had turned back to night.

ANDREA   As if the mountain said: I'm water.

THE LITTLE MONK (*kneels down in tears*)   Lord, I thank Thee.

ANDREA   But now everything has changed. Man is lifting his head, tormented man, and saying: I can live. All this is accomplished when one man gets up and says No!

(*At this moment the big bell of St. Mark's begins to boom. All stand transfixed*)

VIRGINIA (*getting up*)   The bell of St. Mark's. He hasn't been condemned!

(*From the street the announcer is heard reciting Galileo's recantation*)

ANNOUNCER'S VOICE   "I, Galileo Galilei, professor of mathematics and physics in Florence, hereby abjure what I have taught, to wit, that the sun is the center of the world and motionless in its place, and the earth is not the center and not motionless. Out of a sincere heart and unfeigned faith, I abjure, condemn and execrate all these errors and heresies as I do all other errors and all other opinions in opposition to the Holy Church."

(*Darkness*)

(*When it grows light again, the bell is still booming, then it stops. Virginia has left. Galileo's pupils are still there*)

FEDERZONI   He never paid you properly for your work. You couldn't buy a pair of pants or publish anything. You had to put up with all that because you were "working for science"!

ANDREA (*loudly*)   Unhappy the land that has no heroes!

(*Galileo has come in, completely, almost unrecognizably, changed by the trial. He has heard Andrea's exclamation. For a few moments he hesitates at the door, expecting a greeting. As none is forthcoming and his pupils shrink back from him, he goes slowly and because of his bad eyesight uncertainly to the front where he finds a footstool and sits down*)

ANDREA   I can't look at him. I wish he'd go away.

FEDERZONI   Calm yourself.

ANDREA (*screams at Galileo*)   Wine barrel! Snail eater! Have you saved your precious skin? (*Sits down*) I feel sick.

GALILEO (*calmly*)   Get him a glass of water.

(*The little monk goes out to get Andrea a glass of water. The others pay no attention to Galileo who sits on his footstool, listening. From far off the announcer's voice is heard again*)

ANDREA   I can walk now if you'll help me.

(*They lead him to the door. When they reach it, Galileo begins to speak*)

GALILEO   No. Unhappy the land that needs a hero.

A reading in front of the curtain:

Is it not obvious that a horse falling from a height of three or four ells will break its legs, whereas a dog would not suffer any damage, nor would a cat from a height of eight or nine ells, or a cricket from a tower, or an ant even if it were to fall from the moon? And just as smaller animals are comparatively stronger than larger ones, so small plants too stand up better: an oak tree two hundred ells high cannot sustain its branches in the same proportion as a small oak tree, nor can nature let a horse grow as large as twenty horses or produce a giant ten times the size of man unless it changes all the proportions of the limbs and especially of the bones, which would have to be strengthened far beyond the size demanded by mere proportion.—The common assumption that large and small machines are equally durable is apparently erroneous.

Galileo, Discorsi

14

1633–1642. Galileo Galilei spends the rest of his life in a villa near Florence, as a prisoner of the Inquisition. The *Discorsi*.

> Sixteen hundred thirty-three to
> sixteen hundred forty-two
> Galileo Galilei remains a prisoner
> of the church until his death.

A large room with a table, a leather chair and a globe. Galileo, now old and almost blind, is experimenting carefully with a small wooden ball rolling on a curved wooden rail. In the anteroom a monk is sitting on guard. A knock at the door. The monk opens and a peasant comes in carrying two plucked geese. Virginia emerges from the kitchen. She is now about forty years old.

THE PEASANT   I'm supposed to deliver these.

VIRGINIA   Who from? I didn't order any geese.

THE PEASANT   I was told to say from someone that's passing through. (*Out*)
(*Virginia looks at the geese in astonishment. The monk takes them from her and examines them suspiciously. Satisfied, he gives them back and she carries them by the necks to Galileo in the large room*)

VIRGINIA   A present, dropped off by someone who's passing through.

GALILEO   What is it?

VIRGINIA   Can't you see?

GALILEO   No. (*He goes closer*) Geese. Was there any name?

VIRGINIA   No.

GALILEO (*taking one goose from her*)   Heavy. Maybe I'll have some.

VIRGINIA   You can't be hungry again. You just finished dinner. And what's wrong with your eyes today? You ought to be able to see them from where you are.

GALILEO   You're standing in the shadow.

VIRGINIA   I'm not in the shadow. (*She carries the geese out*)

GALILEO   Put in thyme and apples.

VIRGINIA (*to the monk*)   We must send for the eye doctor. Father couldn't see the geese.

THE MONK   I'll need permission from Monsignor Carpula.— Has he been writing again?

VIRGINIA   No. He's dictating his book to me, you know that. You have pages 131 and 132, they were the last.

THE MONK   He's an old fox.

VIRGINIA   He doesn't do anything against the rules. His repentance is real. I keep an eye on him. (*She gives him the geese*) Tell them in the kitchen to fry the liver with an apple and an onion. (*She comes back into the large room*) And now we're going to think of our eyes and stop playing with that ball and dictate a little more of our weekly letter to the archbishop.

GALILEO   I don't feel up to it. Read me some Horace.

VIRGINIA   Only last week Monsignor Carpula, to whom we owe so much—those vegetables the other day—told me the archbishop keeps asking him what you think of the questions and quotations he's been sending you. (*She has sat down ready for dictation*)

GALILEO   Where was I?

VIRGINIA   Section four: Concerning the reaction of the church to the unrest in the arsenal in Venice, I agree with Cardinal Spoletti's attitude concerning the rebellious rope makers . . .

GALILEO   Yes. (*Dictates*) . . . agree with Cardinal Spoletti's attitude concerning the rebellious rope makers, to wit, that it is better to dispense soup to them in the name of Christian charity than to pay them more for their ship's cables and bell ropes. All the more so, since it seems wiser to strengthen their faith than their greed. The Apostle Paul says: Charity never faileth.—How does that sound?

VIRGINIA   It's wonderful, father.

GALILEO   You don't think it could be mistaken for irony?

VIRGINIA   No, the archbishop will be very pleased. He's a practical man.

GALILEO   I rely on your judgment. What's the next point?

VIRGINIA   A very beautiful saying: "When I am weak then I am strong."

GALILEO No comment.

VIRGINIA Why not?

GALILEO What's next?

VIRGINIA "And to know the love of Christ, which passeth knowledge." Paul to the Ephesians three nineteen.

GALILEO I must especially thank Your Eminence for the magnificent quotation from the epistle to the Ephesians. Inspired by it, I found the following in our incomparable "Imitation": (*He quotes from memory*) "He to whom speaketh the eternal word is free from much questioning." May I seize this opportunity to say something on my own behalf? To this day I am being reproached for once having written a book on celestial bodies in the language of the market place. In so doing, I did not mean to suggest, or to express my approval of the writing of books on such important subjects as theology in the jargon of spaghetti vendors. The argument in favor of the service in Latin—that the universality of this language enables all nations to hear mass in exactly the same way—seems less than fortunate since the scoffers, who are never at a loss, may well argue that the use of this language prevents all nations from understanding the text. I for my part prefer to forego the cheap intelligibility of things holy. The Latin tongue, which protects the eternal verities of the church from the prying of the ignorant, inspires confidence when recited by priests, sons of the lower classes, in the pronunciation of their local dialects.—No, strike that out.

VIRGINIA The whole thing?

GALILEO Everything after the spaghetti vendors.

(*A knocking at the door. Virginia goes into the anteroom. The monk opens the door. Andrea Sarti appears. He is a man in his middle years*)

ANDREA Good evening. I am leaving Italy. To do scientific work in Holland. I was asked to see him on my way through and bring the latest news of him.

VIRGINIA I don't know if he'll want to see you. You never came to visit us.

ANDREA Ask him.

(*Galileo has recognized the voice. He sits motionless. Virginia goes in to him*)

GALILEO   Is it Andrea?

VIRGINIA   Yes. Should I send him away?

GALILEO (*after a pause*)   Bring him in.

(*Virginia leads Andrea inside*)

VIRGINIA (*to the monk*)   He's harmless. He was his pupil. So now he's his enemy.

GALILEO   Leave us alone, Virginia.

VIRGINIA   I want to hear what he says. (*She sits down*)

ANDREA (*cool*)   How are you?

GALILEO   Come closer. What are you doing? Tell me about your work. I hear you're on hydraulics.

ANDREA   Fabricius in Amsterdam has asked me to inquire about your health.

(*Pause*)

GALILEO   I'm well. I receive every attention.

ANDREA   I shall be glad to report that you are well.

GALILEO   Fabricius will be glad to hear it. And you may add that I am living in reasonable comfort. The depth of my repentance has moved my superiors to allow me limited scientific pursuits under clerical control.

ANDREA   Oh yes. We too have heard that the church is pleased with you. Your total submission has borne fruit. The authorities, I am told, are most gratified to note that since your submission no work containing any new hypothesis has been published in Italy.

GALILEO (*listening in the direction of the anteroom*)   Unfortunately there are countries which elude the protection of the church. I fear the condemned doctrines are being perpetuated in those countries.

ANDREA   There too your recantation has resulted in a setback most gratifying to the church.

GALILEO   You don't say. (*Pause*) Nothing from Descartes? No news from Paris?

ANDREA   Oh yes. When he heard you had recanted he stuffed his treatise on the nature of light in his desk drawer.

(*Long pause*)

GALILEO   I keep worrying about some of my scientific friends whom I led down the path of error. Has my recantation helped them to mend their ways?

ANDREA   I am going to Holland to carry on my work. The ox is not allowed to do what Jupiter denies himself.

GALILEO   I understand.

ANDREA   Federzoni is back at his lens grinding, in some shop in Milan.

GALILEO (*laughs*)   He doesn't know Latin.

(*Pause*)

ANDREA   Fulganzio, our little monk, has given up science and returned to the fold.

GALILEO   Yes. (*Pause*) My superiors are looking forward to my complete spiritual recovery. I'm making better progress than expected.

ANDREA   I see.

VIRGINIA   The Lord be praised.

GALILEO (*gruffly*)   Attend to the geese, Virginia.

(*Virginia leaves angrily. In passing she is addressed by the monk*)

THE MONK   I don't like that man.

VIRGINIA   He's harmless. You heard what he said. (*On her way out*) We've got fresh goat cheese.

(*The monk follows her out*)

ANDREA   I'm going to travel through the night so as to cross the border by morning. May I go now?

GALILEO   I can't see why you've come, Sarti. To stir me up? I've been living prudently and thinking prudently since I came here. I have my relapses even so.

ANDREA   I have no desire to upset you, Mr. Galilei.

GALILEO   Barberini called it the itch. He wasn't entirely free from it himself. I've been writing again.

ANDREA   You have?

GALILEO   I've finished the *Discorsi*.

ANDREA   What? The *Discourses Concerning Two New Sciences: Mechanics and Local Motion?* Here?

GALILEO   Oh, they let me have paper and pen. My superiors aren't stupid. They know that ingrained vices can't be uprooted overnight. They protect me from unpleasant consequences by locking up page after page.

ANDREA   Oh God!

GALILEO   Did you say something?

ANDREA   They let you plow water! They give you pen and

paper to quiet you! How could you ever write under such conditions?

GALILEO Oh, I'm a slave of habit.

ANDREA The *Discorsi* in the hands of monks! When Amsterdam and London and Prague are clamoring for them!

GALILEO I can just hear Fabricius wailing, demanding his pound of flesh, while he himself sits safely in Amsterdam.

ANDREA Two new branches of science as good as lost!

GALILEO No doubt he and some others will feel uplifted when they hear that I jeopardized the last pitiful remnants of my comfort to make a copy, behind my own back so to speak, for six months using up the last ounces of light on the clearer nights.

ANDREA You have a copy?

GALILEO So far my vanity has prevented me from destroying it.

ANDREA Where is it?

GALILEO "If thine eye offend thee, pluck it out." Whoever wrote that knew more about comfort than I do. I'm sure it's the height of folly to let it out of my hands. But since I've been unable to leave science alone, you may just as well have it. The copy is in the globe. Should you consider taking it to Holland, you would of course have to bear full responsibility. You'd say you bought it from someone with access to the Holy Office.

(*Andrea has gone to the globe. He takes out the copy*)

ANDREA The *Discorsi!* (*He leafs through the manuscript. He reads*) "It is my purpose to establish an entirely new science in regard to a very old problem, namely, motion. By means of experiments I have discovered some of its properties, which are worth knowing."

GALILEO I had to do something with my time.

ANDREA This will be the foundation of a new physics.

GALILEO Put it under your coat.

ANDREA And we thought you had deserted us! My voice was the loudest against you!

GALILEO You were absolutely right. I taught you science and I denied the truth.

ANDREA That changes everything. Everything.

GALILEO   You think so?

ANDREA   You were hiding the truth. From the enemy. Even in ethics you were centuries ahead of us.

GALILEO   Explain that to me, Andrea.

ANDREA   With the man on the street we said: He'll die, but he'll never recant.—You came back and said: I've recanted but I shall live.—Your hands are stained, we said.—You said: Better stained than empty.

GALILEO   Better stained than empty. Sounds realistic. Sounds like me. A new science, a new ethics.

ANDREA   I should have known—better than anyone else. I was eleven when you sold another man's telescope to the senate in Venice. And I watched you make immortal use of that instrument. Your friends shook their heads when you humbled yourself to that child in Florence: But science found an audience. You've always laughed at heroes. "People who suffer bore me," you said. "Bad luck comes from faulty calculations," and "If there are obstacles the shortest line between two points may well be a crooked line."

GALILEO   I remember.

ANDREA   And in thirty-three when you decided to abjure a popular item of your doctrine, I should have known that you were merely withdrawing from a hopeless political brawl in order to further the true interests of science.

GALILEO   Which consist in . . .

ANDREA   . . . the study of the properties of motion, the mother of machines, which alone will make the earth so good to live on that we shall be able to do without heaven.

GALILEO   Hm.

ANDREA   You won the leisure to write a scientific work which you alone could write. Had you perished in the fiery halo of the stake, the others would have been the victors.

GALILEO   They are the victors. Besides, there is no scientific work that one man alone can write.

ANDREA   Then why did you recant?

GALILEO   I recanted because I was afraid of physical pain.

ANDREA   No!

GALILEO   They showed me the instruments.

ANDREA   Then it was not premeditated?

GALILEO It was not.

(*Pause*)

ANDREA (*loud*) In science only one thing counts: contribution to knowledge.

GALILEO And that I have supplied. Welcome to the gutter, brother in science and cousin in treason! You like fish? I have fish. What stinks is not my fish, it's me. I'm selling out, you are the buyer. Oh, irresistible sight of a book, that hallowed commodity. The mouth waters, the curses are drowned. The great Babylonian whore, the murderous beast, the scarlet woman, opens her thighs, and everything is different! Hallowed be our haggling, whitewashing, death-shunning community!

ANDREA To shun death is human. Human weaknesses are no concern of science.

GALILEO No?!—My dear Sarti, even in my present condition I believe I can give you a few hints about the science you are devoting yourself to.

(*A short pause*)

GALILEO (*in lecture style, hands folded over his paunch*) In my free time, and I've got plenty of that, I have reviewed my case and asked myself how the world of science, of which I no longer consider myself a member, will judge it. Even a wool merchant, in addition to buying cheap and selling dear, has to worry about the obstacles that may be put in the way of the wool trade itself. In this sense, the pursuit of science seems to call for special courage. Science trades in knowledge distilled from doubt. Providing everybody with knowledge of everything, science aims at making doubters of everybody. But princes, landlords and priests keep the majority of the people in a pearly haze of superstition and outworn words to cover up their own machinations. The misery of the many is as old as the hills and is proclaimed in church and lecture hall to be as indestructible as the hills. Our new art of doubting delighted the common people. They grabbed the telescope out of our hands and focused it on their tormentors—princes, landlords, priests. Those self-seeking violent men greedily exploited the fruits of science for their own ends but at the same time they felt the cold stare of science focused upon the millennial, yet artificial miseries which mankind could obviously get rid of by getting rid of them. They showered us with threats and bribes, which weak souls cannot resist. But can we turn our backs on the people and still remain scientists? The movements of the heavenly bodies have become more comprehensible; but the movements of their rulers remain unpredictable to the people. The battle to measure the sky was won by doubt; but credulity still prevents the Roman housewife from winning her battle for milk. Science, Sarti, is involved in both battles. If mankind goes on stumbling in a pearly haze of superstition and outworn words and remains too ignorant to make full use of its own strength, it will never be able to use the forces of nature which science has discovered. What end are you scientists working for? To my mind, the only purpose of science is to lighten the toil of human existence. If scientists, browbeaten by selfish rulers, confine themselves to the accumulation of knowledge for the sake of knowledge, science will be crippled and your new machines will only mean new hardships. Given time, you may well discover everything there is to discover, but your progress will be a progression away from humanity. The gulf between you and humanity may one day be so wide that the response to your exultation about some new achievement will be a universal outcry of horror.—As a scientist, I had a unique opportunity. In my time astronomy reached the market place. Under these very special circumstances, one man's steadfastness might have had tremendous repercussions. If I had held out, scientists might have developed something like the physicians' Hippocratic oath, the vow to use their knowledge only for the good of mankind. As things stand now, the best we can hope for is a generation of inventive dwarfs who can be hired for any purpose. Furthermore, I have come to the conclusion, Sarti, that I was never in any real danger. For a few years I was as strong as the authorities. And yet I handed the powerful my knowledge to use, or not to use, or to misuse as served their purposes.

(*Virginia has come in with a dish and stops now*)

I have betrayed my calling. A man who does what I have done, cannot be tolerated in the ranks of science.

VIRGINIA   You have been received in the ranks of the faithful.
(*She walks on and sets the dish on the table*)
GALILEO   Yes.—I must eat now.
(*Andrea offers him his hand. Galileo sees it but does not take it*)
GALILEO   You are teaching now yourself. Can you afford to
shake a hand such as mine? (*He goes to the table*) Somebody on
the way through has sent me two geese. I still like to eat.
ANDREA   Then you no longer believe that a new era has
dawned?
GALILEO   I do.—Take good care of yourself when you pass
through Germany with the truth under your coat.
ANDREA (*unable to leave*)   Regarding your opinion of the author
we discussed I cannot answer you. But I refuse to believe that
your devastating analysis can be the last word.
GALILEO   Thank you, sir. (*He begins to eat*)
VIRGINIA (*seeing Andrea out*)   We don't like visitors from the past.
They upset him.
(*Andrea leaves. Virginia comes back*)
GALILEO   Any idea who could have sent the geese?
VIRGINIA   Not Andrea.
GALILEO   Maybe not. How is the night?
VIRGINIA (*at the window*)   Clear.

15

1637. Galileo's book *Discorsi* crosses the Italian border.

> The great book o'er the border went
> And, good folk, that was the end.
> But we hope you'll keep in mind
> You and I were left behind.
> May you now guard science' light
> Keep it up and use it right
> Lest it be a flame to fall
> One day to consume us all.

A small Italian border town. Early morning. Children are playing by the turnpike near the guard house. Andrea, beside a coachman, is waiting for his papers to be examined by the guards. He is sitting on a small box reading in Galileo's manuscript. The coach is on the far side of the turnpike.

THE CHILDREN (*sing*)

> Mary sat upon a stone
> Had a pink shift of her own
> The shift was full of shit.
> But when cold weather came along
> Mary put her shift back on
> Shitty is better than split.

THE BORDER GUARD   Why are you leaving Italy?

ANDREA   I'm a scholar.

THE BORDER GUARD (*to the clerk*)   Write under "Reason for Leaving": Scholar.
(*The clerk does so*)

THE FIRST BOY (*to Andrea*)   Don't sit there. (*He points at the hut in front of which Andrea is sitting*) A witch lives there.

THE SECOND BOY   Old Marina isn't a witch.

THE FIRST BOY   Want me to twist your arm?

THE THIRD BOY   She is too. She flies through the air at night.

THE FIRST BOY   If she's not a witch, why can't she get any milk anywhere in town?

THE SECOND BOY   How can she fly through the air? Nobody can do that. (*To Andrea*) Or can they?

THE FIRST BOY (*referring to the second boy*)   That's Giuseppe. He doesn't know anything, because he doesn't go to school, because his pants are torn.

THE BORDER GUARD   What's that book?

ANDREA (*without looking up*)   It's by Aristotle, the great philosopher.

THE BORDER GUARD (*suspiciously*)   What's he up to?

ANDREA   He's dead.

(*To tease Andrea, the boys walk around him in a way indicating that they too are reading books*)

THE BORDER GUARD (*to the clerk*)   See if there's anything about religion in it.

THE CLERK (*turning leaves*)   Can't see anything.

THE BORDER GUARD   Anyway there's no point in looking. Nobody'd be so open about anything he wanted to hide. (*To Andrea*) You'll have to sign a paper saying we examined everything.

(*Andrea hesitantly gets up and reading all the time goes into the house with the guards*)

THE THIRD BOY (*to the clerk, pointing at the box*)   Look, there's something else.

THE CLERK   Wasn't it here before?

THE THIRD BOY   The devil's put it there. It's a box.

THE SECOND BOY   No, it belongs to the traveler.

THE THIRD BOY   I wouldn't go near it. She's bewitched Passi the coachman's horses. I looked through the hole in the roof that the snowstorm made, and I heard them coughing.

THE CLERK (*almost at the box hesitates and goes back*)   Witchery, ha? Well, we can't examine everything. We'd never get through.

(*Andrea returns with a pitcher of milk. He sits down on the box again and continues to read*)

THE BORDER GUARD (*following him with papers*)   Close the boxes. Is that all?

THE CLERK   Yes.

THE SECOND BOY (*to Andrea*)   You say you're a scholar. Then tell me: Can people fly through the air?

ANDREA   Just a moment.

THE BORDER GUARD   You may proceed.

(*The luggage has been picked up by the coachman. Andrea takes his box and prepares to go*)

THE BORDER GUARD   Wait! What's in that box?

ANDREA (*taking up his book again*)   Books.

THE FIRST BOY   It's the witch's box.

THE BORDER GUARD   Nonsense. How could she hex a box?

THE THIRD BOY   If the devil's helping her!

THE BORDER GUARD (*laughs*)   Not in our rule book. (*To the clerk*) Open it.

(*The box is opened*)

THE BORDER GUARD (*listlessly*)   How many?

ANDREA   Thirty-four.

THE BORDER GUARD (*to the clerk*)   How long will it take you?

THE CLERK (*who has started rummaging superficially through the box*)   All printed stuff. You'd have no time for breakfast, and when do you expect me to collect the overdue toll from Passi the coachman when his house is auctioned off, if I go through all these books?

THE BORDER GUARD   You're right, we've got to get that money. (*He kicks at the books*) What could be in them anyway? (*To the coachman*) Pfftt!

(*Andrea and the coachman who carries the box cross the border. Beyond it Andrea puts Galileo's manuscript in his bag*)

THE THIRD BOY (*points at the pitcher which Andrea had left behind*)   Look!

THE FIRST BOY   And the box is gone! Now do you see it was the devil?

ANDREA (*turning around*)   No, it was me. You must learn to use your eyes. The milk and the pitcher are paid for. Give them to the old woman. Oh yes, Giuseppe, I haven't answered your question. No one can fly through the air on a stick. Unless it has some sort of machine attached to it. Such machines don't exist yet. Maybe they never will because man is too heavy. But of course, we don't know. We don't know nearly enough, Giuseppe. We've hardly begun.

The Trial
of Lucullus

A Play for Radio

Collaborator: M. Steffin

Translator: Frank Jones

CHARACTERS

LUCULLUS, a Roman general
THE SPEAKER OF THE COURT OF
    THE DEAD
THE JUDGE OF THE DEAD
JURORS OF THE DEAD: THE
    TEACHER, THE COURTESAN,
    THE BAKER, THE FISHWIFE,
    THE FARMER
FIGURES ON A FRIEZE: THE
    KING, THE QUEEN, TWO
    VIRGINS WITH A TABLET,
    TWO SLAVES WITH A
    GOLDEN GOD, TWO
    LEGIONARIES, LUCULLUS'
    COOK, THE BEARER OF THE
    CHERRY TREE

THE TONELESS VOICE
AN OLD WOMAN
THE THREEFOLD VOICE
TWO SHADES
THE CRIER
TWO YOUNG GIRLS
TWO MERCHANTS
TWO WOMEN
TWO PLEBEIANS
A CART DRIVER
CHORUS OF SOLDIERS
CHORUS OF SLAVES
CHORUS OF CHILDREN
VOICES

1

The Funeral Procession

Sounds of a great mass of people.

THE CRIER

5   Hear ye: great Lucullus is dead!
The general who conquered the east
Who overthrew seven kings
Who filled Rome, our city, with riches.
Before his catafalque
10   Which is borne by soldiers
Walk the most respected men of mighty Rome
Their faces veiled. Beside him
Walk his philosopher, his lawyer, and his favorite horse.

SONG OF THE SOLDIERS CARRYING THE CATAFALQUE

15   Hold it steady, hold it shoulder-high!
Let it not sway before these thousand eyes
Now that the lord of the eastern earth
Is passing to the shades. Careful, men, don't stumble!
The thing you bear of flesh and metal
20   Was master of the world.

THE CRIER

Behind him they are hauling a colossal frieze, which
Shows his deeds and is destined for his tomb.
Once again
25   All the people admire his glorious life
Of victories and conquests

And remember the time of his triumph.
VOICES
Think of the invincible, the mighty one!
Think of the scourge of both Asias
5   The darling of Rome and the gods
When he rode through the city
In his golden chariot, bringing you
Foreign kings and foreign animals!
Elephant, camel, panther
10   And carriage loads of captured ladies
Baggage wagons rattling with utensils
Ships, images, fine vessels
All carved in ivory, a whole Corinthful
Of brazen statues, hauled
15   Through the roaring ocean of the people! Think of the sight!
Think of the coins for the children
And the wines and sausages!
When he rode through the city
In his golden chariot
20   He, the invincible, he, the mighty one
He, the scourge of both Asias
Darling of Rome and the Gods!
SONG OF THE SLAVES HAULING THE FRIEZE
Watch out, men, don't stumble!
25   You haulers of the frieze portraying the triumph
Never mind if sweat gets in your eyes
Keep a grip on the stone! Think, if you let it drop
It may shatter into dust.
YOUNG GIRL
30   Look at red-helmet! No, the tall one there!
ANOTHER GIRL
Cross-eyed.
FIRST MERCHANT
All the senators have come!
35 SECOND MERCHANT
And all the tailors too.
FIRST MERCHANT
He got as far as India! Let's be fair!

SECOND MERCHANT
    But he was finished long before he died.
    It's sad but true.
FIRST MERCHANT
5   Greater than Pompey, I tell you!
    Without that man there'd be no Rome.
    The victories he won!
SECOND MERCHANT
    Flukes most of them and gory!
10 FIRST WOMAN
    My son
    Was killed in Asia. All this hullabaloo
    Won't bring him back.
FIRST MERCHANT
15   I know of quite a few
    Who thanks to him have done extremely well.
SECOND WOMAN
    My brother's boy—one more that won't come home.
FIRST MERCHANT
20   We know how well he served the city
    Just think of all that glory!
FIRST WOMAN
    If it wasn't for the lies they tell
    Not a man would fall into their sack.
25 FIRST MERCHANT
    Heroism—what a pity—
    Is on its way out.
FIRST PLEBEIAN
    Man
30   That glory stuff grinds on and on.
SECOND PLEBEIAN
    In Cappadocia, three legions gone
    Up the spout.
A CART DRIVER
35   Can
    I get through?
SECOND WOMAN
    No, it's barred.

FIRST PLEBEIAN
When we're laying our generals in the ground
Even oxcarts are bound
To bide their time.

5 SECOND WOMAN
They've dragged my Pulcher into court:
Owing taxes was his crime!

FIRST MERCHANT
But for him it's plain
10 We wouldn't have our Asian colonies.

FIRST WOMAN
Is tuna up again?

SECOND WOMAN
Yes, and so is cheese!

15 (*The shouting of the crowd swells*)

THE CRIER
Now
They are passing through the triumphal arch
Which the city has erected for its great son.
20 The women lift their children up. The horsemen
Push back the rows of onlookers.
The street behind the procession lies orphaned.
For the last time
Great Lucullus has passed this way.

25 (*The noise of the crowd dies away, as does the martial tread of the procession*)

2

Quick Fade-out, and the Daily Round Resumes

THE CRIER
  The procession has vanished, now
5   The street fills up again. The wagoners drive their oxcarts
  Out of the choked alleys. The garrulous
  Crowd takes up its occupations.
  Busy Rome
  Goes back to work.

10

3

In the Schoolbooks

CHORUS OF CHILDREN
  In the schoolbooks
  Are written the names of the great generals.
15   You learn their battles by heart
  You study their wonderful lives
  If you long to be like them.
  To aim for that
  To rise above the crowd
20   Is our appointed task. Our city
  Is eager to write our names one day
  On the tablets of the immortals.
  Sextus conquers Pontus.
  And you, Flaccus, conquer the three Gauls.
25   But you, Quintilian
  March across the Alps!

4

The Burial

THE CRIER
Out on the Appian Way
5   Stands a small edifice, built ten years ago
Destined to shelter
The great man in death.
Ahead of him
The group of slaves hauling the triumphal frieze
10   Turns off the road. Then
The small rotunda with the clump of boxwood
Receives him too.
A TONELESS VOICE
Halt, soldiers!
15 THE CRIER
A voice comes from
The other side of the wall.
From now on, it commands.
THE TONELESS VOICE
20   Tilt the bier! Beyond this wall
No one is carried. Beyond this wall
A man goes on his own feet.
THE CRIER
The soldiers tilt the bier. The general
25   Stands upright now, a bit shaky.
His philosopher wants to join him
A wise maxim on his lips. But . . .
THE TONELESS VOICE
Stand back, philosopher! Behind this wall
30   You can wheedle no one.
THE CRIER
Says the voice that commands there, and
Next the lawyer comes forward
To raise an objection.

THE TONELESS VOICE
 Overruled.
THE CRIER
 Says the voice that commands there.
5 And it says to the general:
THE TONELESS VOICE
 Now step up to the gate!
THE CRIER
 And the general walks to the little gate
10 Stands still a moment to look around
 And solemnly beholds the soldiers
 Beholds the slaves hauling the frieze
 Beholds the boxwood, final green. He hesitates.
 As the hall is open, the wind gets in
15 From the road.
 (*A gust of wind is heard*)
THE TONELESS VOICE
 Take off your helmet. Our gate is low.
THE CRIER
20 And the general takes his splendid helmet off.
 And steps in, crouching. With signs of relief the soldiers
 Pour out of the tomb, talking cheerfully.

5

Farewell of the Living

25 CHORUS OF SOLDIERS
 So long, Lacallous!
 We're quits, old goat!
 Let's leave this cavern
 And find a tavern!
30 He's earned his palace
 He's in his glory

That's not the whole story
There's living to do.
We'll drink till we float!
You were out of step too.
5 I'll come with you.
Trust me, I will.
Who'll buy the wine?
They'll put it on the bill.
Now he looks fine!
10 As for me, I'll look around for meat.
The little dark one? We'll come too.
No, that wouldn't do.
When you go in threes, she's not so sweet.
The slut!
15 Then let's watch the greyhounds race.
But
There's a gate charge. Not if they know your face.
I'll come too.
All right! One, two . . .
20 Break step! Forward march!

6

The Reception

The toneless voice is the voice of the gatekeeper of the realm of shades.
It takes over the narration.

25 THE TONELESS VOICE
Since the newcomer entered
He has been standing by the door, motionless, his helmet
under his arm

A statue of himself.
The other dead who are new arrivals
Sit on the bench and wait
As formerly they waited many a time
5   For happiness and for death
In the tavern, until they got their wine
And by the fountain, until the loved one came
And in the thicket, in battle, until the command was given.
But this new one
10   Seems not to have learned to wait.

LUCULLUS

By Jupiter, what
Does this mean? I stand here waiting!
The greatest city on the globe still rings
15   With laments for me, and here
There's no one to receive me!
Outside my battle tent
Seven kings waited for me!
Is there no order in this place?
20   What's become of Lasus, my cook, at least?
A man who can turn thin air
Into a nice little bite to eat!
Supposing, now, that he'd been sent to meet me
Since he's staying down here too
25   I'd feel more at home.—Oh, Lasus!
Your lamb with bay leaves and dill!
Cappadocian venison! Those lobsters from Pontus
And those Phrygian cakes with bitter berries!
(Silence)
30   Escort me from this place. That is an order.
(Silence)
Must I stand here among these people?
(Silence)
I protest. Two hundred
35   Iron-armored ships, five legions
Advanced when I raised my little finger.
I protest.
(Silence)

THE TONELESS VOICE
No answer, but on the bench where people wait
An old woman says:
VOICE OF AN OLD WOMAN WAITING
5   Sit down, newcomer.
All that metal you're lugging, that heavy helmet
And breastplate must surely make you tired.
So sit down.
(Lucullus is silent)
10   Don't be stubborn. You can't stand the whole time.
You're going to have a long wait. I'm ahead of you.
You can't tell how long a hearing in there will last.
It's understandable. After all, everyone must be
Strictly appraised before it is decided
15   Whether he shall enter gloomy Hades or
The fields of the blest. Sometimes
The proceedings are brief, a look is enough for the judges.
That man, they say
Led a guiltless life and managed
20   To be useful to his fellows, for
A person's usefulness
Is what they value most. Please, they say to him
Take your rest. Of course in other cases
The trial can last for days, especially in the case of one
25   Who sent another down here to the realm
Of shades before his apportioned span
Of life had passed. The man in there right now
Won't take very long. A harmless little baker. As for me
I'm a bit worried, but I find some hope
30   In what I hear: that some of the jurors in there
Are little people who fully understand
How hard life is for the likes of us in warring times.
Newcomer, I advise you . . .
THE THREEFOLD VOICE *(interrupting)*
35   Tertullia!
THE OLD WOMAN
I'm being called.
Well, newcomer, you'll have to see how you get along.
Take a seat.

THE TONELESS VOICE

The newcomer has been standing obstinately by the gate
But the burden of his medals
His own bellowing
5   And the old woman's kind words have changed him.
He looks around to see if he is really alone. Now
He is moving over to the bench.
But before he can sit down
He will be called. In the old woman's case
10   A look was enough for the judges.

THE THREEFOLD VOICE

Lacallous!

LUCULLUS

Lucullus is my name. Don't you people know that?
15   I come of an illustrious line
Of statesmen and generals. Only in slums
Docks and soldiers' taverns, in the unwashed mouths
Of uncouth persons and scum
Am I called Lacallous.

20 THE THREEFOLD VOICE

Lacallous!

THE TONELESS VOICE

And so, summoned more than once
In the scorned parlance of the slums
25   Lucullus, the general
Who conquered the east
Who overthrew seven kings
Who filled the city of Rome with riches
Reports at eventide, when Rome sits down above the graves
30   to eat
To the highest court in the realm of shades.

7

Choosing a Sponsor

THE SPEAKER OF THE COURT OF THE DEAD
    Before the highest court in the realm of shades
5   Appears General Lacallous, who calls himself Lucullus.
    The judge of the dead presiding
    Five jurors conduct the questioning.
    One formerly a farmer
    One a slave who had been a teacher
10 One a fishwife
    One a baker
    One a courtesan.
    They sit on a high bench
    And have no hands for taking or mouths for eating
15 Their long-extinguished eyes impervious to glamor.
    Incorruptible they are, the ancestors of posterity.
    The judge of the dead opens the trial.

THE JUDGE OF THE DEAD
    Shade, you shall now be questioned.
20 You shall render an account of your life among men.
    Whether you have been of use or harm to them
    Whether the sight of your face will be welcome
    In the fields of the blest.
    You need a sponsor.
25 Have you a sponsor in the fields of the blest?

LUCULLUS
    I request that the great Alexander of Macedon be called.
    That he speak to you as an expert
    On deeds like mine.

30 THE THREEFOLD VOICE (*calls out in the fields of the blest*)
    Alexander of Macedon!
    (*Silence*)

THE SPEAKER
   The man does not answer.
THE THREEFOLD VOICE
   There is no Alexander of Macedon
5   In the fields of the blest.
THE JUDGE
   Shade, your expert
   Is unknown in the fields of the well-remembered.
LUCULLUS
10   What? The man who conquered all Asia to the Indus
   The unforgettable one
   Who unmistakably imprinted his boot upon the globe
   The mighty Alexander . . .
THE JUDGE
15   Is not known here.
   (Silence)
THE JUDGE
   Unfortunate man! The names of the great
   Arouse no fear among us below.
20   Here
   They can no longer threaten. Their utterances
   Pass for lies. Their deeds
   Are not recorded. And their glory
   Is to us like smoke, a sign
25   That a fire has raged.
   Shade, your bearing indicates
   That enterprises of some scope
   Are associated with your name.
   Those enterprises
30   Are not known here.
LUCULLUS
   Then I request
   That the frieze for my tomb be brought
   On which my triumphal procession is shown.
35   But how can it
   Be brought? It's hauled by slaves. No doubt
   The living are
   Denied admission here.

THE JUDGE
    Not slaves. So little
    Separates them from the dead.
    They can barely
5   Be said to live. The step from the world above
    Down to the realm of shades
    Is for them but a short one.
    Let the frieze be brought.

8

¹⁰ Bringing in the Frieze

THE TONELESS VOICE
    His slaves still linger
    Uncertainly by the wall.
    Where is the frieze to go? Then suddenly
15   A voice speaks through the wall.
THE SPEAKER
    Come in.
THE TONELESS VOICE
    And, changed to shades
20   By these two words
    They haul their load
    Through the wall by the boxwood.
CHORUS OF SLAVES
    Out of life and into death
25   We haul our load ungrudgingly
    For years our time was not our own
    Unknown to us our destination.
    So we follow the new voice
    As we did the old one. Why ask questions?
30   We leave nothing behind, expect nothing.

THE SPEAKER
    And so they go through the wall
    For men held back by nothing
    Are not held back by this wall either.
5   And they set down their load
    Before the supreme court of the shades
    The frieze with the triumphal procession.
    You, jurors of the dead, behold it:
    A captured king with mournful gaze
10   A sloe-eyed queen with seductive thighs
    A man with a little cherry tree, eating a cherry
    A golden god, carried by two slaves, very fat
    Two virgins with a tablet bearing the names of 53 cities
    Two legionaries
15   One standing, one dying and saluting his general
    A cook with a fish.

THE JUDGE
    Are these your witnesses, shade?

LUCULLUS
20   They are. But how
    Shall they speak? They're stones, they're mute.

THE JUDGE
    Not for us. They will speak.
    Are you ready, stony shades
25   To testify?

CHORUS OF FIGURES
    We figures, fashioned to stay in the light
    Stony shades of long-vanished victims
    To speak on earth and be silent on earth
30   We figures, once fashioned to represent
    In the light, at the victor's command, those flung
    To the ground, robbed of breath, struck dumb and forgotten
    Are ready for silence and ready for speech.

THE JUDGE
35   Shade, the witnesses to your greatness
    Are ready to testify.

9

The Trial

THE SPEAKER
   And the general steps forward and
5   Points at the king.
   LUCULLUS
   Here you see a man whom I defeated.
   In the few days between new moon and full moon
   I smashed his army with all its chariots and armored riders.
10   In those few days
   His empire collapsed like a hut struck by lightning.
   When I appeared on his border he took flight
   And the few days of the war
   Were barely enough for both of us
15   To reach the other border of his empire.
   The campaign was of such brief duration that a ham
   Which my cook hung up to smoke
   Was not fully smoked when I got back
   And of seven whom I smashed he was but one.
20 THE JUDGE
   Is this true, king?
   THE KING
   It is true.
   THE JUDGE
25   Your questions, jurors.
   THE SPEAKER
   And the slave shade who was once a teacher
   Leans forward sternly and asks a question:
   THE TEACHER
30   How did it happen?
   THE KING
   As he says, we were overrun.

The farmer loading his hay
Still stood with pitchfork lifted as
His wagon, just now fully loaded
Was driven away.
5   The baker's loaf was not yet baked
When foreign hands reached out for it.
Everything he tells you about the lightning
That struck a hut is true. The hut
Is wrecked. Here
10   Stands the lightning.

THE TEACHER
And of seven you were . . .

THE KING
But one.

15 THE SPEAKER
The jurors of the dead consider
The testimony of the king.
(Silence)

THE SPEAKER
20 And the shade who was once a courtesan
Asks a question:

COURTESAN
You there, queen
How did you get here?

25 THE QUEEN
As I went in Taurion to
Bathe one morning early
Fifty foreign soldiers came
Down the hill of olives
30 And I was defeated.

For defense I had a sponge
For a screen clear water
But this armor that I had
Could not long protect me.
35 I was soon defeated.

Terrified, I looked around
Cried out for my handmaids
And the maids cried out in fright

From behind the bushes.
They were all defeated.

THE COURTESAN
And why do you walk in this procession?

5   THE QUEEN
Oh! To show the victory.

THE COURTESAN
What victory? Over you?

THE QUEEN
10   Me and lovely Taurion.

THE COURTESAN
And what did he call a triumph?

THE QUEEN
That the king, my wedded lord
15   Could not save with all his might
His possessions and his country
From the all-devouring Rome.

THE COURTESAN
Sister, my fate equals yours
20   For the all-devouring Rome
Could in my day not protect me
From the all-devouring Rome.

THE SPEAKER
The jurors of the dead consider
25   The testimony of the queen.
(Silence)

THE SPEAKER
And the judge of the dead turns
To the general.

30   THE JUDGE
Shade, do you wish to continue?

LUCULLUS
Yes, I notice that the losers
Have sweet voices. Once
35   They were harsher, though. The king there
Who is prevailing on your pity was in his lifetime
Exceeding cruel. Of tithe and tax
He took no less than I did. The cities
I wrested from him never missed him, but through me
40   Rome gained 53 cities.

TWO VIRGINS WITH A TABLET
>With streets and people and houses
>With temples and waterworks
>We stood in the landscape, now
5 Only our names are left upon this tablet.
THE SPEAKER
>And the juror shade who was once a baker
>Leans forward sternly and asks a question:
THE BAKER
10 Why is that?
THE TWO VIRGINS
>One day at noon an uproar was heard
>A river surged into the street
>It had human waves and swept
15 All that was ours away. By evening
>Only a pillar of smoke showed
>That a city had once stood there.
THE BAKER
>And what
20 Did he carry off, this man who sent the river and says
>That he gave the Romans 53 cities?
THE SPEAKER
>And the slaves who are hauling the golden god
>Begin to tremble and cry out.
25 THE SLAVES
>Us.
>Happy once, now cheaper than oxen
>To haul the booty, ourselves booty.
THE TWO VIRGINS
30 Once the builders
>Of 53 cities, of which only
>Names and smoke remain.
LUCULLUS
>Yes, I carried them away. They were
35 Twice a hundred and fifty thousand.
>At one time foes, but foes no longer.
THE SLAVES
>At one time men, but men no longer.
LUCULLUS
40 And with them I carried away their god

So that the world might look upon our gods
As greater than all other gods

THE SLAVES
And the god was very welcome
5   Because he was of gold and weighed two hundredweight
And each of us is worth a piece of gold
The size of a knucklebone.

THE SPEAKER
And the juror shade who was once a baker
10   In Marsilia, the city by the sea
Makes a proposal:

THE BAKER
Then in your favor, shade, we shall write down
Simply this: brought gold to Rome.

15 THE SPEAKER
The jurors of the dead consider
The testimony of the cities.
(Silence)

THE JUDGE
20   The defendant seems tired.
I declare a recess.

10

Back in Rome

THE SPEAKER
25   The court withdraws.
The defendant sits down.
Head thrown back, he squats
By the doorpost.

He is exhausted, but he overhears
A conversation behind the door
Where new shades have appeared.

A SHADE

5   I came to grief because of an oxcart.

LUCULLUS (*softly*)

Oxcart.

THE SHADE

It was hauling yet another load of sand to a building-site.

10 LUCULLUS (*softly*)

Building-site. Sand.

ANOTHER SHADE

Isn't it time to eat?

FIRST SHADE

15   Time to eat? I had my bread and onions
With me. I've lost my room.
The mob of slaves they're driving in
From the four quarters of the earth
Have ruined the shoemaker's trade.

20 SECOND SHADE

I was a slave too. Let's say the unlucky
Bring bad luck to the lucky.

LUCULLUS (*a bit louder*)

You: does the wind still blow up there?

25 SECOND SHADE

Hear that? Somebody's asking something.

FIRST SHADE (*loudly*)

Does the wind still blow up there? Maybe.
Possibly in the gardens.

30   In the stifling alleys
It can't be noticed.

11

The Trial Continues

THE SPEAKER
   The jurors return.
5   The trial resumes.
   And the shade, once a fishwife
   Speaks up:
THE FISHWIFE
   There was talk of gold just now.
10   I lived in Rome myself.
   But I never noticed any gold where I lived.
   I'd be glad to know what became of it.
LUCULLUS
   What a question!
15   Was I to set out
   With my legions to capture
   A stool for a fishwife?
THE FISHWIFE
   If you brought nothing to the fish market
20   You certainly took something away from the fish market:
   Our sons.
THE SPEAKER
   And the juror
   Addresses the warriors on the frieze:
25 THE FISHWIFE
   Tell me, what did he do to you in both Asias?
FIRST LEGIONARY
   I ran away.
SECOND LEGIONARY
30   I was wounded.
FIRST LEGIONARY
   I carried him.

SECOND LEGIONARY
So he got killed too.
THE FISHWIFE
Why did you leave Rome?
5 FIRST LEGIONARY
I was starving.
THE FISHWIFE
And what did you get out there?
SECOND LEGIONARY
10 I got nothing.
THE FISHWIFE
You're holding your hand out.
Was it to salute the general?
SECOND LEGIONARY
15 I wanted to show him
That it was still empty.
LUCULLUS
I protest.
I rewarded the legionaries
20 After each campaign.
THE FISHWIFE
But not the dead ones.
LUCULLUS
I protest.
25 How can people judge war
When they don't understand it?
THE FISHWIFE
I understand it. My
Son was killed in battle. I
30 Was a fishwife in the Forum market.
One day there was news: the galleys
With the men back from the war in Asia
Had come in. I ran out of the market
And stood many hours by the Tiber
35 While they disembarked; by nightfall
All the ships were empty. But my son had
Not come down the gangplank.
It was windy in the harbor. I took
Fever, and in my fever went on looking

For my son. The more I looked, the
Colder I felt, and then, in death, I came here
To the realm of shades and kept on looking.
Faber, I called, for that was his name.
5   Faber, my son Faber
Whom I bore and whom I reared
My son Faber!
And I ran and ran among the shades
Calling Faber, until a gatekeeper
10   At the camps for soldiers killed in action
Caught me by the sleeve and said to me:
There are many Fabers here, old lady.
Sons of many mothers, all much missed
But they've lost their names, forgot them.
15   They were useful only for the army
But are useless here. These men no longer
Wish to meet their mothers, not since the
Day they let them go to bloody war.
There I stood, caught by my sleeve
20   And my cry stuck in my throat.
Silent I turned back, for I had lost
All desire to see my son again.

THE SPEAKER

And the judge of the dead seeks
25   The eyes of the jurors and announces:

THE JUDGE

The court's opinion: the fallen man's mother
Understands war.

THE SPEAKER

30   The jurors of the dead consider
The testimony of the warriors.
(Silence)

THE JUDGE

But the lady juror is shaken.
35   The scales may tremble in
Her wavering hand. She requires
A recess.

12

Rome—A Last Time

THE SPEAKER
And again
5 The defendant sits down and listens
To the talk of the shades behind the door.
Once more
From above, from the world
A breath comes down.
10 SECOND SHADE
Why were you running so?
FIRST SHADE
To make inquiries. I'd heard they're recruiting legionaries
In the taverns by the Tiber, for the war in the west
15 Which is to be conquered next.
The country's name is Gaul.
SECOND SHADE
Never heard of it.
FIRST SHADE
20 Those countries are known only to the high and mighty.

13

The Trial Continues

THE SPEAKER
    And the judge smiles at the lady juror
5   Summons the defendant and contemplates him sadly.
    THE JUDGE
    Time is running out. You're not making use of it.
    Better stop provoking us with your triumphs.
    Have you no witnesses
10 To any weakness, man?
    Your case looks bad. Your virtues
    Don't seem very useful, maybe
    Your weaknesses would make gaps
    In the chain of your violent deeds?
15 Call your weaknesses to mind
    That's my advice to you, shade.
    THE SPEAKER
    And the juror, once a baker
    Asks a question:
20 THE BAKER
    I see a cook there with a fish.
    He looks cheerful. Cook
    Tell us how you came to be in the procession.
    THE COOK
25 Just to show
    That, busy as he was with war, he still found time
    To find a recipe for a fish.
    I was his cook. Even now
    I often think of the splendid meats
30 The fowl and dark venison
    That he had me roast.
    And he didn't just sit there eating
    He gave me a word of praise

Often stood beside me over the pan
And mixed a dish himself.
Lamb à la Lucullus
Made our kitchen famous.
5   From Syria to Pontus
People spoke of Lucullus' cook.

THE SPEAKER
Then spoke the juror
Who was once a teacher:

10 THE TEACHER
What's it to us that he liked to eat?

THE COOK
But he let me cook
To my heart's content. I thank him for it.

15 THE BAKER
I understand him, I, who was a baker.
How often I had to put bran in my dough
Because my customers were poor. That man
Had a chance to be an artist.

20 THE COOK
Thanks to him!
In the triumph
He paraded me behind the kings
And showed respect for my art.
25 Therefore I call him human.

THE SPEAKER
The jurors of the dead consider
The testimony of the cook.
(Silence)

30 THE SPEAKER
And the juror, once a farmer
Asks a question:

THE FARMER
There's a man carrying a fruit tree.

35 THE CHERRY TREE BEARER
It's a cherry tree.
We brought it from Asia. We carried it
In the triumph. And planted it
On the slopes of the Apennines.

THE FARMER

Oh, so it's you who brought it, Lacallous?
I planted it too, but I didn't know
It came from you.

5   THE SPEAKER

And, smiling amiably
The juror who was once a farmer
Chats with the shade
Who was once a general
10   About the tree.

THE FARMER

It doesn't need much soil.

LUCULLUS

But it won't take much wind.

15   THE FARMER

The red cherries are meatier.

LUCULLUS

And the black ones are sweeter.

THE FARMER

20   My friends, of all that has been conquered
In bloody war of hated memory
I call this best. This little tree lives on.
A friendly newcomer, it takes its place
Beside the vine and the hard-working berry bush
25   And, growing with the growing generations
Bears fruit for them. And therefore I commend you
For bringing it to us. When all the plunder
Of both Asias has long turned to rot
This, the smallest of your trophies
30   Will stand upon the windy hills and wave
Each spring its bloom-white branches to the living.

14

The Verdict

THE SPEAKER
  And the juror, once a fishwife in the market, springs to her
5   feet.
THE FISHWIFE
  So, after all
  You've found a penny in those
  Bloody hands? And the robber is bribing
10   The court with his spoils?
THE TEACHER
  One cherry tree! He could have made
  That conquest with
  One man only! Instead he has sent
15   80,000 down here!
THE BAKER
  How much
  Do they have to pay up there
  For a glass of wine and a roll?
20 THE COURTESAN
  Will they always have to sell their skins
  When they want to lie with a woman? Send him to nothing-
    ness!
THE FISHWIFE
25 Yes, to nothingness!
THE TEACHER
  Yes, to nothingness!
THE BAKER
  Yes, to nothingness!
30 THE SPEAKER
  And they look at the farmer
  The praiser of the cherry tree.
  What say you, farmer?
  (Silence)

THE FARMER
    80,000 for a cherry tree!
    Yes, to nothingness!
THE JUDGE
5   Yes, to nothingness! For
    With all the violence and conquest
    Only one realm increases:
    The realm of shades.
THE JURORS
10 And our gray world below
    Is already full
    Of half-lived lives. Yet here
    We have no plows for sinewy arms, or
    Hungry mouths, of which up there
15 You have so many! What but dust
    Could we heap upon
    The 80,000 slaughtered ones! And you
    Up there need houses! How often
    Shall we meet them on our
20 Paths that lead nowhere and hear them asking their eager
    Terrible questions, what
    The summer of the years is like, and the autumn
    And the winter?
THE SPEAKER
25 And the legionaries on the frieze of the dead
    Move and cry out:
THE LEGIONARIES
    Yes, send him to nothingness! What province
    Tips the scales against
30 Our unlived years that held so much?
THE SPEAKER
    And the slaves, haulers of the frieze
    Move and cry out:
THE SLAVES
35 Yes, to nothingness! How long
    Will they sit, he and his
    Inhuman kind, over men and lift
    Lazy hands and hurl the peoples
    Into bloody wars against each other?

How long shall we
Endure them and our kind endure them?

ALL

Yes, to nothingness
5   With him and all his kind!

THE SPEAKER

And from the high bench rise
The spokesmen of a posterity
Many-handed for taking
10   Many-mouthed for eating
Eagerly reaping
Rejoicing in life.

Mother Courage
and Her Children

A Chronicle of the Thirty Years' War

Translator: Ralph Manheim

CHARACTERS

MOTHER COURAGE
KATTRIN, her mute daughter
EILIF, her elder son
SWISS CHEESE, her younger
    son
THE RECRUITER
THE SERGEANT
THE COOK
THE GENERAL
THE CHAPLAIN
THE ORDNANCE OFFICER
YVETTE POTTIER
THE MAN WITH THE PATCH
    OVER HIS EYE
THE OTHER SERGEANT

THE OLD COLONEL
A CLERK
A YOUNG SOLDIER
AN OLDER SOLDIER
A PEASANT
THE PEASANT'S WIFE
THE YOUNG MAN
THE OLD WOMAN
ANOTHER PEASANT
THE PEASANT WOMAN
A YOUNG PEASANT
THE LIEUTENANT
SOLDIERS
A VOICE

1

Spring, 1624. General Oxenstjerna recruits troops in Dalarna for the Polish campaign. The canteen woman, Anna Fierling, known as Mother Courage, loses a son.

Highway near a city.

A sergeant and a recruiter stand shivering.

THE RECRUITER   How can anybody get a company together in a place like this? Sergeant, sometimes I feel like committing suicide. The general wants me to recruit four platoons by the twelfth, and the people around here are so depraved I can't sleep at night. I finally get hold of a man, I close my eyes and pretend not to see that he's chicken-breasted and he's got varicose veins, I get him good and drunk and he signs up. While I'm paying for the drinks, he steps out, I follow him to the door because I smell a rat: Sure enough, he's gone, like a fart out of a goose. A man's word doesn't mean a thing, there's no honor, no loyalty. This place has undermined my faith in humanity, sergeant.

THE SERGEANT   It's easy to see these people have gone too long without a war. How can you have morality without a war, I ask you? Peace is a mess, it takes a war to put things in order. In peacetime the human race goes to the dogs. Man and beast are treated like so much dirt. Everybody eats what they like, a big piece of cheese on white bread, with a slice of meat on top of the cheese. Nobody knows how many young men or good horses there are in that town up ahead, they've never been counted. I've been in places where they hadn't had a war in as much as seventy years, the people had no names, they didn't even know who they were. It takes a war before you get decent lists and records; then your boots are done up in bales and your grain in sacks, man and beast are properly counted and marched away, because people realize that without order they can't have a war.

THE RECRUITER   How right you are!

THE SERGEANT   Like all good things, a war is hard to get started. But once it takes root, it's vigorous; then people are as scared of peace as dice players are of laying off, because they'll have to reckon up their losses. But at first they're scared of war. It's the novelty.

THE RECRUITER   Say, there comes a wagon. Two women and two young fellows. Keep the old woman busy, sergeant. If this is another flop, you won't catch me standing out in this April wind any more.

(A Jew's harp is heard. Drawn by two young men, a covered wagon approaches. In the wagon sit Mother Courage and her mute daughter Kattrin)

MOTHER COURAGE   Good morning, sergeant.

SERGEANT *(barring the way)*   Good morning, friends. Who are you?

MOTHER COURAGE   Business people. *(Sings)*

Hey, Captains, make the drum stop drumming
And let your soldiers take a seat.
Here's Mother Courage, with boots she's coming
To help along their aching feet.
How can they march off to the slaughter
With baggage, cannon, lice and fleas
Across the rocks and through the water
Unless their boots are in one piece?
    The spring is come. Christian, revive!
    The snowdrifts melt. The dead lie dead.
    And if by chance you're still alive
    It's time to rise and shake a leg.

O Captains, don't expect to send them
To death with nothing in their crops.
First you must let Mother Courage mend them
In mind and body with her schnapps.

On empty bellies it's distressing
To stand up under shot and shell.
But once they're full, you have my blessing
To lead them to the jaws of hell.
　The spring is come. Christian, revive!
　The snowdrifts melt, the dead lie dead.
　And if by chance you're still alive
　It's time to rise and shake a leg.

THE SERGEANT　Halt, you scum. Where do you belong?

THE ELDER SON　Second Finnish Regiment.

THE SERGEANT　Where are your papers?

MOTHER COURAGE　Papers?

THE YOUNGER SON　But she's Mother Courage!

THE SERGEANT　Never heard of her. Why Courage?

MOTHER COURAGE　They call me Courage, sergeant, because when I saw ruin staring me in the face I drove out of Riga through cannon fire with fifty loaves of bread in my wagon. They were getting moldy, it was high time, I had no choice.

THE SERGEANT　No wisecracks. Where are your papers?

MOTHER COURAGE (*fishing a pile of papers out of a tin box and climbing down*)　Here are my papers, sergeant. There's a whole missal, picked it up in Alt-Ötting to wrap cucumbers in, and a map of Moravia, God knows if I'll ever get there, if I don't it's a total loss. And this here certifies that my horse hasn't got foot-and-mouth disease, too bad, he croaked on us, he cost fifteen guilders, but not out of my pocket, glory be. Is that enough paper?

THE SERGEANT　Are you trying to pull my leg? I'll teach you to get smart. You know you need a license.

MOTHER COURAGE　You mind your manners and don't go telling my innocent children that I'd go anywhere near your leg, it's indecent. I want no truck with you. My license in the Second Regiment is my honest face, and if you can't read it, that's not my fault. I'm not letting anybody put his seal on it.

THE RECRUITER　Sergeant, I detect a spirit of insubordination in this woman. In our camp we need respect for authority.

MOTHER COURAGE　Wouldn't sausage be better?

THE SERGEANT　Name.

MOTHER COURAGE　Anna Fierling.

THE SERGEANT   Then you're all Fierlings?

MOTHER COURAGE   What do you mean? Fierling is my name. Not theirs.

THE SERGEANT   Aren't they all your children?

MOTHER COURAGE   That they are, but why should they all have the same name? (*Pointing at the elder son*) This one, for instance. His name is Eilif Nojocki. How come? Because his father always claimed to be called Kojocki or Mojocki. The boy remembers him well, except the one he remembers was somebody else, a Frenchman with a goatee. But aside from that, he inherited his father's intelligence; that man could strip the pants off a peasant's ass without his knowing it. So, you see, we've each got our own name.

THE SERGEANT   Each different, you mean?

MOTHER COURAGE   Don't act so innocent.

THE SERGEANT   I suppose that one's a Chinaman? (*Indicating the younger son*)

MOTHER COURAGE   Wrong. He's Swiss.

THE SERGEANT   After the Frenchman?

MOTHER COURAGE   What Frenchman? I never heard of any Frenchman. Don't get everything balled up or we'll be here all day. He's Swiss, but his name is Fejos, the name has nothing to do with his father. He had an entirely different name, he was an engineer, built fortifications, but he drank.

(*Swiss Cheese nods, beaming; the mute Kattrin is also tickled*)

THE SERGEANT   Then how can his name be Fejos?

MOTHER COURAGE   I wouldn't want to offend you, but you haven't got much imagination. Naturally his name is Fejos because when he came I was with a Hungarian, it was all the same to him, he was dying of kidney trouble though he never touched a drop, a very decent man. The boy takes after him.

THE SERGEANT   But you said he wasn't his father?

MOTHER COURAGE   He takes after him all the same. I call him Swiss Cheese, how come, because he's good at pulling the wagon. (*Pointing at her daughter*) Her name is Kattrin Haupt, she's half German.

THE SERGEANT   A fine family, I must say.

MOTHER COURAGE   Yes, I've been all over the world with my wagon.

THE SERGEANT   It's all being taken down. (*He takes it down*)
You're from Bamberg, Bavaria. What brings you here?

MOTHER COURAGE   I couldn't wait for the war to kindly come to
Bamberg.

THE RECRUITER   You wagon pullers ought to be called Jacob Ox
and Esau Ox. Do you ever get out of harness?

EILIF   Mother, can I clout him one on the kisser? I'd like to.

MOTHER COURAGE   And I forbid you. You stay put. And now,
gentlemen, wouldn't you need a nice pistol, or a belt buckle,
yours is all worn out, sergeant.

THE SERGEANT   I need something else. I'm not blind. Those
young fellows are built like tree trunks, big broad chests,
sturdy legs. Why aren't they in the army? That's what I'd like
to know.

MOTHER COURAGE (*quickly*)   Nothing doing, sergeant. My children aren't cut out for soldiers.

THE RECRUITER   Why not? There's profit in it, and glory. Peddling shoes is woman's work. (*To Eilif*) Step up; let's feel if
you've got muscles or if you're a sissy.

MOTHER COURAGE   He's a sissy. Give him a mean look and he'll
fall flat on his face.

THE RECRUITER   And kill a calf if it happens to be standing in
the way. (*Tries to lead him away*)

MOTHER COURAGE   Leave him alone. He's not for you.

THE RECRUITER   He insulted me. He referred to my face as a
kisser. Him and me will now step out in the field and discuss
this thing as man to man.

EILIF   Don't worry, mother. I'll take care of him.

MOTHER COURAGE   You stay put. You no-good! I know you,
always fighting. He's got a knife in his boot, he's a knifer.

THE RECRUITER   I'll pull it out of him like a milk tooth. Come
on, boy.

MOTHER COURAGE   Sergeant, I'll report you to the colonel. He'll
throw you in the lock-up. The lieutenant is courting my
daughter.

THE SERGEANT   No rough stuff, brother. (*To Mother Courage*)
What have you got against the army? Wasn't his father a
soldier? Didn't he die fair and square? You said so yourself.

MOTHER COURAGE   He's only a child. You want to lead him off to slaughter, I know you. You'll get five guilders for him.

THE RECRUITER   He'll get a beautiful cap and top boots.

EILIF   Not from you.

MOTHER COURAGE   Oh, won't you come fishing with me? said the fisherman to the worm. (*To Swiss Cheese*) Run and yell that they're trying to steal your brother. (*She pulls a knife*) Just try and steal him. I'll cut you down, you dogs. I'll teach you to put him in your war! We do an honest business in ham and shirts, we're peaceful folk.

THE SERGEANT   I can see by the knife how peaceful you are. You ought to be ashamed of yourself, put that knife away, you bitch. A minute ago you admitted you lived off war, how else would you live, on what? How can you have a war without soldiers?

MOTHER COURAGE   It doesn't have to be my children.

THE SERGEANT   I see. You'd like the war to eat the core and spit out the apple. You want your brood to batten on war, tax-free. The war can look out for itself, is that it? You call yourself Courage, eh? And you're afraid of the war that feeds you. Your sons aren't afraid of it, I can see that.

EILIF   I'm not afraid of any war.

THE SERGEANT   Why should you be? Look at me: Has the soldier's life disagreed with me? I was seventeen when I joined up.

MOTHER COURAGE   You're not seventy yet.

THE SERGEANT   I can wait.

MOTHER COURAGE   Sure. Under ground.

THE SERGEANT   Are you trying to insult me? Telling me I'm going to die?

MOTHER COURAGE   But suppose it's the truth? I can see the mark on you. You look like a corpse on leave.

SWISS CHEESE   She's got second sight. Everybody says so. She can tell the future.

THE RECRUITER   Then tell the sergeant his future. It might amuse him.

THE SERGEANT   I don't believe in that stuff.

MOTHER COURAGE   Give me your helmet. (*He gives it to her*)

THE SERGEANT   It doesn't mean any more than taking a shit in the grass. But go ahead for the laugh.

MOTHER COURAGE (*takes a sheet of parchment and tears it in two*)
Eilif, Swiss Cheese, Kattrin: That's how we'd all be torn apart
if we got mixed up too deep in the war. (*To the sergeant*) Seeing
it's you, I'll do it for nothing. I make a black cross on this
piece. Black is death.

SWISS CHEESE   She leaves the other one blank. Get it?

MOTHER COURAGE   Now I fold them, and now I shake them up
together. Same as we're all mixed up together from the cradle
to the grave. And now you draw, and you'll know the answer.
(*The sergeant hesitates*)

THE RECRUITER (*to Eilif*)   I don't take everybody, I'm known to
be picky and choosy, but you've got spirit, I like that.

THE SERGEANT (*fishing in the helmet*)   Damn foolishness! Hocus-
pocus!

SWISS CHEESE   He's pulled a black cross. He's through.

THE RECRUITER   Don't let them scare you, there's not enough
bullets for everybody.

THE SERGEANT (*hoarsely*)   You've fouled me up.

MOTHER COURAGE   You fouled yourself up the day you joined
the army. And now we'll be going, there isn't a war every day,
I've got to take advantage.

THE SERGEANT   Hell and damnation! Don't try to hornswoggle
me. We're taking your bastard to be a soldier.

EILIF   I'd like to be a soldier, mother.

MOTHER COURAGE   You shut your trap, you Finnish devil.

EILIF   Swiss Cheese wants to be a soldier too.

MOTHER COURAGE   That's news to me. I'd better let you draw
too, all three of you. (*She goes to the rear to mark crosses on slips
of parchment*)

THE RECRUITER (*to Eilif*)   It's been said to our discredit that a lot
of religion goes on in the Swedish camp, but that's slander to
blacken our reputation. Hymn singing only on Sunday, one
verse! And only if you've got a voice.

MOTHER COURAGE (*comes back with the slips in the sergeant's helmet*)
Want to sneak away from their mother, the devils, and run
off to war like calves to a salt lick. But we'll draw lots on it,
then they'll see that the world is no vale of smiles with a
"Come along, son, we're short on generals." Sergeant, I'm
very much afraid they won't come through the war. They've

got terrible characters, all three of them. (*She holds out the helmet to Eilif*) There. Pick a slip. (*He picks one and unfolds it. She snatches it away from him*) There you have it. A cross! Oh, unhappy mother that I am, oh, mother of sorrows. Has he got to die? Doomed to perish in the springtime of his life? If he joins the army, he'll bite the dust, that's sure. He's too brave, just like his father. If he's not smart, he'll go the way of all flesh, the slip proves it. (*She roars at him*) Are you going to be smart?

EILIF   Why not?

MOTHER COURAGE   The smart thing to do is to stay with your mother, and if they make fun of you and call you a sissy, just laugh.

THE RECRUITER   If you're shitting in your pants, we'll take your brother.

MOTHER COURAGE   I told you to laugh. Laugh! And now you pick, Swiss Cheese. I'm not so worried about you, you're honest. (*He picks a slip*) Oh! Why, have you got that strange look? It's got to be blank. There can't be a cross on it. No, I can't lose you. (*She takes the slip*) A cross? Him too? Maybe it's because he's so stupid. Oh, Swiss Cheese, you'll die too, unless you're very honest the whole time, the way I've taught you since you were a baby, always bringing back the change when I sent you to buy bread. That's the only way you can save yourself. Look, sergeant, isn't that a black cross?

THE SERGEANT   It's a cross all right. I don't see how I could have pulled one. I always stay in the rear. (*To the recruiter*) It's on the up and up. Her own get it too.

SWISS CHEESE   I get it too. But I can take a hint.

MOTHER COURAGE (*to Kattrin*)   Now you're the only one I'm sure of, you're a cross yourself because you've got a good heart. (*She holds up the helmet to Kattrin in the wagon, but she herself takes out the slip*) It's driving me to despair. It can't be right, maybe I mixed them wrong. Don't be too good-natured, Kattrin, don't, there's a cross on your path too. Always keep very quiet, that ought to be easy seeing you're dumb. Well, now you know. Be careful, all of you, you'll need to be. And now we'll climb up and drive on. (*She returns the sergeant's helmet and climbs up into the wagon*)

THE RECRUITER (*to the sergeant*) Do something!

THER SERGEANT I'm not feeling so good.

THE RECRUITER Maybe you caught cold when you took your helmet off in the wind. Tell her you want to buy something. Keep her busy. (*Aloud*) You could at least take a look at that buckle, sergeant. After all, selling things is these good people's living. Hey, you, the sergeant wants to buy that belt buckle.

MOTHER COURAGE Half a guilder. A buckle like that is worth two guilders. (*She climbs down*)

THE SERGEANT It's not new. This wind! I can't examine it here. Let's go where it's quiet. (*He goes behind the wagon with the buckle*)

MOTHER COURAGE I haven't noticed any wind.

THE SERGEANT Maybe it is worth half a guilder. It's silver.

MOTHER COURAGE (*joins him behind the wagon*) Six solid ounces.

THE RECRUITER (*to Eilif*) And then we'll have a drink, just you and me. I've got your enlistment bonus right here. Come on. (*Eilif stands undecided*)

MOTHER COURAGE All right. Half a guilder.

THE SERGEANT I don't get it. I always stay in the rear. There's no safer place for a sergeant. You can send the men up forward to win glory. You've spoiled my dinner. It won't go down, I know it, not a bite.

MOTHER COURAGE Don't take it to heart. Don't let it spoil your appetite. Just keep behind the lines. Here, take a drink of schnapps, man. (*She hands him the bottle*)

THE RECRUITER (*has taken Eilif's arm and is pulling him away toward the rear*) A bonus of ten guilders, and you'll be a brave man and you'll fight for the king, and the women will tear each other's hair out over you. And you can clout me one on the kisser for insulting you. (*Both go out*)

(*Mute Kattrin jumps down from the wagon and emits raucous sounds*)

MOTHER COURAGE Just a minute, Kattrin, just a minute. The sergeant's paying up. (*Bites the half guilder*) I'm always suspicious of money. I'm a burnt child, sergeant. But your coin is good. And now we'll be going. Where's Eilif?

SWISS CHEESE He's gone with the recruiter.

MOTHER COURAGE (*stands motionless, then*)   You simple soul. (*To Kattrin*) I know. You can't talk, you couldn't help it.

THE SERGEANT   You could do with a drink yourself, mother. That's the way it goes. Soldiering isn't the worst thing in the world. You want to live off the war, but you want to keep you and yours out of it. Is that it?

MOTHER COURAGE   Now you'll have to pull with your brother, Kattrin.

(*Brother and sister harness themselves to the wagon and start pulling. Mother Courage walks beside them. The wagon rolls off*)

THE SERGEANT (*looking after them*)

If you want the war to work for you

You've got to give the war its due.

2

In 1625 and 1626 Mother Courage crosses Poland in the train of the Swedish armies. Outside the fortress of Wallhof she meets her son again.—A capon is successfully sold, the brave son's fortunes are at their zenith.

The general's tent.

Beside it the kitchen. The thunder of cannon. The cook is arguing with Mother Courage, who is trying to sell him a capon.

THE COOK   Sixty hellers for that pathetic bird?

MOTHER COURAGE   Pathetic bird? You mean this plump beauty? Are you trying to tell me that a general who's the biggest eater for miles around—God help you if you haven't got anything for his dinner—can't afford a measly sixty hellers?

THE COOK   I can get a dozen like it for ten hellers right around the corner.

MOTHER COURAGE   What, you'll find a capon like this right around the corner? With a siege on and everybody so starved you can see right through them. Maybe you'll scare up a rat, maybe, I say, 'cause they've all been eaten, I've seen five men chasing a starved rat for hours. Fifty hellers for a giant capon in the middle of a siege.

THE COOK   We're not besieged; they are. We're the besiegers, can't you get that through your head?

MOTHER COURAGE   But we haven't got anything to eat either, in fact we've got less than the people in the city. They've hauled it all inside. I hear their life is one big orgy. And look at us. I've been around to the peasants, they haven't got a thing.

THE COOK   They've got plenty. They hide it.

MOTHER COURAGE (*triumphantly*)   Oh, no! They're ruined, that's what they are. They're starving. I've seen them. They're so hungry they're digging up roots. They lick their fingers when they've eaten a boiled strap. That's the situation. And here I've got a capon and I'm supposed to let it go for forty hellers.

THE COOK   Thirty, not forty. Thirty, I said.

MOTHER COURAGE   It's no common capon. They tell me this bird was so talented that he wouldn't eat unless they played music, he had his own favorite march. He could add and subtract, that's how intelligent he was. And you're trying to tell me forty hellers is too much. The general will bite your head off if there's nothing to eat.

THE COOK   You know what I'm going to do? (*He takes a piece of beef and sets his knife to it*) Here I've got a piece of beef. I'll roast it. Think it over. This is your last chance.

MOTHER COURAGE   Roast and be damned. It's a year old.

THE COOK   A day old. That ox was running around only yesterday afternoon, I saw him with my own eyes.

MOTHER COURAGE   Then he must have stunk on the hoof.

THE COOK   I'll cook it five hours if I have to. We'll see if it's still tough. (*He cuts into it*)

MOTHER COURAGE   Use plenty of pepper, maybe the general won't notice the stink.

(*The general, a chaplain and Eilif enter the tent*)

THE GENERAL (*slapping Eilif on the back*)   All right, son, into your
general's tent you go, you'll sit at my right hand. You've done
a heroic deed and you're a pious trooper, because this is a war
of religion and what you did was done for God, that's what
counts with me. I'll reward you with a gold bracelet when I
take the city. We come here to save their souls and what do
those filthy, shameless peasants do? They drive their cattle
away. And they stuff their priests with meat, front and back.
But you taught them a lesson. Here's a tankard of red wine
for you. (*He pours*) We'll down it in one gulp. (*They do so*) None
for the chaplain, he's got his religion. What would you like
for dinner, sweetheart?

EILIF   A scrap of meat. Why not?

THE GENERAL   Cook! Meat!

THE COOK   And now he brings company when there's nothing
to eat.

(*Wanting to listen, Mother Courage makes him stop talking*)

EILIF   Cutting down peasants whets the appetite.

MOTHER COURAGE   God, it's my Eilif.

THE COOK   Who?

MOTHER COURAGE   My eldest. I haven't seen hide nor hair of
him in two years, he was stolen from me on the highway. He
must be in good if the general invites him to dinner, and what
have you got to offer? Nothing. Did you hear what the general's guest wants for dinner? Meat! Take my advice, snap up
this capon. The price is one guilder.

THE GENERAL (*has sat down with Eilif. Bellows*)   Food, Lamb, you
lousy, no-good cook, or I'll kill you.

THE COOK   All right, hand it over. This is extortion.

MOTHER COURAGE   I thought it was a pathetic bird.

THE COOK   Pathetic is the word. Hand it over. Fifty hellers! It's
highway robbery.

MOTHER COURAGE   One guilder, I say. For my eldest son, the
general's honored guest, I spare no expense.

THE COOK (*gives her the money*)   Then pluck it at least while I
make the fire.

MOTHER COURAGE (*sits down to pluck the capon*)   Won't he be glad
to see me! He's my brave, intelligent son. I've got a stupid one
too, but he's honest. The girl's a total loss. But at least she
doesn't talk, that's something.

THE GENERAL   Take another drink, son, it's my best Falerno,
I've only got another barrel or two at the most, but it's worth
it to see that there's still some true faith in my army. The good
shepherd here just looks on, all he knows how to do is preach.
Can he do anything? No. And now, Eilif my son, tell us all
about it, how cleverly you hoodwinked those peasants and
captured those twenty head of cattle. I hope they'll be here
soon.

EILIF   Tomorrow. Maybe the day after.

MOTHER COURAGE   Isn't my Eilif considerate, not bringing those
oxen in until tomorrow, or you wouldn't have even said hello
to my capon.

EILIF   Well, it was like this: I heard the peasants were secretly
—mostly at night—rounding up the oxen they'd hidden in a
certain forest. The city people had arranged to come and get
them. I let them round the oxen up, I figured they'd find them
easier than I would. I made my men ravenous for meat, put
them on short rations for two days until their mouths watered if they even heard a word beginning with *me* . . . like
measles.

THE GENERAL   That was clever of you.

EILIF   Maybe. The rest was a pushover. Except the peasants had
clubs and there were three times more of them and they fell
on us like bloody murder. Four of them drove me into a
clump of bushes, they knocked my sword out of my hand and
yelled: Surrender! Now what'll I do, I says to myself, they'll
make hash out of me.

THE GENERAL   What did you do?

EILIF   I laughed.

THE GENERAL   You laughed?

EILIF   I laughed. Which led to a conversation. The first thing
you know, I'm bargaining. Twenty guilders is too much for
that ox, I say, how about fifteen? Like I'm meaning to pay.
They're flummoxed, they scratch their heads. Quick, I reach
for my sword and mow them down. Necessity knows no law.
See what I mean?

THE GENERAL   What do you say to that, shepherd?

CHAPLAIN   Strictly speaking, that maxim is not in the Bible. But
our Lord was able to turn five loaves into five hundred. So
there was no question of poverty; he could tell people to love

their neighbors because their bellies were full. Nowadays it's different.

THE GENERAL (*laughs*)   Very different. All right, you Pharisee, take a swig. (*To Eilif*) You mowed them down, splendid, so my fine troops could have a decent bite to eat. Doesn't the Good Book say: "Whatsoever thou doest for the least of my brethren, thou doest for me"? And what have you done for them? You've got them a good chunk of beef for their dinner. They're not used to moldy crusts; in the old days they had a helmetful of white bread and wine before they went out to fight for God.

EILIF   Yes, I reached for my sword and I mowed them down.

THE GENERAL   You're a young Caesar. You deserve to see the king.

EILIF   I have, in the distance. He shines like a light. He's my ideal.

THE GENERAL   You're something like him already, Eilif. I know the worth of a brave soldier like you. When I find one, I treat him like my own son. (*He leads him to the map*) Take a look at the situation, Eilif; we've still got a long way to go.

MOTHER COURAGE (*who has been listening starts plucking her capon furiously*)   He must be a rotten general.

THE COOK   Eats like a pig, but why rotten?

MOTHER COURAGE   Because he needs brave soldiers, that's why. If he planned his campaigns right, what would he need brave soldiers for? The run-of-the-mill would do. Take it from me, whenever you find a lot of virtues, it shows that something's wrong.

THE COOK   I'd say it proves that something is all right.

MOTHER COURAGE   No, that something's wrong. See, when a general or a king is real stupid and leads his men up shit creek, his troops need courage, that's a virtue. If he's stingy and doesn't hire enough soldiers, they've all got to be Herculeses. And if he's a slob and lets everything go to pot, they've got to be as sly as serpents or they're done for. And if he's always expecting too much of them, they need an extra dose of loyalty. A country that's run right, or a good king or a good general, doesn't need any of these virtues. You don't need virtues in a decent country, the people can all be perfectly ordinary, medium-bright, and cowards too for my money.

THE GENERAL   I bet your father was a soldier.

EILIF   A great soldier, I'm told. My mother warned me about it. Makes me think of a song.

THE GENERAL   Sing it! (*Bellowing*) Where's that food!

EILIF   It's called: The Song of the Old Wife and the Soldier. (*He sings, doing a war dance with his saber*)

A gun or a pike, they can kill who they like
And the torrent will swallow a wader
You had better think twice before battling with ice
Said the old wife to the soldier.
Cocking his rifle he leapt to his feet
Laughing for joy as he heard the drum beat
The wars cannot hurt me, he told her.
He shouldered his gun and he picked up his knife
To see the wide world. That's the soldier's life.
Those were the words of the soldier.

Ah, deep will they lie who wise counsel defy
Learn wisdom from those that are older
Oh, don't venture too high or you'll fall from the sky
Said the old wife to the soldier.
But the young soldier with knife and with gun
Only laughed a cold laugh and stepped into the run.
The water can't hurt me, he told her.
And when the moon on the rooftop shines white
We'll be coming back. You can pray for that night.
Those were the words of the soldier.

MOTHER COURAGE (*in the kitchen, continues the song, beating a pot with a spoon*)

Like the smoke you'll be gone and no warmth linger on
And your deeds only leave me the colder!
Oh, see the smoke race. Oh, dear God keep him safe!
That's what she said of the soldier.

EILIF   What's that?
MOTHER COURAGE (*goes on singing*)

And the young soldier with knife and with gun
Was swept from his feet till he sank in the run
And the torrent swallowed the waders.
Cold shone the moon on the rooftop white
But the soldier was carried away with the ice
And what was it she heard from the soldiers?

Like the smoke he was gone and no warmth lingered on
And his deeds only left her the colder.
Ah, deep will they lie who wise counsel defy!
That's what she said to the soldiers.

THE GENERAL   What do they think they're doing in my kitchen?
EILIF (*has gone into the kitchen. He embraces his mother*)   Mother! It's you! Where are the others?
MOTHER COURAGE (*in his arms*)   Snug as a bug in a rug. Swiss Cheese is paymaster of the Second Regiment; at least he won't be fighting, I couldn't keep him out altogether.
ELLIE   And how about your feet?
MOTHER COURAGE   Well, it's hard getting my shoes on in the morning.
THE GENERAL (*has joined them*)   Ah, so you're his mother. I hope you've got more sons for me like this fellow here.
EILIF   Am I lucky! There you're sitting in the kitchen hearing your son being praised.
MOTHER COURAGE   I heard it all right! (*She gives him a slap in the face*)
EILIF (*holding his cheek*)   For capturing the oxen?
MOTHER COURAGE   No. For not surrendering when the four of them were threatening to make hash out of you! Didn't I teach you to take care of yourself? You Finnish devil!
(*The general and the chaplain laugh*)

3

Three years later Mother Courage and parts of a
Finnish regiment are taken prisoner. She is able to
save her daughter and her wagon, but her honest son
dies.

Army camp.

*Afternoon. On a pole the regimental flag. Mother Courage has stretched
a clothesline between her wagon, on which all sorts of merchandise is
hung in display, and a large cannon. She and Kattrin are folding
washing and piling it on the cannon. At the same time she is negotiating
with an ordnance officer over a sack of bullets. Swiss Cheese, now in the
uniform of a paymaster, is looking on. A pretty woman, Yvette Pottier,
is sitting with a glass of brandy in front of her, sewing a gaudy-colored
hat. She is in her stocking feet, her red high-heeled shoes are on the ground
beside her.*

THE ORDNANCE OFFICER   I'll let you have these bullets for two
 guilders. It's cheap, I need the money, because the colonel's
 been drinking with the officers for two days and we're out of
 liquor.
MOTHER COURAGE   That's ammunition for the troops. If it's
 found here, I'll be court-martialed. You punks sell their bullets and the men have nothing to shoot at the enemy.
THE ORDNANCE OFFICER   Don't be hard-hearted, you scratch my
 back, I'll scratch yours.
MOTHER COURAGE   I'm not taking any army property. Not at
 that price.
THE ORDNANCE OFFICER   You can sell it for five guilders, maybe
 eight, to the ordnance officer of the Fourth before the day is
 out, if you're quiet about it and give him a receipt for twelve.
 He hasn't an ounce of ammunition left.
MOTHER COURAGE   Why don't you do it yourself?

THE ORDNANCE OFFICER   Because I don't trust him, he's a friend of mine.

MOTHER COURAGE (*takes the sack*)   Hand it over. (*To Kattrin*) Take it back there and pay him one and a half guilders. (*In response to the ordnance officer's protest*) One and a half guilders, I say. (*Kattrin drags the sack behind the wagon, the ordnance officer follows her. Mother Courage to Swiss Cheese*) Here's your underdrawers, take good care of them, this is October, might be coming on fall, I don't say it will be, because I've learned that nothing is sure to happen the way we think, not even the seasons. But whatever happens, your regimental funds have to be in order. Are your funds in order?

SWISS CHEESE   Yes, mother.

MOTHER COURAGE   Never forget that they made you paymaster because you're honest and not brave like your brother, and especially because you're too simple-minded to get the idea of making off with the money. That's a comfort to me. And don't go mislaying your drawers.

SWISS CHEESE   No, mother. I'll put them under my mattress. (*Starts to go*)

ORDNANCE OFFICER   I'll go with you, paymaster.

MOTHER COURAGE   Just don't teach him any of your tricks. (*Without saying good-bye the ordnance officer goes out with Swiss Cheese*)

YVETTE (*waves her hand after the ordnance officer*)   You might say good-bye, officer.

MOTHER COURAGE (*to Yvette*)   I don't like to see those two together. He's not the right kind of company for my Swiss Cheese. But the war's getting along pretty well. More countries are joining in all the time, it can go on for another four, five years, easy. With a little planning ahead, I can do good business if I'm careful. Don't you know you shouldn't drink in the morning with your sickness?

YVETTE   Who says I'm sick, it's slander.

MOTHER COURAGE   Everybody says so.

YVETTE   Because they're all liars. Mother Courage, I'm desperate. They all keep out of my way like I'm a rotten fish on account of those lies. What's the good of fixing my hat? (*She throws it down*) That's why I drink in the morning, I never used to, I'm getting crow's-feet, but it doesn't matter now. In

the Second Finnish Regiment they all know me. I should have
stayed home when my first love walked out on me. Pride isn't
for the likes of us. If we can't put up with shit, we're through.

MOTHER COURAGE   Just don't start in on your Pieter and how it
all happened in front of my innocent daughter.

YVETTE   She's just the one to hear it, it'll harden her against
love.

MOTHER COURAGE   Nothing can harden them.

YVETTE   Then I'll talk about it because it makes me feel better.
It begins with my growing up in fair Flanders, because if I
hadn't I'd never have laid eyes on him and I wouldn't be here
in Poland now, because he was an army cook, blond, a Dutchman, but skinny. Kattrin, watch out for the skinny ones, but
I didn't know that then, and another thing I didn't know is
that he had another girl even then, and they all called him
Pete the Pipe, because he didn't even take his pipe out of his
mouth when he was doing it, that's all it meant to him. (*She
sings the Song of Fraternization*)

When I was only sixteen
The foe came into our land.
He laid aside his sabre
And with a smile he took my hand.
   After the May parade
   The May light starts to fade.
   The regiment dressed by the right
   Then drums were beaten, that's the drill.
   The foe took us behind the hill
   And fraternized all night.

There were so many foes came
And mine worked in the mess.
I loathed him in the daytime.
At night I loved him none the less.
   After the May parade
   The May light starts to fade.
   The regiment dressed by the right
   Then drums were beaten, that's the drill.
   The foe took us behind the hill
   And fraternized all night.

The love which came upon me
Was wished on me by fate.
My friends could never grasp why
I found it hard to share their hate.
  The fields were wet with dew
  When sorrow first I knew.
  The regiment dressed by the right
  Then drums were beaten, that's the drill
  And then the foe, my lover still
  Went marching from our sight.

Well, I followed him, but I never found him. That was five years ago. (*She goes behind the wagon with an unsteady gait*)

MOTHER COURAGE   You've left your hat.

YVETTE   Anybody that wants it can have it.

MOTHER COURAGE   Let that be a lesson to you, Kattrin. Have no truck with soldiers. It's love that makes the world go round, so you'd better watch out. Even with a civilian it's no picnic. He says he'd kiss the ground you put your little feet on, talking of feet, did you wash yours yesterday, and then you're his slave. Be glad you're dumb, that way you'll never contradict yourself or want to bite your tongue off because you've told the truth, it's a gift of God to be dumb. Here comes the general's cook, I wonder what he wants.

(*The cook and the chaplain enter*)

THE CHAPLAIN   I've got a message for you from your son Eilif. The cook here thought he'd come along, he's taken a shine to you.

THE COOK   I only came to get a breath of air.

MOTHER COURAGE   You can always do that here if you behave, and if you don't, I can handle you. Well, what does he want? I've got no money to spare.

THE CHAPLAIN   Actually he wanted me to see his brother, the paymaster.

MOTHER COURAGE   He's not here any more, or anywhere else either. He's not his brother's paymaster. I don't want him leading him into temptation and being smart at his expense. (*Gives him money from the bag slung around her waist*) Give him this, it's a sin, he's speculating on mother love and he ought to be ashamed.

THE COOK   He won't do it much longer, then he'll be marching off with his regiment, maybe to his death, you never can tell. Better make it a little more, you'll be sorry later. You women are hard-hearted, but afterwards you're sorry. A drop of brandy wouldn't have cost much when it was wanted, but it wasn't given, and later, for all you know, he'll be lying in the cold ground and you can't dig him up again.

THE CHAPLAIN   Don't be sentimental, cook. There's nothing wrong with dying in battle, it's a blessing, and I'll tell you why. This is a war of religion. Not a common war, but a war for the faith, and therefore pleasing to God.

THE COOK   That's a fact. In a way you could call it a war, because of the extortion and killing and looting, not to mention a bit of rape, but it's a war of religion, which makes it different from all other wars, that's obvious. But it makes a man thirsty all the same, you've got to admit that.

THE CHAPLAIN (to Mother Courage, pointing at the cook)   I tried to discourage him, but he says you've turned his head, he sees you in his dreams.

THE COOK (lights a short-stemmed pipe)   All I want is a glass of brandy from your fair hand, nothing more sinful. I'm already so shocked by the jokes the chaplain's been telling me, I bet I'm still red in the face.

MOTHER COURAGE   And him a clergyman! I'd better give you fellows something to drink or you'll be making me immoral propositions just to pass the time.

THE CHAPLAIN   This is temptation, said the deacon, and succumbed to it. (Turning toward Kattrin as he leaves) And who is this delightful young lady?

MOTHER COURAGE   She's not delightful, she's a respectable young lady.

(The chaplain and the cook go behind the wagon with Mother Courage. Kattrin looks after them, then she walks away from the washing and approaches the hat. She picks it up, sits down and puts on the red shoes. From the rear Mother Courage is heard talking politics with the chaplain and the cook)

MOTHER COURAGE   The Poles here in Poland shouldn't have

butted in. All right, our king marched his army into their country. But instead of keeping the peace, the Poles start butting into their own affairs and attack the king while he's marching quietly through the landscape. That was a breach of the peace and the blood is on their head.

THE CHAPLAIN   Our king had only one thing in mind: freedom. The emperor had everybody under his yoke, the Poles as much as the Germans; the king had to set them free.

THE COOK   I see it this way, your brandy's first-rate, I can see why I liked your face, but we were talking about the king. This freedom he was trying to introduce into Germany cost him a fortune, he had to levy a salt tax in Sweden, which, as I said, cost the poor people a fortune. Then he had to put the Germans in jail and break them on the rack because they liked being the emperor's slaves. Oh yes, the king made short shrift of anybody that didn't want to be free. In the beginning he only wanted to protect Poland against wicked people, especially the emperor, but the more he ate the more he wanted, and pretty soon he was protecting all of Germany. But the Germans didn't take it lying down and the king got nothing but trouble for all his kindness and expense, which he naturally had to defray from taxes, which made for bad blood, but that didn't discourage him. He had one thing in his favor, the word of God, which was lucky, because otherwise people would have said he was doing it all for himself and what he hoped to get out of it. As it was, he always had a clear conscience and that was all he really cared about.

MOTHER COURAGE   It's easy to see you're not a Swede, or you wouldn't talk like that about the Hero-King.

THE CHAPLAIN   You're eating his bread, aren't you?

THE COOK   I don't eat his bread, I bake it.

MOTHER COURAGE   He can't be defeated because his men believe in him. (Earnestly) When you listen to the big wheels talk, they're making war for reasons of piety, in the name of everything that's fine and noble. But when you take another look, you see that they're not so dumb; they're making war for profit. If they weren't, the small fry like me wouldn't have anything to do with it.

THE COOK   That's a fact.

THE CHAPLAIN   And it wouldn't hurt you as a Dutchman to take a look at that flag up there before you express opinions in Poland.

MOTHER COURAGE   We're all good Protestants here! Prosit! (*Kattrin has started strutting about with Yvette's hat on, imitating Yvette's gait.*)

(*Suddenly cannon fire and shots are heard. Drums. Mother Courage, the cook and the chaplain run out from behind the wagon, the two men still with glasses in hand. The ordnance officer and a soldier rush up to the cannon and try to push it away*)

MOTHER COURAGE   What's going on? Let me get my washing first, you lugs. (*She tries to rescue her washing*)

THE ORDNANCE OFFICER   The Catholics. They're attacking. I don't know as we'll get away. (*To the soldier*) Get rid of the gun! (*Runs off*)

THE COOK   Christ, I've got to find the general. Courage, I'll be back for a little chat in a day or two. (*Rushes out*)

MOTHER COURAGE   Stop, you've forgotten your pipe.

THE COOK (*from the distance*)   Keep it for me! I'll need it.

MOTHER COURAGE   Just when we were making a little money!

THE CHAPLAIN   Well, I guess I'll be going too. It might be dangerous though, with the enemy so close. Blessed are the peaceful is the best motto in wartime. If only I had a cloak to cover up with.

MOTHER COURAGE   I'm not lending any cloaks, not on your life. I've had bitter experience in that line.

THE CHAPLAIN   But my religion puts me in special danger.

MOTHER COURAGE (*bringing him a cloak*)   It's against my better conscience. And now run along.

THE CHAPLAIN   Thank you kindly, you've got a good heart. But maybe I'd better sit here a while. The enemy might get suspicious if they see me running.

MOTHER COURAGE (*to the soldier*)   Leave it lay, you fool, you won't get paid extra. I'll take care of it for you, you'd only get killed.

THE SOLDIER (*running away*)   I tried. You're my witness.

MOTHER COURAGE   I'll swear it on the Bible. (*Sees her daughter with the hat*) What are you doing with that floozy hat? Take it off, have you gone out of your mind? Now of all times, with the enemy on top of us? (*She tears the hat off Kattrin's head*) You want them to find you and make a whore out of you? And those shoes! Take them off, you woman of Babylon! (*She tries to pull them off*) Jesus Christ, chaplain, make her take those shoes off! I'll be right back. (*She runs to the wagon*)

YVETTE (*enters, powdering her face*)   What's this I hear? The Catholics are coming? Where's my hat? Who's been stamping on it? I can't be seen like this if the Catholics are coming. What'll they think of me? I haven't even got a mirror. (*To the chaplain*) How do I look? Too much powder?

THE CHAPLAIN   Just right.

YVETTE   And where are my red shoes? (*She doesn't see them because Kattrin hides her feet under her skirt*) I left them here. I've got to get back to my tent. In my bare feet. It's disgraceful! (*Goes out*)

(*Swiss Cheese runs in carrying a small box*)

MOTHER COURAGE (*Comes out with her hands full of ashes. To Kattrin*)   Ashes. (*To Swiss Cheese*) What you got there?

SWISS CHEESE   The regimental funds.

MOTHER COURAGE   Throw it away! No more paymastering for you.

SWISS CHEESE   I'm responsible for it. (*He goes rear*)

MOTHER COURAGE (*to the chaplain*)   Take your clergyman's coat off, chaplain, or they'll recognize you, cloak or no cloak. (*She rubs Kattrin's face with ashes*) Hold still! There. With a little dirt you'll be safe. What a mess! The sentries were drunk. Hide your light under a bushel, as the Good Book says. When a soldier, especially a Catholic, sees a clean face, she's a whore before she knows it. Nobody feeds them for weeks. When they finally loot some provisions, the next thing they want is women. That'll do it. Let me look at you. Not bad. Like you'd been wallowing in a pigsty. Stop shaking. You're safe now. (*To Swiss Cheese*) What did you do with the cashbox?

SWISS CHEESE   I thought I'd put it in the wagon.

MOTHER COURAGE (*horrified*)   What! In my wagon? Of all the sinful stupidity! If my back is turned for half a second! They'll hang us all!

SWISS CHEESE   Then I'll put it somewhere else, or I'll run away with it.

MOTHER COURAGE   You'll stay right here. It's too late.

THE CHAPLAIN (*still changing, comes forward*)   Heavens, the flag!

MOTHER COURAGE (*takes down the regimental flag*)   Bozhe moi! I'm so used to it I don't see it. Twenty-five years I've had it. (*The cannon fire grows louder*)

(*Morning, three days later. The cannon is gone. Mother Courage, Kattrin, the chaplain and Swiss Cheese are sitting dejectedly over a meal*)

SWISS CHEESE   This is the third day I've been sitting here doing nothing; the sergeant has always been easy on me, but now he must be starting to wonder: where can Swiss Cheese be with the cashbox?

MOTHER COURAGE   Be glad they haven't tracked you down.

THE CHAPLAIN   What about me? I can't hold a service here either. The Good Book says: "Whosoever hath a full heart, his tongue runneth over." Heaven help me if mine runneth over.

MOTHER COURAGE   That's the way it is. Look what I've got on my hands: one with a religion and one with a cashbox. I don't know which is worse.

THE CHAPLAIN   Tell yourself that we're in the hands of God.

MOTHER COURAGE   I don't think we're that bad off, but all the same I can't sleep at night. If it weren't for you, Swiss Cheese, it'd be easier. I think I've put myself in the clear. I told them I was against the antichrist; he's a Swede with horns, I told them, and I'd noticed the left horn was kind of worn down. I interrupted the questioning to ask where I could buy holy candles cheap. I knew what to say because Swiss Cheese's father was a Catholic and he used to make jokes about it. They didn't really believe me, but their regiment had no provisioner, so they looked the other way. Maybe we stand to gain. We're prisoners, but so are lice on a dog.

THE CHAPLAIN   This milk is good. Though there's not very much of it or of anything else. Maybe we'll have to cut down on our Swedish appetites. But such is the lot of the vanquished.

MOTHER COURAGE   Who's vanquished? Victory and defeat don't
always mean the same thing to the big wheels up top and the
small fry underneath. Not by a long shot. In some cases defeat
is a blessing to the small fry. Honor's lost, but nothing else.
One time in Livonia our general got such a shellacking from
the enemy that in the confusion I laid hands on a beautiful
white horse from the baggage train. That horse pulled my
wagon for seven months, until we had a victory and they
checked up. On the whole, you can say that victory and defeat
cost us plain people plenty. The best thing for us is when
politics gets bogged down. (*To Swiss Cheese*) Eat!
SWISS CHEESE   I've lost my appetite. How's the sergeant going
to pay the men?
MOTHER COURAGE   Troops never get paid when they're running
away.
SWISS CHEESE   But they've got it coming to them. If they're not
paid, they don't need to run. Not a step.
MOTHER COURAGE   Swiss Cheese, you're too conscientious, it
almost frightens me. I brought you up to be honest, because
you're not bright, but somewhere it's got to stop. And now
me and the chaplain are going to buy a Catholic flag and some
meat. Nobody can buy meat like the chaplain, he goes into a
trance and heads straight for the best piece, I guess it makes
his mouth water and that shows him the way. At least they
let me carry on my business. Nobody cares about a shop-
keeper's religion, all they want to know is the price. Protestant pants are as warm as any other kind.
THE CHAPLAIN   Like the friar said when somebody told him the
Lutherans were going to stand the whole country on its head.
They'll always need beggars, he says. (*Mother Courage disappears into the wagon*) But she's worried about that cashbox.
They've taken no notice of us so far, they think we're all part
of the wagon, but how long can that go on?
SWISS CHEESE   I can take it away.
THE CHAPLAIN   That would be almost more dangerous. What if
somebody sees you? They've got spies. Yesterday morning,
just as I'm relieving myself, one of them jumps out of the
ditch. I was so scared I almost let out a prayer. That would
have given me away. I suppose they think they can tell a

Protestant by the smell of his shit. He was a little runt with a patch over one eye.

MOTHER COURAGE (*climbing down from the wagon with a basket*) Look what I've found. You shameless slut! (*She holds up the red shoes triumphantly*) Yvette's red shoes! She's swiped them in cold blood. It's your fault. Who told her she was a delightful young lady? (*She puts them into the basket*) I'm giving them back. Stealing Yvette's shoes! She ruins herself for money, that I can understand. But you'd like to do it free of charge, for pleasure. I've told you, you'll have to wait for peace. No soldiers! Just wait for peace with your worldly ways.

THE CHAPLAIN   She doesn't seem very worldly to me.

MOTHER COURAGE   Too worldly for me. In Dalarna she was like a stone, which is all they've got around there. The people used to say: We don't see the cripple. That's the way I like it. That way she's safe. (*To Swiss Cheese*) You leave that box where it is, hear? And keep an eye on your sister, she needs it. The two of you will be the death of me. I'd sooner take care of a bag of fleas. (*She goes off with the chaplain. Kattrin starts clearing away the dishes*)

SWISS CHEESE   Won't be many more days when I can sit in the sun in my shirtsleeves. (*Kattrin points to a tree*) Yes, the leaves are all yellow. (*Kattrin asks him, by means of gestures, whether he wants a drink*) Not now. I'm thinking. (*Pause*) She says she can't sleep. I'd better get the cashbox out of here, I've found a hiding place. All right, get me a drink. (*Kattrin goes behind the wagon*) I'll hide it in the rabbit hole down by the river until I can take it away. Maybe late tonight. I'll go get it and take it to the regiment. I wonder how far they've run in three days? Won't the sergeant be surprised! Well, Swiss Cheese, this is a pleasant disappointment, that's what he'll say. I trust you with the regimental cashbox and you bring it back.

(*As Kattrin comes out from behind the wagon with a glass of brandy, she comes face to face with two men. One is a sergeant. The other removes his hat and swings it through the air in a ceremonious greeting. He has a patch over one eye*)

THE MAN WITH THE PATCH   Good morning, my dear. Have you by any chance seen a man from the headquarters of the Second Finnish Regiment?

(Scared out of her wits, Kattrin runs front, spilling the brandy. The two exchange looks and withdraw after seeing Swiss Cheese sitting there)

SWISS CHEESE *(starting up from his thoughts)*   You've spilled half of it. What's the fuss about? Poke yourself in the eye? I don't understand you. I'm getting out of here, I've made up my mind, it's best. *(He stands up. She does everything she can think of to call his attention to the danger. He only evades her)* I wish I could understand you. Poor thing, I know you're trying to tell me something, you just can't say it. Don't worry about spilling the brandy, I'll be drinking plenty more. What's one glass? *(He takes the cashbox out of the wagon and hides it under his jacket)* I'll be right back. Let me go, you're making me angry. I know you mean well. If only you could talk.

(When she tries to hold him back, he kisses her and tears himself away. He goes out. She is desperate, she races back and forth, uttering short inarticulate sounds. The chaplain and Mother Courage come back. Kattrin gesticulates wildly at her mother)

MOTHER COURAGE   What's the matter? You're all upset. Has somebody hurt you? Where's Swiss Cheese? Tell it to me in order, Kattrin. Your mother understands you. What, the no-good's taken the cashbox? I'll hit him over the head with it, the sneak. Take your time, don't talk nonsense, use your hands, I don't like it when you howl like a dog, what will the chaplain think? It gives him the creeps. A one-eyed man?

THE CHAPLAIN   The one-eyed man is a spy. Did they arrest Swiss Cheese? *(Kattrin shakes her head and shrugs her shoulders)* We're done for.

MOTHER COURAGE *(takes a Catholic flag out of her basket. The chaplain fastens it to the flagpole)*   Hoist the new flag!

THE CHAPLAIN *(bitterly)*   All good Catholics here.

(Voices are heard from the rear. The two men bring in Swiss Cheese)

SWISS CHEESE   Let me go, I haven't got anything. Stop twisting my shoulder, I'm innocent.

THE SERGEANT   He belongs here. You know each other.

MOTHER COURAGE   What makes you think that?

SWISS CHEESE   I don't know them. I don't even know who they are. I had a meal here, it cost me ten hellers. Maybe you saw me sitting here, it was too salty.

THE SERGEANT   Who are you anyway?

MOTHER COURAGE   We're respectable people. And it's true. He had a meal here. He said it was too salty.

THE SERGEANT   Are you trying to tell me you don't know each other?

MOTHER COURAGE   Why should I know him? I don't know everybody. I don't ask people what their name is or if they're heathens; if they pay, they're not heathens. Are you a heathen?

SWISS CHEESE   Of course not.

THE CHAPLAIN   He ate his meal and he behaved himself. He didn't open his mouth except when he was eating. Then you have to.

THE SERGEANT   And who are you?

MOTHER COURAGE   He's only my bartender. You gentlemen must be thirsty, I'll get you a drink of brandy, you must be hot and tired.

THE SERGEANT   We don't drink on duty. (To Swiss Cheese) You were carrying something. You must have hidden it by the river. You had something under your jacket when you left here.

MOTHER COURAGE   Was it really him?

SWISS CHEESE   I think you must have seen somebody else. I saw a man running with something under his jacket. You've got the wrong man.

MOTHER COURAGE   That's what I think too, it's a misunderstanding. These things happen. I'm a good judge of people, I'm Mother Courage, you've heard of me, everybody knows me. Take it from me, this man has an honest face.

THE SERGEANT   We're looking for the cashbox of the Second Finnish Regiment. We know what the man in charge of it looks like. We've been after him for two days. You're him.

SWISS CHEESE   I'm not.

THE SERGEANT   Hand it over. If you don't you're a goner, you know that. Where is it?

MOTHER COURAGE (with urgency)   He'd hand it over, wouldn't he, knowing he was a goner if he didn't? I've got it, he'd say, take it, you're stronger. He's not that stupid. Speak up, you stupid idiot, the sergeant's giving you a chance.

SWISS CHEESE   But I haven't got it.

THE SERGEANT   In that case come along. We'll get it out of you.
  (They lead him away)

MOTHER COURAGE *(shouts after them)*   He'd tell you. He's not that
  stupid. And don't twist his shoulder off! *(Runs after them)*

  *(The same evening. The chaplain and mute Kattrin are washing
  dishes and scouring knives)*

THE CHAPLAIN   That boy's in trouble. There are cases like that
  in the Bible. Take the Passion of our Lord and Saviour.
  There's an old song about it. *(He sings the Song of the Hours)*

In the first hour Jesus mild
Who had prayed since even
Was betrayed and led before
Pontius the heathen.

Pilate found him innocent
Free from fault and error.
Therefore, having washed his hands
Sent him to King Herod.

In the third hour he was scourged
Stripped and clad in scarlet
And a plaited crown of thorns
Set upon his forehead.

On the Son of Man they spat
Mocked him and made merry.
Then the cross of death was brought
Given him to carry.

At the sixth hour with two thieves
To the cross they nailed him
And the people and the thieves
Mocked him and reviled him.

This is Jesus King of Jews
Cried they in derision
Till the sun withdrew its light
From that awful vision.

At the ninth hour Jesus wailed
Why hast thou me forsaken?
Soldiers brought him vinegar
Which he left untaken.

Then he yielded up the ghost
And the earth was shaken.
Rended was the temple's veil
And the saints were wakened.

Soldiers broke the two thieves' legs
As the night descended
Thrust a spear in Jesus' side
When his life had ended.

Still they mocked, as from his wound
Flowed the blood and water
Thus blasphemed the Son of Man
With their cruel laughter.

MOTHER COURAGE (*enters in a state of agitation*)   His life's at stake.
But they say the sergeant will listen to reason. Only it mustn't
come out that he's our Swiss Cheese, or they'll say we've been
giving him aid and comfort. All they want is money. But
where will we get the money? Hasn't Yvette been here? I met
her just now, she's latched onto a colonel, he's thinking of
buying her a provisioner's business.

THE CHAPLAIN   Are you really thinking of selling?

MOTHER COURAGE   How else can I get the money for the sergeant?

THE CHAPLAIN   But what will you live on?

MOTHER COURAGE   That's the hitch.

(*Yvette Pottier comes in with a doddering colonel*)

YVETTE (*embracing Mother Courage*)   My dear Mother Courage.
Here we are again! (*Whispering*) He's willing. (*Aloud*) This is
my dear friend who advises me on business matters. I just
chanced to hear that you wish to sell your wagon, due to
circumstances. I might be interested.

MOTHER COURAGE   Mortgage it, not sell it, let's not be hasty. It's
not so easy to buy a wagon like this in wartime.

YVETTE (*disappointed*)   Only mortgage it? I thought you wanted to sell it. In that case, I don't know if I'm interested. (*To the colonel*) What do you think?

THE COLONEL   Just as you say, my dear.

MOTHER COURAGE   It's only being mortgaged.

YVETTE   I thought you needed money.

MOTHER COURAGE (*firmly*)   I need the money, but I'd rather run myself ragged looking for an offer than sell now. The wagon is our livelihood. It's an opportunity for you, Yvette, God knows when you'll find another like it and have such a good friend to advise you. See what I mean?

YVETTE   My friend thinks I should snap it up, but I don't know. If it's only being mortgaged ... Don't you agree that we ought to buy?

THE COLONEL   Yes, my dear.

MOTHER COURAGE   Then you'll have to look for something that's for sale, maybe you'll find something if you take your time and your friend goes around with you. Maybe in a week or two you'll find the right thing.

YVETTE   Then we'll go looking, I love to go looking for things, and I love to go around with you, Poldi, it's a real pleasure. Even if it takes two weeks. When would you pay the money back if you get it?

MOTHER COURAGE   I can pay it back in two weeks, maybe one.

YVETTE   I can't make up my mind, Poldi, chéri, tell me what to do. (*She takes the colonel aside*) I know she's got to sell, that's definite. The lieutenant, you know who I mean, the blond one, he'd be glad to lend me the money. He's mad about me, he says I remind him of somebody. What do you think?

THE COLONEL   Keep away from that lieutenant. He's no good. He'll take advantage. Haven't I told you I'd buy you something, pussykins?

YVETTE   I can't accept it from you. But then if you think the lieutenant might take advantage ... Poldi, I'll accept it from you.

THE COLONEL   I hope so.

YVETTE   Your advice is to take it?

THE COLONEL   That's my advice.

YVETTE (*goes back to Mother Courage*)   My friend advises me to do it. Write me out a receipt, say the wagon belongs to me complete with stock and furnishings when the two weeks are up. We'll take inventory right now, then I'll bring you the two hundred guilders. (*To the colonel*) You go back to camp, I'll join you in a little while, I've got to take inventory, I don't want anything missing from my wagon. (*She kisses him. He leaves. She climbs up in the wagon*) I don't see very many boots.

MOTHER COURAGE   Yvette. This is no time to inspect your wagon if it is yours. You promised to see the sergeant about my Swiss Cheese, you've got to hurry. They say he's to be court-martialed in an hour.

YVETTE   Just let me count the shirts.

MOTHER COURAGE (*pulls her down by the skirt*)   You hyena, it's Swiss Cheese, his life's at stake. And don't tell anybody where the offer comes from, in heaven's name say it's your gentleman friend, or we'll all get it, they'll say we helped him.

YVETTE   I've arranged to meet One-Eye in the woods, he must be there already.

THE CHAPLAIN   And there's no need to start out with the whole two hundred, offer a hundred and fifty, that's plenty.

MOTHER COURAGE   Is it your money? You just keep out of this. Don't worry, you'll get your bread and soup. Go on now and don't haggle. It's his life. (*She gives Yvette a push to start her on her way*)

THE CHAPLAIN   I didn't mean to butt in, but what are we going to live on? You've got an unemployable daughter on your hands.

MOTHER COURAGE   You muddlehead, I'm counting on the regimental cashbox. They'll allow for his expenses, won't they?

THE CHAPLAIN   But will she handle it right?

MOTHER COURAGE   It's in her own interest. If I spend her two hundred, she gets the wagon. She's mighty keen on it, how long can she expect to hold on to her colonel? Kattrin, you scour the knives, use pumice. And you, don't stand around like Jesus on the Mount of Olives, bestir yourself, wash those glasses, we're expecting at least fifty for dinner, and then it'll be the same old story: "Oh my feet, I'm not used to running around, I don't run around in the pulpit." I think they'll set him free. Thank God they're open to bribery. They're not wolves, they're human and out for money. Bribe-taking in humans is the same as mercy in God. It's our only hope. As long as people take bribes, you'll have mild sentences and even the innocent will get off once in a while.

YVETTE (*comes in panting*) They want two hundred. And we've got to be quick. Or it'll be out of their hands. I'd better take One-Eye to see my colonel right away. He confessed that he'd had the cashbox, they put the thumb screws on him. But he threw it in the river when he saw they were after him. The box is gone. Should I run and get the money from my colonel?

MOTHER COURAGE The box is gone? How will I get my two hundred back?

YVETTE Ah, so you thought you could take it out of the cashbox? You thought you'd put one over on me. Forget it. If you want to save Swiss Cheese, you'll just have to pay, or maybe you'd like me to drop the whole thing and let you keep your wagon?

MOTHER COURAGE This is something I hadn't reckoned with. But don't rush me, you'll get the wagon, I know it's down the drain, I've had it for seventeen years. Just let me think a second, it's all so sudden. What'll I do, I can't give them two hundred, I guess you should have bargained. If I haven't got a few guilders to fall back on, I'll be at the mercy of the first Tom, Dick, or Harry. Say I'll give them a hundred and twenty, I'll lose my wagon anyway.

YVETTE They won't go along. One-Eye's in a hurry, he's so keyed-up he keeps looking behind him. Hadn't I better give them the whole two hundred?

MOTHER COURAGE (*in despair*) I can't do it. Thirty years I've worked. She's twenty-five and no husband. I've got her to keep too. Don't needle me, I know what I'm doing. Say a hundred and twenty or nothing doing.

YVETTE It's up to you. (*Goes out quickly*)

(*Mother Courage looks neither at the chaplain nor at her daughter. She sits down to help Kattrin scour the knives*)

MOTHER COURAGE Don't break the glasses. They're not ours any more. Watch what you're doing, you'll cut yourself. Swiss Cheese will be back, I'll pay two hundred if I have to.

You'll have your brother. With eighty guilders we can buy a peddler's pack and start all over. Worse things have happened.

THE CHAPLAIN   The Lord will provide.

MOTHER COURAGE   Rub them dry. (*They scour the knives in silence. Suddenly Kattrin runs sobbing behind the wagon*)

YVETTE (*comes running*)   They won't go along. I warned you. One-Eye wanted to run out on me, he said it was no use. He said we'd hear the drums any minute, meaning he'd been sentenced. I offered a hundred and fifty. He didn't even bother to shrug his shoulders. When I begged and pleaded, he promised to wait till I'd spoken to you again.

MOTHER COURAGE   Say I'll give him the two hundred. Run. (*Yvette runs off. They sit in silence. The chaplain has stopped washing the glasses*) Maybe I bargained too long. (*Drums are heard in the distance. The chaplain stands up and goes to the rear. Mother Courage remains seated. It grows dark. The drums stop. It grows light again. Mother Courage has not moved*)

YVETTE (*enters, very pale*)   Now you've done it with your haggling and wanting to keep your wagon. Eleven bullets he got, that's all. I don't know why I bother with you any more, you don't deserve it. But I've picked up a little information. They don't believe the cashbox is really in the river. They suspect it's here and they think you were connected with him. They're going to bring him here, they think maybe you'll give yourself away when you see him. I'm warning you: You don't know him, or you're all dead ducks. I may as well tell you, they're right behind me. Should I keep Kattrin out of the way? (*Mother Courage shakes her head*) Does she know? Maybe she didn't hear the drums or maybe she didn't understand.

MOTHER COURAGE   She knows. Get her. (*Yvette brings Kattrin, who goes to her mother and stands beside her. Mother Courage takes her by the hand. Two soldiers come in with a stretcher on which something is lying under a sheet. The sergeant walks beside them. They set the stretcher down*)

THE SERGEANT   We've got a man here and we don't know his name. We need it for the records. He had a meal with you. Take a look, see if you know him. (*He removes the sheet*) Do you know him? (*Mother Courage shakes her head*) What? You'd never seen him before he came here for a meal? (*Mother Courage shakes her head*) Pick him up. Throw him on the dump. Nobody knows him. (*They carry him away*)

4

Mother Courage sings the Song of the Great Capitulation.

Outside an officer's tent.

Mother Courage is waiting. A clerk looks out of the tent.

THE CLERK   I know you. You had a Protestant paymaster at your place, he was hiding. I wouldn't put in any complaints if I were you.

MOTHER COURAGE   I'm putting in a complaint. I'm innocent. If I take this lying down, it'll look as if I had a guilty conscience. First they ripped up my whole wagon with their sabers, then they wanted me to pay a fine of five talers for no reason at all.

THE CLERK   I'm advising you for your own good: Keep your trap shut. We haven't got many provisioners and we'll let you keep on with your business, especially if you've got a guilty conscience and pay a fine now and then.

MOTHER COURAGE   I'm putting in a complaint.

THE CLERK   Have it your way. But you'll have to wait till the captain can see you. (*Disappears into the tent*)

A YOUNG SOLDIER (*enters in a rage*)   Bouque la Madonne! Where's that stinking captain? He embezzled my reward and now he's drinking it up with his whores. I'm going to get him!

AN OLDER SOLDIER (*comes running after him*)   Shut up. They'll put you in the stocks!

THE YOUNG SOLDIER   Come on out, you crook! I'll make chops

out of you. Embezzling my reward! Who jumps in the river? Not another man in the whole squad, only me. And I can't even buy myself a beer. I won't stand for it. Come on out and let me cut you to pieces!

THE OLDER SOLDIER   Holy Mary! He'll ruin himself.

MOTHER COURAGE   They didn't give him a reward?

THE YOUNG SOLDIER   Let me go. I'll run you through too, the more the merrier.

THE OLDER SOLDIER   He saved the colonel's horse and they didn't give him a reward. He's young, he hasn't been around long.

MOTHER COURAGE   Let him go, he's not a dog, you don't have to tie him up. Wanting a reward is perfectly reasonable. Why else would he distinguish himself?

THE YOUNG SOLDIER   And him drinking in there! You're all a lot of yellowbellies. I distinguished myself and I want my reward.

MOTHER COURAGE   Young man, don't shout at me. I've got my own worries and besides, go easy on your voice, you may need it. You'll be hoarse when the captain comes out, you won't be able to say boo and he won't be able to put you in the stocks till you're blue in the face. People that yell like that don't last long, maybe half an hour, then they're so exhausted you have to sing them to sleep.

THE YOUNG SOLDIER   I'm not exhausted and who wants to sleep? I'm hungry. They make our bread out of acorns and hemp seed, and they skimp on that. He's whoring away my reward and I'm hungry. I'll murder him.

MOTHER COURAGE   I see. You're hungry. Last year your general made you cut across the fields to trample down the grain. I could have sold a pair of boots for ten guilders if anybody'd had ten guilders and if I'd had any boots. He thought he'd be someplace else this year, but now he's still here and everybody's starving. I can see that you might be good and mad.

THE YOUNG SOLDIER   He can't do this to me, save your breath, I won't put up with injustice.

MOTHER COURAGE   You're right, but for how long? How long won't you put up with injustice? An hour? Two hours? You see, you never thought of that, though it's very important, because it's miserable in the stocks when it suddenly dawns on you that you *can* put up with injustice.

THE YOUNG SOLDIER   I don't know why I listen to you. Bouque la Madonne! Where's the captain?

MOTHER COURAGE   You listen to me because I'm not telling you anything new. You know your temper has gone up in smoke, it was a short temper and you need a long one, but that's a hard thing to come by.

THE YOUNG SOLDIER   Are you trying to say I've no right to claim my reward?

MOTHER COURAGE   Not at all. I'm only saying your temper isn't long enough, it won't get you anywhere. Too bad. If you had a long temper, I'd even egg you on. Chop the bastard up, that's what I'd say, but suppose you don't chop him up, because your tail's drooping and you know it. I'm left standing there like a fool and the captain takes it out on me.

THE OLDER SOLDIER   You're right. He's only blowing off steam.

THE YOUNG SOLDIER   We'll see about that. I'll cut him to pieces. (*He draws his sword*) When he comes out, I'll cut him to pieces.

THE CLERK (*looks out*)   The captain will be here in a moment. Sit down.

(*The young soldier sits down*)

MOTHER COURAGE   There he sits. What did I tell you? Sitting, aren't you? Oh, they know us like a book, they know how to handle us. Sit down! And down we sit. You can't start a riot sitting down. Better not stand up again, you won't be able to stand the way you were standing before. Don't be embarrassed on my account, I'm no better, not a bit of it. We were full of piss and vinegar, but they've bought it off. Look at me. No back talk, it's bad for business. Let me tell you about the great capitulation. (*She sings the Song of the Great Capitulation*)

When I was young, no more than a spring chicken
I too thought that I was really quite the cheese
(No common peddler's daughter, not I with my looks and my
    talent and striving for higher things!)
One little hair in the soup would make me sicken
And at me no man would dare to sneeze.
(It's all or nothing, no second best for me. I've got what it
    takes, the rules are for somebody else!)

But a chickadee
Sang wait and see!
   And you go marching with the show
   In step, however fast or slow
   And rattle off your little song:
   It won't be long.
   And then the whole thing slides.
   You think God provides—
   But you've got it wrong.

And before one single year had wasted
I had learned to swallow down the bitter brew
(Two kids on my hands and the price of bread and who do
    they take me for anyway!)
Man, the double-edged shellacking that I tasted
On my ass and knees I was when they were through.
(You've got to get along with people, one good turn deserves
    another, no use trying to ram your head through the wall!)
And the chickadee
Sang wait and see!
   And she goes marching with the show
   In step, however fast or slow
   And rattles off her little song:
   It won't be long.
   And then the whole thing slides
   You think God provides—
   But you've got it wrong.

I've seen many fired by high ambition
No star's big or high enough to reach out for.
(It's ability that counts, where there's a will there's a way, one
    way or another we'll swing it!)
Then while moving mountains they get a suspicion
That to wear a straw hat is too big a chore.
(No use being too big for your britches!)
And the chickadee
Sings wait and see!
   And they go marching with the show
   In step, however fast or slow
   And rattle off their little song:
   It won't be long.

And then the whole thing slides!
You think God provides—
But you've got it wrong!

MOTHER COURAGE (*to the young soldier*)   So here's what I think:
Stay here with your sword if your anger's big enough, I know
you have good reason, but if it's a short quick anger, better
make tracks!

THE YOUNG SOLDIER   Kiss my ass! (*He staggers off, the older soldier
after him*)

THE CLERK (*sticking his head out*)   The captain is here. You can
put in your complaint now.

MOTHER COURAGE   I've changed my mind. No complaint. (*She
goes out*)

5

Two years have passed. The war has spread far and
wide. With scarcely a pause Mother Courage's little
wagon rolls through Poland, Moravia, Bavaria, Italy,
and back again to Bavaria. 1631. Tilly's victory at Mag-
deburg costs Mother Courage four officers' shirts.

Mother Courage's wagon has stopped in a devastated village.

*Thin military music is heard from the distance. Two soldiers at the bar
are being waited on by Kattrin and Mother Courage. One of them is
wearing a lady's fur coat over his shoulders.*

MOTHER COURAGE   What's that? You can't pay? No money, no
schnapps. Plenty of victory marches for the Lord but no pay
for the men.

THE SOLDIER   I want my schnapps. I came too late for the looting. The general skunked us: permission to loot the city for
exactly one hour. Says he's not a monster; the mayor must
have paid him.

THE CHAPLAIN (*staggers in*)   There's still some wounded in the
house. The peasant and his family. Help me, somebody, I
need linen.

(*The second soldier goes out with him. Kattrin gets very excited and
tries to persuade her mother to hand out linen*)

MOTHER COURAGE   I haven't got any. The regiment's bought up
all my bandages. You think I'm going to rip up my officers'
shirts for the likes of them?

THE CHAPLAIN (*calling back*)   I need linen, I tell you.

MOTHER COURAGE (*sitting down on the wagon steps to keep Kattrin
out*)   Nothing doing. They don't pay, they got nothing to
pay with.

THE CHAPLAIN (*bending over a woman whom he has carried out*)
Why did you stay here in all that gunfire?

THE PEASANT WOMAN (*feebly*)   Farm.

MOTHER COURAGE   You won't catch them leaving their property. And I'm expected to foot the bill. I won't do it.

THE FIRST SOLDIER   They're Protestants. Why do they have to be
Protestants?

MOTHER COURAGE   Religion is the least of their worries. They've
lost their farm.

THE SECOND SOLDIER   They're no Protestants. They're Catholics
like us.

THE FIRST SOLDIER   How do we know who we're shooting at?

A PEASANT (*whom the Chaplain brings in*)   They got my arm.

THE CHAPLAIN   Where's the linen?

(*All look at Mother Courage, who does not move*)

MOTHER COURAGE   I can't give you a thing. What with all my
taxes, duties, fees and bribes! (*Making guttural sounds, Kattrin
picks up a board and threatens her mother with it*)   Are you crazy?
Put that board down, you slut, or I'll smack you. I'm not
giving anything, you can't make me, I've got to think of
myself. (*The chaplain picks her up from the step and puts her down
on the ground. Then he fishes out some shirts and tears them into
strips*)

My shirts! Half a guilder apiece! I'm ruined!
(The anguished cry of a baby is heard from the house)
THE PEASANT   The baby's still in there!
(Kattrin runs in)
THE CHAPLAIN *(to the woman)*   Don't move. They're bringing him out.
MOTHER COURAGE   Get her out of there. The roof'll cave in.
THE CHAPLAIN   I'm not going in there again.
MOTHER COURAGE *(torn)*   Don't run hog-wild with my expensive linen.
(Kattrin emerges from the ruins carrying an infant)
MOTHER COURAGE   Oh, so you've found another baby to carry around with you? Give that baby back to its mother this minute, or it'll take me all day to get it away from you. Do you hear me? *(To the second soldier)* Don't stand there gaping, go back and tell them to stop that music, I can see right here that they've won a victory. Your victory's costing me a pretty penny.
(Kattrin rocks the baby in her arms, humming a lullaby)
MOTHER COURAGE   There she sits, happy in all this misery; give it back this minute, the mother's coming to. *(She pounces on the first soldier who has been helping himself to the drinks and is now making off with the bottle)* Pshagreff! Beast! Haven't you had enough victories for today? Pay up.
FIRST SOLDIER   I'm broke.
MOTHER COURAGE *(tears the fur coat off him)*   Then leave the coat here, it's stolen anyway.
THE CHAPLAIN   There's still somebody in there.

6

Outside Ingolstadt in Bavaria Mother Courage attends the funeral of Tilly, the imperial field marshal. Conversations about heroes and the longevity of the war. The chaplain deplores the waste of his talents. Mute Kattrin gets the red shoes. 1632.

Inside Mother Courage's tent.

A bar open to the rear. Rain. In the distance drum rolls and funeral music. The chaplain and the regimental clerk are playing a board game. Mother Courage and her daughter are taking inventory.

THE CHAPLAIN The procession's starting.
MOTHER COURAGE It's a shame about the general—socks: twenty-two pairs—I hear he was killed by accident. On account of the fog in the fields. He's up front encouraging the troops. "Fight to the death, boys," he sings out. Then he rides back, but he gets lost in the fog and rides back forward. Before you know it he's in the middle of the battle and stops a bullet —lanterns: we're down to four. (*A whistle from the rear. She goes to the bar*) You men ought to be ashamed, running out on your late general's funeral! (*She pours drinks*)
THE CLERK They shouldn't have been paid before the funeral. Now they're getting drunk instead.
THE CHAPLAIN (*to the clerk*) Shouldn't you be at the funeral?
THE CLERK In this rain?
MOTHER COURAGE With you it's different, the rain might spoil your uniform. It seems they wanted to ring the bells, naturally, but it turned out the churches had all been shot to pieces by his orders, so the poor general won't hear any bells when they lower him into his grave. They're going to fire a three-gun salute instead, so it won't be too dull—seventeen sword belts.

CRIES (*from the bar*)   Hey! Brandy!

MOTHER COURAGE   Money first! No, you can't come into my tent with your muddy boots! You can drink outside, rain or no rain. (*To the clerk*) I'm only letting officers in. It seems the general had been having his troubles. Mutiny in the Second Regiment because he hadn't paid them. It's a war of religion, he says, should they profit by their faith?

(*Funeral march. All look to the rear*)

THE CHAPLAIN   Now they're marching past the body.

MOTHER COURAGE   I feel sorry when a general or an emperor passes away like this, maybe he thought he'd do something big, that posterity would still be talking about and maybe put up a statue in his honor, conquer the world, for instance, that's a nice ambition for a general, he doesn't know any better. So he knocks himself out, and then the common people come and spoil it all, because what do they care about greatness, all they care about is a mug of beer and maybe a little company. The most beautiful plans have been wrecked by the smallness of the people that are supposed to carry them out. Even an emperor can't do anything by himself, he needs the support of his soldiers and his people. Am I right?

THE CHAPLAIN (*laughing*)   Courage, you're right, except about the soldiers. They do their best. With those fellows out there, for instance, drinking their brandy in the rain, I'll undertake to carry on one war after another for a hundred years, two at once if I have to, and I'm not a general by trade.

MOTHER COURAGE   Then you don't think the war might stop?

THE CHAPLAIN   Because the general's dead? Don't be childish. They grow by the dozen, there'll always be plenty of heroes.

MOTHER COURAGE   Look here, I'm not asking you for the hell of it. I've been wondering whether to lay in supplies while they're cheap, but if the war stops, I can throw them out the window.

THE CHAPLAIN   I understand. You want a serious answer. There have always been people who say: "The war will be over some day." I say there's no guarantee the war will ever be over. Naturally a brief intermission is conceivable. Maybe the war needs a breather, a war can even break its neck, so to speak. There's always a chance of that, nothing is perfect here below. Maybe there never will be a perfect war, one that lives up to all our expectations. Suddenly, for some unforeseen reason, a war can bog down, you can't think of everything. Some little oversight and your war's in trouble. And then you've got to pull it out of the mud. But the kings and emperors, not to mention the pope, will always come to its help in adversity. On the whole, I'd say this war has very little to worry about, it'll live to a ripe old age.

A SOLDIER (*sings at the bar*)

A drink, and don't be slow!
A soldier's got to go
And fight for his religion.

Make it double, this is a holiday.

MOTHER COURAGE   If I could only be sure . . .
THE CHAPLAIN   Figure it out for yourself. What's to stop the war?
THE SOLDIER (*sings*)

Your breasts, girl, don't be slow!
A soldier's got to go
And ride away to Pilsen.

THE CLERK (*suddenly*)   But why can't we have peace? I'm from Bohemia, I'd like to go home when the time comes.
THE CHAPLAIN   Oh, you'd like to go home? Ah, peace! What becomes of the hole when the cheese has been eaten?
THE SOLDIER (*sings*)

Play cards, friends, don't be slow!
A soldier's got to go
No matter if it's Sunday.

A prayer, priest, don't be slow!
A soldier's got to go
And die for king and country.

THE CLERK   In the long run nobody can live without peace.

THE CHAPLAIN The way I see it, war gives you plenty of peace.
It has its peaceful moments. War meets every need, including
the peaceful ones, everything's taken care of, or your war
couldn't hold its own. In a war you can shit the same as in
the dead of peace, you can stop for a beer between battles, and
even on the march you can always lie down on your elbows
and take a little nap by the roadside. You can't play cards
when you're fighting; but then you can't when you're plowing in the dead of peace either, but after a victory the sky's
the limit. Maybe you've had a leg shot off, at first you raise
a howl, you make a big thing of it. But then you calm down
or they give you schnapps, and in the end you're hopping
around again and the war's no worse off than before. And
what's to prevent you from multiplying in the thick of the
slaughter, behind a barn or someplace, in the long run how
can they stop you, and then the war has your progeny to help
it along. Take it from me, the war will always find an answer.
Why would it have to stop?
(Kattrin has stopped working and is staring at the chaplain)
MOTHER COURAGE Then I'll buy the merchandise. You've convinced me. (*Kattrin suddenly throws down a basket full of bottles
and runs out*) Kattrin! (*Laughs*) My goodness, the poor thing's
been hoping for peace. I promised her she'd get a husband
when peace comes. (*She runs after her*)
THE CLERK (*getting up*) I win, you've been too busy talking. Pay
up.
MOTHER COURAGE (*comes back with Kattrin*) Be reasonable, the
war'll go on a little longer and we'll make a little more money,
then peace will be even better. Run along to town now, it
won't take you ten minutes, and get the stuff from the Golden
Lion, only the expensive things, we'll pick up the rest in the
wagon later, it's all arranged, the regimental clerk here will
go with you. They've almost all gone to the general's funeral,
nothing can happen to you. Look sharp, don't let them take
anything away from you, think of your dowry.
(Kattrin puts a kerchief over her head and goes with the clerk)
THE CHAPLAIN Is it all right letting her go with the clerk?
MOTHER COURAGE Who'd want to ruin her? She's not pretty
enough.

THE CHAPLAIN   I've come to admire the way you handle your business and pull through every time. I can see why they call you Mother Courage.

MOTHER COURAGE   Poor people need courage. Why? Because they're sunk. In their situation it takes gumption just to get up in the morning. Or to plow a field in the middle of a war. They even show courage by bringing children into the world, because look at the prospects. The way they butcher and execute each other, think of the courage they need to look each other in the face. And putting up with an emperor and a pope takes a whale of a lot of courage, because those two are the death of the poor. (*She sits down, takes a small pipe from her pocket and smokes*) You could be making some kindling.

THE CHAPLAIN   (*reluctantly takes his jacket off and prepares to chop*) Chopping wood isn't really my trade, you know, I'm a shepherd of souls.

MOTHER COURAGE   Sure. But I have no soul and I need firewood.

THE CHAPLAIN   What's that pipe?

MOTHER COURAGE   Just a pipe.

THE CHAPLAIN   No, it's not "just a pipe," it's a very particular pipe.

MOTHER COURAGE   Really?

THE CHAPLAIN   It's the cook's pipe from the Oxenstjerna regiment.

MOTHER COURAGE   If you know it all, why the mealy-mouthed questions?

THE CHAPLAIN   I didn't know if *you* knew. You could have been rummaging through your belongings and laid hands on some pipe and picked it up without thinking.

MOTHER COURAGE   Yes. Maybe that's how it was.

THE CHAPLAIN   Except it wasn't. You knew who that pipe belongs to.

MOTHER COURAGE   What of it?

THE CHAPLAIN   Courage, I'm warning you. It's my duty. I doubt if you ever lay eyes on the man again, but that's no calamity, in fact you're lucky. If you ask me, he wasn't steady. Not at all.

MOTHER COURAGE   What makes you say that? He was a nice man.

THE CHAPLAIN Oh, you think he was nice? I differ. Far be it from me to wish him any harm, but I can't say he was nice. I'd say he was a scheming Don Juan. If you don't believe me, take a look at his pipe. You'll have to admit that it shows up his character.

MOTHER COURAGE I don't see anything. It's beat up.

THE CHAPLAIN It's half bitten through. A violent man. That is the pipe of a ruthless, violent man, you must see that if you've still got an ounce of good sense.

MOTHER COURAGE Don't wreck my chopping block.

THE CHAPLAIN I've told you I wasn't trained to chop wood. I studied theology. My gifts and abilities are being wasted on muscular effort. The talents that God gave me are lying fallow. That's a sin. You've never heard me preach. With one sermon I can whip a regiment into such a state that they take the enemy for a flock of sheep. Then men care no more about their lives than they would about a smelly old sock that they're ready to throw away in hopes of final victory. God has made me eloquent. You'll swoon when you hear me preach.

MOTHER COURAGE I don't want to swoon. What good would that do me?

THE CHAPLAIN Courage, I've often wondered if maybe you didn't conceal a warm heart under that hard-bitten talk of yours. You too are human, you need warmth.

MOTHER COURAGE The best way to keep this tent warm is with plenty of firewood.

THE CHAPLAIN Don't try to put me off. Seriously, Courage, I sometimes wonder if we couldn't make our relationship a little closer. I mean, seeing that the whirlwind of war has whirled us so strangely together.

MOTHER COURAGE Seems to me it's close enough. I cook your meals and you do chores, such as chopping wood, for instance.

THE CHAPLAIN (goes toward her) You know what I mean by "closer"; it has nothing to do with meals and chopping wood and such mundane needs. Don't harden your heart, let it speak.

MOTHER COURAGE Don't come at me with that ax. That's too close a relationship.

THE CHAPLAIN   Don't turn it to ridicule. I'm serious, I've given it careful thought.

MOTHER COURAGE   Chaplain, don't be silly. I like you, I don't want to have to scold you. My aim in life is to get through, me and my children and my wagon. I don't think of it as mine and besides I'm not in the mood for private affairs. Right now I'm taking a big risk, buying up merchandise with the general dead and everybody talking peace. What'll you do if I'm ruined? See? You don't know. Chop that wood, then we'll be warm in the evening, which is a good thing in times like these. Now what? (*She stands up*)

(*Enter Kattrin out of breath, with a wound across her forehead and over one eye. She is carrying all sorts of things, packages, leather goods, a drum, etc.*)

MOTHER COURAGE   What's that? Assaulted? On the way back? She was assaulted on the way back. Must have been that soldier that got drunk here! I shouldn't have let you go! Throw the stuff down! It's not bad, only a flesh wound. I'll bandage it, it'll heal in a week. They're worse than wild beasts. (*She bandages the wound*)

THE CHAPLAIN   I can't find fault with them. At home they never raped anybody. I blame the people that start wars, they're the ones that dredge up man's lowest instincts.

MOTHER COURAGE   Didn't the clerk bring you back? That's because you're respectable, they don't give a damn. It's not a deep wound, it won't leave a mark. There, all bandaged. Don't fret, I've got something for you. I've been keeping it for you on the sly, it'll be a surprise. (*She fishes Yvette's red shoes out of a sack*) See? You've always wanted them. Now you've got them. Put them on quick before I regret it. It won't leave a mark, though I wouldn't mind if it did. The girls that attract them get the worst of it. They drag them around till there's nothing left of them. If you don't appeal to them, they won't harm you. I've seen girls with pretty faces, a few years later they'd have given a wolf the creeps. They can't step behind a bush without fearing the worst. It's like trees. The straight tall ones get chopped down for ridgepoles, the crooked ones enjoy life. In other words, it's a lucky break. The shoes are still in good condition, I've kept them nicely polished.

(Kattrin leaves the shoes where they are and crawls into the wagon)

THE CHAPLAIN   I hope she won't be disfigured.

MOTHER COURAGE   There'll be a scar. She can stop waiting for peace.

THE CHAPLAIN   She didn't let them take anything.

MOTHER COURAGE   Maybe I shouldn't have drummed it into her. If I only knew what went on in her head. One night she stayed out, the only time in all these years. Afterwards she traipsed around as usual, except she worked harder. I never could find out what happened. I racked my brains for quite some time. *(She picks up the articles brought by Kattrin and sorts them angrily)* That's war for you! A fine way to make a living! *(Cannon salutes are heard)*

THE CHAPLAIN   Now they're burying the general. This is a historic moment.

MOTHER COURAGE   To me it's a historic moment when they hit my daughter over the eye. She's a wreck, she'll never get a husband now, and she's so crazy about children. It's the war that made her dumb too, a soldier stuffed something in her mouth when she was little. I'll never see Swiss Cheese again and where Eilif is, God knows. God damn the war.

7

Mother Courage at the height of her business career.

Highway.

The chaplain, Mother Courage and her daughter Kattrin are pulling the wagon. New wares are hanging on it. Mother Courage is wearing a necklace of silver talers.

MOTHER COURAGE   Stop running down the war. I won't have it.
I know it destroys the weak, but the weak haven't a chance
in peacetime either. And war is a better provider. (*Sings*)

If you're not strong enough to take it
The victory will find you dead.
A war is only what you make it.
It's business, not with cheese but lead.

And what good is it staying in one place? The stay-at-homes
are the first to get it. (*Sings*)

Some people think they'd like to ride out
The war, leave danger to the brave
And dig themselves a cozy hideout—
They'll dig themselves an early grave.
I've seen them running from the thunder
To find a refuge from the war
But once they're resting six feet under
They wonder what they hurried for.

(*They plod on*)

8

In the same year Gustavus Adolphus, King of Sweden, is killed at the battle of Lützen. Peace threatens to ruin Mother Courage's business. Her brave son performs one heroic deed too many and dies an ignominious death.

A camp.

A summer morning. An old woman and her son are standing by the wagon. The son is carrying a large sack of bedding.

MOTHER COURAGE'S VOICE (*from the wagon*)   Does it have to be at this unearthly hour?

THE YOUNG MAN   We've walked all night, twenty miles, and we've got to go back today.

MOTHER COURAGE'S VOICE   What can I do with bedding? The people haven't any houses.

THE YOUNG MAN   Wait till you've seen it.

THE OLD WOMAN   She won't take it either. Come on.

THE YOUNG MAN   They'll sell the roof from over our heads for taxes. Maybe she'll give us three guilders if you throw in the cross. (*Bells start ringing*) Listen, mother!

VOICES (*from the rear*)   Peace! The king of Sweden is dead!

MOTHER COURAGE (*sticks her head out of the wagon. She has not yet done her hair*)   Why are the bells ringing in the middle of the week?

THE CHAPLAIN (*crawls out from under the wagon*)   What are they shouting?

MOTHER COURAGE   Don't tell me peace has broken out when I've just taken in more supplies.

THE CHAPLAIN (*shouting toward the rear*)   Is it true? Peace?

VOICE   Three weeks ago, they say. But we just found out.

THE CHAPLAIN (*to Mother Courage*)   What else would they ring the bells for?

VOICE   There's a whole crowd of Lutherans, they've driven their carts into town. They brought the news.

THE YOUNG MAN   Mother, it's peace. What's the matter?

(*The old woman has collapsed*)

MOTHER COURAGE (*going back into the wagon*)   Heavenly saints! Kattrin, peace! Put your black dress on! We're going to church. We owe it to Swiss Cheese. Can it be true?

THE YOUNG MAN   The people here say the same thing. They've made peace. Can you get up? (*The old woman stands up, still stunned*) I'll get the saddle shop started again. I promise. Everything will be all right. Father will get his bed back. Can you walk? (*To the chaplain*) She fainted. It was the news. She thought peace would never come again. Father said it would. We'll go straight home. (*Both go out*)

MOTHER COURAGE'S VOICE   Give her some brandy.

THE CHAPLAIN   They're gone.

MOTHER COURAGE'S VOICE   What's going on in camp?

THE CHAPLAIN   A big crowd. I'll go see. Shouldn't I put on my clericals?

MOTHER COURAGE'S VOICE   Better make sure before you step out in your antichrist costume. I'm glad to see peace, even if I'm ruined. At least I've brought two of my children through the war. Now I'll see my Eilif again.

THE CHAPLAIN   Look who's coming down the road. If it isn't the general's cook!

THE COOK (*rather bedraggled, carrying a bundle*)   Can I believe my eyes? The chaplain!

THE CHAPLAIN   Courage! A visitor!

(*Mother Courage climbs down*)

THE COOK   Didn't I promise to come over for a little chat as soon as I had time? I've never forgotten your brandy, Mrs. Fierling.

MOTHER COURAGE   Mercy, the general's cook! After all these years! Where's Eilif, my eldest?

THE COOK   Isn't he here yet? He left ahead of me, he was coming to see you too.

THE CHAPLAIN   I'll put on my clericals, wait for me. (*Goes out behind the wagon*)

MOTHER COURAGE   Then he'll be here any minute. (*Calls into the wagon*) Kattrin, Eilif's coming! Bring the cook a glass of brandy! (*Kattrin does not appear*) Put a lock of hair over it, and forget it! Mr. Lamb is no stranger. (*Gets the brandy herself*) She won't come out. Peace doesn't mean a thing to her, it's come too late. They hit her over the eye, there's hardly any mark, but she thinks people are staring at her.

THE COOK   Ech, war! (*He and Mother Courage sit down*)

MOTHER COURAGE   Cook, you find me in trouble. I'm ruined.

THE COOK   What? Say, that's a shame.

MOTHER COURAGE   Peace has done me in. Only the other day I stocked up. The chaplain's advice. And now they'll all demobilize and leave me sitting on my merchandise.

THE COOK   How could you listen to the chaplain? If I'd had time, I'd have warned you against him, but the Catholics came too soon. He's a fly-by-night. So now he's the boss here?

MOTHER COURAGE   He washed my dishes and helped me pull the wagon.

THE COOK   Him? Pulling? I guess he's told you a few of his jokes too, I wouldn't put it past him, he has an unsavory attitude toward women, I tried to reform him, it was hopeless. He's not steady.

MOTHER COURAGE   Are you steady?

THE COOK   If nothing else, I'm steady. Prosit!

MOTHER COURAGE   Steady is no good. I've only lived with one steady man, thank the Lord. I never had to work so hard, he sold the children's blankets when spring came, and he thought my harmonica was unchristian. In my opinion you're not doing yourself any good by admitting you're steady.

THE COOK   You've still got your old bite, but I respect you for it.

MOTHER COURAGE   Don't tell me you've been dreaming about my old bite.

THE COOK   Well, here we sit, with the bells of peace and your world-famous brandy, that hasn't its equal.

MOTHER COURAGE   The bells of peace don't strike my fancy right now. I don't see them paying the men, they're behindhand already. Where does that leave me with my famous brandy? Have you been paid?

THE COOK (*hesitantly*)   Not really. That's why we demobilized ourselves. Under the circumstances, I says to myself, why should I stay on? I'll go see my friends in the meantime. So here we are.

MOTHER COURAGE   You mean you're out of funds?

THE COOK   If only they'd stop those damn bells! I'd be glad to go into some kind of business. I'm sick of being a cook. They give me roots and shoe leather to work with, and then they throw the hot soup in my face. A cook's got a dog's life these days. I'd rather be in combat, but now we've got peace. (*The chaplain appears in his original dress*) We'll discuss it later.

THE CHAPLAIN   It's still in good condition. There were only a few moths in it.

THE COOK   I don't see why you bother. They won't take you back. Who are you going to inspire now to be an honest soldier and earn his pay at the risk of his life? Besides, I've got a bone to pick with you. Advising this lady to buy useless merchandise on the ground that the war would last forever.

THE CHAPLAIN (*heatedly*)   And why, I'd like to know, is it any of your business?

THE COOK   Because it's unscrupulous. How can you meddle in other people's business and give unsolicited advice?

THE CHAPLAIN   Who's meddling? (*To Mother Courage*) I didn't know you were accountable to this gentleman, I didn't know you were so intimate with him.

MOTHER COURAGE   Don't get excited, the cook is only giving his private opinion. And you can't deny that your war was a dud.

THE CHAPLAIN   Courage, don't blaspheme against peace. You're a battlefield hyena.

MOTHER COURAGE   What am I?

THE COOK   If you insult this lady, you'll hear from me.

THE CHAPLAIN   I'm not talking to you. Your intentions are too obvious. (*To Mother Courage*) But when I see you picking up peace with thumb and forefinger like a snotty handkerchief, it revolts my humanity; you don't want peace, you want war, because you profit by it, but don't forget the old saying: "He hath need of a long spoon that eateth with the devil."

MOTHER COURAGE   I've no use for war and war hasn't much use for me. Anyway, I'm not letting anybody call me a hyena, you and me are through.

THE CHAPLAIN   How can you complain about peace when it's such a relief to everybody else? On account of the old rags in your wagon?

MOTHER COURAGE   My merchandise isn't old rags, it's what I live off, and so did you.

THE CHAPLAIN   Off war, you mean. Aha!

THE COOK (*to the chaplain*)   You're a grown man, you ought to know there's no sense in giving advice. (*To Mother Courage*) The best thing you can do now is to sell off certain articles quick, before the prices hit the floor. Dress yourself and get started, there's no time to lose.

MOTHER COURAGE   That's very sensible advice. I think I'll do it.

THE CHAPLAIN   Because the cook says so!

MOTHER COURAGE   Why didn't *you* say so? He's right, I'd better run over to the market. (*She goes into the wagon*)

THE COOK   My round, chaplain. No presence of mind. Here's what you should have said: me give you advice? All I ever did was talk politics! Don't try to take me on. Cockfighting is undignified in a clergyman.

THE CHAPLAIN   If you don't shut up, I'll murder you, undignified or not.

THE COOK (*taking off his shoe and unwinding the wrappings from his feet*)   If the war hadn't made a godless bum out of you, you could easily come by a parsonage now that peace is here. They won't need cooks, there's nothing to cook, but people still do a lot of believing, that hasn't changed.

THE CHAPLAIN   See here, Mr. Lamb. Don't try to squeeze me out. Being a bum has made me a better man. I couldn't preach to them any more.

(*Yvette Pottier enters, elaborately dressed in black, with a cane. She is much older and fatter and heavily powdered. Behind her a servant*)

YVETTE   Hello there! Is this the residence of Mother Courage?

CHAPLAIN   Right you are. With whom have we the pleasure?

YVETTE   The Countess Starhemberg, my good people. Where is Mother Courage?

THE CHAPLAIN (*calls into the wagon*)   Countess Starhemberg wishes to speak to you!

MOTHER COURAGE   I'm coming.

YVETTE   It's Yvette!

MOTHER COURAGE'S VOICE   My goodness! It's Yvette!

YVETTE   Just dropped in to see how you're doing. (*The cook has turned around in horror*) Pieter!

THE COOK   Yvette!

YVETTE   Blow me down! How did you get here?

THE COOK   In a cart.

THE CHAPLAIN   Oh, you know each other? Intimately?

YVETTE   I should think so. (*She looks the cook over*) Fat!

THE COOK   You're not exactly willowy yourself.

YVETTE   All the same I'm glad I ran into you, you bum. Now I can tell you what I think of you.

THE CHAPLAIN   Go right ahead, spare no details, but wait until Courage comes out.

MOTHER COURAGE (*comes out with all sorts of merchandise*)   Yvette! (*They embrace*) But what are you in mourning for?

YVETTE   Isn't it becoming? My husband the colonel died a few years ago.

MOTHER COURAGE   The old geezer that almost bought my wagon?

YVETTE   His elder brother.

MOTHER COURAGE   You must be pretty well fixed. It's nice to find somebody that's made a good thing out of the war.

YVETTE   Oh well, it's been up and down and back up again.

MOTHER COURAGE   Let's not say anything bad about colonels. They make money by the bushel.

THE CHAPLAIN   If I were you, I'd put my shoes back on again. (*To Yvette*) Countess Starhemberg, you promised to tell us what you think of this gentleman.

THE COOK   Don't make a scene here.

MOTHER COURAGE   He's a friend of mine, Yvette.

YVETTE   He's Pete the Pipe, that's who he is.

THE COOK   Forget the nicknames, my name is Lamb.

MOTHER COURAGE (*laughs*)   Pete the Pipe! That drove the women crazy! Say, I've saved your pipe.

THE CHAPLAIN   And smoked it.

YVETTE   It's lucky I'm here to warn you. He's the worst rotter that ever infested the coast of Flanders. He ruined more girls than he's got fingers.

THE COOK   That was a long time ago. I've changed.

YVETTE   Stand up when a lady draws you into a conversation!

How I loved this man! And all the while he was seeing a little bandylegged brunette, ruined her too, naturally.

THE COOK   Seems to me I started you off on a prosperous career.

YVETTE   Shut up, you depressing wreck! Watch your step with him, his kind are dangerous even when they've gone to seed.

MOTHER COURAGE (*to Yvette*)   Come along, I've got to sell my stuff before the prices drop. Maybe you can help me, with your army connections. (*Calls into the wagon*) Kattrin, forget about church, I'm running over to the market. When Eilif comes, give him a drink. (*Goes out with Yvette*)

YVETTE (*in leaving*)   To think that such a man could lead me astray! I can thank my lucky stars that I was able to rise in the world after that. I've put a spoke in your wheel, Pete the Pipe, and they'll give me credit for it in heaven when my time comes.

THE CHAPLAIN   Our conversation seems to illustrate the old adage: The mills of God grind slowly. What do you think of my jokes now?

THE COOK   I'm just unlucky. I'll come clean: I was hoping for a hot meal. I'm starving. And now they're talking about me, and she'll get the wrong idea. I think I'll beat it before she comes back.

THE CHAPLAIN   I think so too.

THE COOK   Chaplain, I'm fed up on peace already. Men are sinners from the cradle, fire and sword are their natural lot. I wish I were cooking for the general again, God knows where he is, I'd roast a fine fat capon, with mustard sauce and a few carrots.

THE CHAPLAIN   Red cabbage. Red cabbage with capon.

THE COOK   That's right, but he wanted carrots.

THE CHAPLAIN   He was ignorant.

THE COOK   That didn't prevent you from gorging yourself.

THE CHAPLAIN   With repugnance.

THE COOK   Anyway you'll have to admit those were good times.

THE CHAPLAIN   I might admit that.

THE COOK   Now you've called her a hyena, your good times here are over. What are you staring at?

THE CHAPLAIN   Eilif! (*Eilif enters, followed by soldiers with pikes. His hands are fettered. He is deathly pale*) What's wrong?

EILIF   Where's mother?

THE CHAPLAIN   Gone to town.

EILIF   I heard she was here. They let me come and see her.

THE COOK (*to the soldiers*)   Where are you taking him?

A SOLDIER   No good place.

THE CHAPLAIN   What has he done?

THE SOLDIER   Broke into a farm. The peasant's wife is dead.

THE CHAPLAIN   How could you do such a thing?

EILIF   It's what I've been doing all along.

THE COOK   But in peacetime!

EILIF   Shut your trap. Can I sit down till she comes?

THE SOLDIER   We haven't time.

THE CHAPLAIN   During the war they honored him for it, he sat at the general's right hand. Then it was bravery. Couldn't we speak to the officer?

THE SOLDIER   No use. What's brave about taking a peasant's cattle?

THE COOK   It was stupid.

EILIF   If I'd been stupid, I'd have starved, wise guy.

THE COOK   And for being smart your head comes off.

THE CHAPLAIN   Let's get Kattrin at least.

EILIF   Leave her be. Get me a drink of schnapps.

THE SOLDIER   No time. Let's go!

THE CHAPLAIN   And what should we tell your mother?

EILIF   Tell her it wasn't any different, tell her it was the same. Or don't tell her anything.

(*The soldiers drive him away*)

THE CHAPLAIN   I'll go with you on your hard journey.

EILIF   I don't need any sky pilot.

THE CHAPLAIN   You don't know yet. (*He follows him*)

THE COOK (*calls after them*)   I'll have to tell her, she'll want to see him.

THE CHAPLAIN   Better not tell her anything. Or say he was here and he'll come again, maybe tomorrow. I'll break it to her when I get back. (*Hurries out*)

(*The cook looks after them, shaking his head, then he walks anxiously about. Finally he approaches the wagon*)

THE COOK   Hey! Come on out! I can see why you'd hide from peace. I wish I could do it myself. I'm the general's cook, remember? Wouldn't you have a bite to eat, to do me till your mother gets back? A slice of ham or just a piece of bread while

I'm waiting. (*He looks in*) She's buried her head in a blanket.
(*The sound of gunfire in the rear*)

MOTHER COURAGE (*runs in. She is out of breath and still has her merchandise*)   Cook, the peace is over, the war started up again three days ago. I hadn't sold my stuff yet when I found out. Heaven be praised! They're shooting each other up in town, the Catholics and Lutherans. We've got to get out of here. Kattrin, start packing. What have *you* got such a long face about? What's wrong?

THE COOK   Nothing.

MOTHER COURAGE   Something's wrong, I can tell by your expression.

THE COOK   Maybe it's the war starting up again. Now I probably won't get anything hot to eat before tomorrow night.

MOTHER COURAGE   That's a lie, cook.

THE COOK   Eilif was here. He couldn't stay.

MOTHER COURAGE   He was here? Then we'll see him on the march. I'm going with our troops this time. How does he look?

THE COOK   The same.

MOTHER COURAGE   He'll never change. The war couldn't take him away from me. He's smart. Could you help me pack? (*She starts packing*) Did he tell you anything? Is he in good with the general? Did he say anything about his heroic deeds?

THE COOK (*gloomily*)   They say he's been at one of them again.

MOTHER COURAGE   Tell me later, we've got to be going. (*Kattrin emerges*) Kattrin, peace is over. We're moving. (*To the cook*) What's the matter with you?

THE COOK   I'm going to enlist.

MOTHER COURAGE   I've got a suggestion. Why don't . . . ? Where's the chaplain?

THE COOK   Gone to town with Eilif.

MOTHER COURAGE   Then come a little way with me, Lamb. I need help.

THE COOK   That incident with Yvette . . .

MOTHER COURAGE   It hasn't lowered you in my estimation. Far from it. Where there's smoke there's fire. Coming?

THE COOK   I won't say no.

MOTHER COURAGE   The Twelfth Regiment has shoved off. Take the shaft. Here's a chunk of bread. We'll have to circle around

to meet the Lutherans. Maybe I'll see Eilif tonight. He's my
favorite. It's been a short peace. And we're on the move again.
(*She sings, while the cook and Kattrin harness themselves to the
wagon*)

From Ulm to Metz, from Metz to Pilsen
Courage is right there in the van.
The war both in and out of season
With shot and shell will feed its man.
But lead alone is not sufficient
The war needs soldiers to subsist!
Its diet elseways is deficient.
The war is hungry! So enlist!

9

The great war of religion has been going on for sixteen years. Germany has lost more than half its population. Those whom the slaughter has spared have
been laid low by epidemics. Once-flourishing coun-
trysides are ravaged by famine. Wolves prowl
through the charred ruins of the cities. In the fall of
1634 we find Mother Courage in Germany, in the
Fichtelgebirge, at some distance from the road followed by the Swedish armies. Winter comes early
and is exceptionally severe. Business is bad, begging
is the only resort. The cook receives a letter from
Utrecht and is dismissed.

Outside a half-demolished presbytery.

*Gray morning in early winter. Gusts of wind. Mother Courage and the
cook in shabby sheepskins by the wagon.*

THE COOK   No light. Nobody's up yet.

MOTHER COURAGE   But it's a priest. He'll have to crawl out of bed to ring the bells. Then he'll get himself a nice bowl of hot soup.

THE COOK   Go on, you saw the village, everything's been burned to a crisp.

MOTHER COURAGE   But somebody's here, I heard a dog bark.

THE COOK   If the priest's got anything, he won't give it away.

MOTHER COURAGE   Maybe if we sing . . .

THE COOK   I've had it up to here. (*Suddenly*) I got a letter from Utrecht. My mother's died of cholera and the tavern belongs to me. Here's the letter if you don't believe me. It's no business of yours what my aunt says about my evil ways, but never mind, read it.

MOTHER COURAGE (*reads the letter*)   Lamb, I'm sick of roaming around, myself. I feel like a butcher's dog that pulls the meat cart but doesn't get any for himself. I've nothing left to sell and the people have no money to pay for it. In Saxony a man in rags tried to foist a cord of books on me for two eggs, and in Württemberg they'd have let their plow go for a little bag of salt. What's the good of plowing? Nothing grows but brambles. In Pomerania they say the villagers have eaten up all the babies, and that nuns have been caught at highway robbery.

THE COOK   It's the end of the world.

MOTHER COURAGE   Sometimes I have visions of myself driving through hell, selling sulphur and brimstone, or through heaven peddling refreshments to the roaming souls. If me and the children I've got left could find a place where there's no shooting, I wouldn't mind a few years of peace and quiet.

THE COOK   We could open up the tavern again. Think it over, Anna. I made up my mind last night; with or without you, I'm going back to Utrecht. In fact I'm leaving today.

MOTHER COURAGE   I'll have to talk to Kattrin. It's kind of sudden, and I don't like to make decisions in the cold with nothing in my stomach. Kattrin! (*Kattrin climbs out of the wagon*) Kattrin, I've got something to tell you. The cook and me are thinking of going to Utrecht. They've left him a tavern there. You'd be living in one place, you'd meet people. A lot of men would be glad to get a nice, well-behaved girl, looks aren't everything. I'm all for it. I get along fine with the cook. I've got to hand it to him: He's got a head for business. We'd eat regular meals, wouldn't that be nice? And you'd have your own bed, wouldn't you like that? It's no life on the road, year in year out. You'll go to rack and ruin. You're crawling with lice already. We've got to decide, you see, we could go north with the Swedes, they must be over there. (*She points to the left*) I think we'll do it, Kattrin.

THE COOK   Anna, could I have a word with you alone?

MOTHER COURAGE   Get back in the wagon, Kattrin.

(Kattrin climbs back in)

THE COOK   I interrupted you because I see there's been a misunderstanding. I thought it was too obvious to need saying. But if it isn't, I'll just have to say it. You can't take her, it's out of the question. Is that plain enough for you?

(Kattrin sticks her head out of the wagon and listens)

MOTHER COURAGE   You want me to leave Kattrin?

THE COOK   Look at it this way. There's no room in the tavern. It's not one of those places with three taprooms. If the two of us put our shoulder to the wheel, we can make a living, but not three, it can't be done. Kattrin can keep the wagon.

MOTHER COURAGE   I'd been thinking she could find a husband in Utrecht.

THE COOK   Don't make me laugh! How's she going to find a husband? At her age? And dumb! And with that scar!

MOTHER COURAGE   Not so loud.

THE COOK   Shout or whisper, the truth's the truth. And that's another reason why I can't have her in the tavern. The customers won't want a sight like that staring them in the face. Can you blame them?

MOTHER COURAGE   Shut up. Not so loud, I say.

THE COOK   There's a light in the presbytery. Let's sing.

MOTHER COURAGE   How could she pull the wagon by herself? She's afraid of the war. She couldn't stand it. The dreams she must have! I hear her groaning at night. Especially after battles. What she sees in her dreams, God knows. It's pity that makes her suffer so. The other day the wagon hit a hedgehog, I found it hidden in her blanket.

THE COOK   The tavern's too small. (*He calls*) Worthy gentleman

and members of the household! We shall now sing the Song
of Solomon, Julius Caesar, and other great men, whose greatness didn't help them any. Just to show you that we're God-
fearing people ourselves, which makes it hard for us,
especially in the winter. (*They sing*)

You saw the wise King Solomon
You know what came of him.
To him all hidden things were plain.
He cursed the hour gave birth to him
And saw that everything was vain.
How great and wise was Solomon!
Now think about his case. Alas
A useful lesson can be won.
It's wisdom that had brought him to that pass!
How happy is the man with none!

Our beautiful song proves that virtues are dangerous things,
better steer clear of them, enjoy life, eat a good breakfast, a
bowl of hot soup, for instance. Take me, I haven't got any
soup and wish I had, I'm a soldier, but what has my bravery
in all those battles got me, nothing, I'm starving, I'd be better
off if I'd stayed home like a yellowbelly. And I'll tell you why.

You saw the daring Caesar next
You know what he became.
They deified him in his life
But then they killed him just the same.
And as they raised the fatal knife
How loud he cried: "You too, my son!"
Now think about his case. Alas
A useful lesson can be won.
It's daring that had brought him to that pass!
How happy is the man with none!

(*In an undertone*) They're not even looking out. Worthy gentleman and members of the household! Maybe you'll say, all
right, if bravery won't keep body and soul together, try
honesty. That may fill your belly or at least get you a drop
to drink. Let's look into it.

You've heard of honest Socrates
Who never told a lie.
They weren't so grateful as you'd think
Instead they sentenced him to die
And handed him the poisoned drink.
How honest was the people's noble son!
Now think about his case. Alas
A useful lesson can be won.
His honesty had brought him to that pass.
How happy is the man with none!

Yes, they tell us to be charitable and to share what we have,
but what if we haven't got anything? Maybe philanthropists
have a rough time of it too, it stands to reason, they need a
little something for themselves. Yes, charity is a rare virtue,
because it doesn't pay.

St. Martin couldn't bear to see
His fellows in distress.
He saw a poor man in the snow.
"Take half my cloak!" He did, and lo!
They both of them froze none the less.
He thought his heavenly reward was won.
Now think about his case. Alas
A useful lesson can be won.
Unselfishness had brought him to that pass.
How happy is the man with none!

That's our situation. We're God-fearing folk, we stick together, we don't steal, we don't murder, we don't set fire to
anything! You could say that we set an example which bears
out the song, we sink lower and lower, we seldom see any
soup, but if we were different, if we were thieves and murder-
ers, maybe our bellies would be full. Because virtue isn't
rewarded, only wickedness, the world needn't be like this,
but it is.

And here you see God-fearing folk
Observing God's ten laws.
So far He hasn't taken heed.

You people sitting warm indoors
Help to relieve our bitter need!
Our virtue can be counted on.
Now think about our case. Alas
A useful lesson can be won.
The fear of God has brought us to this pass.
How happy is the man with none!

VOICE (*from above*)   Hey, down there! Come on up! We've got some good thick soup.
MOTHER COURAGE   Lamb, I couldn't get anything down. I know what you say makes sense, but is it your last word? We've always been good friends.
THE COOK   My last word. Think it over.
MOTHER COURAGE   I don't need to think it over. I won't leave her.
THE COOK   It wouldn't be wise, but there's nothing I can do. I'm not inhuman, but it's a small tavern. We'd better go in now, or there won't be anything left, we'll have been singing in the cold for nothing.
MOTHER COURAGE   I'll get Kattrin.
THE COOK   Better bring it down for her. They'll get a fright if the three of us barge in. (*They go out*)
(*Kattrin climbs out of the wagon. She is carrying a bundle. She looks around to make sure the others are gone. Then she spreads out an old pair of the cook's trousers and a skirt belonging to her mother side by side on a wheel of the wagon so they can easily be seen. She is about to leave with her bundle when Mother Courage comes out of the house*)
MOTHER COURAGE (*with a dish of soup*)   Kattrin! Stop! Kattrin! Where do you think you're going with that bundle? Have you taken leave of your wits? (*She examines the bundle*) She's packed her things. Were you listening? I've told him it's no go with Utrecht and his lousy tavern, what would we do there? A tavern's no place for you and me. The war still has a thing or two up its sleeve for us. (*She sees the trousers and skirt*) You're stupid. Suppose I'd seen that and you'd been gone? (*Kattrin tries to leave, Mother Courage holds her back*) And don't go thinking I've given him the gate on your account. It's the wagon.

I won't part with the wagon, I'm used to it, it's not you, it's the wagon. We'll go in the other direction, we'll put the cook's stuff out here where he'll find it, the fool. (*She climbs up and throws down a few odds and ends to join the trousers*) There. Now we're shut of him, you won't see me taking anyone else into the business. From now on it's you and me. This winter will go by like all the rest. Harness up, it looks like snow.
(*They harness themselves to the wagon, turn it around and pull it away. When the cook comes out he sees his things and stands dumbfounded*)

10

Throughout 1635 Mother Courage and her daughter Kattrin pull the wagon over the roads of central Germany in the wake of the increasingly bedraggled armies.

Highway.

Mother Courage and Kattrin are pulling the wagon. They come to a peasant's house. A voice is heard singing from within.

THE VOICE

> The rose bush in our garden
> Rejoiced our hearts in spring
> It bore such lovely flowers.
> We planted it last season
> Before the April showers.
> A garden is a blessèd thing
> It bore such lovely flowers.
>
> When winter comes a-stalking
> And gales great snow storms bring
> They trouble us but little.
> We've lately finished caulking
> The roof with moss and wattle.
> A sheltering roof's a blessèd thing
> When winter comes a-stalking.

(Mother Courage and Kattrin have stopped to listen. Then they move on)

11

January 1636. The imperial troops threaten the Protestant city of Halle. The stone speaks. Mother Courage loses her daughter and goes on alone. The end of
the war is not in sight.

*The wagon, much the worse for wear, is standing beside a peasant house
with an enormous thatch roof. The house is built against the side of a
stony hill. Night.*

A lieutenant and three soldiers in heavy armor step out of the woods.

THE LIEUTENANT   I don't want any noise. If anybody yells, run
him through with your pikes.

FIRST SOLDIER   But we need a guide. We'll have to knock if we
want them to come out.

THE LIEUTENANT   Knocking sounds natural. It could be a cow
bumping against the barn wall.
(*The soldiers knock on the door. A peasant woman opens. They hold
their hands over her mouth. Two soldiers go in*)

A MAN'S VOICE (*inside*)   Who's there?
(*The soldiers bring out a peasant and his son*)

THE LIEUTENANT (*points to the wagon, in which Kattrin has appeared*)   There's another one. (*A soldier pulls her out*) Anybody
else live here?

THE PEASANT COUPLE   This is our son.—That's a dumb girl.—
Her mother's gone into the town on business.—Buying up
people's belongings, they're selling cheap because they're getting out.—They're provisioners.

THE LIEUTENANT   I'm warning you to keep quiet, one squawk
and you'll get a pike over the head. All right. I need somebody
who can show us the path into the city. (*Points to the young
peasant*) You. Come here!

THE YOUNG PLEASANT   I don't know no path.

THE SECOND SOLDIER (*grinning*)   He don't know no path.

THE YOUNG PEASANT   I'm not helping the Catholics.

THE LIEUTENANT (*to the second soldier*)   Give him a feel of your pike!

THE YOUNG PEASANT (*forced down on his knees and threatened with the pike*)   You can kill me. I won't do it.

THE FIRST SOLDIER   I know what'll make him think twice. (*He goes over to the barn*) Two cows and an ox. Get this: If you don't help us, I'll cut them down.

THE YOUNG PEASANT   Not the animals!

THE PEASANT WOMAN (*in tears*)   Captain, spare our animals or we'll starve.

THE LIEUTENANT   If he insists on being stubborn, they're done for.

THE FIRST SOLDIER   I'll start with the ox.

THE YOUNG PEASANT (*to the old man*)   Do I have to? (*The old woman nods*) I'll do it.

THE PEASANT WOMAN   And thank you kindly for your forbearance, Captain, for ever and ever, amen.

(*The peasant stops her from giving further thanks*)

THE FIRST SOLDIER   Didn't I tell you? With them it's the animals that come first.

(*Led by the young peasant, the lieutenant and the soldiers continue on their way*)

THE PEASANT   I wish I knew what they're up to. Nothing good.

THE PEASANT WOMAN   Maybe they're only scouts.—What are you doing?

THE PEASANT (*putting a ladder against the roof and climbing up*)   See if they're alone. (*On the roof*) Men moving in the woods. All the way to the quarry. Armor in the clearing. And a cannon. It's more than a regiment. God have mercy on the city and everybody in it.

THE PEASANT WOMAN   See any light in the city?

THE PEASANT   No. They're all asleep. (*He climbs down*) If they get in, they'll kill everybody.

THE PEASANT WOMAN   The sentry will see them in time.

THE PEASANT   They must have killed the sentry in the tower on the hill, or he'd have blown his horn.

THE PEASANT WOMAN   If there were more of us . . .

THE PEASANT   All by ourselves up here with a cripple . . .

THE PEASANT WOMAN   We can't do a thing. Do you think . . .

THE PEASANT   Not a thing.

THE PEASANT WOMAN   We couldn't get down there in the dark.

THE PEASANT   The whole hillside is full of them. We can't even give a signal.

THE PEASANT WOMAN   They'd kill us.

THE PEASANT   No, we can't do a thing.

THE PEASANT WOMAN   (*to Kattrin*)   Pray, poor thing, pray! We can't stop the bloodshed. If you can't talk, at least you can pray. He'll hear you if nobody else does. I'll help you. (*All kneel, Kattrin behind the peasants*) Our Father which art in heaven, hear our prayer. Don't let the town perish with everybody in it, all asleep and unsuspecting. Wake them, make them get up and climb the walls and see the enemy coming through the night with cannon and pikes, through the fields and down the hillside. (*Back to Kattrin*) Protect our mother and don't let the watchman sleep, wake him before it's too late. And succor our brother-in-law, he's in there with his four children, let them not perish, they're innocent and don't know a thing. (*To Kattrin, who groans*) The littlest is less than two, the oldest is seven. (*Horrified, Kattrin stands up*) Our Father, hear us, for Thou alone canst help, we'll all be killed, we're weak, we haven't any pikes or anything, we are powerless and in Thine hands, we and our animals and the whole farm, and the city too, it's in Thine hands, and the enemy is under the walls with great might.

(*Kattrin has crept unnoticed to the wagon, taken something out of it, put it under her apron and climbed up the ladder to the roof of the barn*)

THE PEASANT WOMAN   Think upon the children in peril, especially the babes in arms and the old people that can't help themselves and all God's creatures.

THE PEASANT   And forgive us our trespasses as we forgive them that trespass against us. Amen.

(*Kattrin, sitting on the roof, starts beating the drum that she has taken out from under her apron*)

THE PEASANT WOMAN   Jesus! What's she doing?

THE PEASANT   She's gone crazy.
THE PEASANT WOMAN   Get her down, quick!
(The peasant runs toward the ladder, but Kattrin pulls it up on the roof)
THE PEASANT WOMAN   She'll be the death of us all.
THE PEASANT   Stop that, you cripple!
THE PEASANT WOMAN   She'll have the Catholics down on us.
THE PEASANT *(looking around for stones)*   I'll throw rocks at you.
THE PEASANT WOMAN   Have you no pity? Have you no heart? We're dead if they find out it's us! They'll run us through!
(Kattrin stares in the direction of the city, and goes on drumming)
THE PEASANT WOMAN *(to the peasant)*   I told you not to let those tramps stop here. What do they care if the soldiers drive our last animals away?
THE LIEUTENANT *(rushes in with his soldiers and the young peasant)*   I'll cut you to pieces!
THE PEASANT WOMAN   We're innocent, captain. We couldn't help it. She sneaked up there. We don't know her.
THE LIEUTENANT   Where's the ladder?
THE PEASANT   Up top.
THE LIEUTENANT *(to Kattrin)*   Throw down that drum. It's an order!
(Kattrin goes on drumming)
THE LIEUTENANT   You're all in this together! This'll be the end of you!
THE PEASANT   They've felled some pine trees in the woods over there. We could get one and knock her down . . .
THE FIRST SOLDIER *(to the lieutenant)*   Request permission to make a suggestion. *(He whispers something in the lieutenant's ear. He nods)* Listen. We've got a friendly proposition. Come down, we'll take you into town with us. Show us your mother and we won't touch a hair of her head.
(Kattrin goes on drumming)
THE LIEUTENANT *(pushes him roughly aside)*   She doesn't trust you. No wonder with your mug. *(He calls up)* If I give you my word? I'm an officer, you can trust my word of honor.
(She drums still louder)
THE LIEUTENANT   Nothing is sacred to her.

THE YOUNG PEASANT   It's not just her mother, lieutenant!

THE FIRST SOLDIER   We can't let this go on. They'll hear it in the city.

THE LIEUTENANT   We'll have to make some kind of noise that's louder than the drums. What could we make noise with?

THE FIRST SOLDIER   But we're not supposed to make noise.

THE LIEUTENANT   An innocent noise, stupid. A peaceable noise.

THE PEASANT   I could chop wood.

THE LIEUTENANT   That's it, chop! (*The peasant gets an ax and chops at a log*) Harder! Harder! You're chopping for your life. (*Listening, Kattrin has been drumming more softly. Now she looks anxiously around and goes on drumming as before*)

THE LIEUTENANT (*to the peasant*)   Not loud enough. (*To the first soldier*) You chop too.

THE PEASANT   There's only one ax. (*Stops chopping*)

THE LIEUTENANT   We'll have to set the house on fire. Smoke her out.

THE PEASANT   That won't do any good, captain. If the city people see fire up here, they'll know what's afoot. (*Sill drumming, Kattrin has been listening again. Now she laughs*)

THE LIEUTENANT   Look, she's laughing at us. I'll shoot her down, regardless. Get the musket! (*Two soldiers run out. Kattrin goes on drumming*)

THE PEASANT WOMAN   I've got it, captain. That's their wagon over there. If we start smashing it up, she'll stop. The wagon's all they've got.

THE LIEUTENANT (*to the young peasant*)   Smash away. (*To Kattrin*) We'll smash your wagon if you don't stop. (*The young peasant strikes a few feeble blows at the wagon*)

THE PEASANT WOMAN   Stop it, you beast! (*Kattrin stares despairingly at the wagon and emits pitiful sounds. But she goes on drumming*)

THE LIEUTENANT   Where are those stinkers with the musket?

THE FIRST SOLDIER   They haven't heard anything in the city yet, or we'd hear their guns.

THE LIEUTENANT (*to Kattrin*)   They don't hear you. And now we're going to shoot you down. For the last time: Drop that drum!

THE YOUNG PEASANT (*suddenly throws the plank away*) Keep on
drumming! Or they'll all be killed! Keep on drumming, keep
on drumming . . .
(*The soldier throws him down and hits him with his pike. Kattrin
starts crying, but goes on drumming*)
THE PEASANT WOMAN Don't hit him in the back! My God,
you're killing him.
(*The soldiers run in with the musket*)
THE SECOND SOLDIER The colonel's foaming at the mouth. We'll
be court-martialed.
THE LIEUTENANT Set it up! Set it up! (*To Kattrin, while the musket
is being set up on its stand*) For the last time: Stop that drum-
ming! (*Kattrin in tears drums as loud as she can*) Fire!
(*The soldiers fire. Kattrin is hit. She beats the drum a few times more
and then slowly collapses*)
THE LIEUTENANT Now we'll have some quiet.
(*But Kattrin's last drumbeats are answered by the city's cannon.
A confused hubbub of alarm bells and cannon is heard in the dis-
tance*)
FIRST SOLDIER She's done it.

12

Night, toward morning. The fifes and drums of troops marching away.

Outside the wagon Mother Courage sits huddled over her daughter. The peasant couple are standing beside them.

THE PEASANT (*hostile*) You'll have to be going, woman. There's only one more regiment to come. You can't go alone.

MOTHER COURAGE Maybe I can get her to sleep. (*She sings*)

> Lullaby baby
> What stirs in the hay?
> The neighbor brats whimper
> Mine are happy and gay.
> They go in tatters
> And you in silk down
> Cut from an angel's
> Best party gown.
>
> They've nothing to munch on
> And you will have pie
> Just tell your mother
> In case it's too dry.
> Lullaby baby
> What stirs in the hay?
> The one lies in Poland
> The other—who can say?

Now she's asleep. You shouldn't have told her about your brother-in-law's children.

THE PEASANT Maybe it wouldn't have happened if you hadn't gone to town to swindle people.

MOTHER COURAGE I'm glad she's sleeping now.

THE PEASANT WOMAN   She's not sleeping, you'll have to face it, she's dead.

THE PEASANT   And it's time you got started. There are wolves around here, and what's worse, marauders.

MOTHER COURAGE   Yes. (*She goes to the wagon and takes out a sheet of canvas to cover the body with*)

THE PEASANT WOMAN   Haven't you anybody else? Somebody you can go to?

MOTHER COURAGE   Yes, there's one of them left. Eilif.

THE PEASANT (*while Mother Courage covers the body*)   Go find him. We'll attend to this one, give her a decent burial. Set your mind at rest.

MOTHER COURAGE   Here's money for your expenses. (*She gives the peasant money*)

(*The peasant and his son shake hands with her and carry Kattrin away*)

THE PEASANT WOMAN (*on the way out*)   Hurry up!

MOTHER COURAGE (*harnesses herself to the wagon*)   I hope I can pull the wagon alone. I'll manage, there isn't much in it. I've got to get back in business.

(*Another regiment marches by with fifes and drums in the rear*)

MOTHER COURAGE   Hey, take me with you! (*She starts to pull*)

(*Singing is heard in the rear:*)

With all the killing and recruiting
The war will worry on a while.
In ninety years they'll still be shooting.
It's hardest on the rank-and-file.
Our food is swill, our pants all patches
The higher-ups steal half our pay
And still we dream of God-sent riches.
Tomorrow is another day!
  The spring is come! Christian, revive!
  The snowdrifts melt, the dead lie dead!
  And if by chance you're still alive
  It's time to rise and shake a leg.

Notes and Variants

LIFE OF GALILEO

Texts by Brecht

Foreword

It is well known how beneficially people can be influenced by
the conviction that they are poised on the threshold of a new
age. At such a moment their environment appears to be still
entirely unfinished, capable of the happiest improvements, full
of dreamt-of and undreamt-of possibilities, like malleable raw
material in their hands. They themselves feel as if they have
awakened to a new day, rested, strong, resourceful. Old beliefs
are dismissed as superstitions, what yesterday seemed a matter
of course is today subject to fresh examination. We have been
ruled, says mankind, but now we shall be the rulers.

Around the turn of this century no other line from a song so
powerfully inspired the workers as the line: "Now a new age
is dawning"; old and young marched to it, the poorest, the
down-and-outs and those who had already won something of
civilization for themselves—all felt young. Under a house
painter the unprecedented seductive power of these selfsame
words was also tried and proved; for he too promised a new age.
Here the words revealed their emptiness and vagueness. Their
strength lay in their very indefiniteness, which was now being
exploited in demoralizing the masses. The new age—that was
something and is something that affects everything, leaves nothing unchanged, but is also still only unfolding its character
gradually; something in which all imagination has scope to
flower, and which is only restricted by too precise description.
Glorious is the feeling of beginning, of pioneering; the fact of
being a beginner inspires enthusiasm. Glorious is the feeling of

happiness in those who oil a new machine before it is to display
its strength, in those who fill in a blank space on an old map,
in those who dig the foundation of a new house, their house.

This feeling comes to the researcher who makes a discovery
that will change everything, to the orator who prepares a speech
that will create an entirely new situation. Terrible is the disappointment when men discover, or think they discover, that they
have fallen victims to an illusion, that the old is stronger than
the new, that the "facts" are against them and not for them, that
their age—the new age—has not yet arrived. Then things are
not merely as bad as before, but much worse because people
have made immense sacrifices for their schemes and have lost
everything; they have ventured and are now defeated; the old
is taking its revenge on them. The researcher or the discoverer
—an unknown but also unpersecuted man before he has published his discovery—when once his discovery has been dis-
proved or discredited is a swindler and a charlatan, and all too
well known; the victim of oppression and exploitation, when
once his insurrection has been crushed, is a rebel who is subject
to special repression and punishment. Exertion is followed by
exhaustion, possibly exaggerated hope by possibly exaggerated
hopelessness. Those who do not relapse into indifference and
apathy fall into worse; those who have not sacrificed their energies for their ideals now turn those selfsame energies against
those very ideals! There is no more remorseless reactionary
than a frustrated innovator, no crueler enemy of the wild elephant than the tame elephant.

And yet these disappointed men may still go on existing in
a new age, an age of great upheaval. Only, they know nothing
of new ages.

In these days the conception of the new is itself falsified. The
Old and the Very Old, now re-entering the arena, proclaim
themselves as new, or else it is held to be new when the Old or
the Very Old are put over in a new way. But the really New,
having been deposed today, is declared old-fashioned, degraded
to being a transitory phase whose day is done. The "new" for
example is the system of waging wars, whereas "old," so they
say, is a system of economy, proposed but never put into prac-

tice, which makes wars superfluous. In the new system, society is being entrenched in classes; and the old, so they say, is the desire to abolish classes. The hopes of mankind do not so much become discouraged in these times; rather, they become diverted. Men had hoped that one day there would be bread to eat. Now they may hope that one day there will be stones to eat.

Amid the darkness gathering fast over a fevered world, a world surrounded by bloody deeds and no less bloody thoughts, by increasing barbarism which seems to be leading irresistibly to perhaps the greatest and most terrible war of all time, it is difficult to adopt an attitude appropriate to people on the threshold of a new and happier age. Does not everything point to night's arrival and nothing to the dawning of a new age? So shouldn't one, therefore, assume an attitude appropriate to people heading towards the night?

What is this talk of a "new age"? Is not this expression itself obsolete? When it is shouted at us, it is bellowed from hoarse throats. Now indeed, it is mere barbarism which impersonates the new age. It says of itself that it hopes it will last a thousand years.

So should one hold fast to the old times? Should one discuss sunk Atlantis?

Am I already lying down for the night and thinking, when I think of the morning, of the one that has passed, so as to avoid thinking of the one to come? Is that why I occupy myself with that epoch of the flowering of the arts and sciences three hundred years ago? I hope not.

These images of the morning and the night are misleading. Happy times do not come in the same way as a morning follows a night's sleep.

[Dated 1939; not revised by Brecht. From Werner Hecht (ed.): *Materialien zu Brechts "Leben des Galilei,"* Frankfurt, Suhrkamp, 1968, pp. 7 ff.]

The *Life of Galileo* Is Not a Tragedy

So, from the point of view of the theater, the question will arise
whether the *Life of Galileo* is to be presented as a tragedy or as
an optimistic play. Is the keynote to be found in Galileo's "Salu-
tation to the New Age" in scene 1 or in certain parts of scene
14? According to the prevailing rules of play-construction, the
end of a drama must carry the greater weight. But this play is
not constructed according to these rules. The play shows the
dawn of a new age and tries to correct some of the prejudices
about the dawn of a new age.

[Dated 1939. From Werner Hecht (ed.), *ibid.*, p. 13.]

Portrayal of the Church

For the theater it is important to understand that this play must
lose a great part of its effect if its performance is directed chiefly
against the Catholic Church.

 Of the dramatis personae, many wear the church's garb. Actors who, because of that, try to portray these characters as
odious would be doing wrong. But neither, on the other hand,
has the church the right to have the human weaknesses of its
members glossed over. It has all too often encouraged these
weaknesses and suppressed their exposure. But in this play
there is also no question of the church being admonished:
"Hands off science!" Modern science is a legitimate daughter of
the church, a daughter who has emancipated herself and turned
against the mother.

 In the present play the church functions, even when it op-
poses free investigation, simply as authority.

 Since science was a branch of theology, the church is the
intellectual authority, the ultimate scientific court of appeal.
But it is also the temporal authority, the ultimate political court
of appeal. The play shows the temporary victory of authority,
not the victory of the priesthood. It corresponds to the historical

truth in that the Galileo of the play never turns directly against the church. There is not a sentence uttered by Galileo in that sense. If there had been, such a thorough commission of investigation as the Inquisition would undoubtedly have brought it to light. And it equally corresponds to the historical truth that the greatest astronomer of the Papal Roman College, Christopher Clavius, confirmed Galileo's discoveries (scene 6). It is also true that clerics were among his pupils (scenes 8, 9, and 13).

To take satirical aim at the worldly interests of high dignitaries seems to me cheap (it would be in scene 7). But the casual way in which these high officials treat the physicist is only meant to show that, by reason of their past experiences, they think they can count on ready complaisance from Galileo. They are not mistaken.

Considering our bourgeois politicians, one cannot but extol the spiritual (and scientific) interests of those politicians of old.

The play, therefore, ignores the falsifications made to the protocol of 1616 by the Inquisition of 1633, falsifications established by the recent historical studies under the direction of the German scholar Emil Wohlwill. Doubtless the judgment and sentence of 1633 were thereby made juridically possible. Anybody who understands the point of view outlined above will appreciate that the author was not concerned with this legal side of the trial.

There is no doubt that Urban VIII was personally incensed at Galileo and, in the most detestable manner, played a personal part in the proceedings against him. The play passes this over.

Anyone who understands the standpoint of the author will appreciate that this attitude implies no reverence for the church of the seventeenth, let alone of the twentieth century.

Casting the church as the embodiment of authority in this theatrical trial of the persecutors of the champions of free research certainly does not help to secure an acquittal for the church. But it would be highly dangerous, particularly nowadays, to treat a matter like Galileo's fight for freedom of research as a religious one; for thereby attention would be most unhappily deflected from present-day reactionary authorities of a totally unecclesiastical kind.

[Dated 1939. From Werner Hecht (ed.), *ibid.*, pp. 14 f.]

Three Notes on the Character of Galileo

1. [The new type of physicist]

[. . .] It's important that you shouldn't idealize Galileo: You know the kind of thing—the stargazer, the pallid intellectual-ized idealist. I know you wouldn't if left to yourself, but the pictures you'll see in the books are already idealized. My Galileo is a powerful physicist with a tummy on him, a face like Socra-tes, a vociferous, full-blooded man with a sense of humor, the new type of physicist, earthly, a great teacher. Favorite attitude: stomach thrust forward, both hands on the buttocks, head back, using one meaty hand all the time to gesticulate with, but with precision; comfortable trousers for working in, shirtsleeves or (particularly at the end) a long whitish-yellow robe with broad sleeves, tied with a cord round his stomach. You get the idea—preferably an etching of this figure or some kind of steel engrav-ing or wood engraving to maintain its historical flavor: in other words, realistic. Or for that matter one could have pen drawings standing freely on the page. Don't be scared of a bit of humor. History without humor is a ghastly thing . . .

N.B. As far as I know, Galileo's telescope was about two-and-a-half feet long and the thickness of a man's arm. You can stand it on an ordinary tripod. The model of the Ptolemaic system (in scene 1) is of wood, some twenty inches in diameter. You could probably get a rough idea from the keeper of the planetarium.

2. The Sensual Element in Galileo

Galileo of course is not a Falstaff: He insists on his physical pleasures because of his materialist convictions. He wouldn't, for instance, drink at his work; the point is that he *works* in a sensual way. He gets pleasure from handling his instruments with elegance. A great part of his sensuality is of an intellectual kind: for instance, the "beauty" of an experiment, the little theatrical performance with which he gives shape to each of his lessons, the often abrupt way in which he will confront somebody with the truth, not to mention those passages in his speeches (in 1, 7, 13) where he picks good words and tests them like a spice. (This has nothing to do with that bel canto of the actor who may produce his arias as if he enjoyed them, but fails to show the enjoyment of the character he is playing.)

3. About the Part of Galileo

What gives this new historical character his quality of strangeness, novelty, strikingness, is the fact that he, Galileo, looks at the world of 1600 around him as if he himself were a stranger. He studies this world and finds it remarkable, out-dated, in need of explanation. He studies:

in scene 1, Ludovico Marsili and Priuli
in scene 2, the way in which the senators look through the telescope (When am I going to be able to buy one of these things?)
in scene 3, Sagredo (the prince being a child of nine)
in scene 4, the court scholars
in scene 5, the monks
in scene 7, the young monk
in scene 8, Federzoni and Ludovico
in scene [11], (for just one second) Virginia
in scene [13], his pupils
in scene [14], Andrea and Virginia.

[From Werner Hecht (ed.), *ibid.* pp. 27 f. The first section comes from a letter from Brecht to the painter Hans Tom-brock in March 1941, and refers to the first version of the play, which Tombrock illustrated for a proposed publication in the USSR which never materialized. The second and third are undated, but appear to refer to the second, American version.]

Drafts for a Foreword to *Life of Galileo*

The *Life of Galileo* was written in those last dark months of 1938, when many people felt fascism's advance to be irresistible and the final collapse of Western civilization to have arrived. And

indeed we were approaching the end of that great age to which
the world owes the development of the natural sciences, together with such new arts as music and the theater. There was
a more or less general expectation of a barbaric age "outside
history." Only a minority saw the evolution of new forces and
sensed the vitality of the new ideas. Even the significance of
expressions like "old" and "new" had been obscured. The doctrines of the socialist classics had lost the appeal of novelty, and
seemed to belong to a vanished day.

The bourgeois single out science from the scientist's conscious-
ness, setting it up as an island of independence so as to be
able in practice to interweave it with *their* politics, *their* eco-
nomics, *their* ideology. The research scientist's object is "pure"
research; the product of that research is not so pure. The for-
mula $E = mc^2$ is conceived of as eternal, not tied to anything.
Hence other people can do the tying: Suddenly the city of
Hiroshima became very short-lived. The scientists are claiming
the irresponsibility of machines.

Let us think back to the founding father of experimental
science, Francis Bacon, whose phrase that one must obey nature
in order to command her was not written in vain. His contem-
poraries obeyed his nature by bribing him with money, and so
thoroughly commanded him when he was Lord Chief Justice
that in the end Parliament had to lock him up. Macaulay, the
puritan, drew a distinction between Bacon the scientist, whom
he admired, and Bacon the politician, of whom he disapproved.
Should we be doing the same thing with the German doctors
of Nazi times?
    Among other things, war promotes the sciences. What an
opportunity! It creates discoverers as well as thieves. A higher
responsibility (that of the higher ranks) replaces the lower (that
for the lowly). Obedience is the midwife of arbitrariness. Disorder is perfectly in order. Those doctors who combatted yellow
fever had to use themselves as guinea pigs; the fascist doctors
had material supplied them. Justice played a part too; they had
to freeze only "criminals," in other words those who did not
share their opinions. For their experiments in using "animal

warmth" as a means of thawing they were given prostitutes, women who had transgressed the rule of chastity. They had served sin; now they were being allowed to serve science. It incidentally emerged that hot water restores life better than a woman's body; in its small way it can do more for the fatherland. (Ethics must never be overlooked in war.) Progress all round. At the beginning of this century the lower classes' politicians were forced to treat the prisons as their universities. Now the prisons became universities for the warders (and doctors). Their experiments would of course have been perfectly in order —"from a scientific point of view," that is—even if the state had been forced to exceed the ethical bounds. None the less the bourgeois world still has a certain right to be outraged. Even if it is only a matter of degrees it is a matter of degrees. When Generals von Mackensen and Mältzer were being tried in Rome for shooting hostages, the English prosecutor, a certain Colonel Halse, admitted that "reprisal killings" in war were not illegal so long as the victims were taken from the scene of the incident in question, an attempt was made to find the persons responsible for it, and there were not too many executions. The German generals however had gone too far. They took ten Italians for every German soldier killed (not twenty, though, as demanded by Hitler), and dispatched the whole lot too quickly, within some twenty-four hours. The Italian police, by an oversight, handed over several Italians too many, and by another oversight the Germans shot them too, out of a misplaced reliance on the Italians. But here again they had ransacked the prisons for hostages, taking criminals or suspects awaiting trial, and filling the gaps with Jews. So a certain humanity asserted itself, and not merely in the errors of arithmetic. All the same, bounds were exceeded in this case, and something had to be done to punish the excess.

It can none the less be shown that, in this period when the bourgeoisie has gone completely to pieces, those pieces are still made of the same stuff as the original polished article.

And so in the end the scientists get what they want: state resources, large-scale planning, authority over industry; their Golden Age has come. And their great production starts as the production of weapons of destruction; their planning leads to extreme anarchy, for they are arming the state against other states. As soon as he represents such a threat to the world, the people's traditional contempt for the unworldly professor turns into naked fear. And just when he has wholly cut himself off from the people as the complete specialist, he is appalled to see himself once again as one of the people, because the threat applies to him too; he has reason to fear for his own life, and the best reason of anybody to know just how much. His protests, of which we have heard quite a number, refer not only to the attacks on his science, which is to be hampered, sterilized, and perverted, but also to the threat which his knowledge represents to the world, and also to the threat to himself.

The Germans have just undergone one of those experiences that are so difficult to convert into usable conclusions. The leadership of the state had fallen to an ignorant person who associated himself with a gang of violent and "uneducated" politicians to proclaim a vast war and utterly ruin the country. Shortly before the catastrophic end, and for some time after it, the blame was attributed to these people. They had conducted an almost total mobilization of the intellectuals, providing every branch with trained manpower, and although they made a number of clumsy attempts to interfere, the catastrophe cannot be ascribed to clumsy interference alone. Not even the military and political strategy appears to have been all that wrong, while the courage of the army and of the civil population is beyond dispute. What won in the end was the enemy's superiority in men and technology, something that had been brought into play by a series of almost unpredictable events.

Many of those who see, or at any rate suspect, capitalism's shortcomings are prepared to put up with them for the sake of the personal freedom which capitalism appears to guarantee. They believe in this freedom mainly because they scarcely ever make use of it. Under the scourge of Hitler they saw this freedom more or less abrogated; it was like a little nest-egg in the savings bank which could normally be drawn on at any time, though it was clearly more sensible not to touch it, but had now as it were been frozen—i.e., could not be drawn on, although it was still there. They regarded the Hitler period as abnormal; it was a matter of some warts on capitalism, or even of an anticapitalist movement. The latter was something that one could only believe if one accepted the Nazis' own definition of capitalism, while as for the wart theory one was after all dealing with a system where warts flourished, and there was no question of the intellectuals being able to prevent them or make them go away. In either case freedom could only be restored by a catastrophe. And when the catastrophe came, not even it was able to restore freedom, not even it.

Among the various descriptions of the poverty prevailing in denazified Germany was that of spiritual poverty. "What they want, what they're waiting for is a message," people said. "Didn't they have one?" I asked. "Look at the poverty," they said, "and at the lack of leadership." "Didn't they have leadership enough?" I asked, pointing to the poverty. "But they must have something to look forward to," they said. "Aren't they tired of looking forward to such things?" I asked. "I understand they lived quite a while on looking forward either to getting rid of their leader or to having him lay the world at their feet for them to pillage."

The hardest time to get along without knowledge is the time when knowledge is hardest to get. It is the condition of bottommost poverty where it seems possible to get along without knowledge. Nothing is calculable any longer, the measures went up in the fire, short-range objectives hide those in the distance; at that point chance decides.

> [From Werner Hecht (ed.): *ibid.*, pp. 16 ff. These different items are given in the same order as there, though they appear to date from after the Second World War and not, as there suggested, mainly from 1938–1939.]

Unvarnished Picture of a New Age

PREAMBLE TO THE AMERICAN VERSION

When, during my first years in exile in Denmark, I wrote the play *Life of Galileo*, I was helped in the reconstruction of the Ptolemaic cosmology by assistants of Niels Bohr who were working on the problem of splitting the atom. My intention was, among others, to give an unvarnished picture of a new age —a strenuous undertaking since all those around me were convinced that our own era lacked every attribute of a new age. Nothing of this aspect had changed when, years later, I began together with Charles Laughton to prepare an American version of the play. The "atomic" age made its debut at Hiroshima in the middle of our work. Overnight the biography of the founder of the new system of physics read differently. The infernal effect of the great bomb placed the conflict between Galileo and the authorities of his day in a new, sharper light. We had to make only a few alterations—not a single one to the structure of the play. Already in the original version the church was portrayed as a secular authority, its ideology as, fundamentally, interchangeable with many others. From the first the keystone of the gigantic figure of Galileo was his conception of a science for the people. For hundreds of years and throughout the whole of Europe people had paid him the honor, in the Galileo legend, of not believing in his recantation, just as they had for long derided scientists as biased, unpractical and eunuch-like old fogeys. [. . .]

> [Dated 1946. From Werner Hecht (ed.), *ibid.*, pp. 10 ff. The rest of the note, here omitted, was incorporated in the Model Book (see p. 238–239 below).]

Praise or Condemnation of Galileo?

It would be a great weakness in this work if those physicists were right who said to me—in a tone of approval—that Galileo's recantation of his teachings was, despite one or two "wa-

verings," portrayed as being sensible, with the argument that
this recantation enabled him to carry on with his scientific work
and to hand it down to posterity. The fact is that Galileo en-
riched astronomy and physics by simultaneously robbing these
sciences of a greater part of their social importance. By discred-
iting the Bible and the church, these sciences stood for a while
at the barricades on behalf of all progress. It is true that a
forward movement took place in the following centuries, and
these sciences were involved in it, but it was a slow movement,
not a revolution; the scandal, so to speak, degenerated into a
dispute between experts. The church, and with it all the forces
of reaction, was able to bring off an organized retreat and more
or less reassert its power. As far as these particular sciences are
concerned, they never again regained their high position in
society, neither did they ever again come into such close contact
with the people.

Galileo's crime can be regarded as the "original sin" of modern natural sciences. From the new astronomy, which deeply
interested a new class—the bourgeoisie—since it gave an impetus to the revolutionary social current of the time, he made
a sharply defined special science which—admittedly through its
very "purity," i.e., its indifference to modes of production—was
able to develop comparatively undisturbed.

The atom bomb is, both as a technical and as a social phenomenon, the classical end-product of his contribution to
science and his failure to contribute to society.

Thus, the "hero" of this work is not Galileo but the people,
as Walter Benjamin has said. This seems to me to be rather too
briefly expressed. I hope this work shows how society extorts
from its individuals what it needs from them. The urge to
research, a social phenomenon no less delightful or compulsive
than the urge to reproduce, steers Galileo into that most dangerous territory, drives him into agonizing conflict with his violent
desires for other pleasures. He raises his telescope to the stars
and delivers himself to the rack. In the end he indulges his
science like a vice, secretly and probably with pangs of conscience. Confronted with such a situation, one can scarcely wish
only to praise or only to condemn Galileo.

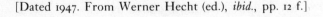

[Dated 1947. From Werner Hecht (ed.), *ibid.*, pp. 12 f.]

Prologue to the American Production

Respected public of the way called Broad
Tonight we invite you to step on board
A world of curves and measurements, where you'll descry
The newborn physics in their infancy.
Here you will see the life of the great Galileo Galilei.
The law of falling bodies versus the GRATIAS DEI
Science's fight versus the rulers, put on stage
At the beginning of the modern age.
Here you'll see science in its blooming youth
Also its first compromises with the truth.
The Good, so far, has not been turned to goods
But already there's something nasty in the woods
Which stops that truth from reaching the majority
And won't relieve, but aggravate their poverty.
We think such sights are relevant today
The modern age is so quick to pass away
We hope you'll lend a charitable ear
To what we say, since otherwise we fear
If you won't learn from Galileo's experience
The Bomb will put in a personal appearance.

[From Werner Hecht (ed.), *ibid.*, p. 38.]

Epilogue of the Scientists

And the lamp his work ignited
We have tried to keep alight
Stooping low, and yet high-minded
Unrestrained, yet laced up tight.
Making moon and stars obey us
Groveling at our rulers' feet
We sell our brains for what they'll pay us
To satisfy our bodies' need.
So, despised by those above us

Ridiculed by those below
We've found out the laws that move us
Keep this planet on the go.
Knowledge grows too large for nitwits
Servitude expands as well
Truth becomes so many titbits
Liberators give us hell.
Riding in new railway coaches
To the new ships on the waves
Who is it that now approaches?
Only slave-owners and slaves.
Only slaves and slave-owners
Leave the trains
Taking the new aeroplanes
Through the heaven's age-old blueness.
Till the latest one arrives
Astronomic
White, atomic
Obliterating all our lives.

[From Werner Hecht (ed.), *ibid.*, pp. 38 f.]

Notes on Individual Scenes

[*Scene 11*]

Could Galileo have acted any differently?

This scene gives ample reasons for Galileo's hesitation about escaping from Florence and seeking asylum in the North Italian cities. None the less the audience can imagine him putting himself in the hands of Matti the iron founder, and discover various tendencies in his character and situation which would support this.

The actor Laughton showed Galileo in a state of great inner agitation during his talk with the iron founder. He played it as a moment of decision—the wrong one. (Connoisseurs of dialec-

tics will find Galileo's possibilities further clarified in the ensuing scene "The Pope," where the inquisitor insists that Galileo
must be forced to recant his theory because the Italian maritime
cities need his star charts, which derive from it and of which it
would not be possible to deprive them.)
An objectivist approach is not permissible here.*

[Scene 14]

Galileo after his recantation

His crime has made a criminal of him. When he reflects on
the *scale* of his crime he is pleased with himself. He defends
himself against the outside world's impertinent expectations of
its geniuses. What has Andrea done to oppose the Inquisition?
Galileo applies his intellect to solving the problems of the
clergy, which these blockheads have overlooked. His mind
functions automatically, like a motor in neutral. His appetite
for knowledge feels to him like the impetus that makes him
twitch. Scholarly activity, for him, is a sin: mortally dangerous,
but impossible to do without. He has a fanatical hatred for
humanity. Andrea's readiness to revise his damning verdict as
soon as he sees the book means that he has been corrupted. As
to a lame and starving wolf, Galileo tosses him a crust, the
logical scientific analysis of the Galileo phenomenon. Behind
this lies his rejection of the moral demands of a humanity which
does nothing to relieve the deadliness of that morality and those
demands.
[. . .]
Once Galileo knows that his book has set out on its journey
towards publication he changes his attitude again. He proposes
that the book should be prefaced by an introduction sharply
condemning the author's treachery. Andrea passionately
refuses to pass on such a request, pointing out that everything
is different now, that Galileo's recantation gave him the chance
to finish this immensely significant work. What needs to be

*Objectivists who prove the necessity of a given sequence of facts are always
in danger of slipping into the position of justifying those facts (Lenin).

altered is the popular concept of heroism, ethical precepts and
so on. The one thing that counts is one's contribution to science,
and so forth.

At first Galileo listens in silence to Andrea's speech, which
builds a golden bridge for his return to the esteem of his fellow
scientists, then contemptuously and cuttingly contradicts him,
accusing Andrea of squalidly recanting every principle of
science. Starting with a denunciation of "bad thinking" which
seems designed as a brilliant demonstration of how the trained
scientist ought to analyse a case like his own, he proves to
Andrea that no achievement is valuable enough to make up for
the damage caused by a betrayal of mankind.

Galileo's portrayal in scene 14

The fact that the author is known to all and sundry as an
opponent of the church might lead a theater to give the play's
performance a primarily anticlerical slant. The church, however, is mainly being treated here as a secular establishment. Its
specific ideology is being looked at in the light of its function
as a prop to practical rule. The old cardinal (in scene 6) can be
turned into a Tory or a Louisiana Democrat without much
adjustment. Galileo's illusions concerning a "scientist in the
chair of St. Peter" have more than one parallel in contemporary
history, and these are scarcely related to the church. In scene
13 Galileo is not returning "to the bosom of the church"; as we
know, he never left it. He is simply trying to make his peace
with those in power. One can judge his demoralization by his
social attitude; he buys his comfort (even his scientific activity
has degenerated to the status of a comfort) by means of hack-
work, unashamedly prostituting his intellect. (His use of clerical quotations is thus sheer blasphemy.) On no account should
the actor make use of his self-analysis to endear the hero to the
audience by his self-reproaches. All it does is to show that his
brain is unimpaired, never mind what area he directs it to.
Andrea Sarti's final remark in no sense represents the playwright's own view of Galileo, merely his opinion of Andrea
Sarti. The playwright was not out to have the last word.

Galileo is a measure of the standard of Italian intellectuals in the first third of the seventeenth century, when they were defeated by the feudal nobility. Northern countries like Holland and England developed productive forces further by means of what is called the Industrial Revolution. In a sense Galileo was responsible both for its technical creation and for its social betrayal.

[*Crime and Cunning*]

The first version of the play ended differently. Galileo had written the *Discorsi* in the utmost secrecy. He uses the visit of his favorite pupil Andrea to get him to smuggle the book across the frontier. His recantation had given him the chance to create a seminal work. He had been wise.

In the Californian version [...] Galileo interrupts his pupil's hymns of praise to prove to him that his recantation had been a crime, and was not to be compensated by this work, important as it might be.

In case anybody is interested, this is also the opinion of the playwright.

> [Shortened from Werner Hecht (ed.), *ibid.*, pp. 32–37. These notes were written at various times, those on scene 14 mainly during Brecht's work on the Berliner Ensemble production. The reference to a new critical introduction to the *Discorsi* must relate to a proposed change which Brecht never made; it is not to be found in our text.]

Building up a Part: Laughton's Galileo

PREFACE

In describing Laughton's Galileo Galilei the playwright is setting out not so much to try and give a little more permanence to one of those fleeting works of art that actors create, as to pay tribute to the pains a great actor is prepared to take over a fleeting work of this sort. This is no longer at all common. It is not just that the under-rehearsing in our hopelessly commer-

cialized theater is to blame for lifeless and stereotyped portraits
—give the average actor more time, and he would hardly do
better. Nor is it simply that this century has very few outstand-
ing individualists with rich characteristics and rounded con-
tours—if that were all, care could be devoted to the portrayal
of lesser figures. Above all it is that we seem to have lost any
understanding and appreciation of what we may call a *theatrical
conception:* what Garrick did when, as Hamlet, he met his father's ghost; Sorel when, as Phèdre, she knew that she was
going to die; Bassermann when, as Philip, he had finished listening to Posa. It is a question of inventiveness.

The spectator could isolate and detach such theatrical concep-
tions, but they combined to form a single rich texture. Odd
insights into men's nature, glimpses of their particular way of
living together, were brought about by the ingenious contriv-
ance of the actors.

With works of art, even more than with philosophical systems, it is impossible to find out how they are made. Those who
make them work hard to give the impression that everything
just happens, as it were of its own accord, as though an image
were forming in a clear mirror that is itself inert. Of course this
is a deception, and apparently the idea is that if it comes off it
will increase the spectator's pleasure. In fact it does not. What
the spectator, anyway the experienced spectator, enjoys about
art is the making of art, the active creative element. In art we
view nature herself as if she were an artist.

The ensuing account deals with this aspect, with the process
of manufacture rather than with the result. It is less a matter
of the artist's temperament than of the notions of reality which
he has *and communicates;* less a matter of his vitality than of the
observations which underlie his portraits and can be derived
from them. This means neglecting much that seemed to us to
be "inimitable" in Laughton's achievement, and going on
rather to what can be learned from it. For we cannot create
talent; we can only set it tasks.

It is unnecessary here to examine how the artists of the past
used to astonish their public. Asked why he acted, L. answered:
"Because people don't know what they are like, and I think I

can show them." His collaboration in the rewriting of the play showed that he had all sorts of ideas which were begging to be disseminated, about how people *really* live together, about the motive forces that need to be taken into account here. L.'s attitude seemed to the playwright to be that of a realistic artist of our time. For whereas in relatively stationary ("quiet") periods artists may find it possible to merge wholly with their public and to be a faithful "embodiment" of the general conception, our profoundly unsettled time forces them to take special measures to penetrate to the truth. Our society will not admit of its own accord what makes it move. It can even be said to exist purely through the secrecy with which it surrounds itself. What attracted L. about *Life of Galileo* was not only one or two formal points but also the subject matter; he thought this might become what he called a contribution. And so great was his anxiety to show things as they really are that despite all his indifference (indeed timidity) in political matters he suggested and even demanded that not a few of the play's points should be made sharper, on the simple ground that such passages seemed "somehow weak" to him, by which he meant that they did not do justice to things as they are.

We usually met in L.'s big house above the Pacific, as the dictionaries of synonyms were too bulky to lug about. He had continual and inexhaustibly patient recourse to these tomes, and used in addition to fish out the most varied literary texts in order to examine this or that gest, or some particular mode of speech: Aesop, the Bible, Molière, Shakespeare. In my house he gave readings of Shakespeare's works to which he would devote perhaps a fortnight's preparation. In this way he read *The Tempest* and *King Lear*, simply for me and one or two guests who happened to have dropped in. Afterward we would briefly discuss what seemed relevant, an "aria" perhaps or an effective scene opening. These were exercises and he would pursue them in various directions, assimilating them in the rest of his work. If he had to give a reading on the radio he would get me to hammer out the syncopated rhythms of Whitman's poems (which he found somewhat strange) on a table with my fists, and once he hired a studio where we recorded half a dozen ways of telling the story of the creation, in which he was an African planter telling the Negroes how he had created the world, or an English butler ascribing it to His Lordship. We needed such broadly ramified studies, because he spoke no German whatever and we had to decide the gest of each piece of dialogue by my acting it all in bad English or even in German and his then acting it back in proper English in a variety of ways until I could say: That's it. The result he would write down sentence by sentence in longhand. Some sentences, indeed many, he carried around for days, changing them continually. This system of performance-and-repetition had one immense advantage in that psychological discussions were almost entirely avoided. Even the most fundamental gests, such as Galileo's way of observing, or his showmanship, or his craze for pleasure, were established in three dimensions by actual performance. Our first concern throughout was for the smallest fragments, for sentences, even for exclamations—each treated separately, each needing to be given the simplest, freshly fitted form, giving so much away, hiding so much or leaving it open. More radical changes in the structure of entire scenes or of the work itself were meant to help the story to move and to bring out fairly general conclusions about people's attitudes to the great physicist. But this reluctance to tinker with the psychological aspect remained with L. all through our long period of collaboration, even when a rough draft of the play was ready and he was giving various readings in order to test reactions, and even during the rehearsals.

The awkward circumstance that one translator knew no German and the other scarcely any English compelled us, as can be seen, from the outset to use acting as our means of translation. We were forced to do what better-equipped translators should do too: to translate gests. For language is theatrical in so far as it primarily expresses the mutual attitude of the speakers. (For the "arias," as has been described, we brought in the playwright's own gest, by observing the bel canto of Shakespeare or the writers of the Bible.)

In a most striking and occasionally brutal way L. showed his lack of interest in the "book," to an extent the playwright could not always share. What we were making was just a text; the performance was all that counted. Impossible to lure him to translate passages which the playwright was willing to cut for the proposed performance but wanted to keep in the book. The theatrical occasion was what mattered, the text was only there to make it possible: It would be expended in the production, would be consumed in it like gunpowder in a firework. Although L.'s theatrical experience had been in London, which had become thoroughly indifferent to the theater, the old Elizabethan London still lived in him, the London where theater was such a passion that it could swallow immortal works of art greedily and barefacedly as so many "texts." These works which have survived the centuries were in fact like improvisations thrown off for an all-important moment. Printing them at all was a matter of little interest, and probably only took place so that the spectators, in other words, those who were present at the actual event, the performance, might have a souvenir of their enjoyment. And the theater seems in those days to have been so potent that the cuts and interpolations made at rehearsal can have done little harm to the text.

We used to work in L.'s small library, in the mornings. But often L. would come and meet me in the garden, running barefoot in shirt and trousers over the damp grass, and would show me some changes in his flowerbeds, for his garden always occupied him, providing many problems and subtleties. The gaiety and the beautiful proportions of this world of flowers overlapped in a most pleasant way into our work. For quite a while our work embraced everything we could lay our hands on. If we discussed gardening it was only a digression from one of the scenes in *Galileo;* if we combed a New York museum for technical drawings by Leonardo to use as background pictures in the performance we would digress to Hokusai's graphic work. L., I could see, would make only marginal use of such material. The parcels of books or photocopies from books, which he persistently ordered, never turned him into a bookworm. He obstinately sought for the external: not for physics but for the physicists' behavior. It was a matter of putting together a bit of theater, something slight and superficial. As the material piled up, L. became set on the idea of getting a good draftsman to produce entertaining sketches in the manner of

Caspar Neher, to expose the anatomy of the action. "Before you amuse others you have to amuse yourself," he said.

For this no trouble was too great. As soon as L. heard of Caspar Neher's delicate stage sketches, which allow the actors to group themselves according to a great artist's compositions and to take up attitudes that are both precise and realistic, he asked an excellent draftsman from the Walt Disney Studios to make similar sketches. They were a little malicious; L. used them, but with caution.

What pains he took over the costumes, not only his own, but those of all the actors! And how much time we spent on the casting of the many parts!

First we had to look through works on costume and old pictures in order to find costumes that were free of any element of fancy dress. We sighed with relief when we found a small sixteenth-century panel that showed long trousers. Then we had to distinguish the classes. There the elder Brueghel was of great service. Finally we had to work out the color scheme. Each scene had to have its basic tone: the first, e.g., a delicate morning one of white, yellow, and gray. But the entire sequence of scenes had to have its development in terms of color. In the first scene a deep and distinguished blue made its entrance with Ludovico Marsili, and this deep blue remained, set apart, in the second scene with the upper bourgeoisie in their blackish-green coats made of felt and leather. Galileo's social ascent could be followed by means of color. The silver and pearl-gray of the fourth (court) scene led into a nocturne in brown and black (where Galileo is jeered by the monks of the Collegium Romanum), then on to the seventh, the cardinals' ball, with delicate and fantastic individual masks (ladies and gentlemen) moving about the cardinals' crimson figures. That was a burst of color, but it still had to be fully unleashed, and this occurred in the tenth scene, the carnival. After the nobility and the cardinals the poor people too had their masquerade. Then came the descent into dull and somber colors. The difficulty of such a plan of course lies in the fact that the costumes and their wearers wander through several scenes; they have always to fit in and contribute to the color scheme of the new scene.

We filled the parts mainly with young actors. The speeches

presented certain problems. The American stage shuns speeches except in (maybe because of) its frightful Shakespearean productions. Speeches just mean a break in the story and, as commonly delivered, that is what they are. L. worked with the young actors in a masterly and conscientious manner, and the playwright was impressed by the freedom he allowed them, by the way in which he avoided anything Laughtonish and simply taught them the structure. To those actors who were too easily influenced by his own personality he read passages from Shakespeare, without rehearsing the actual text at all; to none did he read the text itself. The actors were incidentally asked on no account to prove their suitability for the part by putting something "impressive" into it.

We jointly agreed on the following points:

1. The decorations should not be of a kind to suggest to the spectators that they are in a medieval Italian room or the Vatican. The audience should be conscious of being in a theater.

2. The background should show more than the scene directly surrounding Galileo; in an imaginative and artistically pleasing way, it should show the historical setting, but still remain background. (This can be achieved when the decoration itself is not independently colorful, but helps the actors' costumes and enhances the roundedness of the figures by remaining two-dimensional even when it contains three-dimensional elements, etc.)

3. Furniture and props (including doors) should be realistic and above all be of social and historical interest. Costumes must be individualized and show signs of having been worn. Social differences were to be underlined since we find it difficult to distinguish them in ancient fashions. The colors of the various costumes should harmonize.

4. The characters' groupings must have the quality of historical paintings (but not to bring out the historical aspect as an esthetic attraction; this is a directive which is equally valid for contemporary plays). The director can achieve this by inventing historical titles for the episodes. (In the first scene such titles might be: *Galileo the physicist explains the new Copernican theory to his subsequent collaborator Andrea Sarti and predicts the great historical importance of astronomy—To make a living the great Galileo teaches rich pupils—Galileo who has requested support for his continued*

investigations is admonished by the university officials to invent profitable instruments—Galileo constructs his first telescope based on information from a traveler.)

5. The action must be presented calmly and in a large sweep. Frequent changes of position involving irrelevant movements of the characters must be avoided. The director must not for a moment forget that many of the actions and speeches are hard to understand and that it is therefore necessary to express the underlying idea of an episode by the positioning. The audience must be assured that when someone walks, or gets up, or makes a gesture it has meaning and deserves attention. But groupings and movements must always remain realistic.

6. In casting the ecclesiastical dignitaries realism is of more than ordinary importance. No caricature of the church is intended, but the refined manner of speech and the "breeding" of the seventeenth-century hierarchy must not mislead the director into picking spiritual types. In this play, the church mainly represents authority; as types the dignitaries should resemble our present-day bankers and senators.

7. The portrayal of Galileo should not aim at rousing the audience to sympathy or empathy; they should rather be encouraged to adopt a deliberate attitude of wonder and criticism. Galileo should be portrayed as a phenomenon of the order of Richard III; the audience's emotions will be engaged by the vitality of this strange figure.

8. The more profoundly the historical seriousness of a production is established, the more scope can be given to humor. The more sweeping the over-all plan, the more intimately individual scenes can be played.

9. There is no reason why *Life of Galileo* cannot be performed without drastically changing the present-day style of production, as a historical "war-horse," for instance, with a star part. Any conventional performance, however (which need not seem at all conventional to the actors, especially if it contained interesting inventions), would weaken the play's real strength considerably without making it any easier for the audience. The play's main effects will be missed unless the theater changes its attitude. The stock reply, "Won't work here," is familiar to the author; he heard it at home too. Most directors treat such plays

as a coachman would have treated an automobile when it was first invented. On the arrival of the machine, mistrusting the practical instructions accompanying it, this coachman would have harnessed horses in front—more horses, of course, than to a carriage, since the new car was heavier—and then, his attention being drawn to the engine, he would have said, "Won't work here."*

The performance took place in a small theater in Beverly Hills, and L.'s chief worry was the prevailing heat. He asked that trucks full of ice be parked against the theater walls and fans be set in motion "so that the audience can think."

NOTES ON INDIVIDUAL SCENES

1

The Scholar, a Human Being

The first thing L. did when he set to work was to rid the figure of Galileo of the pallid, spiritual, stargazing aura of the text books. Above all, the scholar must be made into a man. The very term "scholar" [Gelehrter] sounds somewhat ridiculous when used by simple people; there is an implication of having been prepared and fitted, of something passive. In Bavaria people used to speak of the Nuremberg Funnel by which simpletons were more or less forcibly fed undue quantities of knowledge, a kind of enema for the brain. When someone had "crammed himself with learning," that too was considered unnatural. The educated—again one of those hopelessly passive words—talked of the revenge of the "uneducated," of their innate hatred for the mind; and it is true that their contempt was often mixed with hatred; in villages and working-class districts, the mind was considered something alien, even hostile. The same contempt, however, could also be found among the "better

*[Brecht added Note 9 at a later date for inclusion in his Notes to the Play.]

classes." A scholar was an impotent, bloodless, quaint figure, conceited and barely fit to live. He was an easy prey for romantic treatment. L.'s Galileo never strayed far from the engineer at the great arsenal in Venice. His eyes were there to see with, not to flash, his hands to work with, not to gesticulate. Everything worth seeing or feeling L. derived from Galileo's profession, his pursuit of physics and his teaching, the teaching, that is, of something very concrete with its concomitant real difficulties. And he portrayed the external side not just for the sake of the inner man—that is to say, research and everything connected with it, not just for the sake of the resulting psychological reactions—these reactions, rather, were never separated from the everyday business and conflicts, they never became "universally human," even though they never lost their universal appeal. In the case of the Richard III of Shakespeare's theater, the spectator can easily change himself along with the actor, since the king's politics and warfare play only a very vague role; there is hardly more of it than a dreaming man would understand. But with Galileo it is a continual handicap to the spectator that he knows much less about science than does Galileo. It is a piquant fact that in representing the history of Galileo, both playwright and actor had to undo the notion which Galileo's betrayal had helped to create, the notion that schoolteachers and scientists are by nature absent-minded, hybrid, castrated. (Only in our own day when, in the shape of ruling-class hirelings remote from the people, they delivered the latest product of Galileo's laws of motion, did popular contempt change to fear.) As for Galileo himself, for many centuries, all over Europe, the people honored him for his belief in a popularly based science by refusing to believe in his recantation.

Subdivisions and Line

We divided the first scene into several parts:

We had the advantage that the beginning of the story was also a beginning for Galileo, that is, his encounter with the telescope, and since the significance of this encounter is hidden from him for the time being, our solution was to derive the joy of beginning from the early morning: having him wash with cold water—L., with bare torso, lifted a copper pitcher with a quick sweeping motion to let the jet of water fall into the basin —find his open books on the high desk, have his first sip of milk, and give his first lesson, as it happens, to a young boy. As the scene unfolds, Galileo keeps coming back to his reading at the high desk, annoyed at being interrupted by the returning student with his shallow preference for new-fangled inventions such as this spyglass, and by the procurator of the university who denies him a grant; finally reaching the last obstacle that keeps him from his work, the testing of the lenses which, however, would not have been possible without the two prior interruptions and makes an entirely new field of work accessible.

Interest in Interest and Thinking as Expression of Physical Contentment

Two elements in the action with the child may be mentioned:

Washing himself in the background, Galileo observes the boy's interest in the armillary sphere as little Andrea circles around the strange instrument. L. emphasized what was novel in G. at that time by letting him look at the world around him as if he were a stranger and as if it needed explanation. His chuckling observation made fossils out of the monks at the Collegium Romanum. In that scene he also showed amusement at their primitive method of proof.

Some people objected to L.'s delivering his speech about the new astronomy in the first scene with a bare torso, claiming that it would confuse the audience if it were to hear such intellectual utterances from a half-naked man. But it was just this mixture of the physical and the intellectual that attracted L. "Galileo's physical contentment" at having his back rubbed by the boy is transformed into intellectual production. Again, in the ninth scene, L. brought out the fact that Galileo recovers his taste for wine on hearing of the reactionary pope's expected demise. His sensual walking, the play of his hands in his pockets while he is planning new researches, came close to being offensive. Whenever Galileo is creative, L. displayed a mixture of aggressiveness and defenseless softness and vulnerability.

Rotation of the Earth and Rotation of the Brain

L. arranges the little demonstration of the earth's rotation to be quick and offhand, leaving his high desk where he has begun to read and returning to it. He avoids anything emphatic, seems to pay no attention to the child's intellectual capacity, and at the end leaves him sitting there alone with his thoughts.

This casual manner, in keeping with his limited time, simultaneously admits the boy to the community of scholars. Thus L. demonstrated how for Galileo learning and teaching are one and the same—which makes his subsequent betrayal all the more horrible.

Balanced Acting

During this demonstration of the earth's rotation Galileo is surprised by Andrea's mother. Questioned about the nonsensical notions he is teaching the child he answers: "Apparently we are on the threshold of a new era, Mrs. Sarti." The way in which L. caressingly emptied his glass of milk while he said it was enchanting.

Response to a Good Answer

A small detail: The housekeeper has gone to let the new student in. Galileo feels constrained to make a confession to Andrea. His science is in no very good state, its most important concerns must be concealed from the authorities, and for the moment they are only hypotheses. "I want to become an astronomer," Andrea says quickly. At this answer Galileo looks at him with an almost tender smile. Usually actors do not rehearse such details separately, or often, enough to render them quickly in the performance.

[Dismissal of Andrea]

The dismissal of Andrea during the conversation with Ludovico is a piece of stage business for which time must be allowed. Galileo now drinks his milk as if it were the only pleasure to be had, and one which will not last very long. He is fully aware of Andrea's presence. Ill-humoredly he sends him away. One of those unavoidable everyday compromises!

Galileo Underestimates the New Invention

Ludovico Marsili describes a new spyglass which he has seen in Holland and cannot understand. Galileo asks for detailed information and makes a sketch which solves the problem. He holds the cardboard with the sketch without showing it to his pupil, who expected to have a look. (L. insisted that the actor playing Ludovico should expect this.) The sketch itself he drew casually, just to solve a problem that offered some relief from the conversation. Then, his way of asking the housekeeper to send Andrea for lenses and borrowing a scudo from the entering procurator—all that had an automatic and routine quality. The whole incident seemed only to demonstrate that Galileo too was capable of plowing water.

A New Commodity

The birth of the telescope as a commodity took a long time to emerge clearly in the rehearsals. We found out why: L. had reacted too quickly and arrogantly to the university's refusal of a grant. All was well as soon as he accepted the blow in hurt silence and then went on, almost sadly, to speak like a poor man. As a natural result, Galileo's "Mr. Priuli, I may have something for you," came out in a way to make Galileo's dismissal of the new spyglass as "bosh" perfectly clear.

[Interruption of Work]

When Andrea returns with the lenses he finds Galileo deep in his work. (L. has shown, during a by no means brief interval, how the scholar handles his books.) He has already forgotten the lenses, he lets the boy wait, then proceeds, almost guiltily because he has no desire to take up the lucrative bosh, to arrange the two lenses on a piece of cardboard. Finally he takes the "thing" away, not without a little demonstration of his showmanship.

2

Fraud and Representation

Lesser actors would have delivered Galileo's speech representing the telescope as his own invention in a comical manner, simply in order to provide a strong contrast to the few excited words in which he tells his friend Sagredo about the instrument's scientific importance. This would have robbed the handing-over ceremony of all significance and belittled the fraud as a moral trifle. L. delivered the speech seriously, in a businesslike way (what Goethe called "artig"), that is, as a matter of routine, the sort of way in which the chief engineer at the great arsenal of Venice behaves on official occasions. Only when he mentioned the "Christian principles" according to which the "optical tube or telescope" was constructed was there a hint of the great gainsayer's delight in provocation.

It was highly entertaining to see how shamelessly the colossus bowed to his betters when, after a glance through the telescope, they applauded him, and how, on the other hand, he warded off their jovial and somewhat too familiar jokes while at the same time telling his friend, with supreme authority and passion, that he has turned the thing on the night sky.

Patience Guarantees Tempo

During rehearsals L. completely freed himself of the fever of an evening performance, that feeling that nothing is going fast enough which so easily infects the rehearsals. In this case things cannot go slowly enough. One has to rehearse as if the play could go on for twelve hours. L. rigorously rejected any suggestion of makeshift "bridges" to avoid loss of tempo. There were effects everywhere; the smallest detail could reveal peculiarities or habits of people's living together. (Loss of tempo occurs most often when a point is muddled and bungled and has to be glossed over.) For instance, the relatively cursory ending of the second scene cannot be staged adequately without very patient and detailed rehearsing.

The senators surround and congratulate Galileo and draw him to the rear, but the tiny exchange with Ludovico Marsili, with its imputation of plagiarism, must as it were still hover in the air; for when the half-curtain closes behind them [Ludovico and Virginia] and in front of Galileo and the others, they continue and conclude the conversation while exiting along the footlights. And Ludovico's cynical remark, "I am beginning to understand science," serves as a springboard for the ensuing third scene—that of the great discoveries.

3

[Confidence in Objective Judgment]

Galileo lets his friend Sagredo look through the telescope at the moon and Jupiter. L. sat down, his back to the instrument, relaxed, as though his work were done and he only wanted his friend to pass impartial judgment on what he saw, and that this were all he needed to do since his friend was now seeing for himself. By this means he established that the new possibilities of observation must bring all controversy about the Copernican system to an end.

This attitude explains at the very beginning of the scene the boldness of his application for the lucrative position at the court of Florence.

The Historical Moment

L. conducted the exchange with his friend at the telescope without any emphasis. The more casually he acted, the more clearly one could sense the historic night; the more soberly he spoke, the more solemn the moment appeared.

An Embarrassment

When the procurator of the university comes in to complain about the fraud of the telescope, L.'s Galileo shows noticeable embarrassment by studiously looking through the telescope, obviously less to observe the sky than to avoid looking the procurator in the eye. Shamelessly he exploits the "higher" function of the instrument which the Venetians have found not to be very profitable.

It is true that he also shows his behind to the angry man who has trusted him. But, far from trying to put him off with the discoveries of "pure" science, he at once offers him another profitable item, the astronomical clock for ships. When the procurator has left, he sits glumly before the telescope, scratching his neck and telling Sagredo about his physical and intellectual needs which must be satisfied in one way or another. Science is a milch cow for all to milk, he himself of course included. While at this point in time Galileo's attitude is still helpful to science, later on, in his fight with Rome, it is going to push science to the brink of the abyss, in other words, deliver it into the hands of the rulers.

The Wish Is Father to the Thought

Looking up from their calculations of the movements of Jupiter's moons, Sagredo voices his concern for the man about to publish a discovery so embarrassing to the church. Galileo mentions the seductive power of evidence. He fishes a pebble from his pocket and lets it fall from palm to palm, following gravity: "Sooner or later everybody must succumb to it" [the evidence]. As he argued along these lines, L. never forgot for a moment to do it in such a way that the audience would remember it later when he announced his decision to hand over his dangerous discoveries to the Catholic court of Florence.

[Rejection of Virginia]

L.'s Galileo used the little scene with his daughter Virginia to indicate how far he might be blamed for Virginia's subsequent behavior as a spy for the Inquisition. He does not take her interest in the telescope seriously and sends her off to matins. L. scrutinized his daughter after her question, "May I look through it?" before replying, "What for? It's not a toy."

The Fun in Contradictions

Saying, "I am going to Florence," Galileo carefully signs his letter of application. In this hasty capitalization of his discoveries as well as in his discourse on the seductive power of evidence and the representative value of great discoveries, L. left the spectator completely at liberty to study, criticize, admire Galileo's contradictory personality.

4

The Acting of Anger

Vis-à-vis the court scholars who refuse to look through the telescope, because to do so would either confirm Aristotle's doctrine or show up Galileo as a swindler, what L. acted was not so much anger as the attempt to dominate anger.

Servility

After Galileo, erupting at last, has threatened to take his new science to the dockyards, he sees the court depart abruptly. Deeply alarmed and disturbed, he follows the departing prince in cringing servility, stumbling, all dignity gone. In such a case an actor's greatness can be seen in the degree to which he can make the character's behavior incomprehensible or at least objectionable.

4 and 6*

The Fight and the Particular Manner of Fighting

L. insisted that throughout the two following scenes, 4 and 6, the sketch of Jupiter's moons from Galileo's original report should remain projected on the backdrop screen. It was a re-

---

* Scene 5 was not played in this production.

minder of the fight. To show one of its aspects, the heel-cooling for the sake of truth, L., at the end of scene 4, when the chamberlain stays behind after the hasty departure of the court to inform him of the appeal to Rome, let himself be driven out of the space that stood for his house and stood in front of the half-curtain. He stood there between scenes 4 and 6 and again between scenes 6 and 7, waiting, and occasionally verifying that the pebble from his pocket continued to fall from one raised hand to the other stretched out below.

6

[*Observation of the Clergy*]

Galileo is not entirely devoid of appreciation when he observes the jeering monks at the Collegium Romanum—after all, by pretending to stand on a rolling globe they are trying to *prove* the absurdity of his propositions. The very old cardinal fills him with pity.

After the astronomer Clavius has confirmed Galileo's findings, Galileo shows his pebble to the hostile cardinal who retreats in dismay; L. did this by no means triumphantly, rather as if he wanted to offer his adversary a last chance to convince himself.

7

Fame

Invited to the masked ball of Cardinals Bellarmine and Barberini, Galileo lingers for a moment in the anteroom, alone with the clerical secretaries who later turn out to be secret agents. He has been greeted on his arrival by distinguished masked guests with great respect: obviously he stands in high favor. From the halls a boys' choir is heard, and Galileo listens to one of these melancholic stanzas which are sung amid the joy of life. L. needed no more than this brief listening and the word

"Rome!" to express the pride of the conqueror who has the capital of the world at his feet.

The Duel of Quotations

In the brief duel of Bible quotations with Cardinal Barberini, L.'s Galileo shows, beside the fun he has with such intellectual sport, that the possibility of an unfavorable outcome to his affairs is dawning on him. For the rest, the effectiveness of the scene depends on the elegance of its performance; L. made full use of his heavy body.

Two Things at Once

The brief argument about the capacity of the human brain (which the playwright was delighted to have heard formulated by Albert Einstein) furnished L. the opportunity to show two traits: 1) a certain arrogance of the professional when his field is invaded by laymen, and 2) an awareness of the difficulty of such a problem.

[Disarmed by Lack of Logic]

When the decree is read out forbidding the guest to teach a theory acknowledged to have been proven, L.'s Galileo reacts by twice turning abruptly from the reading secretaries to the liberal Barberini. Thunderstruck, he lets the two cardinals drag him to the ball as if he were a steer stunned by the ax. L. was able, in a manner the playwright cannot describe, to give the impression that what mainly disarmed Galileo was the lack of logic.

8

[Indomitable Urge to Research]

If in the seventh scene Galileo experiences the *No* of the church, in the eighth he is confronted with the *No* of the people. It comes from the lips of the little monk, himself a physicist.

Galileo is disturbed, then recognizes the situation: in the fight against science it is not the church that defends the peasant, but the peasant who defends the church. It was L.'s theatrical conception to let Galileo be so profoundly upset that he delivers his counter-arguments in a spirit of defense, even of angry self-defense, and makes the throwing down of the manuscript into a gesture of helplessness. He blamed his indomitable urge to research like a sex offender blaming his glands.

Laughton Does Not Forget to Tell the Story

In the eighth scene one of Galileo's lines contains a sentence which continues the story: "Should I condone this decree . . ." L. distilled this small but important detail with great care.

9

[The Impatience of Galileo the Scientist]

Whereas L. insisted he must be allowed to give Galileo's character a markedly criminal evolution after the recantation in scene 13, he did not feel a similar need at the beginning of scene 9. Here too, to oblige the church, Galileo has for many years abstained from publicizing his discoveries, but this cannot be considered a betrayal like the later one. At this point the people know very little about the new science, the cause of the new astronomy has not yet been taken up by the North Italian bourgeoisie, the battle fronts are not yet political. There may not be an open declaration on his part, but there is no recantation either. In this scene therefore it is still the scientist's personal impatience and dissatisfaction which must be portrayed.

When Does Galileo Become Antisocial?

The issue in Galileo's case is not that a man must stand up for his opinion as long as he holds it to be true; that would entitle him to be called a "character." The man who started it all, Copernicus, did not stand up for his opinion; it would be truer to say that he lay down for it inasmuch as he had it published only after his death; and yet, quite rightly, no one has ever reproached him for this. Something had been laid down to be picked up by anybody.

The man who had laid it down had gone, out of range of blame or thanks. Here was a scientific achievement which allowed simpler, shorter and more elegant calculations of celestial motions—let humanity make use of it. Galileo's life work is on the whole of the same order, and humanity used it. But unlike Copernicus who had avoided a battle, Galileo fought it and betrayed it. If Giordano Bruno, of Nola, who did not avoid the battle and had been burned twenty years earlier, had recanted, no great harm might have come of it; it could even be argued that his martyrdom deterred scientists more than it aroused them. In Bruno's time the battle was still a feeble one. But time did not stand still: A new class, the bourgeoisie with its new industries, had assertively entered the scene; no longer was it only scientific achievements that were at stake, but battles for their large-scale general exploitation. This exploitation had many aspects because the new class, in order to pursue its interests, had to come to power and smash the prevailing ideology that obstructed it. The church, which defended the privileges of princes and landowners as God-given and therefore natural, did not rule by means of astronomy, but it ruled within astronomy, as in everything else. And in no field could it allow its rule to be smashed. The new class, clearly, could exploit a victory in any field including that of astronomy. But once it had singled out a particular field and concentrated the battle in it, the new class became broadly vulnerable there. The maxim, "A chain is as strong as its weakest link," applies to chains that bind (such as the ideology of the church) as well as to transmission chains (such as the new class's new ideas about property, law, science, etc.). Galileo became antisocial when he led his science into this battle and then abandoned the fight.

Teaching

Words cannot do justice to the lightness and elegance with which L. conducted the little experiment with the pieces of ice in the copper basin. A fairly long reading from books was followed by the rapid demonstration. Galileo's relationship with his pupils is like a duel in which the fencing master uses all his feints—using them against the pupil to serve the pupil. Catching Andrea out in a hasty conclusion, Galileo crosses out his wrong entry in the record book with the same matter-of-fact patience as he displays in correcting the ice's position in the submersion experiment.

Silence

With his own pupils he uses his tricks mainly to quell their dissatisfaction with him. They are offended by his keeping silent in the European controversy about sunspots, when his views are constantly being solicited as those of the greatest authority in the field. He knows he owes his authority to the church, and hence owes the clamor for his views to his silence. His authority was given him on condition that he should not use it. L. shows how Galileo suffers by the episode of the book on sunspots, which has been brought along and is discussed by his pupils. He pretends complete indifference, but how badly he does it! He is not allowed to leaf through the book, probably full of errors and thus twice as attractive. In little things he supports their revolt, though not himself revolting: When the lens grinder Federzoni angrily drops the scales on the floor because he cannot read Latin, Galileo himself picks them up—casually, like a man who would pick up anything that fell down.

Resumption of Research—a Sensual Pleasure

L. used the arrival of Ludovico Marsili, Virginia's fiancé, to show his own disgust at the routine nature of his work. He organized the reception of his guest in such a way that it interrupted the work and made his pupils shake their heads. On being told that the reactionary pope was on his deathbed Galileo visibly began to enjoy his wine. His bearing changed completely. Sitting at the table, his back to the audience, he experienced a rebirth; he put his hands in his pockets, placed one leg on the bench in a delicious sprawl. Then he rose slowly and walked up and down, with his glass of wine. At the same

252 Life of Galileo: Notes and Variants

time he let it be seen how his future son-in-law, the landowner and reactionary, displeased him more with every sip. His instructions to the pupils for the new experiment were so many challenges to Ludovico. With all this, L. still took care to make it plain that he was seizing the opportunity for new research not by the forelock, but just by a single little hair.

The Gest of Work

The speech about the need for caution with which Galileo resumes a scientific activity that defies all caution shows L. in a rare gest of creative, very vulnerable softness.

Even Virginia's fainting spell upon finding her fiancé gone barely interests Galileo. As the pupils hover over her, he says painfully: "I've got to know." And in saying it he did not seem hard.

10

Political Attitude on Dramatic Grounds

L. took the greatest interest in the tenth (carnival) scene, where the Italian people are shown relating Galileo's revolutionary doctrine to their own revolutionary demands. He helped sharpen it by suggesting that representatives of the guilds, wearing masks, should toss a rag doll representing a cardinal in the air. It was so important to him to demonstrate that property relationships were being threatened by the doctrine of the earth's rotation that he declined a New York production where this scene was to be omitted.

11

Decomposition

The eleventh scene is the decomposition scene. L. begins it with the same authoritative attitude as in the ninth scene. He does not permit his increasing blindness to detract one iota from his virility. (Throughout, L. strictly refused to exploit this ailment which Galileo had contracted in the pursuit of his profession, and which of course could easily have won him the sympathy of the audience. L. did not want Galileo's surrender to be ascribable to his age or physical defects. Even in his last scene he was a man who was spiritually, not physically, broken.)

The playwright would sooner have Galileo's recantation in this scene, rather than let it take place before the Inquisition. Galileo executes it when he rejects the offer of the progressive bourgeoisie, in the person of the iron founder Vanni, to support him in his fight against the church, and insists that what he has written is an apolitical scientific work. L. acted this rejection with the utmost abruptness and strength.

Two Versions

In the New York production L. changed his gest for the meeting with the cardinal inquisitor as he emerges from the inner chambers. In the California production he remained seated, not recognizing the cardinal, while his daughter bowed. This created the impression of something ominous passing through, unrecognizable, but bowing. In New York, L. rose and himself acknowledged the cardinal's bow. The playwright finds no merit in the change, since it establishes a relationship between Galileo and the cardinal inquisitor which is irrelevant, and turns Galileo's ensuing remark, "His attitude was respectful, I think," into a statement rather than a question.

The Arrest

As soon as the chamberlain appears at the head of the stairs, Galileo hastily puts the book under his arm and runs upstairs, passing the startled chamberlain. Stopped short by the chamberlain's words, he leafs through the book as though its quality was all that mattered. Left standing on the lower part of the staircase, he must now retrace his steps. He stumbles. Almost at the footlights—his daughter has run to meet him—he completely pulls himself together and gives his instructions firmly and to the point. It becomes clear that he has taken certain precautions. Holding his daughter close and supporting her, he sets out to leave the hall at a rapid, energetic pace. When he reaches the wings the chamberlain calls him back. He receives the fateful decision with great composure. Acting thus, L. shows that this is neither a helpless nor an ignorant man who is being caught, but one who has made great mistakes.

13

A Difficulty for the Actor: Some Effects become Apparent only when the Play is seen a Second Time

In preparing for the recantation scene L. never neglected in the preceding scenes to exhibit in all their fine shades the compliance and non-compliance in Galileo's conduct vis-à-vis the authorities, even those instances which would only mean anything to a spectator who had already seen the entire play once. Both he and the playwright recognized that in this type of play certain details unavoidably depend on a knowledge of the whole.

The Traitor

In the book there is a stage direction for Galileo when he returns to his pupils after he recanted to the Inquisition: *"He is changed, almost unrecognizable."* The change in L. was not of a physical nature as the playwright had intended. There was something infantile, bed-wetting in his loose gait, his grin, indicating a self-release of the lowest order, as if restraints had been thrown off that had been very necessary.

This, like what follows, can best be seen on photographs of the California production.

Andrea Sarti is feeling sick; Galileo has asked for a glass of water for him, and now the little monk passes by him, his face averted. Galileo's gaze is answered by Federzoni, the artisan-scholar, and for some time the two stare at each other until the monk returns with the water. This is Galileo's punishment: it will be the Federzonis of the future centuries who will have to pay for his betrayal at the very inception of their great career.

"Unhappy the Land"

The pupils have abandoned the fallen man. Sarti's last word had been: "Unhappy is the land that breeds no hero." Galileo has to think of an answer, then calls after them, too late for them to hear: "Unhappy is the land that needs a hero." L. says it soberly, as a statement by the physicist who wants to take away nature's privilege to ordain tragedies and mankind's need to produce heroes.

14

The Goose

Galileo spends the last years of his life on an estate near Florence as a prisoner of the Inquisition. His daughter Virginia, whom he has neglected to instruct, has become a spy for the Inquisition. He dictates his *Discorsi* to her, in which he lays down his main teachings. But to conceal the fact that he is making a copy of the book he exaggerates the extent of his failing eyesight. Now he pretends not to recognize a goose which she shows him, the gift of a traveler. His wisdom has been degraded to cunning. But his zest for food is undiminished: He instructs his daughter carefully how he wants the liver prepared. His daughter conceals neither her disbelief in his inability to see nor her contempt for his gluttony. And Galileo, aware that she defends him vis-à-vis the Inquisition's guards, sharpens the conflicts of her troubled conscience by hinting that he may be deceiving the Inquisition. Thus in the basest manner he experiments with her filial love and her devotion to the church. Nonetheless, L. succeeded brilliantly in eliciting from the spectator not only a measure of contempt but also a measure of horror at degradations that debase. And for all this he had only a few sentences and pauses at his disposal.

Collaboration

Anxious to show that crime makes the criminal more criminal, L. insisted, during the adaptation of the original version, on a scene in which Galileo collaborates with the authorities in full view of the audience. There was another reason for this: During the scene Galileo makes the most dignified use of his well-preserved intellectual powers by analyzing his betrayal for the benefit of his former pupil. So he now dictates to his daughter, to whom he had for many weeks been dictating his main work, the *Discorsi*, an abject letter to the archbishop in which he advises him how the Bible may be used for the suppression of starving artisans. In this he quite frankly shows his daughter his cynicism without being entirely able to conceal the effort this ignominious exercise costs him. L. was fully aware of the recklessness with which he swam against the stream by thus throwing away his character—no audience can stand a thing like that.

The Voice of the Visitor

Virginia has laid down the manuscript of the letter to the archbishop and gone out to receive a belated visitor. Galileo hears the voice of Andrea Sarti, formerly his favorite pupil who had broken with him after the recantation. To those readers of the play who complained that it gave no description of the spiritual agonies to which our nuclear physicists were subjected by the authorities ordering the bombs, L. could show that no first-rate actor needs more than a fleeting moment to indicate such spiritual discomfort. It is of course right to compare Galileo's submissiveness towards his authorities with that of our physicists towards rulers whom they distrust, but it would be wrong to go all the way into their stomach pains. What would be gained by that? L. was simply making this the moment to display his bad conscience, which could not have been shown

later in the scene when his betrayal is analyzed, without getting
in his way.

The Laughter

The laughter in the picture [in the Model Book] was not
suggested by the text, and it was frightening. Sarti, the former
favorite pupil, calls and Virginia overhears the strained conversation. When Galileo inquires about his former collaborators,
Sarti answers with utter frankness calculated to hurt his master.
They get to Federzoni, a lens grinder whom Galileo had made
his scientific collaborator even though he had no Latin. When
Sarti reports he is back in a shop grinding lenses Galileo answers: "He can't read the books": Then L. makes him laugh.
The laugh however does not contain bitterness about a society
that treats science as something secret reserved for the well-to-
do, but a disgraceful mocking of Federzoni's inadequacies together with a brazen complicity in his degradation, though this
is simply (and completely) explained by his being inadequate.
L. thus intended to make the fallen man a provocateur. Sarti,
naturally, responds with indignation and seizes the opportunity
to inflict a blow on the shameless recanter when Galileo cautiously inquires about Descartes's further work. Sarti coldly
reports that Descartes shelved his investigations into the nature
of light when he heard that Galileo had recanted. And Galileo
once had exclaimed that he would willingly be "imprisoned a
thousand feet beneath the earth, if in exchange he could find out
what light is." L. inserted a long pause after this unpleasant
information.

The Right to Submit

During the first sentences of his exchange with Sarti he listens inconspicuously for the footsteps of the Inquisition's official in the anteroom, who stops every now and then,
presumably in order to eavesdrop. Galileo's inconspicuous listening is difficult to act since it must remain concealed from
Sarti but not from the audience; concealed from Sarti because
otherwise he would not take the prisoner's repentant remarks

at face value. But Galileo must convey them to him at face value so that his visitor can change them when he reaches foreign parts; it would not do at all if it were rumored abroad that the prisoner was recalcitrant. Then the conversation reaches a point where Galileo abandons this way of speaking for the benefit of hostile ears, and proclaims, authoritatively and forcefully, that it is his right to submit. Society's command to its members to produce is but vague and accompanied by no manner of guarantee; a producer produces at his own risk, and Galileo can prove any time that being productive endangers his comfort.

Handing over the Book

L. made the disclosure about the existence of the *Discorsi* quickly and with exaggerated indifference; but in a way suggesting that the old man was only trying to get rid of the fruits of a regrettable lapse, with yet another implication beneath this: anxiety lest the visitor reject the imposition together with the risk involved in taking the book with him. As he was protesting ill-humoredly that he wrote the book only as a slave of habit— the thoroughly vicious habit of thinking—the spectator could see that he was also listening. (Having made his eyesight worse by secretly copying the book which is endangered by the Inquisition, when he wants to gauge Sarti's reaction, he is wholly dependent on his ears.) Toward the end of his appeal he virtually abandons his attitude of "condescending grandeur" and comes close to begging. The remark about having continued his scientific work simply to kill time, uttered when Sarti's exclamation "The *Discorsi!*" had made him aware of his visitor's enthusiasm, came so falsely from L.'s lips that it could deceive no one.

It is furthermore important to realize that when Galileo so strongly emphasizes his own condemnation of the teaching activities which are now forbidden to him he is mainly trying to deceive himself. Since working, let alone sharing the results with the outside world, would threaten whatever was left of his comfort, he himself is passionately against this "weakness" which makes him like a cat that cannot stop catching mice.

Indeed the audience is witnessing his defeat when it sees him yield so reluctantly yet helplessly to an urge fostered in him by society. He must consider the risks to be larger than ever because now he is wholly in the hands of the Inquisition; his punishment would no longer be a public one; and the body of people who formerly would have protested has dispersed—thanks to his own fault. And not only has the danger increased, but he would be too late now with any contribution anyway, since astronomy has become apolitical, the exclusive concern of scientists.

Watchfulness

After the young physicist has found the book for which the scientific community no longer dares to hope, he at once changes his opinion about his former teacher and launches, with great passion, into a rationalization of Galileo's motives for the betrayal; motives, he finds, which exonerate him completely. Galileo has recanted so that he can go on with his work and find more evidence for the truth. Galileo listens for a while, interjecting monosyllables. What he is hearing now may well be all that he can expect posterity to say in recognition of his difficult and dangerous endeavor. First, he seems to be testing his pupil's improvised theory, just in the same way as any other theory must be tested for its validity. But presently he discovers that it is not tenable. At this point, immersed in the world of his scientific concerns, he forgets his watchfulness vis-à-vis a possible eavesdropper: he stops listening for steps.

The Analysis

Galileo's great counterattack against the golden bridge opens with a scornful outburst that abandons all grandeur: "Welcome to my gutter, dear colleague in science and brother in treason! I sold out, you are a buyer." This is one of the few passages which gave L. trouble. He doubted whether the spectator would get the meaning of the words, apart from the fact that the words are not taken from Galileo's usual, purely logical vocabulary. L. could not accept the playwright's argument that

there must be some gest simply showing how the opportunist
damns himself by damning all who accept the rewards of oppor-
tunism; what he understood even less was that the playwright
would be quite satisfied with the exhibition of a state of mind
that defies rational analysis. The omission of a spiteful and
strained grin at this point robbed the opening of the great
instructional speech of its malice. It was not fully brought out
that deriding the ignorant is the lowest form of instruction and
that it is an ugly light that is shed solely for the purpose of
letting one's own light shine. Because the lowest starting point
was missing some spectators were unable to gauge the full
height which L. undoubtedly reached in the course of the great
speech, nor was it entirely possible to see the collapse of Galileo's vain and violently authoritarian attitude that colored even
his scientific statements. The theatrical content of the speech,
in fact, is not directly concerned with the ruthless demonstration of bourgeois science's fall from grace at the beginning of
its rise—its surrender of scientific knowledge to the rulers who
are authorized "to use it, not use it, abuse it, as it suits their
ends." The theatrical content derives from the whole course of
the action, and the speech should show how well this perfect
brain functions when it has to judge its owner. That man, the
spectator should be able to conclude, is sitting in a hell, more
terrible than Dante's, where the true function of intellect has
been gambled away.

Background of the Performance

It is important to realize that our performance took place at
the time and in the country of the atom bomb's recent production and military application and where nuclear physics was
then shrouded in deepest secrecy. The day the bomb was
dropped will not easily be forgotten by anyone who spent it in
the U.S.

The Japanese war had cost the U.S. real sacrifices. The troop
ships left from the west coast, and the wounded and the victims
of tropical diseases returned there. When the news reached Los
Angeles it was at once clear that this was the end of the hateful
war, that sons and brothers would soon come home. But the

great city rose to an astonishing display of mourning. The playwright heard bus drivers and saleswomen in fruit markets express nothing but horror. It was victory, but it was the shame
of defeat. Next came the suppression of the tremendous energy
source by the military and politicians, and this upset the intellectuals. Freedom of investigation, the exchange of scientific
discoveries, the international community of scholars were jetti-
soned by authorities that were strongly distrusted. Great physicists left the service of their bellicose government in headlong
flight; one of the best known took an academic position where
he was forced to waste his working time in teaching rudimen-
tary essentials solely to escape working for the government. It
had become ignominious to make new discoveries.

[From *Aufbau einer Rolle/Laughtons
Galilei*, East Berlin, Henschel, 1956.]

APPENDICES TO "BUILDING UP A PART"

Sense and sensuality

The demonstrative style of acting, which depicts life in such
a way that it is laid open to intervention by the human reason,
and which strikes Germans as thoroughly doctrinaire, presented no special difficulty to the Englishman L. What makes
the sense seem so striking and insistent once it is "lugged in"
is our particular lack of sensuality. To lack sensuality in art is
certainly senseless, nor can any sense remain healthy if it is not
sensual. Reason, for us, immediately implies something cold,
arbitrary, mechanical, presenting us with such pairs of alterna-
tives as ideas and life, passion and thinking, pleasure and utility.
Hence when we stage a performance of our *Faust*—a regular
occurrence for educational reasons—we strip it of all sensuality
and thus transport the audience into an indefinite atmosphere
where they feel themselves confronted with all sorts of
thoughts, no single one of which they can grasp clearly. L.
didn't even need any kind of theoretical information about the

required "style." He had enough taste not to make any distinction between the supposedly lofty and the supposedly base, and
he detested preaching. And so he was able to unfold the great
physicist's contradictory personality in a wholly corporeal
form, without either suppressing his own thoughts about the
subject or forcing them on us.

Beard or no beard

In the California production L. acted without a beard, in the
New York with one. This order has no significance, nor were
there any fundamental discussions about it. It is the sort of case
where the desire for a change can be the deciding factor. At the
same time it does of course lead to modifications in the character. People who had seen the New York production confirmed
what can be seen from the pictures [in the Model Book], namely
that L. acted rather differently. But everything essential was
still there, and the experiment can be taken as evidence to show
how much play is left for the "personal" element.

The leavetaking

Certainly nothing could have been more horrible than the
moment when L. has finished his big speech and hastens to the
table saying "I must eat now," as though in delivering his insights Galileo has done everything that can be expected of him.
His leavetaking from Sarti is cold. Standing absorbed in the
sight of the goose he is about to eat, he replies to Sarti's repeated
attempt to express his regard for him with a formal "Thank
you, sir." Then, relieved of all further responsibility, he sits
down pleasurably to his food.

Concluding remark

Though it resulted from several years of preparation and was
brought about by sacrifices on the part of all concerned, the
production of *Galileo* was seen by a bare ten thousand people.
It was put on in two small theaters, a dozen times in each: first
in Beverly Hills, Los Angeles, and then with a competely new

cast in New York. Though all the performances were sold out the notices in the main papers were bad. Against that could be set the favorable remarks of such people as Charles Chaplin and Erwin Piscator, as well as the interest of the public, which looked like being enough to fill the theater for some considerable time. But the large cast meant that the potential earnings were low even if business was really good, and when an artistically interested producer made an offer it had to be rejected because L., having already turned down a number of film engagements and made considerable sacrifices, could not afford to turn down another. So the whole thing remained a private operation by a great artist who, while earning his keep outside the theater, indulged himself by displaying a splendid piece of work to a (not very large) number of interested parties. Though this is something that needed to be said, it does not however convey the complete picture. Given the way the American theater was organized in those years, it was impossible that such plays and such productions should reach their audience. Productions like this one, therefore, should be treated as examples of a kind of theater that might become possible under other political and economic conditions. Their achievements, like their mistakes, make them object lessons for anyone who is looking for a theater of great themes and rewarding acting.

> [From Werner Hecht (ed.), *Materialien zu Brechts "Leben des Galilei,"* pp. 78–80. In the last of these notes Brecht is perhaps being undeservedly kind to Laughton, since the actor's wariness of Communist associations, at a time when Brecht and Hanns Eisler were being heard by the Un-American Activities Committee, appears to have been another strong factor in deciding him to close the play.]

Note of two conversations with Caspar Neher about *Life of Galileo*

After the Italian fashion, a lightly built stage that is recognizable as having been lightly built. Nothing stony, weighty, massive. No interior decoration.

Color to emerge from the costumes, i.e. in movement.

The stage shows Galileo's background, making use of contemporary evidence (Leonardo's technical drawings, Romulus and Remus with the she-wolf, a man of war from the Venice arsenal, and so on).

No projections, since this would prevent the full illumination of the stage. Giant photographs, maybe, nobly suspended. A flagged floor.

> [Dated October 3 and 5, 1955. From Werner Hecht (ed.), *ibid.*, p. 88. The eventual stage set for the Berliner Ensemble's production, completed by Erich Engel after Brecht's death and first performed on January 15, 1957, was somewhat different from this.]

Editorial Note

Much of the information that follows, including some of the quotations from Brecht, is derived from Ernst Schumacher's *Drama und Geschichte. Bertolt Brecht's "Leben des Galilei" und andere Stücke*, Henschel, East Berlin 1965, whose usefulness is gratefully acknowledged.

1. General

Judging by the proportion of Brecht's papers devoted to it in the Brecht Archive in Berlin, *Galileo* is much the most heavily worked-over of all his plays. None of the others went through such stages, for not only did *Galileo* occupy him during the last nineteen years of his life, but its linguistic, theatrical, and thematic bases all changed drastically during that period, as did the dramatist's own circumstances. Thus it was written in German, then entirely rewritten in English (with Brecht himself contributing in a mixture of English and German), then rewritten in German again largely on the basis of the English-language version. Again, it was first written with no clear prospect of production, then rewritten for a specific actor, Laughton, and a specific production before an American audience, then rewritten once more for Brecht's own Berliner Ensemble to play in East Berlin. During Brecht's work on the first version, it became known that Niels Bohr had split the uranium atom; while he and Laughton were preparing the second, the first atom bomb dropped on Hiroshima, on August 6, 1945. Finally, Brecht himself was at first living as an exile, close to Germany, on the eve of an impending war; he rewrote the play once in the aura of Hollywood, when an allied victory was at last certain, then again after his own successful reestablishment in his country, within a bitterly divided world.)

There are thus three principal versions of the play whose differences will be described in what follows. The first is the German version whose earliest typescript was entitled *The Earth Moves* and which was originally written in November 1938. What appear to be early sketches lay down a structure as follows:

Life of Galileo

1. PADUA/Welcoming the new age/Copernicus's hypothesis/ authoritarian economy in Italy.
2. SIGNORIA/Landscape.
3. RESEARCH/Danger of the truth/speech about reason and its seductions.
4. DEMONSTRATIONS/The addicts of authority exhorted to see.
5. PLAGUE.
6. COLLEGIUM ROMANUM/The Copernican system ridiculed.
7. THE DECREE/On the church's responsibilities/the ch. system too all-embracing.
7a. CONVERSATION/The monk's parents/Horace.
8. THE SUNSPOTS/On science/Keunos.
9. The new age without fear/strict research/hope in working people.
9a. BALLAD.
10. THE INQUISITION'S SUMMONS.
11. INQUISITION/Condemnation of doubt.
12. RECANTATION/Praise of steadfastness.
13. THE PRISONER/Passage from the *Discorsi*/On the scientist's duty/On expropriation/The new age, a harridan.
14. SMUGGLING.

It did not take long to complete. On November 17 his secretary-collaborator Margarete Steffin wrote to Walter Benjamin:

Ten days ago Brecht began getting *Galileo* down in dramatic form, after it had been plaguing his mind for some time. He has already finished nine of the fourteen scenes, and very fine they are.

A mere six days after that, according to his diary, he had completed it, commenting that

The only scene to present difficulties was the last one. As in *St. Joan* [*of the Stockyards*] I needed some sort of twist at the end to make absolutely certain of the necessary detachment on the part of the audience. At any rate, now even a man subject to unthinking empathy must experience the A-effect in the course of identifying himself with Galileo. A legitimate degree of empathy occurs, given strictly epic presentation.

On January 6, 1939, the *Berlingske Tidende* published an interview in which he said that the play was "really written for New York"; though it is not clear just what he had in mind. A few weeks later he carefully revised it under the title *Life of Galileo* and had a number of duplicated copies run off, of which Walter Benjamin and Fritz Sternberg each appear to have been given one. This was also to all intents and purposes the version sent to Zurich and staged there in the middle of the war. But already Brecht was dissatisfied with it:

Technically, *Life of Galileo* is a great step backwards, far too opportunist, like *Señora Carrar's Rifles*. The play would need to be completely rewritten to convey that "breeze that comes from new shores," that rosy dawn of science. It would all have to be more direct, without the interiors, the atmospherics, the empathy. And all switched to planetary demonstration. The division into scenes can be kept, Galileo's characterization likewise, but work, the pleasures of work, would need to be realized in practical form, through contact with a theater. The first thing would be to study the *Fatzer* and *Breadshop* fragments. Technically those represent the highest standard.

So he noted on February 25. On the 27th he heard a Danish radio interview with three of Niels Bohr's assistants, one of whom, Professor C. Møller, knew Brecht and recalls discussing Galileo and the *Discorsi* with him early the previous year. This interview described the splitting of the uranium atom, which (so Ernst Schumacher suggests) may have prompted the passage in

the revised text about "the greatest discoveries . . . being made
at one or two places." The revision, however, certainly did
nothing to change the play "technically." Though an early but
undated note speaks of a *Life of Galileo* version for workers,
there appears to be no indication that a start was ever made on
this.

The second or American version dates from April 1944, when
Brecht took up the play again as a result of a meeting with Jed
Harris, the producer of Thornton Wilder's *Our Town*. A translation of the first version had already been made by Desmond
Vesey; in addition Brecht now got a rough interlinear translation made by one of his own collaborators, followed by a new
acting version by two of Orson Welles's associates, Brainerd
Duffield and Emerson Crocker. The two last-named had been
recommended to him by Charles Laughton, who seems to have
become interested in the play some time that autumn and to
have used their version for his own work with Brecht on the
adaptation. "Now working systematically with Laughton on
the translation and stage version of *The Life of the Physicist
Galileo*" said a diary note of December 10. In the course of this
activity, which lasted off and on until December 1945, Brecht
redrafted many passages in a remarkable mixture of German
and English; thus his sketch for the beginning of scene 4 runs:

Rede des Mathematikers

Das Universum des göttlichen Aristoteles mit seinen

mystisch musizierenden Sphären und Kristallnen Gewöl-
        circles   heavenly bodies
ben sowie den Kreisläufen seiner Himmelskörper,
        obliquity of the eclyptic
seinem Schiefenwinkel der Sonnenbahn/den Geheimnissen
     . Sternen
der Table of Cords, dem/Reichtum des Catalogue
        inspirierten
for the southern hemisphere/der/construction of a

celestial globe is ein Gebäude von grosser Ordnung

und Schönheit.

The Universe of the divine Classics.

For the New York production, which took place after Brecht's return to Europe, there were, according to its director Joseph Losey, "Different words, thanks in part to the collaboration of George Tabori in rewriting with Laughton and me from notes left behind in New York by Brecht."

The text as we reproduce it in the appendix (pp. 403–467) was published by Indiana University Press in 1952 in *From the Modern Repertoire, Series Two*, edited by Eric Bentley, then in *Seven Plays by Bertolt Brecht*, Grove Press, New York, 1961, and separately by Grove Press again in 1966. The play still struck Brecht himself as formally conventional, to judge from a note of January 1945 which found that

> with its interiors and atmospheric effects the construction of the scenes, derived from the epic theatre, makes a singularly theatrical impact.

He also told an interviewer somewhat apologetically that summer that "Galileo is anyway interesting as a contrast to my parables. Where they embody ideas, it extracts ideas from a subject."

In 1953, six years after the Hollywood and New York productions, he got Elisabeth Hauptmann and Benno Besson of the Berliner Ensemble, with some advice from Ruth Berlau (who had helped with, and photographed, the American version) to draft a third version in German, using the best parts of the previous texts. This he himself revised to form the play which was given its German première at Cologne in April 1955, published as *Versuche 14* and subsequently rehearsed by him for some three months with his own company. With minor amendments it is the text of the *Gesammelte Werke* on which our edition is based. It differs substantially from the second version.

2. The first version, 1938–1943

From Brecht's first completed typescript, dating presumably from November 1938, to the text used for the Zurich production of 1943, the play remained essentially the same, the only changes of real substance being those in the last scene but one which define the nature of Galileo's crime. The general structure of this first version was already very similar to that of the text which we have followed, and certain scenes, or large parts of them, were taken into the latter without drastic rewriting, for instance the first half of scene 1, scene 3, the start of scene 4, scene 5b (Plague), scene 6 (Collegium Romanum), much of scene 8, scene 11 (The Pope) and the last (Smuggling) scene. Even the carnival scene (10) had the same place, gist and purpose, though the ballad round which it centers was later rewritten. There were, however, some striking differences among the characters. To sum these up briefly:

Mrs. Sarti originally died of the plague in scene 5b. The character in 9 was "the housekeeper." This was altered after the first typescript.

Ludovico, Virginia's fiancé, did not appear till scene 7 (The Ball). He was then called Sitti, and was not a member of the landowning aristocracy; indeed in scene 9 (Sunspots) he lamented that he has no fortune of his own. His function of introducing Galileo to the principle of the telescope (scenes 1 and 2) was performed by a silly-ass character called Doppone, son of a wool merchant, whose only other appearance was, briefly, as a papal chamberlain in the ball scene.

Virginia was much less contemptuously treated by her father. Her relations with Andrea were friendlier, though her role in the penultimate scene was the same.

Federzoni the lens grinder did not figure in the play at all. Some of his lines were spoken by an "elderly scholar."

Vanni the iron founder did not figure in the play either. Stove-fitter and doctor appeared in the penultimate scene.

In the first typescript the play was called *The Earth Moves* (Die Erde bewegt sich) and the scenes bore no titles. The title *Life*

of Galileo, together with the individual scene titles, more or less
in their final form, are to be found in the revised scripts of early
1939. The verses before each scene are absent from this version.
The following is a scene-by-scene account of it.

I

Galileo Galilei, teacher of mathematics in Padua, sets out to demonstrate the new Copernican system.

Galileo's long speech about the "new age" (pp. 4–6) is about ten
lines shorter, omitting inter alia the passages about the ships
previously hugging the shores and about the masons in Siena,
but taking in the lines about "The ancient doctrines that have
been accepted for a thousand years" which come at the close of
the scene in the final text (p. 14). Andrea's age was not originally
specified, but the revised versions make him thirteen (as opposed to eleven in the final text).

The whole episode with Ludovico is absent. Instead Galileo
explains to Andrea the nature of a hypothesis. Copernicus, he
says, knows that the earth rotates

> only because he has worked it out. Actually he doesn't
> know it at all. He's assuming it. It's simply what is called
> a hypothesis. No facts. No proofs. They're being looked
> for. A few people in Prague and in England are looking for
> the proofs. It's the greatest hypothesis there has ever been,
> but it's no more than that. Hence the great flaw in the new
> system is that nobody who isn't a mathematician *can* under-
> stand why it's like that and can't be any other way. All I've
> showed you is that it can be that way. There's no reason
> why not, if you see what I mean.
>
> ANDREA   Can't I become a mathematician and find out the
> reason why it should?
>
> GALILEO   And how am I going to pay the butcher and the
> milkman and the bookseller if I start giving you lessons for
> nothing? Off you go, now; I must get on with my work.

In the revised versions Andrea asks "What's a hypothesis?" and
gets the answer which the final text puts at the end of the scene,
down to "that see very little" (p. 14), concluding "Copernicus's

hypothesis is the greatest hypothesis there has ever been, but it's no more than that."

ANDREA   Then what about what the church is saying? What's that?

GALILEO   Oh, that's a hypothesis too, but not such a good one. Lots of laws that don't explain very much. But the great flaw of the new system . . .

—and so on, as above.

The episode with the procurator of the university, which follows, is close to the final text, though the reference to the scientific implications of "the campaign for better looms" is lacking. Doppone appears *after* this, and is taken on as a private pupil for thirty scudi a month; his father wants him to become a theologian, since he likes arguing. Before leaving, he tells Galileo about the telescope, which Galileo then constructs from two lenses bought for him by Andrea. The scene ends with them looking through it.

GALILEO   You didn't eat the apple—which shows you've got the makings of a mathematician. A taste for unrewarding art. I'll teach you. It won't break me. This flimflam is worth five hundred scudi.

ANDREA   (*after Galileo has allowed him another look*) How clearly one sees. Here's Signor Gambione the bailiff coming up to our house.

GAMBIONE   Quick, shove those forty-five scudi in your pocket!

2

Galileo presents a new invention to the Republic of Venice.

Federzoni and Ludovico do not figure in this scene, which is dated August 24, 1609. Nor does Virginia. The telescope is handed over by Andrea, who however has nothing to say. The scene starts with Galileo's telling Sagredo that he has used it to look at the moon. Then his presentation speech is read for him by the procurator, including as Galileo's own the emphasis on the instrument's military usefulness; he adds a comment that

Galileo hopes to continue serving the Venetians. During this speech Doppone appears and tries to catch the eye of Galileo, who is annoyed and embarrassed: "It's one of my pupils, an unbelievable idiot. I can't imagine what he wants." As the city fathers try the instrument Galileo goes on talking to Sagredo about its relevance to Copernican theory.

> GALILEO (*without looking at him*) How about this? Flecks of light on the dark portion of the disk, dark patches on the bright sickle. It fits almost too well. Of course, I'm very skeptical, extremely skeptical.

The scene ends with Doppone breaking through the palace guards and saying breathlessly:

> Signor Galilei, why wouldn't you listen to me before the presentation? It's all wrong. The cover ought to be green.

It was green; trust Doppone.

3

January 10, 1610: By means of the telescope Galileo discovers celestial phenomena which prove the Copernican system. Warned by his friend of the possible consequences of his investigations, Galileo affirms his faith in reason.

Up to Mrs. Sarti's exit two-thirds of the way through (p. 25) this scene is very close to the final text, the main differences being the omission of Galileo's six lines on the value of star charts for navigation (p. 21); the fact that Sarti appears "in night attire"; and the doubling of Galileo's eventual salary (one thousand scudi in this version, as against the final five hundred). The episode with Virginia is then shifted to the end of the scene, after Sagredo's second "Galileo, don't go to Florence!" (p. 27), which leads to a cross-fade, thus:

> GALILEO You'd do better helping me write my letter to the Florentines.
>
> SAGREDO You really mean to go there?
>
> GALILEO Certainly. And with the tube. And with the truth. And with my belief in human reason.

SAGREDO   Then there's nothing more to say, is there? (*He leaves hurriedly without speaking*)

GALILEO (*laughs as he sits down at the telescope and starts making notes. It gets dark. When the lights come on again it is morning. Galileo is still sitting at this table writing by two candles. He has his coat on, as the fire has evidently gone out. A bell is ringing for early mass. Enter Galileo's very young daughter Virginia, warmly dressed*)

As in the final text she announces that she is going to matins, though without mention of Ludovico. In her dialogue with her father, which is rather differently phrased here, he does not snub her with such words as "It's not a toy" (p. 25) and "Nothing for you," though she complains of never being allowed to look through the telescope. He then tells her to read his letter to Duke Cosmo to see if it is humble enough, and she reads out the text which is now at the end of the scene. They discuss it, and in conclusion he sleepily comments:

The only way an unpopular and embarrassing man can get a job that gives him enough free time is by crawling on his belly.

VIRGINIA (*hugging him*)   Shall we have a big house there?

GALILEO   Time, that's the main thing, my dear, time!

Virginia expresses no particular joy about going to court.

4

Galileo has exchanged the Venetian republic for the court of Florence. The discoveries he has made with the help of the telescope are met with disbelief by the court scholars.

The first part, up to the quarrel between the two boys, is close to the final text, apart from the substitution of the court chamberlain for Cosmo's tutor and the fact that in the earliest typescript Mrs. Sarti's opening speech was about a third of its subsequent length. After that, however, the scene was, in the main, differently written (again, without Federzoni) and incorporated scene 5a, thus reducing the plague scene to 5b only. In this version the reason given for Cosmo's sudden departure was not

the court ball but "a particularly important message," leading
the three representatives of orthodox physics to continue the
speculations with which they made their original appearance.

> I wonder what sort of a message His Highness got? I don't
> like those cases of illness in the old town—The message
> couldn't possibly have anything to do with that! The medi-
> cal faculty is quite certain that ... (*There is a knock on the door
> downstairs. Mrs. Sarti opens it. Virginia comes in with a traveling
> bag*) (p. 37)

And so into 5a.

The preceding argument between Galileo and the three scholars (who in the typescript were simply Professors A, B, and C,
before being distinguished in the revised versions as astronomer, mathematician and theologian) is the same in substance,
but largely different in form. There is no formal dispute, no
attempt to use Latin, no accompanying court ladies; the dialogue is slacker and more repetitive. Galileo's references to his
work with the employees of the Venice arsenal and to the sailors
are not yet included (p. 36). On the other hand, he begins his
immediately preceding speech with:

> You must realize that it is up to you to set an example and
> trust your reason. That the meanest stableboy is waiting to
> be encouraged and challenged to trust your reason.

The next lines about "doctrines believed to be unshakeable are
beginning to totter" were already there in the first typescript.

The cannibalized 5a is somewhat differently arranged, since
Galileo appears at the top of the stairs, chuckling at the scholars'
panicky departure, sees Virginia and asks what she is doing here
(when she should be at her convent school). Virginia's presence
in this scene was in fact an amendment to the first typescript,
which originally gave her lines to the neighbor's wife. Sarti
then announced that the neighbor had arranged a carriage to
take them all away, but Brecht changed this to "The court is
sending a carriage" and added the lackey's speech which in this
version finished with a friendly message from Cosmo to Andrea.

After Mrs. Sarti's "But it's not reasonable" (p. 38) Galileo adds:

And I can tell you another reason. In times like these nobody can say how long he's going to remain alive. (*He smiles*) So let's go and paint more stars on the lens. (*Goes into his study*)
The first two of these sentences were added in pen to the original typescript.

5b [5]
Undaunted even by the plague, Galileo continues his investigations.

Originally, after the old woman's "Maybe your mother is there too," Andrea replied "No, she's dead." Brecht, however, amended this on the typescript to read as now. Otherwise the differences from the final text are insignificant. Conceivably this scene was a last-minute addition to the first typescript. The numbering and typing seem to suggest it.

6 [5 on first typescript, 6 in revised versions]
1616: The Collegium Romanum, the research institute of the Vatican, confirms Galileo's discoveries.

Virtually the same as the final text, apart from the ending, which in the first typescript (later reworded) read:
(*The astronomer escorts him in*)
THE ASTRONOMER   That was him, Your Eminence.
THE INQUISITOR (*very politely*)   May I look through the tube? I find this tube extremely interesting.

7 [6 in first typescript only]
But the Inquisition places the Copernican doctrine on the Index (March 5, 1616).

Though the structure and general gist of this, the ball scene, are the same as in the final version, there are considerable differ-

ences in the dialogue. Partly this is due to the fact that
Ludovico, who makes his first appearance here, is not specifi-
cally identified with the aristocracy or even, in the first typescript, given a surname: hence the absence of the first secretary's reference to "All the great families of Italy," with their
resounding names. Doppone also makes a last brief entry,
speaking jerkily like Mr. Jingle:

GALILEO   I've concluded my business here.

DOPPONE   Yes, I know—known to one and all—brilliant tri-
    umph—sat at your feet myself—epicircle and all that.

Neither Galileo's verse ("Your tucker, Thaïs, is askew") nor the
Lorenzo de' Medici madrigal are included. The old cardinal
does not appear, and Bellarmine and Barberini are in different
disguises, the former as a fox, the latter as a donkey.

In Galileo's argument with these two cardinals some of the key
phrases are already there, such as Barberini's reference to astronomy as "the itch," Galileo's pronouncement "I believe in
reason" (only uttered once however), Bellarmine's account of
the Campagna peasants whose situation can only be justified by
positing a Higher Being, and his objection that Galileo is accusing God of "the juiciest boners in astronomy" (p. 51). Bellarmine's reference to star charts and navigation, however, is once
again missing, as is the subsequent bandying of Biblical texts
and Barberini's "Welcome to Rome..." (p. 49) to which it leads.
Instead the dialogue runs (after "the itch"):

BELLARMINE   Unfortunately not only have the new theories
    displaced our good earth, which the Almighty designated
    as our dwelling place, from the center of the cosmos, in an
    almost contemptuous way, but the assumption of utterly
    incredible distances in the cosmos makes the world seem so
    tiny that the interest which God evidently takes in the
    human race becomes almost impossible to understand.

GALILEO   As the Collegium Romanum has at last admit-
    ted . . .

BELLARMINE   What we feel is, that to say it's easier to explain
    phenomena by positing that the earth moves and the sun
    stands still, than by accepting the Ptolemaic cycles and
    epicycles, is a wholly admirable thing, risks nothing and is

all right for mathematicians. But suppose one tried to suggest that the sun is really at the center of our world and
rotates only round itself without moving across from east
to west while the earth circles round the sun at immense
speed, then that would be a very risky affair, don't you
think, because it would upset philosophy and the theologians, who are awkward customers and what's more it
would make the scriptures untrue.

BARBERINI   But don't you see, Bellarmine, the scriptures
don't satisfy his reason? Whereas Copernicus does . . .

After Barberini, leading Bellarmine aside, has asked Galileo
about the possibility of God giving the stars irregular movements, Galileo makes much the same reply as in the final text,
but forgets himself and calls the future pope "my dear man."
Then the instruction to the secretaries not to take the discussion
down comes some two dozen lines later than in the final text,
just before Bellarmine formally tells Galileo of the Holy Office's
decision. This is not repeated by the secretary, but in the revised versions Bellarmine on leaving instructs the secretaries to
"Make a note of the fact that I have today informed Signor
Galileo of the decree of the Holy Office concerning the Copernican doctrine."

The remainder of the scene, with the inquisitor, is almost as in
the final text, except that he enters with two ladies, saying:

Oh, truly I don't know half what you do. You're so much
crueller than I ever could be.

and in asking Virginia about her engagement omits the words
"your fiancé comes of a distinguished family" (p. 53).

8 [*Transformation scene*]

This conversation with the little monk has no title, and is presumably intended to be played before the curtain. Its general
direction, and much of its dialogue, have remained constant
since the first typescript, though Brecht continually added to it.
Notable differences in the first version are:

(1) The start:

THE LITTLE MONK   You're right.

GALILEO   Haven't you read the Index Congregation's decree?

THE LITTLE MONK   I have read it.

GALILEO   After that you can't go on saying I'm right, wearing the habit you wear.

THE LITTLE MONK   I haven't been able to sleep for four nights (etc.).

(2) In the first typescript Galileo's next speech ran:

See that man down there hiding behind the oleanders and peeping up now and again? Since the cardinal inquisitor looked through my tube I've never lacked for company. They're very interested in criminals in Rome. I'll give him one of my tubes to help him observe me better.

THE LITTLE MONK   Please believe me when I say that I have nothing to do with that man and the people who sent him. I'm a mathematician.

GALILEO   And I'm a criminal.

This was removed in revision. Then, after the little monk's long speech about his peasant family, ending "a great goodness of soul?" (p. 57), Galileo originally went straight to the speech about the Priapus (p. 58). The first part of his comment on the situation of the peasants was added on the first typescript, but not the passage about the oyster and the pearls. The important exchange about whether the truth will out ("Truth prevails only when we make it prevail," (p. 58) was added in the process of revision. The ensuing sentence about "divine patience" is not in this version.

9 [8 or 7 in first typescript]

After a silence of eight years Galileo feels encouraged by the enthronement of a new pope, himself a scientist, to resume his research in the forbidden field. The sunspots.

Apart from the penultimate scene, this is the most heavily

amended of them all. In place of Federzoni there is the "elderly scholar," while, in the first typescript only, "the housekeeper" figured instead of Mrs. Sarti. The exchanges with Ludovico are entirely different, as well as shorter; again Ludovico is no aristocrat, and his nervousness about his prospective father-in-law's theories seems to stem from hints dropped at the university where he is a student without private means. The order of events also underwent subsequent changes.

Thus the scene opens with Galileo demonstrating the behavior of floating bodies. He begins with an extended version of the remarks later put after the experiment with the needle (p. 64):

> GALILEO   The aim of science is not to open the door to everlasting wisdom, but to set a limit to everlasting error. Philosophy for the most part is limitless, wild and indefinite, but truth is restricted and contained in small examples. A main cause of poverty in the sciences is the illusion of wealth. We only conquer nature by obeying her. Whatever counts as a cause when we are observing counts as a rule when we are putting something into effect. By observing the small errors on which the great philosophies are erected we arrived in the course of the summer at all kinds of concepts which have been obstructing the advance of science ever since Aristotle's time. Such as cold and thinness, dampness and length, from which some people think they can construct a whole world if they put the words together the right way.

Andrea then puts the Aristotelian case, about the ice and the needle, going on to describe Galileo's disproof of it while Galileo demonstrates. When he succeeds they all laugh, leading the women to make their remarks about laughter (p. 64) up to Sarti's "Who knows?"

Mucius then appears, and is dealt with very much as in the final text. Then after Galileo has gone into his study Virginia and Mrs. Sarti have their chat about horoscopes (p. 61), in its final form—an episode which was not, however, in the first typescript—before Andrea starts asking Galileo about sunspots, saying he has read Fabricius' book. The dialogue here is largely different. Thus when the elderly scholar asks Galileo "Is it really right to keep one's mouth shut?" Galileo replies with the Keuner story about the man who was asked if he would serve his enemy, served him for seven years till he died, and then bundled up his corpse, scrubbed out the room, breathed deeply and replied "No." Only Galileo tells it, in the first typescript, of "Mr. Sarrone, a philosopher in Modena," amended to "the Cretan philosopher Keunos, who was much loved by the Cretans for his libertarian views." As the others laugh Andrea shakes his head and (in the revised versions) says he doesn't care for the story.

Gaffone the rector makes his brief appearance, as on p. 61, followed by some twenty lines of dialogue between the two women, including Virginia's remark about "a very high ecclesiastic" (p. 60), some references to signs of official surveillance, and an inquiry to Andrea about his fiancée:

VIRGINIA   How's Jessica? Are you still quarreling?

ANDREA (*laughing*)   No, I've found out now why she didn't want to marry me. Pangs of conscience. Because astronomers are unholy people, you know. Of course that wasn't a very serious obstacle. We're together again. (*Goes upstairs*)

MRS. SARTI [in the revised versions]   She knows she's doing well for herself. Her father's just an ordinary artisan . . .

Ludovico enters in traveling clothes, followed by a servant, saying he has got to speak to Galileo, about a rumor. Is he writing a book on sunspots? Galileo says what nonsense; did Ludovico come all the way to ask that?

LUDOVICO   I hope you understand. They're all talking about Copernicus again in connection with these sunspots. And I was hoping you weren't getting involved. I've already had hints dropped at the university.

GALILEO   Oh, so you're frightened?

Like the final Ludovico, this one brings the news that Barberini may soon be pope. Much of Galileo's speech in the first typescript about what his election might mean for science—e.g.

This means nothing less than the start of a new century of the arts and sciences. No more fear. Knowledge will be a passion and research a self-indulgence. What a dreadful age, where saying what is, is considered a crime. But now people will say, what a dreadful age it was. Who's scared of discoveries now, they'll ask. Who's got reason to be?

—was shifted to immediately in front of his "Put a grid over the screen" (p. 67), so that his order to focus the telescope on the sun follows instantly on the news, without any of the teasing of Ludovico which is found in the final text. Ludovico begs him not to join in the sunspot controversy, to which Galileo answers:

> . . . Are they to say Galileo hasn't got the courage to open his mouth? People are looking at me, man. The earth rotates—it's I who say that, do you get me? If I keep silent it'll stop!

LUDOVICO   Virginia, I know I love you. But I can't marry you if this is how things are. I haven't any money of my own.

Andrea suggests Galileo should help them. "My Jessica has come to terms with her conscience, but after all she's only risking hell. I don't know what she'd do if the city clergy stopped getting their communion vessels from her father the silversmith. A threat of that sort is far worse." But Galileo turns away to his collaborators.

LUDOVICO   Virginia, I love you, and I love your father the way he is. But his concerns are not mine; I don't understand them and I haven't got the courage.

And because Galileo remains silent, Virginia gives him back his ring.

Thus virtually everything in the final text from Mrs. Sarti's "Pretty near!" (p. 67) to Andrea's interruption (69) is missing in this version. Galileo goes straight on to his big speech (p. 69), including already such key phrases as "My aim is not to prove that I've been right, but to find out whether or not I have been," and "And if there's something we hope to find, we'll regard it with particular distrust when we do find it." As Ludovico embraces Virginia and leaves, Galileo continues (from "yet go on talking")

> Then we'll crush this stupidity underfoot, eh, my boy? We'll peel off its skin to carry as our banner. And we'll write on it in blood: Look out! Or, rather, in ink—which

is more dangerous. At last we're going to bang those narrow-minded heads together till they burst like eggshells. Yes, we're going to make cruel use of our arguments. Perhaps it'll be the first time in history that cruelty has been directed against ignorance. A historic date!

ANDREA   And are you going to write the book on the world systems?

GALILEO   Yes, and not in Latin for the few but in Florentine for the many. Because this book has got to be understood by everybody. For that I need people who work with their hands. Who else is going to want to know the causes of everything? [Then, in the revised versions, as on p. 68 to "she'll probably laugh".] And the peasants who force their plough into the earth, and the weavers at their looms, the people now stirring in every street, are all going to point at the sun and say: It's not a golden coat of arms but a lever. We move it, because it moves us.

Virginia repacks her trousseau, and Andrea closes the scene with his four-line epigram from p. 66.

10 [*9, or 8 in first typescript*]

The Copernican doctrine circulates among the people.

The setting is a street, with a street singer and his wife singing to a hurdy-gurdy and the populace listening from windows. The ballad differs, above all structurally, from that in the final text, and is here translated for the first time:

> Great Galileo told the sun
> (Or so the story says)
> To give up turning around the earth
> On which it casts its rays.
> What a to-do!
> The sun has started turning around itself
> Not around me and you.
>
> And immediately the sun had ceased
> Reserving all its light for us

The verger gave up following after the priest
The apprentice after his boss.
No doubt you've guessed:
They all want to turn around themselves
And do what suits them best.

The bricklayer who was building the house
Is now its occupier.
The woodcutter who chops down trees
Puts the wood on his own fire.
What a to-do!
The woodcutter was telling his wife
His feet were frozen through.

I saw two housewives shopping for fish
The clock was striking twelve.
The fishwife took out a piece of bread
And ate the fish herself.
What a to-do!
The fishwife thought she'd have fish for once
Very nutritious too.

The master appears, the maids don't get up
The footmen omit to bow.
The master observes to his great surprise
Nothing turns around him now.
No doubt you've guessed:
The footmen have their hands too full
The maids won't allow them to rest.

THE WOMAN

I too had been dancing out of line
And said to my husband, "My dear
Whatever you do for me might well be done
By any other star."

THE MAN

What a to-do!

My wife ought to turn around no one but me—
That's always been my view.

The princes clean their boots with their own hands.
The emperor bakes his own bread.
The soldiers no longer obey commands
But stroll in the streets instead.
No doubt you've guessed:
There was too much work for too many to do.
In the end they had to protest.

(*In a confidential undertone*)

The cardinals all stood in St. Peter's Square
When the pope showed himself to the crowd
The cardinals acted as if he weren't there.
And went on talking much too loud.
What a to-do!
Their eminences have taken to kissing their own feet—
You know who that's due to.

Three archangels came down to earth, to complain
It should praise God more audibly.
But the earth said; "There are so many worlds in space
Why do they have to pick on me?"
No doubt you've guessed:
If our earth is just one of a whole lot of worlds
It can share such chores with the rest.

At the end of the ballad *"a Jesuit crosses the square. He crouches when he hears the song, and goes off like a drenched poodle. The people laugh and throw down coins."*

A note then says that the scene can develop into a ballet. *"A popular carnival celebration can be shown in the style of Brueghel's* The Battle Between Carnival and Lent. *Following the first verse of the ballad a carnival procession can move across the square, including a man dressed as a BIBLE with a hole in it, and a cart with a monk stretching out, trying with both hands to hold back a collapsing ST. PETER'S THRONE. Then after the last verse the MOON, SUN, EARTH and*

PLANETS can appear and demonstrate the new system of motion in a dance, to a severe musical setting."

11 [*10, or 9 in first typescript*]

1633. The Inquisition summons the world-famous scholar to Rome.

This short scene in the Medici palace is close to the final text, except that the episode with Vanni the iron founder from Virginia's "There's Mr. Vanni" on p. 74 to Galileo's "and you'll lose your arm" on p. 76 is not in this version. Instead a man passes to whom Galileo vainly calls out "Galliardo! Galliardo!," commenting:

> That was the director of artillery equipment. He must have seen me. He usually eats out of my hand. Today he's running away as if he thought I was infectious.

Then a student passes, who wants to stop and talk to Galileo but is called away by his tutor. Just before Cosmo's entrance Galileo comments:

> After all, we're not here to get polite attentions paid us. I crawled into this position years ago on all fours, since anybody wanting to introduce the truth—or even a morsel of it—into a place like this can only enter through the lowest hole of all, the one for dogs. But it was a good thing to do, as now they'll have to protect me. There's something in the air. If I hadn't got the pope's imprimatur for it I'd think it was the book. But they know the book has passed the censors. The pope would flatly reject any attempt to make a trap for me out of it. And after all the grand duke is my pupil. I shall complain to him.

The passage about Sagredo's invitation (p. 77) and the appearance of the cardinal inquisitor were added before this in revision. Galileo's resolve to escape in Volpi's wine cart is not in this version; nor is the last sentence of the final text.

12 [*11, or 10 in first typescript*]

The pope.

This scene is divided by a "transformation" into two halves, of which the second is not in the later versions and is given in full below. The first half, in the pope's own room, is a slightly shorter version of the final text. It excludes notably the reference to Galileo's star charts and the maritime cities' need for them, the mention of his powerful friends, leading to the pope's order "Hands off!" (p. 80) with the inquisitor's cynical reply and the pope's comment that "Even his thinking is sensual." This half accordingly ends with "Not the whole world, but the best part of it." Then, after the transformation:

Another room. At the window, Galileo, waiting. Here too the stamping and shuffling of many feet of the gathering congregation is heard. In the foreground two officials of the Inquisition.

OFFICIAL (*sotto voce to his companion*) He's got good nerves. He's having a look at all his enemies.

GALILEO I hope the interview with His Holiness will take place before the session. It's important for me, as I want to ask for my evidence and proofs to be investigated before any decision is come to. It is of course quite impossible for me to make any kind of statement in a matter of such importance for the world of science without my evidence and proofs first getting a most scrupulous hearing and examination. I'd be glad of a little water. (*The first official pours him some water from a carafe on the table. Galileo reaches for it uncertainly and spills some.*)

SECOND OFFICIAL (*when the first returns*) Having a look at his enemies, but at nothing else. Had you forgotten he's half blind?

GALILEO I suppose His Holiness really does want to see me?

FIRST OFFICIAL Definitely.

GALILEO Then I'd prefer to wait in another room if that's possible.

SECOND OFFICIAL It's not possible. You wouldn't like His Holiness to arrive and find you weren't here, because you couldn't stand the shuffling.

GALILEO (*looks at him blankly*)

SECOND OFFICIAL   Yes, you must be beginning to realize it isn't just a handful of people gathering there to testify against you. It's the most distinguished minds in Italy, the most learned scholars, the stars of all the universities, in short it's everybody.

GALILEO   Yes. (*He turns to his window again*)

FIRST OFFICIAL   He must feel rather like someone before the flood who was expecting a spring shower, then the real rain came, then came an endless downpour and that turned into the flood, don't you think?

(*A high official appears. Galileo turns to face him and makes a deep bow. He thinks it is the pope*)

THE HIGH OFFICIAL   Has this person eaten?

FIRST OFFICIAL   He was served a substantial meal.

THE HIGH OFFICIAL   The session later may go on a long time. (*Goes out*)

GALILEO (*has risen to his feet in confusion*)   Gentlemen, I know His Holiness personally, having met him once at Cardinal Bellarmine's. But my eyesight is not what it was, and I must beg you to tell me when he is coming.

FIRST OFFICIAL   Shall be done, even though you wouldn't oblige us by making a proper meal.

GALILEO   The fact that the gentleman who just left used the word "later" when speaking about the Inquisition's session today is surely a definite sign that His Holiness wants to speak to me first?

FIRST OFFICIAL (*shrugs his shoulders*)

GALILEO   Did you say something?

FIRST OFFICIAL   I shrugged my shoulders.

13 [*12 or 11 in first typescript*]

Apart from the fact that Federzoni's subsequent lines are given to the elderly scholar, that the end of the scene (after the blackout) was at first conceived as a short scene on its own, and that Andrea's insults ("Wine barrel!" etc., p. 84) are missing, this version is not much different from the final one. In the first typescript a speech for the elderly scholar was written in; it appears to belong after Andrea's "He couldn't write his book there" (p. 82) but was omitted in revision.

> Clearly he didn't pay enough attention to that part. It's true that he said: It's not enough to know something, you have to be able to prove it. And he held his tongue till he was forty-six years old, and only spoke when he was able to prove his knowledge. But then he talked about his proofs to people with bunged-up ears, not to those who were dissatisfied with what had been believed in up to then but to those who were content with it. His mistake was to think that the choice between speaking in a republic and speaking in a grand duchy wasn't an astronomical problem.

14 [*13, or 12 in first typescript*]

1633–1642. A prisoner of the Inquisition, Galileo continues his scientific studies up to his death. He manages to smuggle his principal work out of Italy.

Like 9, this is a heavily altered scene with substantial differences from the final text. To sum them up briefly: (a) Galileo has conspired with the stove-fitter to conceal and smuggle out his writings; (b) Virginia reads him aphorisms by Montaigne, not scribbled texts provided by the archbishop; (c) his big speech (pp. 93–94) is differently conceived, though containing one or two phrases that recur in its final form; it omits all but the most general references to science's social implications, accuses himself only of failure to speak up for reason, and includes neither the warning of a "universal outcry of horror," nor the proposal for a scientists' Hippocratic oath; (d) it is only *after* this speech that Virginia leaves the room and Galileo admits to having written the *Discorsi;* (e) Andrea's enthusiastic reaction in praise of the "new ethics" is missing, as also is Galileo's counter-speech of self-abasement ("Welcome to the gutter" p. 93); thus there are no dramatic reversals of feeling between the handing-over of the *Discorsi* and the end of the scene.

In the opening stage direction Galileo is described as *"old and ill, and moves like a blind man.*" Virginia solicitously serves him his supper ("Now let's eat up our good soup, and try not to spill a drop of it"). He then complains that the stove isn't working properly, and asks when the stove-fitter is coming. The official in the antechamber (the monk of the final text) complains to Virginia that manuscripts have been leaking out:

Don't forget that the *Dialogue Concerning the Two Chief World Systems* was smuggled to Holland from here. And now they've intercepted a letter to Strasbourg, saying a manuscript will be coming. It must already have got out. Who took it? (*Enter a big, broad-shouldered man, the stove-fitter. He has his tools with him*)

The stove-fitter is indeed the agent responsible, but this time he has brought the manuscript back because "They are after us. Villagio has been arrested." The doctor then appears, to check on Galileo's eyesight.

THE OFFICIAL   Can he or can he not see?

THE DOCTOR (*shrugs his shoulders*)   I don't know; very little, I'd say. I'll be making my report.

Virginia then comes in again to read to her father. (The following passage was published in 1957 in *Versuche 15* as an addendum to the play.)

VIRGINIA   Shall I read to you?

GALILEO   Yes, those inscriptions on the beams of M. de Montaigne's library. But only the ones I've marked.

VIRGINIA (*gets the book and reads*)   54th Inscription: Without leaning .

GALILEO   Is that all?

VIRGINIA   Yes.

GALILEO   But that depends on at least three things: the force of the thrust applied to one, the visibility of the objective and the solidity of the base. Some advice! Go on.

VIRGINIA   52nd inscription: I do not understand.

GALILEO   That's good. It's a starting point.

VIRGINIA   13: It is possible and it is not possible.[1]

GALILEO   Good, so long as he gives reasons.

(1) Sextus Empiricus, *Hypotyposes*, I, 21

VIRGINIA   5: It's no more like this than like that or like neither.[2]

GALILEO   Provided one goes on looking.

VIRGINIA   21: He who knows that he knows doesn't know how he knows.[3]

GALILEO   Again, that's very good. But it all tastes of defeatism.

VIRGINIA   10: What are heaven and earth and sea, with all they embrace, against the sum of sums of the immeasurable whole?[4]

GALILEO   One has to start, though. Make a note.

VIRGINIA   2: He gave them curiosity, that he might torment them.[5]

GALILEO   Rubbish.

VIRGINIA   15: Man is too fragile.[6]

GALILEO   Not fragile enough.

VIRGINIA   20: Be wise in moderation, that you may not grow stupid.[7]

GALILEO   Go on.

VIRGINIA   42: Men are not confused by things but by opinions about things.[8]

GALILEO   That could be wrong too. Who confuses the opinions?

VIRGINIA   Should I make a note of that?

GALILEO   No.

VIRGINIA   19: I am a human; nothing human is alien to me.[9]

GALILEO   Good.

(2) Ibid., 1, 19, cited Montaigne *Essays*, 2, 12.

(3) 1 Corinthians 8:2. The A. V. quotation is "And if any man think that he knoweth anything, he knoweth nothing yet as he ought to know."

(4) Lucretius, *De Rerum Natura*, 6, cited Montaigne *Essays* 2, 12.

(5) Ecclesiastes 1, of which verse 13 in A.V. reads "And I gave my heart to seek and search out by wisdom concerning all things that are done under heaven: this sore travail hath God given to the sons of man to be exercised therewith" (*Essays* 2, 17)

(6) Keramos anthropos. Wrongly attributed to Romans 9.

(7) Ecclesiastes 7: ". . . neither make thyself over wise: why shouldest thou destroy thyself?"

(8) Epictetus, cited by Stobaeus. (*Essays* 1, 14)

(9) Terence, *Heautontimoroumenos* Act 1 (*Essays*, 2, 2) This was Karl Marx's favorite saying.

VIRGINIA   37: God has created man like a shadow. Who can judge him once the sun has set?[10]
(*Galileo is silent*)
VIRGINIA   17: You should neither fear your last day nor yearn for it.[11]
GALILEO   I used to find the first point difficult; now it's the second.
VIRGINIA   14: A wondrous thing is goodness.[12]
GALILEO   Louder!
VIRGINIA (*louder*)   A wondrous thing is goodness.

A much shorter alternative to the whole passage, which is also given in the first typescript, with Galileo and Virginia going over proofs, replaces it in the revised versions. In this Virginia reads Galileo the extract from the *Discorsi* which appears at the end of the previous scene in the final text.

At this point Andrea enters, and the dialogue is fairly close to the final text, up to where Galileo asks about his scientific friends: "Has my recantation helped them to mend their ways?" (p. 89). Andrea hardly answers the question; he says nothing about Fulganzio, or, of course, Federzoni; the immediately preceding exchange about Descartes is also missing. Instead the text continues:

ANDREA   For a time there was a considerable difference of opinion about you. Some of your former friends insisted that you had recanted because of services you still hoped to render physics by remaining alive. Because of such works as only you could write.
GALILEO (*brusquely*)   There are no such works.
ANDREA   How do you mean? If you hadn't written the [*Dialogue*] . . .
GALILEO   Then someone else would have written it.
ANDREA   So that wasn't your motive?

(10) Ecclesiastes 7. Or more probably 6: 12, which reads "For who knoweth what is good for man in this life, all the days of his vain life which he spendeth as a shadow? For who can tell a man what shall be after him under the sun?" (*Essays* 2, 12)
(11) *Essays* 2, 37, after Martial, 10.
(12) Plato, *Cratylus.*

GALILEO Shortly after my trial various people who had known me earlier were good enough to credit me with all kinds of noble intentions. I wouldn't have this. To me it simply signified a decline of the critical faculties, brought about by the fact that they found drastic physical changes in me.

After carefully considering all the circumstances, extenuating and otherwise, it is impossible to conclude that a man could arrive at this state of—call it obedience, from any other motive than an undue fear of death. (*Pause*) That is not to deny (*Addressing Virginia*) the profound regret which I, as a son of the church, felt when my superiors induced me, by the most weighty of all arguments, to see the error of my ways. As a rule nothing less than threatening a man with death will serve to dissuade him from something of which his reason, that most dangerous of all God's gifts, has persuaded him. I fully understood that I could now only expect that hell which, so the poet tells, is inhabited by people who have gambled away the gifts of the mind and are accordingly without hope.

He tells Andrea that science should be able to get along without authority (including his own). "Authority and absence of truth doubtless go together, and so do truth and absence of authority." Andrea then sums up the case against him, as it emerges in this version:

... a lot of people everywhere were hanging on your words and actions because they felt what you stood for was not a particular theory about the movements of the stars but the freedom to theorize in any field. Not just for any particular thoughts, in other words, but for the right to think in the first place, which was now being threatened. So as soon as these people heard you recanting all you had said they concluded that it was not merely certain thoughts about celestial motions that were being discredited but thinking itself that was being regarded as unholy, since it operates by means of causes and proofs.

Virginia replies that the church has not forbidden science, but has even absorbed Galileo's main discoveries. "Only he mustn't attack the opinions of theology, which is an entirely different science." The big speech follows, starting very much as it does in the final text (p. 93):

GALILEO   In my free time, and I've got plenty of that, I have asked myself how the world of science, of which I no longer consider myself a member, even if I still know a thing or two about its pursuits, will judge my conduct. (*In lecture style, hands folded over his paunch*) It will have to take into account whether it is good enough for its members to provide it with a given number of sentences, for instance about the tendencies of falling bodies or the motions of certain stars. I have, as I said, excluded myself from the scientific way of thinking; however, I take it that when faced with the threat of destruction that world will be in no position to lay down more far-reaching duties for its members, e.g., that of collaborating in its own maintenance as science. Even a wool merchant, in addition to buying cheap and providing good wool, has to worry about his trade being permitted at all and without restriction. On that principle no member of the scientific world is logically entitled to point to his own possible contributions to research if he has failed to honor his profession as such and to defend it against any use of force. This, however, is a business of vast scope. For science consists, not in a license to subordinate facts to opinions, but in an obligation to subordinate opinions to facts. It is not in any position to permit restriction of these sentences or to establish them only for "certain views" and "those particular facts." In order to make sure that it can apply these sentences unrestrictedly at any one time, science has to fight to be respected in every sphere. For science and humanity as a whole happen to be in the same boat. So it can't say "What business is it of mine if the boat springs a leak at the other end?" [A passage cut from the original typescript here is repeated between two asterisks on p. 296 below.] Science has no use for people who fail to stick up for reason. It must expel them in ignominy, because, however many truths science knows, it could have no future in a world of lies. If the hand that feeds it occasionally seizes it unpredictably by the throat then humanity will have to chop it off. That is why science cannot tolerate a person like me in its ranks.

VIRGINIA (*with passion*)   But you have been received in the ranks of the faithful. (cf. p. 95)

GALILEO   That is the position. In my view I have wrecked every experiment that might have been injurious to blind faith. Only my ingrained habit of making allowances for improbabilities would lead me to say "nearly every experiment." Plainly nothing but the irresistible arguments put forward by the Inquisition could have convinced me of the harmfulness of my researches.

ANDREA (*in a strangled voice*)   Yes.

Virginia leaves the room, and Galileo at once slyly admits that he has had relapses (p. 90). The dialogue then roughly anticipates that in the final text, up to where Andrea takes up the manuscript of the *Discorsi*, with the difference that Andrea never assumes that the work has been irrevocably handed over to "the monks" as occurs, with consequently heightened tension, in the final text. Nor does Galileo simply tell him to "Put it under your coat" (p. 91), but makes more elaborate and self-protective hints as to how he might take it away. Then as Andrea leaves, there is a significantly different exchange, to which the section in square brackets was added in the course of revision:

ANDREA (*who has concealed the manuscript on him*)   Yes, I'm going now. [I realize it's as if a tower had collapsed which was enormously tall and thought to be unshakeable. The noise it made collapsing was louder than the noise of the builders and their machines during the whole period of its construction, and the column of dust which its collapse caused was even higher than it had been. But conceivably when the dust disperses it may turn out that although the top twelve stories fell down the bottom thirty are still standing. In which case the building could be developed further. Is that what you mean? It would be supported by the fact that the inconsistencies in our science are still all in evidence and have been sifted. The difficulty seems to have increased, but at the same time the necessity has become greater.] I'm glad I came. (*He holds out his hand to him*)

GALILEO (*does not take it; hesitantly*)   My eyesight is bad, Andrea. I can't see any more, I only stare. You had better go. (*He walks slowly to* [*the globe and sees if it is shut*) I'm not unresponsive to the kindnesses I'm always being shown. Travelers passing through remember me, and so on. I don't misinterpret such things.] I'm glad too to have talked to you, and to have found you as you are. You have had experiences which could have given you a quite wrong view of what we've always termed the future of reason. But of course, no single man could either bring it to pass or discredit it. *It is too big an affair ever to be contained inside a single head. Reason is something people can be divided into. It can be described as the egoism of all humanity. *Such egoism is not strong enough. But even a person like myself can still see that reason is not coming to an end but beginning. And I still believe that this is a new age. It may look like a bloodstained old harridan, but if so that must be the way new ages look. When light breaks in it does so in the uttermost darkness. While a few places are the scene of the most immense discoveries, which must contribute immeasurably to humanity's resources for happiness, great areas of this world still lie entirely in the dark. In fact the blackness has actually deepened there. Look out for yourself when you travel through Germany with the truth under your coat.

(*Andrea goes out*)

Andrea says nothing about a "devastating analysis" (p. 95). The scene quickly closes, somewhat as in the final text, though not on the word "Clear" but on Galileo's ensuing comment: "That's good. Then he'll be able to see his way."

15 [*14*]

1637. Galileo's book *Discorsi* crosses the Italian border.

Very close to the final text.

3. The American Version, 1944–1947

This English-language version, which Brecht and Laughton worked on from the end of 1944 up to the Hollywood production of July 1947, maintains the general structure of the play, but shortens and very largely rewrites it. The main structural changes are the omission of the first half of scene 4; the cutting of scene 5a off the end of scene 4 and the elimination of it and 5b (the plague scenes); also the cutting of the second half of scene 12 (pp. 287–288 above), with Galileo waiting for the pope. An element of social interest was introduced by making Ludovico an aristocrat and creating two new characters: Federzoni the lens grinder, who helps bring out the point of Galileo's use of the vernacular language, and the iron founder here called Matti, whose function is to appear in scenes 2 and 11 and show that the embryo bourgeoisie is on Galileo's side. Ludovico takes over Doppone's role in scenes 1 and 2; not surprisingly he becomes a little unconvincing. Federzoni too gets some of the elderly scholar's lines in scene 9. In this scene Mucius is cut, in scene 14 the stove-fitter and the doctor. According to Brecht it was Laughton who insisted on transposing the handing-over of the *Discorsi* in this scene so that Galileo's big self-accusatory speech should come after it.

The carnival scene (10) was rewritten entirely, with a new English-language ballad, though the gist of this remained much the same. The actions of the masqueraders and the crowd, while not exactly amounting to the "ballet" proposed in the first version, were described in some detail, finishing with the appearance of the enormous dummy figure of "Galileo, the Bible-killer."

Finally there are no scene titles in the text as published, but short English verses were put at the beginning of each scene,

and at the end of the play, which now finished with the warning:

> May you now guard science' light,
> Kindle it and use it right,
> Lest it be a flame to fall
> Downward to consume us all.

The full text of this version is given on pages 403–467. The
following is a brief scene-by-scene commentary on the changes.
Scene numbers are those of the final text, with the American
version's numbering in square brackets.

1.

The scene begins with the arrival of the Ptolemaic model which
was previously already there. Galileo's speech on the "new age"
is shorter and simpler and more sloppily worded, ("A new age
was coming. I was onto it years ago"), but includes the ships and
the Sienese masons. His second demonstration to Andrea, with
the apple (which is in both the first and the final versions), is cut
from Andrea's "But it's not true" (p. 8) to Galileo's "Aha!" on
p. 9. Ludovico then appears, the gist of the dialogue being much
the same as in the final text, but very much shortened. Galileo's
discussion with Andrea about hypotheses is cut. The procurator, who follows Ludovico's exit, is for some reason a museum
curator; again the dialogue is shortened and simplified, even
vulgarized:

CURATOR   You've never let me down yet, Galilei.

GALILEO   You are always an inspiration to me, Priuli.

The ending of the scene is likewise shorter.

2.

The form of the scene is as in the final text, except that Virginia
makes the presentation, that Matti the (Florentine) iron founder
appears, and that the doge has nothing to say. Note the curator's
"best chamber-of-commerce manner" and the allusion to him as a
businessman, also the new silliness of Virginia as exemplified in
the closing exchanges.

3.

This is the same scene as in the final version, but shortened. It introduces Galileo's remarks about star charts, but cuts the episode with Mrs. Sarti (pp. 24–25) who does not appear at all. Virginia enters earlier—there is no cross-fade as before—and stays long enough to hear Sagredo read out the end of the letter to the grand duke. The scene now ends approximately as in the final text, though rather more abruptly.

4.

The first half of the scene has been cut: Mrs. Sarti's speech, the grand duke's arrival and the episode with the two boys, also Galileo's opening speech and the beginning of the scientific argument up to where Cosmo's three professors are invited to look through the telescope for themselves (p. 33 in the final version). Instead it begins with the philosopher talking Latin and the exchange (p. 32) about the need to use the vernacular for Federzoni's sake. The argument which follows, now interrupted by the court ladies with jarringly improbable comments, follows the same pattern as the final version, though again in shortened form. It introduces notably Galileo's remark, "Why defend shaken teachings? You should be doing the shaking," and the speech that follows about the arsenal workers and the sailors. The professors leave without speculating about Cosmo's hurried departure, now attributed to the state ball.

5.

[is cut]

6. [5]

Apart from the ending, this is a shortened form of the Collegium Romanum scene as we have it. The episode with the two astronomers is cut (from their entry p. 43 to their exit p. 44), apart from the very thin (or in this version infuriated) monk's first remark. His ensuing speech (starting "They degrade the home of mankind") is likewise cut. The scene ends on the little monk's remark about Galileo's having won. Galileo's answer and the appearance of the cardinal inquisitor are omitted. The inscription about astronomical charts which is lowered after the curtain is not found in the other versions.

7. [6]

Again, this is a slightly shortened form of the final text. The great families attending the ball are named, Doppone is omitted, the two cardinals are now lamb and dove, the reference to star charts is new, Barberini swaps Biblical texts with Galileo and welcomes him to Rome, Bellarmine's speech about the Campagna peasants and the "master plan" is cut, the inquisitor greets Virginia with the comment that her fiancé comes "from a fine family." The Lorenzo de' Medici madrigal is still missing.

8. [7]

The scene with the little monk is virtually as in the final version. Most of Galileo's speech about the Priapus is cut, but the beginning is as we now have it, and the phrases about the oyster and the pearl, and the peasants' "divine patience" are included.

9. [8]

The order of events is as in the final text, though the episode with Mucius has been cut. The scene thus starts with Virginia's dialogue with Mrs. Sarti, including the talk about horoscopes. The Keunos story has gone, as have all allusions to Andrea's Jessica. Instead there is the dialogue between the collaborators as the experiment is prepared, including the little monk's remark about "happiness in doubting" but omitting Andrea's account of how he has been observing the sun's rays in the attic. The whole episode with Ludovico corresponds closely to the final text, from his entrance on p. 64 to his exit on p. 69, apart from the omission of Mrs. Sarti's long speech (p. 67) and the little monk's immediately preceding remark about God and

physics. The end of the scene too is the same, except that it stops
at the end of Galileo's important speech.

10. [9]

The rewriting of this scene has already been mentioned (p. 297).

11. [10]

Close to the final text. Half the Vanni episode is here, though
he is called Matti (as in scene 2) and it ends at the equivalent of
"please remember that you have friends in every branch of
industry" (p. 75). (The rest appears to have been written at the
same time, but not included in the published text.) Galliardo
and the student do not appear. The passages about Sagredo's
invitation and the possibility of escape were not in the earlier
version.

12. [11]

The inquisitor's long speech is shortened by half, notably by the
references to papal politics and the abolition of top and bottom,
with the ensuing quotation from Aristotle. The exchange about
Galileo's self-indulgence is new. That about the conclusion of
his book is omitted. The ending, after "but the best part of it"
(p. 81) is new; the final stage instruction (which does not read
like Brecht) being found only in this version. Otherwise this
part of the scene is as we now have it. As already noted, the
second part of the scene is cut.

13. [12]

From Andrea's cry "not to know the truth" (p. 82) to his imitation of Galileo is cut. The rest is as in the final version except
for Federzoni's remark about Andrea not getting paid, and the
shifting of Andrea's "Unhappy is the land that breeds no hero"
to immediately before Galileo's answer.

14. [*13*]

The order of events has been shifted, and is the same as in the final text. There is now nothing about the Inquisition's suspicions that manuscripts are being smuggled out, and the episodes with the doctor and the stove-fitter are cut. The "weekly letter to the archbishop," whose discussion replaces that of the Montaigne inscriptions, is about half as long as in the final text. Andrea's ensuing dialogue with Galileo is as in the final text up to the point where Virginia leaves the room (which now comes very much earlier); that is to say it discusses what has happened to his former collaborators. The revelation of the *Discorsi* then comes before the analysis of Galileo's motives and conduct, which is now without the passages quoted on pp. 293 ff., but introduces Andrea's gradually waning praise of Galileo's behavior, from Andrea's "Two new branches of science" (p. 461) to Galileo's "It was not" (p. 462). The "welcome to the gutter" speech which follows is new, though shorter than its final version. The big speech is likewise about one-third shorter than in the final text, omitting notably the phrases "But can .we turn our backs on the people and still remain scientists?" and "Science, Sarti, is involved in both battles," as well as the suggestion of a Hippocratic oath and the picture of scientists as "inventive dwarfs." The shift of emphasis from intellectual to social betrayal, the stressing of the liberating popular effects of the new science, finally the introduction of allusions to the horrors of the atom bomb, can all best be seen by comparing the actual text with that of the earlier version (pp. 462–463).

Galileo's view of "the new age," in the final exchanges, is expressed in the same terms as in the previous version. Again he ignores Andrea's hand, without comment. There is no mention of Andrea's journey through Germany, and the scene ends with Virginia's final remark.

15. [*14*]

The scene is broadly similar to its earlier version, but has been wholly rewritten, including the song. Among other things, the witch's house is shown, and the children steal her milk jug and kick it over.

4. The Berlin Version, 1953–1956

We can now summarize what happened when Brecht decided to make a new German version of the play after his return to Berlin. Two principal texts are involved: that published in his *Versuche 14* in 1955, and the final revised text of the collected *Stücke* (1957), which incorporates minor changes made in the course of Brecht's rehearsals and as a result of the Cologne production in the former year. This version follows the general structure of the American version, giving more or less the same account of characters, incidents, motivations and social substructure. However, it brings back important stretches of dialogue from the first version, eliminating many of the crudities of the American text and giving more elbow-room to the arguments at the cost, of course, of making a considerably longer play.

The characters remain the same as in the American version, apart from the bringing back of Mucius at the beginning of scene 9, and the renaming of Vanni, who no longer figures in scene 2. So do their social roles. The plague scene is restored in a new form by running together 5a and 5b; this, presumably, being something that Brecht had wished to have "in the book" even though, like Laughton, he was excluding it from the acting version. Scene 4 is restored to its full length, scene 15 put back into its old form. The original German text of the ballad in scene 10 has not been restored; instead it has been (freely) re-translated from the English, so as to fit Eisler's setting, though with the addition of the singer's remarks to the crowd. The same applies to the between-scene verses, which were not done in time for the *Versuche* edition. The Lorenzo de' Medici madrigal in scene 7, (which appears to derive from the sixtieth and last stanzas of his Eclogue "La Ritrozia") now makes its appearance for the first time.

The play again begins as in the first version, though Galileo's speech on the "new age" has been slightly expanded; the second demonstration with Andrea and the full conversation with the procurator are restored. In scene 3 the episode with Mrs. Sarti is brought back, leading to the (shortened) conclusion, "They snatch at it" (p. 25), while immediately before her entry Galileo's speech is given a new last sentence: "Thinking is one of the greatest pleasures of the human race" (p. 24). Virginia is now made to leave before the reading of the letter to the grand duke. In scene 4 some of the fatuous remarks of the court ladies (e.g. "Perfect poise!" and "What diction!") are eliminated; the professors' proposal for a formal disputation is new, as is Federzoni's call for new textbooks.

In the plague scene the second half (b) is virtually as in the (revised) first version, but the first half has been revised, notably cutting Galileo's last remarks, with their reference to the uncertainty of remaining alive "in times like these." In the ball scene (7) Galileo's new poem, which could be a quasi-Horatian variant on Herrick's "Delight in Disorder," replaces the English one; while Bellarmine's remarks about the Campagna peasants and the (social) need to attribute all the world's horrors to a "master plan" are restored. In the sunspot scene (9) the episode with Mucius now comes near the start of the scene, which has been correspondingly rewritten; Mrs. Sarti's speech (p. 67) has also been restored, as has Galileo's call for "people who work with their hands" (p. 68), in lieu of the American version's too simple view that scientific work is not worth doing "for less than the population at large." The end of this scene ("I've got to know") is quite new.

In the carnival scene (10) the procession is now described briefly in a single stage direction at the end. In scene 11 the episode with Vanni is extended to emphasize Galileo's sense of security (and of his own comforts). Scene 12 restores the inquisitor's comments on papal politics and introduces the graffito about the Barberinis' love of art, as well as the exchange about condemning the doctrine and keeping its practical applications. For the slight changes in scenes 13 and 14 see pp. 301–302 above. There is in the Brecht-Archive a sketch for the notion of a Hippocratic oath for scientists which was evidently noted down in America (in Brecht's homemade English) but for some reason not then worked into the play. It goes thus:

ingenious dwarfs

Hypocratic
hypocrades Oath

     Had I resisted, the natural sciences might have

          something like the   of the physicians.
      develloped their own Hypöcratic oath

      mankind
Now, the most we can hope for will be a race of ingenious dwarfs who can

be hired for any purpose who will, as on islands, produce whatever

their masters demand.

                 means
      what's the use of progress, if it is a

      leaving behind of mankind? There even

      a state of things could develop, when our

      inventions

[Spelling and spacing as on Brecht's typescript, but not showing his corrections and deletions. From BBA 609/91, reproduced in Schumacher: *Drama und Geschichte*, 1965, p. 208.]

THE TRIAL
OF LUCULLUS

Texts by Brecht

Notes on the Opera *The Condemnation of Lucullus**

The radio play *The Trial of Lucullus* forms the basis of the opera *The Condemnation of Lucullus*. The earlier work concluded with the end of the trial and the lines:

> The court
> Withdraws to consider its verdict.

Scene 14 "The Verdict" has been added from the opera. The title, however, has been retained to help distinguish the play from the later work.

The opera does not include the testimony of the stone figures on the frieze. Instead, the shades of those represented on the frieze are summoned as witnesses. Here the new scene (cf. p. 114):

Bringing in the Frieze

THE SLAVES WITH THE FRIEZE
Out of life and into death
We haul our load ungrudgingly.
For years our time was not our own
Unknown to us our destination.
So we follow the new voice

*Passages not in *Trial of Lucullus* translated by the Editors.

As we did the old one. Why ask questions?
We leave nothing behind, expect nothing.

LUCULLUS

You, jurors of the dead, behold my frieze.
A captured king, Tigranes of Pontus.
His sloe-eyed queen. Look at her lovely thighs.
A man with a little cherry tree, eating a cherry.
Two virgins with a tablet bearing the names of 53 cities.
Two legionaries
One standing, one dying and saluting his general.
My cook with a fish.

CHORUS

See how they've built themselves a monument
Of stony shades of long-vanished victims, fashioned
To speak on earth or to be silent on earth.
Helpless witnesses called to represent
In the light, at the victor's command, those flung
To the ground, robbed of breath, struck dumb and forgot-
    ten
Ready for silence and ready for speech.

THE SPEAKER

Shade, the jurors have taken
Note of your triumphal frieze.
They are eager to learn more about
Your triumph than the frieze relates.
They suggest that those
Depicted upon your frieze
Be summoned.

THE JUDGE

They shall be called.
For always
It is the victor who writes the history of the vanquished.
The slayer distorts
The features of the slain. The weaker
Vanishes from the world, the lies
Remain. Down here we
Have no need of your stones. There are
So many down here, general, of those
Who crossed your path. Rather than

Portraits we shall call the
Portrayed. We'd rather question
Shades than stones.

LUCULLUS
I object.
I do not wish to see them.

THE VOICES OF THREE WOMAN CRIERS
The victims of General Lacallous
On his campaigns in Asia!
(*From the background emerge the shades of those portrayed on the
triumphal frieze, and line up opposite the frieze*)

The beginning of the next scene had to be changed to correspond.

THE SPEAKER
Bow your head, shade.
These are your witnesses.

LUCULLUS
I protest.

THE SPEAKER
These are your witnesses.

LUCULLUS
But they are enemies!
There you see a man whom I defeated.
In the few days . . .

After the trial performance which the Ministry of Education
arranged at the Berlin State Opera, two interpolations were
made on the basis of prolonged discussions. The first shows why
it was possible for the defeated king, who in the opera appears
as a shade and not merely as a figure on the frieze, to be acquit-
ted in a trial similar to the one in which Lucullus will be condemned. The following interpolation was made in "The Trial"
(p. 118):

LUCULLUS
Yes, I notice that the losers
Have sweet voices. Once
They were different, though. The king there

Who is prevailing on your pity, was in his lifetime
No better than I. Of tithe and tax
He took no less than I did.
The silver that he mined
Never found its way to the people.

THE TEACHER (*to the king*)

Why then
Are you among us, king?

THE KING

Because I built cities.
Because I defended them when you
Romans demanded their surrender.

THE TEACHER

Not us. Him!

THE KING

Because, to defend the country, I proclaimed:
Man, woman and child
In hedgerow and water hole
With mattock, ax and plowshare
By day and night
By their speech, by their silence
Free or captive
In the face of the enemy
In the face of death.

THE TEACHER

I propose that we all
Rise to our feet before this witness
And in honor of those
Who defended their cities.
(*The jurors rise*)

LUCULLUS

What kind of Romans are you!
Applauding the enemy!
I didn't go on my own
It was an order
I was sent by
Rome.

THE TEACHER

Rome! Rome! Rome!

Who is Rome?
Were you sent by the masons who built her?
Were you sent by the bakers and fishermen
Or the peasants and ox drivers
And the gardeners who feed her?
Was it the tailors and furriers
Or the weavers and sheep shearers who clothe her?
Were you sent by the stone polishers
And wool dyers who adorn her?
Or were you sent by the tax farmers
And the silver merchants and the slave traders
And the bankers of the Forum, who plunder her?
(*Silence*)
LUCULLUS
Whoever sent me—
I won
53 cities for Rome.
THE TEACHER
And where are they?
Jurors, let us question the cities.
TWO VIRGINS WITH A TABLET
With streets and people and houses . . .

The second interpolation is at the end of the last scene, where
the legionaries who died on the Asian campaigns join in the
condemnation of Lucullus (p. 130). Instead of:

Yes, send him to nothingness! What province
Tips the scales against
Our unlived years that held so much?

it now reads:

THE LEGIONARIES
Serving the bandit
Committing arson and murder
We the sons of the
People met our death.
Yes, send him to nothingness!
Like the wolf
That breaks into the fold

And has to be killed
So we were killed
In his service.
Yes, send him to nothingness!
If only we
Had deserted the aggressor!
If only we
Had joined the defenders!
Send him to nothingness!

The insertion of the three new arias ("Summons to Defence," "Who is Rome?" "Song of the Fallen Legionaries") was also intended to correct a certain disproportion arising from the fact that less musical expression was given to the court than to the defendant.

> [From GW *Stücke*, pp. 1479–1485. Signed "Brecht. Dessau." For a more exact account of the differences between the final text, as used for our translation, and the original radio play on the one hand and the opera text on the other, see pp. 316 ff. below.]

The Discussion about *The Condemnation of Lucullus*

The opera had already been accepted when the campaign against formalism was launched. Objections were raised at the Ministry of Education. The authors were asked to withdraw the opera. But they were only willing to forego their contract, not to withdraw the opera, because they did not regard it as formalistic. The arguments adduced did not convince them, in fact those raised by the musical advisers struck them as themselves formalistic. The authors stressed the importance of the message, namely, a condemnation of predatory war, and proposed that the rehearsals, which had already begun, should be continued long enough to permit of a closed performance on the strength of which an understanding might be reached between the authors and an audience of government representatives. The proposal was accepted and everything was done to make such an understanding possible. When the performance took place, the theme had a powerful effect on the audience, for one thing because it corresponded to the peace-loving policy of the German Democratic Republic and its condemnation of predatory war. Nevertheless, grave objections were raised, and in the course of a three-hour discussion between the authors and leading members of the government under the chairmanship of the President of the German Democratic Republic, it was shown that in its present form the opera might introduce a certain element of confusion into the newly initiated campaign, which was extremely important because it was designed to bridge the gap which undeniably existed between the arts and their new public. The metaphoric character of the text made it hard to understand, the music was not sufficiently in keeping with the present state of musical education among the general public, and deviated from the classical line. Moreover, the somber, violent music portraying the aggressor dominated the score. Brecht and Dessau declared their willingness to make additions in the spirit of the discussion and to resubmit the work. When at a second discussion among the same persons new texts were submitted and the composer also held out the prospect of certain changes, the members of the government decided that the opera should be produced and thrown open to the criticism of the public.

[From GW *Schriften zum Theater*, pp. 1152–3.]

Changes in the Text of *Lucullus*

1

Question: Can the scene of the children in the mausoleum be so misunderstood as to suggest that we are opposed to the veneration of heroes?

Change: Though it transpires in the following that the hero being honored on this occasion is condemned as a war criminal by the court of posterity, a momentary misunderstanding can be avoided by having the *teacher* exhort the children to become conquerors, while the children merely repeat his words. (TEACHER Sextus conquers Pontus.—PUPIL Pontus.—And so on.)

2

Question: How can it be brought out that only wars of aggression are condemned, not defensive wars?

Change: A new scene is added to the questioning of the king and queen. The king of the invaded country is asked by the jurors how he managed to pass the test of posterity. He repeats the proclamation in which he called on the people to defend their country dauntlessly. (The proclamation is positive and rousing.) The jurors rise from their seats in honor of those who defended their country.

3

Question: How can it be brought out that the primary instigators of war are not the generals, but . . . ?

Change: Lucullus claims that he went out to conquer Asia by order of Rome. A juror asks: Who is Rome? He replies that he was sent to Asia not by the masons, bakers, weavers, and peasants, but by the silver merchants, slave traders, and bankers.

4

Question: In addition to condemning offensive war, would it be possible to say what can be done to combat it?

Change: Toward the end a song of Lucullus' legionaries who died in Asia is added. In it, they castigate themselves for having let themselves be misled and express their regret that they did not refuse to serve Lucullus and instead help his victims to defend their country.

5

The title is to be changed from *The Trial of Lucullus* to *The Condemnation of Lucullus.* And instead of being called *Opera*, it is to be called *A Musical Play.*

> [From GW *Schriften zum Theater*, pp. 1154–6. Paragraphs 1–4 deal with the main changes outlined in "Notes on the Opera *The Condemnation of Lucullus,*" as a result of the discussions held in 1951. Paragraph 5's proposal to change the category of the work to "musical play" was rejected by Dessau; according to Fritz Hennenberg it was originally Hermann Scherchen's suggestion.]

Three Short Notes

The action of the opera *The Trial of Lucullus*—the trial and conviction of predatory war by posterity—takes place in the nether world. This device was frequently used by classical authors (Prologue in Heaven in *Faust*, Classical Walpurgis Night in *Faust*, Gluck's *Orpheus and Euridice*, and so forth and so on). The main importance of this device is not that it serves to camouflage ideas for purposes of contraband—obviously such a work could not be performed in the west today if MacArthur were standing trial—but that art benefits when the spectator, by discovering its relevance for himself, is enabled to respond more deeply and intensely. In general, the enjoyment of art (and the enjoyment of insights and impulses through art) is enhanced when the audience is stimulated to intellectual production, discovery and experience.

We are performing the opera *The Trial of Lucullus* by Paul Dessau. It is based on a radio play written by Brecht in 1939, a year marked by the outbreak of the wars of spoliation and conquest that culminated and ended in the Second World War. It deals with the trial of Lucullus, a Roman general who, in the last century before our era, invaded Asia with his legions and conquered vast territories for the Roman Empire.

The *Condemnation of Lucullus* is an opera based on a radio play. If any of the opera houses accept it, this will, I believe, mark the first appearance in that quarter of a work deriving from the collective effort of modern radio.

> [GW *Schriften zum Theater*, pp. 1151–2. These notes were written for different occasions. The last is signed "Dessau. Brecht."]

Editorial Note

Although Brecht's notes make it appear as if there were two versions of this play, the radio play and the opera libretto, there are basically three: (a) the radio play of 1939, (b) the revised text of 1949–50 as printed in the collected works, and (c) the opera libretto of 1951. The text which we have followed in this volume is in fact a hybrid, halfway between radio play and opera, and as far as we know it was not publicly performed in German in Brecht's lifetime.

The radio play (a) was performed by the Bern studio of the Swiss radio in 1940 and published in the German language Moscow monthly *Internationale Literatur* at the end of that year. Its text is very close to that set down in Brecht's first typescript, and, on paper at least, is much the most effective of the three versions, being shorter and leaving more to the imagination; this is especially the case with the last scene. Already Brecht seems to have had in mind a musical setting, for a page attached to the first script, (and likewise in his own typing) lists the musical numbers as follows:

1
song of the soldiers ("hold it steady")
song of the slaves ("watch out, men, don't stumble")

3
chorus of children ("in the schoolbooks")

4
duet of the crier and the gatekeeper ("out on the appian way")

5
conversation of the soldiers ("so long, lacallous")

6
lucullus' outburst ("by jupiter, what does this mean?")
quartet of lucullus and threefold voice ("lacallous" and
  "lucullus is my name")

7
recitative of the usher ("before the highest court")
trio of the threefold voice ("alexander of macedon")

8
chorus of slaves ("out of life and into death")
chorus of frieze figures ("we figures, fashioned to stay in the
  light")

9
triumphal song of lucullus ("here you see a man whom i
  defeated")
song of the king ("one morning")
song of the queen ("as i went in taurion to")
song of lucullus ("the losers have sweet voices")
song of the virgins ("with streets and people and houses")

10
recitative of the 2 new shades and lucullus ("i came to grief")

11
duet of the warriors ("i ran away")
report of the fishwife ("i was a fishwife in the forum market")

12
duet of the 2 new shades ("why were you running so?")

13
song of the cook ("i was his cook")
duet of the farmer and lucullus ("it doesn't need much soil")

14
recitative of the usher ("and from the high bench rise")

When Brecht and Dessau started work on the opera version
about 1949 they had (according to a note by Elisabeth Hauptmann) the radio play before them. The first version of the opera

libretto consisted essentially of this, with additions designed to give opportunities to the composer: the "voices" in scene 1 ("Think of the Invincible"), Lucullus' tribute to his cook in scene 6, the judge's aria in scene 7 ("Unfortunate Man!"), the third stanza of the queen's song in scene 9 and the invocations of "Faber, my son Faber" in the fishwife's aria in scene 11. In addition Brecht, at Dessau's suggestion, wrote a new, longer final scene, where the jurors, followed by the legionaries and the slaves, agree that Lucullus should be cast into nothingness.

This version is to all intents and purposes (b), that published in the collected works; in *Versuche 11* Brecht prefaced it a shade misleadingly as follows:

> *The Trial of Lucullus*, the 25th *Versuch*, is a radio play and was written in 1939 before the outbreak of the Second World War. It forms the basis of the opera *The Condemnation of Lucullus*, for which Paul Dessau wrote the music.

In the typescripts it is already headed "Opera in 2 x 7 scenes by Bertolt Brecht. Music by Paul Dessau," with a list of characters showing how unorthodox the operatic conception then was:

Singing parts

LUCULLUS	*Buffo tenor,* reminiscent of Julius Liebau
THE QUEEN	*Coloratura soprano*
THE COURTESAN	*Mezzo-soprano*
TWO VIRGINS	*Mezzo-sopranos*

Musically and vocally endowed actors

A TONELESS VOICE

THE OLD WOMAN

THE JUDGE OF THE DEAD

THE KING

THE TEACHER

THE BAKER

TWO SHADES

THE FISHWIFE

TWO WARRIORS

THE COOK

THE FARMER

THE MAN CARRYING THE CHERRY TREE

Speaking parts

THE ANNOUNCER
THE CRIER
TWO GIRLS
TWO MERCHANTS
TWO WOMEN
TWO PLEBEIANS
A CART DRIVER
SPOKESMAN FOR THE COURT OF THE DEAD
SINGING CHORUSES, SPEAKING CHORUSES, CHILDREN'S CHORUSES

From this first opera libretto was evolved the tightened-up second version headed (again in typescript) "Opera in 12 Scenes. By Paul Dessau. Text by Bertolt Brecht." This contains all the major dramaturgical switches and cuts of (c) the final opera text, but not the emendations described in Brecht's notes. Thus scene 2 is telescoped with scene 1, scene 3 is transposed, the courtesan's aria inserted in scene 8, scene 12 omitted, and so on; however, the middle of scene 8 and the end of the last scene (after the entry of the legionaries) are as in (b) the previous text. It was performed in this form in March 1951, on which occasion the East German government intervened and the crucial changes were made.

The published opera libretto (c) (Aufbau-Verlag, East Berlin, and Ars Viva Verlag, Zurich—Fritz Hennenberg has found the two printings to be identical—gives the text as amended, re-titled and finally staged in October, 1951. Its list of characters reads:

LUCULLUS, a Roman general	*Tenor*
FIGURES ON THE FRIEZE:	
THE KING	*Bass*
THE QUEEN	*Soprano*
TWO CHILDREN	*Soprano and Mezzo*
TWO LEGIONARIES	*Basses*
LASUS, Lucullus' cook	*Tenor*
THE MAN CARRYING A CHERRY TREE	*Baritone*
JURORS OF THE DEAD:	
THE FISHWIFE	*Contralto*
THE COURTESAN	*Mezzo-soprano*

THE TEACHER	*Tenor*
THE BAKER	*Tenor*
THE FARMER	*Bass*
TERTULLIA, an old woman	*Mezzo-soprano*
THREE ROMAN WOMEN	*Sopranos*
VOICES OF THE THREE FEMALE CRIERS	
THE JUDGE OF THE DEAD	*High bass*
VOICE OF A WOMAN COMMENTATOR	

Speaking parts

THE SPEAKER OF THE COURT OF THE DEAD
THREE CRIERS
TWO GIRLS
TWO MERCHANTS
TWO WOMEN
TWO PLEBEIANS
A CART DRIVER
CHORUS OF THE CROWD: SOLDIERS, SLAVES, SHADES, CHILDREN

Shortly after approving this version Brecht suggested still further cuts and changes. Some, like the cutting of two stanzas of the queen's song and the beginning of the courtesan's aria, were rejected by Dessau; others however were made, and can be found in the Reclam edition of the text and in the piano score (1951 and 1961). The chorus became a single voice, the soldiers a quintet of officers, the speaker of the court of the dead was eliminated, his part being shared between the judge of the dead and the voice. The opera was staged in this form at its second East German production in Leipzig in 1957; Dessau in a program note confirmed that this was the fifth version of the text to date. After that (i.e., after Brecht's death) Dessau made one or two more dramaturgical changes for the State Opera production of 1960. These included the cutting of Lucullus' tribute to the cook, originally in scene 6, and the composition of a new chorus for the legionaries in the last scene. The composer, it seems, had never been satisfied with this scene and would have liked the work to end with a general chorus.

The two "radio plays" and the 1951 opera libretto

Accordingly, the following notes set out the differences between the text printed in the body of this volume, which calls itself a radio play but is in fact the first opera libretto of 1949–50, and the real radio play, published in *Internationale Literatur* in 1940, on the one hand and the amended opera libretto *Die Verurteilung des Lukullus* published by Aufbau-Verlag in 1951, on the other. By using these notes, both versions can be reconstituted completely, apart from one or two details of layout and punctuation.

CHANGES FROM 1940 RADIO PLAY

References are to page and line

101, 9	before = behind
13	horse. = horse and before him
	They drag (. . . , continue with 101, 22 - 102, 1, followed by 101, 14–20)
102, 2–22	omitted
27	after line, insert subhead
	THE CROWD
105, 23–26	omitted
106, 32	there = here
109, 5	death = death:
11	LUCULLUS = LUCULLUS (*suddenly*)
20–28	omitted
110, 36–39	omitted
113, 17–30	omitted

115, 24	Are you ready, stony shades = Are you ready, you figures You stony shades
116, 28	asks a question: = asks:
117, 36–118, 2	omitted
118, 18–22	omitted
23	after line, insert: And all fall silent.
119, 8	asks a question: = asks:
120, 11	Makes a proposal: = Leans negligently forward and says:
16	The jurors = And all fall silent. The jurors

23	## Back in Rome = Rome

120, 25–121, 3	replace with: And the court withdraws. The defendant sits down. He squats by the doorpost, his head thrown back. He is exhausted, but he overhears a conversation behind the door Where new shades have appeared.
122, 4	The jurors = And the jurors
6–7	replace with: And the shade that was once a fishwife Says:
26	Tell me, what = And what
27	LEGIONARY = WARRIOR (throughout this scene)
30	I was = And I was
124, 5–7	omitted
15	were = are

124, 27   The fallen man's mother = The mother

30   The jurors = And all fell silent. The jurors

36–37   She requires
A recess. =
To restore
Her composure she requires
A recess.

125, 2   ## Rome—A Last Time = Rome Once Again

126, 18   juror, once = juror who was once

127, 21   Thanks to him! = Thanks to him! Therefore I call him human.

25   Therefore I call him human. =
And I also know
That when the city of Amisus, daughter of magnificent Athens
Full to the brim with books and art treasures was being looted
He implored his soldiers with tears in his eyes not to set it on fire.
Drenched in tears, he came to me for his supper.
That too was human. Take account of it.

27   The jurors = And all fell silent. The jurors

31   juror, once = juror who was once

129, 2–131, 2   substitute original version of last scene:

Wheat and Chaff

THE JUDGE
And so I conclude this trial.

Of your witnesses, shade
The most distinguished were not those who
    said most in your favor. However
Lesser ones appeared in the end. Your bloody
    hands
Were not found wholly empty. True enough
Even for your best gift, the cherry tree
The price was very high. That conquest
Could easily have been made with one man
    only, but you
Sent 80,000 to Hades for it. As things stand
We must content ourselves with a few
Hours of happiness for a cook, tears
Wept for the destruction of books and other
    such nonessentials.
Ah, with all the violence and conquest
Only one realm increases:
The realm of the shades.

THE JURORS

We, however, appointed to judge the dead
Take note when they leave the earth
Of what the earth has received from them.

THE SPEAKER

And from the high bench rise
The spokesmen of a posterity
Many-handed for taking
Many-mouthed for eating
Hard to deceive, eagerly reaping
Rejoicing in life.
The court
Withdraws to consider the verdict.

CHANGES MADE FOR 1951 OPERA TEXT

References are to page and line

101, 3   omitted

    4   THE CRIER = FIRST CRIER

101,	8	after line, insert: SECOND CRIER
	21	THE CRIER = THIRD CRIER
102,	2	VOICES = SONG OF THE THREE ROMAN WOMEN
	9–15	omitted
104,	16	THE CRIER = FIRST CRIER
	25–26	omitted
105,	1–2	omitted
	3	THE CRIER = SECOND CRIER
	4	procession has vanished, now = ceremony is over. Now (This speech forms the conclusion of Scene I)
	10–26	Scene 3 is transferred to after the present scene 5 and becomes scene IV
	11	after line, insert: A SPEAKING VOICE From then on the teachers showed the schoolchildren The tomb of the great conqueror.
	14	generals. = conquerors.
	22	after line, insert: TEACHER (*sings last four lines*)
106,	1	4 = II
	3	THE CRIER = CHORUS
106, 13–107, 22		replaced by stage direction: (*The catafalque and the frieze are carried in by soldiers and slaves. After the catafalque has been lowered into the tomb, the enormous frieze is set up in front of it. At the command: "Dismissed!" the soldiers go out*)
107,	23	5 = III
108,	21	6 = V
	23–24	omitted
	25	THE TONELESS VOICE = CHORUS (throughout this scene)

109, 28
with bitter berries! =
      with the bitter berries
And all your innumerable spices:
Sage and olive
Thyme, nutmeg and crushed cinnamon
What sauces, what salads, oh Lasus!

110, 4
VOICE OF AN OLD WOMAN WAITING = TERTULLIA

34
THE THREEFOLD VOICE = VOICES OF THE THREE
WOMEN CRIERS
(throughout this scene)

112, 1
7 = VI

3
THE SPEAKER = SPEAKER (throughout entire text)

18
THE JUDGE = JUDGE (throughout entire text)

30
delete: (*calls out in the fields of the blest*)

113, 1–2
transposed to follow 113, 5

8
well-remembered = blest

16–17
delete: (*Silence*) THE JUDGE

114, 8
after line, add:
VOICES OF THE THREE WOMEN CRIERS
  Let the frieze be brought!

9
8 = VII
(The full text of the scene is as given in Brecht's
  notes, pp. 306–308)

116, 1
9 = VIII

3–7
replace with version in Brecht's notes (p. 308)

27–28
replace by:
  Here the slave
  Shade who was once a teacher, has a question:

117, 16
The jurors of the dead consider = Jurors of the
dead, consider

21
Asks = Has

118, 22	after line insert new stanza: When my flesh was on the market Which began with sixteen summers I too bowed to blows and curses For a little oil and wormy pasta. So I know well what you suffered On the day of your disaster. Woman, I can feel for you.
24	The jurors of the dead consider = Jurors of the dead, consider
27–29	omitted
37–40	replace by the new interpolation from Brecht's notes (pp. 308–310)
119, 1	TWO VIRGINS = TWO CHILDREN
4	We = They
5	our = their
11	TWO VIRGINS = TWO CHILDREN
119, 19–40	replace with: Continue. TWO CHILDREN And in the cities were Two hundred and fifty thousand children. They are no more. The great Lucullus Descended on us with his iron chariots And defeated us all. LUCULLUS Yes, I shattered their insolent cities And took their gold and many kinds of treasure And I carried their people away to be our slaves. For they paid tribute to false gods. But I overthrew them
120, 3–7	omitted
9	juror shade = juror of the dead
16	The jurors of the dead consider = Jurors of the dead, consider

120, 22	10 = IX

23	Back in Rome = Rome

120, 24–121, 3   replace with:
CHORUS
The defendant sits down.
He is exhausted, but he overhears
A conversation in the vestibule
Where new shades have appeared.

121, 4   A SHADE = FIRST SHADE

8   THE SHADE = FIRST SHADE

12   ANOTHER SHADE = SECOND SHADE

13   after line, insert:
LUCULLUS
Time to eat?

15   delete: Time to eat?

21   I was a slave too = I myself am a slave

22   to the lucky = to you lucky ones

23   delete: (*a bit louder*)

122, 1   11 = X

4–5   omitted

6–7   And the shade, once a fishwife
Speaks up =
Here the shade, once a fishwife
Has a question

22–25   omitted

123, 37   after line, insert:
Faber, my son Faber
Whom I bore and whom I reared
My son Faber.

124,	23–25	omitted
	30	The jurors of the dead consider = Jurors of the dead, consider
	36–37	She requires A recess. = To restore Her composure she requires a recess
125,	1–20	omitted
126,	1	13 = XI
	3–7	replace by: CHORUS The lady juror has recovered. SPEAKER Defendant, step forward! JUDGE Lacallous! Time is etc.
	19	Asks = Has
	22	delete: He looks cheerful.
127,	8	Then spoke the juror = Hear the juror
	21	Thanks to him! = Thanks to him! Therefore I call him human.
	22–25	omitted
	27	The jurors of the dead consider = Jurors of the dead, consider
	32	Asks = Has
	34	fruit tree = cherry tree
128,	5	THE SPEAKER = CHORUS
129,	1	14 = XII
	3	THE SPEAKER = CHORUS
	4	And the juror = The juror
	30	THE SPEAKER = CHORUS

129, 34   omitted

130, 4   omitted

    11–14   replaced by:
Of half-lived lives.

FARMER
Yet here we have no plows for sinewy arms!
THE JURORS
Or hungry mouths, etc.

    24–30   replaced by:
CHORUS
Here come the Asian
Legionaries fallen in battle.
(*Roman legionaries appear in formation*)
Then comes the legionaries' chorus as in Brecht's
notes (p. 310), except that the fifth line, ("Yes, send
him to nothingness!"), the tenth line ("In his ser-
vice!"), and the final "Send him to nothingness!"
are all cut.

MOTHER COURAGE AND HER CHILDREN

Texts by Brecht

The Story
CURVE OF THE DRAMATURGY

1

This scene emphasizes that things are at the beginning. Courage's canteen business and the new war as new undertakings of a familiar sort. (They begin and they continue; they begin by continuing.) Needed: energy, enterprise, the prospect of new times, arrival of new business, together with new dangers. She longs for war and at the same time fears it. She wants to join in, but as a peaceable business woman, not in a warlike way. She wants to maintain her family during the war and by means of it. She wants to serve the army and also to keep out of its clutches.

Her children: With her eldest son she is afraid of his bravery, but counts on his cleverness. With the second she is afraid of his stupidity but counts on his honesty. With her daughter she is afraid of her pity but counts on her dumbness. Only her fears prove to be justified.

She is anticipating business; she is going to go bankrupt.

The play begins with the entrance (i.e., hanging about) of the men of war. The vast disorder of war begins with order, the vast disorganization with organization.

The peaceful landscape and the men of iron. Courage arrives four strong, goes away three strong.

2

War as a business idyll. Courage swindles peasants out of a capon; her elder son robs peasants of their oxen. He wins fame and possessions; she profits. She pillages the army somewhat too. The danger for her son becomes more real.

3

Being taken prisoner need be no disadvantage to her business. It seems that she had nothing to say against her younger son's joining the army as a paymaster. All she thinks necessary in his case is honesty. This does him in. If he had not been connected with the army he would not have been killed. Her stubborn bargaining over her wagon costs her son his life. She stops her daughter from becoming a whore—the only career open to her in wartime, and one which brings good fortune to Yvette. In any case she is no Antigone.

4

Courage stifles her human reactions (any kind of outrage, rebellion or criticism) for the sake of her business. She thinks capitulation will do something for her.

5

All the same, human reactions sometimes overrun her business principles. The general's victory leads to financial losses.

6

Business, which is to earn her daughter's (peacetime) dowry, leads to her wartime disfigurement. Courage counts on the length of the war, which is helpful to her finances but means spinsterhood for her daughter. Finally, for the first time she curses the war which, from a business standpoint, she must needs want.

7

Peacetime is pleasant, if also ruinous. As a result of the peace she does not get her son back, but loses him for good. In her daughter's case peace arrives too late. The son falls because he has applied the principles of war in peacetime. The former camp prostitute Yvette Pottier has prospered as a result of the war and married a colonel. The war starts up again. Is business going to start up again too?

8

Business is on the downgrade. The war is too long. Disorganization and disorder on every side. In a song Courage (qua beggar) curses all the human virtues as not only uncommercial but actually dangerous. For her daughter's sake she must give up the cook, who could have provided her with a roof over her head. She is bound to the war by pity for her daughter.

9

The daughter perishes because of her pity for other people's children. Courage goes on dragging her empty wagon, alone, in the wake of the tattered army.

[From Werner Hecht (ed.): *Materialien zu Brechts "Mutter Courage,"* Frankfurt, Suhrkamp, 1967, pp. 7–9.]

The Mother Courage Model

Now, after the great war, life goes on in our ruined cities, but it is a different life, the life of different or differently composed groups, guided or thwarted by new surroundings, new because so much has been destroyed. The great heaps of rubble are piled on the city's invaluable substructure, the water and drainage pipes, the gas mains and electric cables. Even the large building that has remained intact is affected by the damage and rubble around it, and may become an obstacle to planning. Temporary structures must be built and there is always a danger of their becoming permanent. All this is reflected in art, for our way of thinking is part of our way of living. In the theater we set up models to fill the gap. They immediately meet with strong opposition from all supporters of the old ways, of the routine that masquerades as experience and of the conventionality that calls itself creative freedom. And they are endangered by those who take them up without having learned to use them. Though meant to simplify matters, they are not simple to handle. They were designed not to make thought unnecessary, but to provoke it; not to replace but to compel artistic creation.

First of all we must imagine that the information which the printed text provides about certain events, here the adventures of Mother Courage and the losses she incurs, has to some extent been complemented; it has now been established that when the woman's dead son was brought to her she was sitting beside her mute daughter, and so on—the kind of information which an artist painting some historic incident can arrive at by questioning eye-witnesses. Later he can still change certain details as for one reason or another he may think advisable. Until one has learned to copy (and construct) models in a living and intelligent way, one had better not copy too much. Such things as the cook's makeup or Mother Courage's costume should not be imitated. The model should not be used to excess.

Pictures and descriptions of a performance are not enough. One does not learn much by reading that a character moves in a particular direction after a given sentence, even if the tone of the sentence, the way of walking, and a convincing motive can be supplied—which is very difficult. The persons available for the imitation are not the same as those of the pattern; with them it would not have come into being. Anyone deserving of the name of artist is unique; he represents something universal, but in his own individual way. He can neither be perfectly imitated nor give a perfect imitation. Nor is it so important for artists to imitate art as to imitate life. The use of models is a particular kind of art, and there is a limit to what can be learned from it. The aim must be neither to copy the pattern exactly nor to break away from it too quickly.

In studying what follows—a number of explanations and discoveries emerging from the rehearsal of a play—one should, above all, be led by the solutions of certain problems to consider the problems themselves.

Music

Paul Dessau's music for *Mother Courage* is not meant to be particularly easy; like the stage set, it left something to be supplied by the audience; in the act of listening they had to link the voices with the melody. Art is not a land of Cockaigne. In order to make the transition to the musical parts, to let the music have its say, we lowered a musical emblem from the flies whenever there was a song which did not spring directly from the action, or which did spring from it but remained clearly apart. This consisted of a trumpet, a drum, a flag, and electric globes that lit up: a slight and delicate thing, pleasant to look at, even if scene 9 found it badly damaged. Some people regarded this as sheer playfulness, as an unrealistic element. But on the one hand playfulness in the theater should not be condemned out of hand as long as it is kept within bounds, and on the other hand it was not wholly unrealistic, for it served to set the music apart from the reality of the action. We made use of it as a visible sign of the shift to another artistic level—that of music—and in order to give the right impression, that these were musical insertions, rather than to lead people to think quite mistakenly that the songs "sprang from the action." Those who object to this are quite simply opposed to anything intermittent, inorganic, pieced-together—this chiefly because they object to any shattering of illusion. What they ought to have objected to was not the tangible symbol of music, but the manner of fitting the musical numbers into the play: i.e., as insertions.

The musicians were placed so that they could be seen, in a box beside the stage—thus their performances became little concerts, independent contributions made at suitable points in the play. The box communicated with the stage, so that a musician or two could occasionally go backstage for trumpet calls or when music occurred as part of the action.

We began with the overture. It was a bit thin, for it was performed by only four musicians; still, it was a reasonably ceremonious preparation for the confusions of war.

Stage Design

For the production we are describing, at the Deutsches Theater in Berlin, we used the well-known model devised by Teo Otto during the war for the Zurich Schauspielhaus. There was a permanent framework of huge screens, making use of such materials as one would expect to find in the military encampments of the seventeenth century: tenting, wooden posts lashed together with ropes, etc. Three-dimensional structures, realistic both as to construction and as to material, were placed on the stage to represent such buildings as the presbytery and the peasants' house, but in artistic abbreviation, only so much being shown as was necessary for the action. Colored projections were thrown on the cyclorama, and the revolving stage was used to give the impression of travel—we varied the size and position of the screens and used them only for the camp scenes, so as to distinguish these from the scenes on the highway. The Berlin stage designer made his own versions of the buildings (in scenes 2, 4, 5, 9, 10, and 11), but on the same principle. We dispensed with the background projections used in Zurich and suspended the names of the various countries over the stage in large black letters. We used an even, white light, as much of it as our equipment permitted. In this way we eliminated any vestige of "atmosphere" that could easily have given the incidents a romantic tinge. We retained almost everything else down to the smallest details (chopping block, hearth, etc.), particularly the admirable positionings of the wagon. This last was very important because it determined much of the grouping and movement from the outset.

Surprisingly little is lost by the sacrifice of complete freedom of "artistic creation." You have to start somewhere, with something, and it may as well be with something that has already been fully thought out. Freedom will be acquired through the principle of contradiction, which is continually active and vocal in all of us.

Realistic Theater and Illusion

Writing in 1826, Goethe spoke of the "inadequacy of the English wooden stage" of Shakespeare's day. He says: "There is no trace here of the aids to naturalness to which we have gradually become accustomed through the improvement in machinery, in the art of perspective and in costuming." "Who?" he asks, "would tolerate such a thing today? Under those conditions Shakespeare's plays would become highly interesting fairy tales, narrated by a number of persons who tried to increase their effectiveness somewhat by making up as the characters, by coming and going and carrying out the movements necessary to the story, but left it to the audience to imagine as many paradises and palaces as they pleased on the empty stage."

Since he wrote these words, the mechanical equipment of our theaters has been improving for a hundred years, and "aids to naturalness" have led to such emphasis on illusion that we latecomers would be more inclined to put up with Shakespeare on an empty stage than with a Shakespeare who had ceased to require or to provoke any use of the imagination.

In Goethe's day what improvement had been made in the mechanics of illusion was relatively harmless, since the machinery was so imperfect, so much "in the childhood of its beginnings," that theater itself was still a reality and both imagination and ingenuity could still be employed to turn nature into art. The sets were still theatrical displays, in which the stage designer gave an artistic and poetic interpretation of the places concerned.

The bourgeois classical theater occupied a happy halfway point on the road to naturalistic illusionism. Stage machinery provided enough elements of illusion to improve the representation of some aspects of reality, but not so much as to make the audience feel that they were no longer in a theater; art had not yet come to signify the obliteration of all indications that art is at work. Since there was no electricity, lighting effects were still primitive; where poor taste decreed sunset effects, poor equipment prevented total enchantment. The Meiningers' authentic costumes came later; they were usually magnificent, though not always beautiful, and they were after all compensated by an inauthentic manner of speaking. In short, the theater remained the theater, at least where it failed in its business of deception. Today the restoration of the theater's reality as theater is a precondition for any realistic representation of human relations. Too much heightening of the illusion in the setting, along with a "magnetic" manner of acting which gives the spectator the illusion of being present at a fleeting, fortuitous "real" event, create such an impression of naturalness that one can no longer interpose one's judgment, imagination or reactions, and must simply conform by sharing in the experience and becoming one of "nature's" objects. The illusion created by the theater must be a partial one, so that it can always be recognized as illusion. Reality, however completely represented, must be changed by art, in order that it may be seen to be subject to change and treated as such.

That is why we are demanding naturalness today—because we want to change the nature of our human relations.

Elements of Illusion?

No doubt the sight of the cyclorama behind a completely empty stage (in the prologue and in the seventh and last scenes) creates the illusion of a flat landscape with the sky over it. There is no objection to this, because there must be some stirring of poetry in the soul of the spectator if such an illusion is to come about. Thanks to the ease with which it is created, the actors are able to suggest by their manner of playing, at the beginning that a wide horizon lies open to the business enterprise of the little family of provisioners, then at the end that the exhausted seeker after fortune is faced by boundless devastation. And we can always hope that this substantive impression of the play will combine with a formal one: that when the spectator sees the empty stage, soon to be inhabited, he will be able to share in the initial void from which everything arises. On this tabula rasa, he knows, the actors have been working for weeks, testing first one detail, then another, coming to know the incidents of the chronicle by portraying them, and portraying them by judging them. And now the play is starting and Mother Courage's wagon comes rolling onto the stage.

If in big matters such a thing as a beautiful approximation is possible, in matters of detail it is not. A realistic portrayal requires carefully worked-out detail in costumes and props, for here the imagination of the audience can add nothing. All implements connected with working and eating must have been most lovingly made. And the costumes, of course, cannot be as for a folklore festival; they must show signs of individuality and social class. They have been worn for a longer or shorter time, are made of cheaper or more expensive material, are well or not so well taken care of, etc.

The costumes for this production of *Mother Courage* were by [Kurt] Palm.

What is a performance of Mother Courage and Her Children *primarily meant to show?*

That in wartime the big profits are not made by little people. That war, which is a continuation of business by other means, makes the human virtues fatal even to their possessors. That no sacrifice is too great for the struggle against war.

Prologue

By way of a prologue, Mother Courage and her little family were shown on their way to the war zone. Mother Courage sang her business song from scene 1 (so that in scene 1 her answer "Business people" is followed immediately by the sergeant's question: "Halt, you scum. Where do you belong?"). After the overture, to spare the performer the exertion of singing against the rumbling of the revolving stage, the first stanza was played on a record, the house being darkened. Then the prologue begins.

The Long Road to War

The linen half-curtain, on which in the following the titles of the scenes are projected, opens and Mother Courage's wagon is rolled forward against the movement of the revolving stage.

The wagon is a cross between a military vehicle and a general store. A sign affixed to the side of it says: "Second Finnish Regiment" and another "Mother Courage, Groceries." On the canvas Swedish pork sausages are displayed next to a flag with a price tag indicating "Four Guilders." The wagon will undergo several changes in the course of the chronicle. There will be sometimes more, sometimes less merchandise hanging on it, the canvas will be dirtier or cleaner, the letters on the signs will be faded and then again freshly painted, depending on the state of business. Now at the start it is clean and richly covered with wares.

The wagon is pulled by the two sons. They sing the second stanza of Mother Courage's Business Song: "O Captains, don't expect to send them/ To death with nothing in their crops." On the box sit mute Kattrin, playing the Jew's harp, and Mother Courage. Courage is sitting in lazy comfort, swaying with the wagon and yawning. Everything, including her one backward glance, indicates that the wagon has come a long way.

We had conceived of the song as a dramatic entrance, lusty and cocky—we had the last scene of the play in mind. But Weigel saw it as a realistic business song and suggested that it be used to picture the long journey to the war. Such are the ideas of great actors.

Once this was settled, it seemed to us that by showing the business woman's long journey to the war zone we would be showing clearly enough that she was an active and voluntary participant in the war. But certain reviews and many discussions with persons who had seen the play showed that a good many people regarded Mother Courage merely as a representative of the "little people" who "become involved in the war in spite of themselves," who are "helpless victims of the war," and so on. A deeply engrained habit leads the theater-goer to pick out the more emotional utterances of the characters and overlook everything else. Like descriptions of landscapes in novels, references to business are received with boredom. The "business atmosphere" is simply the air one breathes and as such requires no special mention. And so, regardless of all our efforts to represent the war as an aggregate of business deals, the discussions showed time and time again that people regarded it as a timeless abstraction.

Too Short can be Too Long

The two stanzas of the opening song plus the pause between them during which the wagon rolls silently along, take up a certain amount of time, too much time it seemed to us at first in rehearsal. But when we cut the second stanza, the prologue seemed longer, and when we prolonged the pause between the stanzas, it seemed shorter.

[. . .]

Scene 1

The business woman Anna Fierling, known as Mother Courage, encounters the Swedish army

Recruiters are going about the country looking for cannon fodder. Mother Courage introduces her mixed family, acquired in various theaters of war, to a sergeant. The canteen woman defends her sons against the recruiters with a knife. She sees that her sons are listening to the recruiters and predicts that the sergeant will meet an early death. To make her children afraid of the war, she has them too draw black crosses. Because of a small business deal, she nevertheless loses her brave son. And the sergeant leaves her with a prophecy:

"If you want the war to work for you
You've got to give the war its due."

Over-all arrangement

Recruiters are going about the country looking for cannon fodder. On the empty stage the sergeant and the recruiter are standing right front on the lookout, complaining in muffled voices of the difficulty of finding cannon fodder for their general. The city of which the sergeant speaks is assumed to be in the orchestra. Mother Courage's wagon appears and the recruiters' mouths water at the sight of the young men. The sergeant cries "Halt!" and the wagon stops.

Mother Courage introduces her mixed family, acquired in various theaters of war, to a sergeant. The professionals of commerce and of war meet, the war can start. At the sight of the military, the Fierlings may hesitate for a moment as though afraid: the soldiers on their own side are also enemies; the army gives, but it also takes. Mother Courage's "Good morning, sergeant" is spoken in the same curt, military monotone as his "Good morning, friends." Climbing down from her wagon, she makes it clear that she regards showing her papers as a formality, superfluous among professionals ("All right, we'll run through the whole routine"). She introduces her little family, acquired in various theaters of war, in a jocular tone: she puts on a bit of a "Mother Courage" act.

The wagon and the children are on the left, the recruiters on the right. Mother Courage crosses over with her tin box full of papers. She has been summoned, but she is also sallying forth to scout and do business. She describes her children from the other side of the stage, as though better able to take them in from a distance. The recruiter makes forays behind her back, stalking the sons, tempting them. The pivotal point is in the lines: "Wouldn't you need a nice pistol, or a belt buckle?" and "I need something else."

The canteen woman defends her sons against the recruiters with a knife. The sergeant leaves her standing there and goes over to the sons, followed by the recruiter. He thumps their chests, feels their calves. He goes back and stands before Mother Courage: "Why aren't they in the army?" The recruiter has stayed with the sons: "Let's see if you're a sissy." Mother Courage runs over, thrusts herself between the recruiter and her son: "He's a sissy." The recruiter goes over to the sergeant (on the right) and complains: "He insulted me"; Mother Courage snatches her Eilif away. The sergeant tries to reason, but Mother Courage pulls a knife and stands there in a rage, guarding her sons.

Mother Courage sees that her sons are listening to the recruiter and predicts that the sergeant will meet an early death. Again she goes over to the sergeant ("Give me your helmet"). Her children follow her and look on, gaping. The recruiter makes a flank movement, comes up to Eilif from behind and speaks to him.

When after some hesitation the sergeant has drawn his black cross, the children, satisfied, go back to the wagon, but the recruiter follows them. And when Mother Courage turns ("I've got to take advantage"), she sees the recruiter between her sons; he has his arms around their shoulders.

To make her children afraid of the war, Mother Courage has them too draw black crosses. The rebellion in her own ranks is in full swing. She runs angrily behind her wagon to paint black crosses for her children. When she returns to the wagon shaft with the helmet, the recruiter, grinning, leaves the children to her and goes back (right) to the sergeant. When the somber ceremony is over, Mother Courage goes to the sergeant, returns his helmet, and with fluttering skirts climbs up on the seat of the wagon. The sons have harnessed themselves, the wagon starts moving. Mother Courage has mastered the situation.

Because of a small business deal, she nevertheless loses her brave son. But the sergeant has only been half defeated; on the recruiter's advice, he offers to make a purchase. Electrified, Mother Courage climbs down from the wagon and the sergeant draws her off left behind the wagon. While the deal is in progress, the recruiter takes the harness off Eilif and leads him away. Kattrin sees this, climbs down from the wagon and tries in vain to call her mother's attention to Eilif's disappearance. But Mother Courage is deep in her bargaining. Only after she has snapped her moneybag shut does she notice his absence. For a moment she has to sit down on the wagon shaft, still holding her buckles. Then she angrily flings them into the wagon, and the family, with one less member, moves gloomily off.

And the sergeant leaves her with a prophecy. Laughing, he predicts that if she wants to live off the war, she will also have to give the war its due.

[. . .]

The recruiters

The empty stage of the prologue was transformed into a concrete locality by means of a few clumps of wintry grass marking the edge of a highway. Here the military men stand waiting, freezing in their armor.

The great disorder of war begins with order, disorganization with organization. The troublemakers have troubles of their own. We hear complaints to the effect that it takes intelligence to get a war started. The military are businessmen. The sergeant has a little book that he consults, the recruiter has a map to help him fight with geography. The fusion of war and business cannot be established too soon.

Grouping

There will be some difficulty in persuading the actors playing the sergeant and the recruiter to stay together and in one place until Mother Courage's wagon appears. In our theater, groups always show a strong tendency to break up, partly because each actor believes he can heighten audience interest by moving about and changing his position, and partly because he wants to be alone, so as to divert the attention of the audience from the group to himself. But there is no reason not to leave the military men together; on the contrary, both the image and the argument would be impaired by a change of position.

Changes of position

Positions should be retained as long as there is no compelling reason for changing them; and a desire for variety is not a compelling reason. If one gives in to a desire for variety, the consequence is a devaluation of all movement on the stage; the spectator ceases to look for a specific meaning behind each movement, he stops taking movement seriously. But especially at the crucial points in the action, the full impact of a change of position must not be weakened. Legitimate variety is obtained by ascertaining the crucial points and planning the arrangement around them. For example, the recruiters have been listening to Mother Courage; she has succeeded in diverting and entertaining them with her tall talk and so putting them in a good humor; so far there has been only one ominous circumstance: the sergeant has asked for her papers; but he has not examined them—his only purpose was to prolong their stay. She takes the next step (also physically: she goes up to the sergeant, takes hold of his belt buckle, and says: "Wouldn't you need a belt buckle?"), she tries to sell them something, and that is when the recruiters spring into action. The sergeant says ominously: "I need something else" and along with the recruiter goes over to the sons at the wagon shaft. The recruiters look the sons over as they would horses. The crucial point is accented when the sergeant goes back to Mother Courage, comes to a standstill before her, and asks: "Why aren't they in the army?" (The effect of such movements should not be weakened by having the actors speak during them.) If changes of position are needed to make certain developments clear to the audience, the movement must be utilized to express something significant for the action and for this particular moment; if nothing of the sort can be found, it is advisable to review the whole arrangement up to this point, it will probably be seen to be at fault, because the sole purpose of an arrangement is to express the action, and the action (it is to be hoped) involves a logical development of incidents, which the arrangement need only present.

On details

On the brightly lighted stage every detail, even the smallest, must of course be acted out to the full. This is especially true of actions which on our stage are glossed over almost as a matter of principle, such as paying on conclusion of a sale. Here Weigel devised (for the sale of the buckle in 1, the sale of the capon in 2, the sale of drinks in 5 and 6, the handing out of the burial money in 12, etc.) a little gesture of her own: she audibly snaps shut the leather moneybag that she wears slung from her neck. It is indeed difficult in rehearsals to resist the impatience of actors who are in the habit of trying to sweep an audience off its feet, and to work out the details painstakingly and inventively in accordance with the principle of epic theater: *one thing after another*. Even minute details are very revealing, e.g., the fact that when the recruiters step up to her sons and feel their muscles as if they were horses, Mother Courage displays maternal pride for a moment, until the sergeant's question ("Why aren't they in the army?") shows her the danger their qualities put them in: then she rushes between her sons and the recruiters. The pace at rehearsals should be slow, if only to make it possible to work out details; determining the pace of the performance is another matter and comes later.

A detail

In pulling a knife, Mother Courage shows no savagery. She is merely showing how far she will go in defending her chil-

dren. The performer must show that Mother Courage is familiar with such situations and knows how to handle them.

Mother Courage has her children draw lots. Only by a mild tirade
and by eloquently averting her face when Swiss Cheese draws
his slip from the helmet—in other words by a slightly exaggerated display of impartiality (see for yourself, no sleight-of-
hand, no tricks) does the actress show that Mother Courage
knows she has been tampering with fate—otherwise she fully
believes what she says, namely, that in certain situations certain
of her children's qualities and defects could be fatal.

Mother Courage predicts that the sergeant will meet an early death.
We discovered that Mother Courage had to turn around toward
Eilif before stepping up to the sergeant to let him draw his lot.
Otherwise it would not have been understood that she does this
in order to frighten her warlike son away from the war.

The belt-buckle deal. Mother Courage loses her son to the recruiter because she can't resist the temptation to sell a belt
buckle. After climbing down from the wagon to bring the sergeant the buckle, she must at first show a certain amount of
distrust by looking around anxiously for the recruiter. Once the
sergeant seizing the string of buckles has drawn her behind the
wagon, her distrust shifts to the area of business. When she goes
to get schnapps for the sergeant, she takes the buckle, which has
not yet been paid for, out of his hands; and she bites into the
coin. The sergeant is dismayed at her distrust.

If the distrust at the beginning were omitted, we should have
a stupid, utterly uninteresting woman, or a person with a passion for business but no experience. The distrust must not be
absent, it must merely be too weak to do any good.

Pantomine

The recruiter must act out the scene where he removes the
harness from Eilif ("the women will tear each other's hair out
over you"). He is freeing him from his yoke.

He has forced a guilder on him; holding out his fist with the
guilder in it in front of him, Eilif goes off as if in a trance.

Proportion

Weigel showed a masterful sense of proportion in playing Mother Courage's reaction to the abduction of her brave son. She showed dismay rather than horror. In becoming a soldier, her son has not been lost, he is merely in danger. And she will lose other children. To show that she knows very well why Eilif is no longer with her, Weigel let her string of belt buckles drag on the ground and threw it angrily into the wagon after holding it between her legs while sitting on the shaft for a few moments to rest. And she does not look her daughter in the face as she puts her into Eilif's harness.

Scene 2

Before the fortress of Wallhof Mother Courage meets her brave son again

Mother Courage sells provisions at exorbitant prices in the Swedish camp; while driving a hard bargain over a capon, she makes the acquaintance of an army cook who is to play an important part in her life. The Swedish general brings a young soldier into his tent and honors him for his bravery. Mother Courage recognizes her lost son in the young soldier; taking advantage of the meal in Eilif's honor, she gets a steep price for her capon. Eilif relates his heroic deed and Mother Courage, while plucking her capon in the kitchen adjoining the tent, expresses opinions about rotten generals. Eilif does a sword dance and his mother answers with a song. Eilif hugs his mother and gets a slap in the face for putting himself in danger with his heroism.

Over-all arrangement

Mother Courage sells provisions at exorbitant prices in the Swedish camp before the fortress of Wallhof; while driving a hard bargain over a capon she makes the acquaintance of an army cook who is to play an important part in her life. In this scene the movement occurs at the pivotal point ("You know what I'm going to do?"). The cook stops peeling his carrots, fishes a piece of rotten meat out of the garbage barrel and takes it over to the butcher's block. Courage's attempt at blackmail has failed.

The Swedish general brings a young soldier into his tent and makes a short speech commending him for his bravery. A drumroll outside the tent announces the arrival of highly placed persons. It need not be clear whether the general drinks in order to honor the soldier or honors the soldier in order to drink. Meanwhile in the kitchen adjoining the tent the cook is preparing the meal. Courage stays right there with her capon.

Mother Courage recognizes her lost son in the young soldier; taking advantage of the meal in Eilif's honor, she gets a steep price for her capon. Mother Courage is overcome with joy at seeing her son, but not too overcome to turn Eilif's reappearance to her business advantage. Meanwhile, the general has the chaplain bring him a spill to light his clay pipe with.

Eilif relates his heroic deed and Mother Courage, while plucking her capon in the kitchen, expresses opinions about rotten generals. At first the mother beams as she listens to the story, then her face clouds over, and in the end she throws her capon angrily into the tub in front of her. Resuming her work, she lets it be known what she thinks of the general; at the same time the general in the tent shows her son on the map what new deeds of heroism he needs him for.

Eilif does a sword dance and his mother answers with a song. Eilif does his sword dance front stage near the partition between tent and kitchen. Mother Courage creeps up to the partition to finish the song. Then she goes back to her tub but she remains standing.

Eilif hugs his mother and gets a slap in the face for putting himself in danger with his heroism.

The capon deal

The bargaining over the capon between Courage and the cook served among other things to establish the beginning of their tender relations. Both showed pleasure in the bargaining, and the cook expressed his admiration not only for her ready tongue but also for the shrewdness with which she exploited the honoring of her son for business purposes. Courage in turn was amused at the way the cook fished the chunk of rotten beef out of the garbage barrel with the tip of his long meat knife and carried it, carefully as though it were a precious object—though to be kept at a safe distance from one's nose—over to his kitchen table. The actor Bildt played the scene brilliantly, making the cook, a Don Juan fired by budding passion, prepare the capon with theatrical elegance. This dumb show, it should be observed, was performed with restraint, so that it did not distract attention from the scene in the tent.

Bildt even took the trouble to acquire a Dutch accent with the help of a Dutchman.

[. . .]

The general

The general was made into something of a cliché. Too much gruff bluster, and the performance showed too little about the ruling class. It would have been better to make him an effete Swedish aristocrat, who honors the brave soldier as a matter of routine action, almost absently. If this had been done, his very entrance—he is drunk, supports himself on the guest of honor, and heads straight for the wine jug—would have been more instructive. As it was, one saw little more than rowdy drunkenness.

[. . .]

The war of religion

The general's treatment of the chaplain is meant to show the role of religion in a war of religion. This was played rather crudely. The general has him bring the burning spill for his pipe and contemptuously pours wine over his coat; with his eyes on Eilif, the chaplain wipes the hem of his cassock, half protesting, half taking it as a joke. He is not invited to sit down to table like the young murderer, nor is he given anything to drink. But what shows his position most clearly is the undignified way, resulting from the indignity of his position, with which he sits down at table and pours himself wine when the general leads the young soldier, in whose presence all this is enacted, to the map on the tent wall, so leaving the table unoccupied. This position is the source of the chaplain's cynicism.

Eilif's dance

The brave son's short sword dance must be executed with passion as well as ease. The young man is imitating a dance he has seen somewhere. It is not easy to make such things evident.

Costume: Eilif has a cheap, dented breast plate and is still wearing his frayed trousers. Not until scene 8 (the outbreak of peace) does he wear expensive clothing and gear; he dies rich.

A detail

During her angry speech about rotten generals Courage plucks her capon violently, giving the plucking a kind of symbolic significance. Brief bursts of laughter from the amused cook interrupt her blasphemies.

[. . .]

Scene 3

Mother Courage switches from the Lutheran to the Catholic camp and loses her honest son Swiss Cheese

Black marketing in ammunition. Mother Courage serves a camp whore and warns her daughter not to take up with soldiers. While Courage flirts with the cook and the chaplain, mute Kattrin tries on the whore's hat and shoes. The surprise attack. First meal in the Catholic camp. Conversation between brother and sister and arrest of Swiss Cheese.

Mother Courage mortgages her wagon to the camp whore in order to ransom Swiss Cheese. Courage haggles over the amount of the bribe. She haggles too long and hears the volley that lays Swiss Cheese low. Mute Kattrin stands beside her mother to wait for the dead Swiss Cheese. For fear of giving herself away, Courage denies her dead son.

Over-all arrangement

During the whole scene the wagon stands left with its shaft pointed toward the audience, so that those to the left of it are not seen by those on the right. Center rear there is a flagpole, right front a barrel serving as a dining table. The scene is divided into four parts: *The surprise attack, The arrest of the honest son, The bargaining, The denial.* After the first two parts the half-curtain is drawn; after the third part the stage is darkened.

Black marketing in ammunition. Mother Courage enters from the left, followed by an ordnance officer who is trying to talk her into something. For a moment she stands front stage with him; after "Not at that price," she turns away from him and sits down on a box near the wagon, where Swiss Cheese is already sitting. The business is conducted in an undertone. Kattrin is called away from taking down the washing and goes behind the wagon left with the ordnance officer. Courage has started mending Swiss Cheese's underdrawers; while working, she admonishes him to be honest. Returning from the other side of the wagon, the ordnance officer takes him away with him. This and the following scenes have the tone of an idyll.

Mother Courage serves a camp whore and warns her daughter not to take up with soldiers. Taking her sewing, Courage sits down with the Pottier woman. Kattrin listens to their conversation as she takes the washing off the line. After her song, Pottier, with a conspicuously whorish gait, goes behind the wagon.

While Courage flirts with the cook and the chaplain, mute Kattrin tries on the whore's hat and shoes. After some brief banter, Mother Courage leads her guests behind the wagon for a glass of wine and they strike up a political conversation. After the inserted sentence "And this war is a war of religion," the cook ironically starts singing the hymn "A stronghold sure." This gives Kattrin time to try on Yvette's hat and shoes.

The surprise attack. The fixed point amid all the running and shouting of the surprise attack is the chaplain who stands still and gets in everybody's way. The rest of the arrangement follows from the printed text.

First meal in the Catholic camp. The chaplain, now Mother Courage's bartender, joins the little family around the cooking pot; Swiss Cheese keeps slightly to one side; he wants to get away.

Conversation between brother and sister and arrest of Swiss Cheese. The conversation between brother and sister takes place at the improvised dining table. When Kattrin sees the spy behind the wagon, she tries to stop her brother from climbing into it. When Courage comes back with the chaplain, Kattrin runs toward her as far as the center of the stage. Courage, the chaplain, and Kattrin group themselves around the table, waiting for the Catholics.

Mother Courage tries to mortgage her wagon to the camp whore in order to ransom Swiss Cheese. The chaplain runs to meet Courage; she is exhausted and he catches her in his arms in front of the wagon. She quickly frees herself from his embrace, which has restored her strength a little, and starts thinking. Her plan is all ready when Pottier comes along with the colonel. Pottier leaves the colonel standing there, runs over to Courage, gives her the kiss of Judas, runs back to her cavalier, and then crawls avidly into the wagon. Courage pulls her out, curses her, and sends her off with a push to negotiate over Swiss Cheese.

Mother Courage haggles over the amount of the bribe. Courage has set Kattrin and the chaplain to washing glasses and scouring knives, so creating a certain atmosphere of siege. Standing center stage between her family and the whore, she refuses to give up her wagon entirely—she has fought too hard for it. She sits down again to scour knives and does not stand up when Pottier comes back with the news that the soldiers are asking two hundred guilders. Now she is willing to pay.

Mother Courage hears the volley that lays Swiss Cheese low. No sooner has Courage sent Pottier away than she suddenly stands up and says: "Maybe I bargained too long." The volley rings

out, the chaplain leaves her and goes behind the wagon. It
grows dark.

For fear of giving herself away, Courage denies her dead son. Yvette
walks slowly out from behind the wagon. She scolds Courage,
warns her not to give herself away, and brings Kattrin out from
behind the wagon. Her face averted, Kattrin goes to her mother
and stands beside her. Swiss Cheese is brought in. His mother
goes over to him and denies him.

Movements and groupings

The arrangement of the movements and groupings must follow the rhythm of the story and give pictorial expression to the
action.

In scene 3 a camp idyll is disrupted by the enemy's surprise
attack. The idyll should be composed from the start in such a
way as to make it possible to show a maximum of disruption.
It must leave room for people to run back and forth in clearly
laid-out confusion; the parts of the stage must be able to change
their functions.

At the beginning of the scene Kattrin is hanging out washing
on a clothesline stretched between the wagon and the cannon
right rear so that Courage can hurriedly take it down at the end
of the scene. In order to rescue her washing, Courage must go
diagonally right across the stage. Kattrin sits huddled by the
barrel right front, where at the beginning Yvette was being
served as a customer; Courage takes soot from the wagon and
brings it to the barrel to rub on her daughter's face. The same
place which up until then had been devoted exclusively to business is now the scene of a private incident. Carrying the cashbox, Swiss Cheese enters diagonally from right rear to the
wagon left front in such a way that his path crosses that of
Courage hurrying to her daughter. First she runs a few steps
past him, but she has seen the cashbox and turns around toward
him just as he is about to enter the wagon. She stands for a
moment like a hen between two endangered chicks, undecided
which to save first. While she is smearing her daughter's face,
her son hides the cash-box in the wagon; she cannot reprove

him until she has finished with her daughter and he comes back out of the wagon. She is still standing beside him when the chaplain rushes out from behind the wagon and points to the Swedish flag. Courage runs to it center rear and takes it down.

The camp idyll that is disrupted by the attack must be divided into distinct parts. After the shady little deal in black-market ammunition has been completed by the wagon steps, Swiss Cheese followed by the ordnance officer goes out right. The ordnance officer recognizes the camp whore who is sitting by the barrel, sewing her hat; he looks away in disgust. Yvette shouts something after him, and then, when the center of gravity has shifted to the right side of the stage, Courage also comes slowly over to the barrel. (A little later Kattrin follows, coming out from behind the wagon and starting once more to hang up the washing.) The two women talk and Kattrin listens as she hangs up the washing. Yvette sings her song. With a provocative gait, she goes out from right front to left rear. Kattrin watches her and is admonished by her mother. The cook and the chaplain come in from the right rear. After a brief bit of banter during which they attract the attention of the audience to Kattrin by the attention they pay to her, Mother Courage leads them behind the wagon. The political discussion and Kattrin's pantomine follow. She imitates Yvette, walking over the same ground. The alarm begins with the ordnance officer and soldiers running in from right rear. The cook goes out in that direction after Courage has run to the cannon to rescue her washing and Kattrin to the barrel to hide her feet.

Important

Courage's unflagging readiness to work is important. She is hardly ever seen not working. It is her energy and competence that make her lack of success so shattering.

A tiny scene

The tiny scene at the beginning of 3, in which army property is black-marketed, shows the general and matter-of-fact corruption in the army camps during the great war of religion. The honest son listens with half an ear, as to something quite usual; his mother does not conceal the crooked business from him, but admonishes him to be honest because he is not bright. His heeding of this advice is going to cost him his life.

Yvette Pottier

Kattrin has the example of Yvette before her. She herself must work hard, the whore drinks and lolls about. For Kattrin as well the only form of love available in the midst of the war would be prostitution. Yvette sings a song showing that other forms of love lead to grave trouble. At times the whore becomes powerful by selling herself at a high price. Mother Courage who only sells boots must struggle desperately to defend her wagon from her. Mother Courage of course makes no moral condemnation of Yvette and her special type of business.

The colonel

The colonel whom Yvette tows in to buy Courage's wagon for her is difficult to play, because he is a purely negative quantity. His only function is to show the price the whore must pay for her rise in life; consequently he must be repellent. [Georg-Peter] Pilz portrayed the aged colonel subtly, making him mime an ardent passion of which he was not for one moment capable. The old man's lechery erupted as though in response to a cue, and he seemed to forget his surroundings. An instant later he forgot his lechery and stared absently into the void. The actor produced a striking effect with his stick. In his passionate moments he pressed it to the ground so hard that it bent; an instant later it snapped straight—this suggested loathsome aggressive impotence and produced an irresistibly comic effect. Considerable elegance is required to keep such a performance within the limits of good taste.

A detail

Having finished hanging up the washing, Kattrin stares open-mouthed at the visitors from the general's tent. The cook honors her with special attention as he follows Courage behind the wagon. This is probably what gives her the idea of stealing Yvette's weapons.

The two sides

While on one side of the wagon the war is discussed with frank mockery, Kattrin is appropriating some of the tools of the whore's trade and practising Yvette's swaying gait, which she has just seen. Here [Angelika] Hurwicz's facial expression was strained and deeply serious.

"A stronghold sure"

The first part of Kattrin's pantomime occurs after "I can see why I liked your face." (The cook added: "And this is a war of religion.") At this point Courage, the cook and the chaplain placed themselves to one side of the wagon in such a way that they could not see Kattrin, and struck up "A stronghold sure." They sang it with feeling, casting anxious glances around them as though such a song were illegal in the Swedish camp.

The surprise attack

It must be brought out that Courage is used to such surprises and knows how to handle them. Before she thinks about saving the cannon, she rescues her washing. She helps the chaplain to disguise himself, she smears her daughter's face, she tells her son to throw the cashbox away, she takes down the Swedish flag. All this she does as a matter of routine, but by no means calmly.
[. . .]

The meal

Courage has prepared it. Enlarged by the new hired man who was a chaplain only that morning, the little family still seem somewhat flurried; in talking they look around like prisoners, but the mother is making jokes again; the Catholics, she says, need pants as much as the Protestants. They have not learned that honesty is just as mortally dangerous among Catholics as among Lutherans.

The chaplain

The chaplain has found a refuge. He has his own bowl to eat from and he makes himself awkwardly useful, hauls buckets of water, scours knives, and so on. Otherwise he is still an outsider; for this reason or because of his phlegmatic disposition he shows no exaggerated involvement in the tragedy of the honest son. While Courage is engaged in her too-long-drawn-out bargaining, he looks upon her simply as his source of support.

Swiss Cheese

It seems to be hard for an actor to repress his pity for the character he is playing and not to reveal his knowledge of his impending death. In speaking to his sister Swiss Cheese shows no forebodings; that is what makes him so moving when he is taken.

Brother and sister

The short conversation between mute Kattrin and Swiss Cheese is quiet and not without tenderness. Shortly before the destruction we are shown for the last time what is to be destroyed.

The scene goes back to an old Japanese play in which two boys conclude a friendship pact. Their way of doing this is that one shows the other a flying bird, while the second shows the first a cloud.

A detail

Kattrin gesticulates too wildly in telling her mother about the arrest of Swiss Cheese. Consequently Courage does not understand her and says: "Use your hands, I don't like it when you howl like a dog. What will the chaplain think? It gives him the creeps." Hurwicz made Kattrin pull herself together and nod. She understands this argument, it is a strong one.

A detail

While the sergeant was questioning her in the presence of Swiss Cheese, Courage rummaged in a basket—a busy business woman with no time for formalities. But after the sentence: "And don't twist his shoulder off!" she ran after the soldiers who were leading him away.

Yvette's three trips

Yvette runs back and forth three times for the sake of Courage's son and her wagon. Her anger changes from mere anger at Courage's attempt to swindle her by paying her out of the regimental cashbox to anger at Courage's betrayal of her son.

Kattrin and the bargaining over Swiss Cheese

The portrayal of mute Kattrin is not realistic if her goodness is stressed to the point of making her oppose her mother's attempt to get the amount of the bribe reduced. She runs off from scouring the knives when she begins to see that the bargaining has been going on too long. When after the execution Yvette sends her ahead and she goes to her mother with her face averted, there may be a reproach in this—but above all she cannot look her in the face.

The denial

Courage is sitting, holding the hand of her daughter who is standing. When the soldiers come in with the dead boy and she is asked to look at him, she stands up, goes over, looks at him, shakes her head, goes back and sits down. During all this she has an obstinate expression, her lower lip thrust forward. Here Weigel's recklessness in throwing away her character reaches its highest point.

(The actor playing the sergeant can command the spectator's astonishment by looking around at his men in astonishment at such hardness.)

Observation

Her look of extreme suffering after she has heard the shots, her unscreaming open mouth and backward-bent head probably derived from a press photograph of an Indian woman crouched over the body of her dead son during the shelling of Singapore. Weigel must have seen it years before, though when questioned she did not remember it. That is how observations are stored up by actors.—Actually it was only in the later performances that Weigel assumed this attitude.

[. . .]

Scene 4

The Song of the Great Capitulation

Mother Courage is sitting outside the captain's tent; she has come to put in a complaint about damage to her wagon; a clerk advises her in vain to let well enough alone. A young soldier appears, also to make a complaint; she dissuades him. The bitter "Song of the Great Capitula-

tion." Courage herself learns from the lesson she has given the young soldier and leaves without having put in her complaint.

Over-all arrangement

Mother Courage is sitting outside the captain's tent; she has come to put in a complaint about damage to her wagon; a clerk advises her in vain to let well enough alone. The clerk comes up to the bench where Courage is sitting and speaks to her kindly. She remains obstinate.

A young soldier appears, also to make a complaint; she dissuades him, arguing that his anger is too short. Two soldiers enter. The younger wants to rush into the captain's tent and the older is holding him back by main force. Courage intervenes and involves the young man in a conversation about the danger of short attacks of anger.

The bitter "Song of the Great Capitulation." The young soldier, whose anger has evaporated, goes off cursing.

Courage herself learns from the lesson she has given the young soldier, and leaves without putting in her complaint.

Courage's state of mind at the beginning of the scene

In the first rehearsals Weigel opened this scene in an attitude of dejection. This was not right.

Courage learns by teaching. She teaches capitulation and learns it.

The scene calls for bitterness at the start and dejection at the end.

Courage's depravity

In no other scene is Courage so depraved as in this one, where she instructs the young man in capitulation to the higher-ups and then puts her own teaching into effect. Nevertheless Weigel's face in this scene shows a glimmer of wisdom and even of nobility, and that is good. Because the depravity is not so much that of her person as that of her class, and because she herself

at least rises above it somewhat by showing that she understands this weakness and that it even makes her angry.
[. . .]

The scene played without alienation

Such a scene is socially disastrous if by hypnotic action the
actress playing Mother Courage invites the audience to identify
with her. This will only increase the spectator's own tendencies
to resignation and capitulation—besides giving him the pleasure of being superior to himself. It will not put him in a
position to feel the beauty and attraction of a social problem.

Scene 5

Mother Courage loses four officers' shirts and mute Kattrin finds a baby

*After a battle. Courage refuses to give the chaplain her officers' shirts
to bandage wounded peasants with. Kattrin threatens her mother. At the
risk of her life Kattrin saves an infant. Courage laments the loss of her
shirts and snatches a stolen coat away from a soldier who has stolen some
schnapps, while Kattrin rocks the baby in her arms.*

Over-all arrangement

After a battle. Courage is standing with two soldiers outside
her wagon; its sideboard is lowered for use as a bar. Kattrin,
sitting on the wagon steps, is uneasy. Courage gulps down two
glasses of schnapps; she needs it to harden her to the sight of
misery.

*Courage refuses to give the chaplain her officers' shirts to bandage
wounded peasants with.* From inside a peasant's wrecked house
the chaplain shouts for linen. Kattrin is prevented by her
mother from taking officers' shirts from the wagon. Courage

obstinately blocks the wagon steps, letting no one in.

Kattrin threatens her mother. With the help of one soldier the chaplain has carried a wounded woman out of the house, then an old peasant whose arm is dangling. Again he calls for linen and all look at Courage who lapses into silence. Angrily Kattrin seizes a plank and threatens her mother. The chaplain has to take it away from her. He picks Courage up, sets her down on a chest, and takes some officers' shirts.

At the risk of her life Kattrin saves an infant. Still struggling with the chaplain, Courage sees her daughter rush into the house that is threatening to cave in, to save a baby. Tugged both ways, between Kattrin and the officers' shirts, she runs about until the shirts are torn into bandages and Kattrin comes out of the house with the infant. Now she runs after Kattrin to make her get rid of the baby. (Movements: Kattrin with the baby runs counterclockwise around the wounded, then clockwise around the wagon.) Her mother stops in the middle of the stage because the chaplain is coming out of the wagon with the shirts. Kattrin sits down on the chest right.

Courage laments the loss of her shirts and snatches a stolen coat away from a soldier who has stolen some schnapps, while Kattrin rocks the baby in her arms. After springing like a tigress at the soldier who has failed to pay, Mother Courage stuffs his fur coat into the wagon.

A new Courage

A change has taken place in Courage. She has sacrificed her son to the wagon and now she defends the wagon like a tigress. She has been hardened by the hard bargains she drives.

A detail

At the beginning of the scene (after "Plenty of victory marches for the Lord but no pay for the men") Weigel's Courage tosses off two glasses of schnapps. Apart from this extenuating circumstance, she provided no justification for Courage's haggling, scolding and raging throughout the scene.

A detail

There was a kind of by-play between the soldier who gets no schnapps from Courage and the soldier drinking schnapps at the bar. It expressed the hostility between the haves and the have-nots. The drinker grins scornfully and drains his glass with ostentatious enjoyment, the have-not gives him a long hostile stare before turning around in disgust and going defeated to the rear—to wait for a chance to lay hands on the schnapps. Later the drinker will show more sympathy than the thirsty man for the wounded peasant woman.

The contradictions must not disappear

The character of the chaplain is based on a contradiction. He is part scoundrel, part superior intelligence. The actor [Werner] Hinz gave him a wooden, awkward, comical quality, which he retained in his role of good Samaritan. His manner was stiff and cold, as though it were only his clergyman's past that impelled him to turn against his present employer. But something else shone through: his former high position gives him the leadership on the battlefield where he acts in a spirit deriving from the realization that in the last analysis he himself was one of the oppressed. When he helps the injured, it becomes clear that he too is to be pitied.

The scene is dependent on pantomime

The effect of the battlefield scene depends entirely on the meticulous pantomime with which Kattrin shows her mounting anger at her mother's inhumanity. Angelika Hurwicz ran back and forth like an alarmed hen between the wounded peasants and Mother Courage. Up to the point when she began to argue, in gestures, with her mother, she made no attempt to repress the voluptuous curiosity that horror inspires in infantile persons. She carried the baby out of the house like a thief; at the end of the scene she lifts the baby up in the air, prodding it with both hands, as though to make it laugh. If her mother's share in the spoils is the fur coat, hers is the baby.

Kattrin

In the battlefield scene Kattrin threatens to kill her mother because she refuses the wounded peasants her linen. It is necessary to show an intelligent Kattrin from the start. (Her infirmity misleads actors into representing her as dull.) At the beginning she is fresh, gay and even-tempered—Hurwicz gave her a kind of awkward charm even in the conversation with her brother in scene 3. True, the helplessness of her tongue communicates itself to her body; but it is the war that breaks her, not her infirmity; in technical terms, the war must find something that remains to be broken.

The whole point is missed if her love of children is depreciated as mindless animal instinct. Her saving of the city of Halle is an intelligent act. How else would it be possible to bring out what must be brought out, namely, that here the most helpless creature of all is ready to help?

A detail

At the end of the scene Kattrin lifted the baby into the air, while Courage rolled up the fur coat and threw it into the wagon: both women had their share of the spoils.

Music and pauses

Music played an essential part in the fifth (battlefield) scene.
Victory march: from the start to "Help me, somebody."
From after "They got my arm" to "I'm not giving anything."
From after ". . . happy in all this misery" to the end of the scene.

Pauses after:
"The mayor must have paid him."
"Where's the linen?"
"The blood's coming through." [This line spoken by the chaplain is deleted from the final text. It followed "your victory's costing me a pretty penny."]

Scene 6

Prosperity has set in, but Kattrin is disfigured

Mother Courage, grown prosperous, is taking inventory; funeral oration for the fallen field marshal Tilly. Conversation about the duration of the war; the chaplain proves that the war is going to go on for a long time. Kattrin is sent to buy merchandise. Mother Courage declines a proposal of marriage and insists on firewood. Kattrin is permanently disfigured by some soldiers and rejects Yvette's red shoes. Mother Courage curses the war.

Over-all arrangement

Mother Courage, grown prosperous, is taking inventory; funeral oration for the fallen field marshal Tilly. Courage interrupts her counting of merchandise to serve brandy to some soldiers who are playing hooky from the funeral. She virtuously reproves them, declaring that she feels sorry for generals because the common people don't give their grandiose plans proper support. Meanwhile she is looking for worms in a tin box. The regimental clerk listens in vain, hoping to catch her in a subversive utterance.

Conversation about the duration of the war; the chaplain proves that the war will go on for a long time. The right section of the stage is the private part. To the left are the bar and the guest table at which the clerk and the chaplain are sitting. There is by-play between right and left when the drinking soldier sings for Kattrin and she smiles at him, while Courage, with a bundle of belt buckles which she is counting, comes over to the table to ask the chaplain-bartender how long he thinks the war will go on. All through his cynical comments she stands deep in thought: Should she lay in new supplies?

Kattrin is sent to buy merchandise. When the chaplain-bartender says the war will go on for a long time, Kattrin runs angrily behind the wagon. Courage laughs, brings her back and sends her to the camp with a big basket to buy merchandise. "Don't let them take anything away from you, think of your dowry."

Mother Courage declines a proposal of marriage and insists on firewood. Courage has sat down on a stool beside her wagon; she fills a pipe and tells the bartender to chop some firewood. He chops clumsily, complaining that his talents are lying fallow, and, probably with a view to avoiding physical labor, asks her to marry him. She hints that she doesn't want to take anybody into her business, and leads him gently back to the chopping block.

Kattrin is permanently disfigured by some soldiers and rejects Yvette's red shoes. Kattrin staggers in with a basket full of merchandise. She collapses at the entrance to the tent and Courage has to drag her over to her stool and dress her wound. Kattrin rejects the red shoes that her mother brings out to comfort her; they are now useless. With silent reproach she crawls into the wagon.

Mother Courage curses the war. Slowly Courage brings forward the new supplies, which Kattrin has defended at such cost, and gets down on her knees to look them over in the place where she was taking inventory at the beginning of the scene. She recognizes that war is a miserable source of income and for the first and last time curses the war.

Inventory

Again Courage has changed. Increasing prosperity has made her softer and more human. Both qualities attract the chaplain and he proposes to her. For the first time we see her sitting briefly at rest, not working.

Funeral oration for Tilly

In the course of many performances it was found that Courage's funeral oration for the field marshal is more effective if during the pause, when all are looking to the rear and the funeral march has grown loud and solemn, the clerk, who is slightly tipsy, rises from his chair and watches Courage closely, suspecting that in this oration she is ridiculing the field marshal. He sits down again in disappointment, because Courage has not said anything demonstrably incriminating.

(The pause during the funeral march must be long; otherwise the funeral scene will not produce the right effect.)

A detail

In the funeral oration for field marshal Tilly ("I feel sorry when a general or an emperor passes away like this") Weigel added—after "he doesn't know any better"—"Jesus Christ, the worms have got into my biscuits." While saying this she laughed. Here Mother Courage releases the merriment which, with the clerk looking on, she was unable to express in her evasively subversive speech.

Pantomime

The chaplain's remarks on the longevity of the war must not take on an independent existence. They are the answer to Courage's anxious question as to whether she can risk taking in new merchandise. While the chaplain was talking, Weigel mimed Courage's anxiety and calculations.

A detail

The drunken soldier addresses his song to Kattrin. She smiles at him. For the last time before she is disfigured the spectator is reminded that she is capable of love.

A point to consider

Violent occupations lead actors to shout. The actor playing the chaplain shouted occasionally while chopping wood. The scene suffered.
[. . .]

Kattrin

Again sitting huddled on the chest as during the drunken soldier's song, the injured girl merely touches her forehead gingerly once or twice to make sure where the wound is; otherwise, except for the willingness with which she lets herself be bandaged, she gives no indication of knowing what the scar will mean to her. Protest is expressed by her lack of interest in Yvette's red shoes and by the way she crawls into the wagon: she blames her mother for what has happened to her.

Contradiction

Courage has cursed the war while gathering up the supplies in defence of which her daughter has been disfigured.

Resuming the inventory begun at the start of the scene, she now counts the new articles.

Scene 7

Mother Courage at the height of her business career

Mother Courage has corrected her opinion of the war and sings its praises as a good provider.

Over-all arrangement

Mother Courage has corrected her opinion of the war and sings its praises as a good provider. Pulled by Kattrin and the chaplain-bartender, the wagon comes in from the rear and rolls along the footlights. Courage walks beside them, arguing with them; then, while singing, she turns to the audience. Pause.

Signs of prosperity

After some forty performances it seemed to us that in scene 6, where she takes inventory, Courage should have rings on her fingers and a chain of silver talers round her neck as a sign of the relative prosperity she had achieved. But after a few more performances one of us discovered that this weakened her speech about the courage of the poor, and we decided to put the signs of prosperity in scene 7. Here, where she retracts her condemnation of war, her recently acquired signs of prosperity show her up for what she is: bribed.

In this short scene Weigel showed Courage in the full possession of her vitality, as previously only in scene 5 (the battlefield scene); in scene 5, however, she was gloomy; here she was cheerful.

[. . .]

Scene 8

Peace threatens to ruin Mother Courage's business. Her brave son performs one heroic deed too many and dies an ignominious death

Courage and the chaplain hear a rumor that peace has broken out. The cook reappears. The fight for the feedbag. An old friend who has made a good thing of the war; Pete the Pipe is unmasked. The downfall of Eilif, Mother Courage's brave son; he is executed for one of the misdeeds that had brought him rewards during the war. The peace comes to an end; Courage leaves the chaplain and goes on with the cook in the wake of the Swedish army.

Over-all arrangement

Courage and the chaplain hear a rumor that peace has broken out. On the right stand an old woman and her son who have come from the city with all sorts of household goods to sell. It is early in the morning, and Courage, still half asleep, answers sulkily from the wagon left. Then bells are heard from the right, the chaplain crawls out from under the wagon where he has been sleeping and Courage sticks her head out of the wagon. The bells seem to have made the old woman happy—not Mother Courage.

The cook reappears. The bells of peace bring all sorts of visitors. First comes—from the right like the rest—the cook, ragged, with all his possessions in a bundle. The chaplain is not pleased to see him, but Courage, who is braiding her hair, runs out to meet him and shakes his hand heartily. She invites him over to a wooden bench in front of the wagon, while the chaplain goes behind the wagon to put on his clericals. Amid the ringing of the bells they sit there almost like lovers, telling each other about the bankruptcy that peace has brought them.

The fight for the feedbag. When the chaplain comes back—he stands in the middle of the stage like a last incisor in a toothless mouth—the cook begins to demolish him. Courage climbs into her wagon to get her pack ready; she is going to sell the merchandise she bought when the chaplain promised her a long war. The cook starts unwrapping his feet because he means to stay, and the chaplain is obliged to beg him humbly not to drive him out. The cook merely shrugs his shoulders.

An old friend who has made a good thing of the war; Pete the Pipe is unmasked. Another visitor. Fat and asthmatic, walking with the help of a cane, the Countess Starhemberg, the former camp whore, enters, clothed in black silk and followed by a servant. She has dismounted from her carriage to call on Mother Courage. She catches sight of the cook, known to her as Pete the Pipe, and angrily denounces him to Courage, who has difficulty in preventing her from attacking him with her cane.

The downfall of Eilif, Mother Courage's brave son; he is executed for one of the misdeeds that brought him rewards during the war. When the women have left, the cook gloomily puts his foot bindings on again and the chaplain relishes his triumph. Their conversation turns to melancholy recollections of the good old war days. Blown in by the bells of peace, soldiers with arquebuses bring in a richly dressed lieutenant—Eilif. His courage deserts him when he hears that his mother is not there. The chaplain gives him a swallow of brandy and, a clergyman once again, accompanies him to the place of execution.

The peace comes to an end; Courage goes on with the cook, in the wake of the Swedish army. The cook tries to get Kattrin to come out of the wagon so he can beg some bread from her. Courage comes running in, overjoyed. The peace is over. The cook does not mention Eilif's death. With the cook's help she packs her belongings into the wagon and they go on without the chaplain.

Advance preparation

In her conversation with the chaplain in scene 6 Weigel very carefully laid the groundwork for her conversation with the cook in scene 8. She said "He was a nice man" a little more warmly and thoughtfully than required by her good-natured rebuff of the chaplain. Consequently in scene 8 she had an audience who knew what was what. This enabled her to take a dry, matter-of-fact tone with the cook. Knowing what it knew, the audience could be touched as well as amused that the subject of their love dialogue should be the fact that they were both ruined.

The dignity of misery

In the cockfight between the chaplain and the cook, Hinz as the chaplain obtained a powerful and natural effect when, suddenly throwing all arrogance to the winds, he begged the cook not to squeeze him out of his place with Courage because, having become a better man, he could no longer practice the clergyman's profession. His fear of losing his job lent him a new dignity.

Humiliations

The cook too is capable of enduring humiliations. At the end of the dialogue in which he triumphs over the chaplain, he removes his shoes and foot wrappings like a man who has come to the end and goal of a long peregrination. Yvette finds him barefooted, which embarrasses the aging Don Juan. After he has been unmasked and the chaplain has lectured him, he sorrowfully puts his footwear back on. The episode in which he begs Kattrin for food was played brilliantly by Bildt. His bundle slung over his shoulder, ready to hit the road, he first tapped his stick nonchalantly on the drum hanging from the wagon. Talking into the wagon, he uttered the words "ham" and "bread" in the tone of a gourmet and connoisseur: the starving cook.

Good business

Yvette Pottier is the only character in the play who strikes it rich; she has sold herself for a good price. She has been as badly disfigured by good food as Kattrin by her scar; she is so fat one has the impression that eating has become her only passion. She speaks with the accent of the Austrian aristocracy. [. . .]

War the provider

Courage comes back from the village exhausted from running but overjoyed that the war has started up again. In high spirits she lets the cook relieve her of her pack. The prospect of good business will enable her to take the cook in. She speaks light-heartedly of the possibility of seeing her son again. "Now there's war again, everything will work out all right" [not in the final text]. She is going to ride over his grave.

A detail

While they are packing, Kattrin appears. She sees the cook staring at her scar, covers it with her hand and turns away. She has come to fear the light.

Again in scene II, when the soldiers drag her out of the wagon, she holds her hand over her eye.

Scene 9

Times are hard, the war is going badly. Because of her daughter, she refuses the offer of a home

The cook has inherited a tavern in Utrecht. Kattrin hears the cook refuse to take her along to Utrecht. The "Song of the Temptations of the Great." Kattrin decides to spare her mother the need to make a decision, packs her bundle and leaves a message. Mother Courage stops Kattrin from running away and goes on alone with her. The cook goes to Utrecht.

Over-all arrangement

Times are hard. The cook has inherited a tavern in Utrecht. In the early dawn of a stormy winter day Courage and the cook, both in rags, bring the wagon to a stop outside a presbytery. The cook morosely unharnesses himself and admits to Courage that he means to go to Utrecht where he has inherited a tavern. He asks her to go with him. Sitting shivering on the shaft, Courage complains of the bad business situation: the war is no longer finding much to feed on.

Kattrin hears the cook refuse to take her along to Utrecht. The cook interrupts the conversation between mother and daughter about the peaceful life in Utrecht, and motions Courage to step to one side with him (to the right, in front of the presbytery). Hidden beside the wagon, Kattrin hears the cook refuse to take her along.

The cook and Courage sing the "Song of the Temptations of the Great." While they sing their begging song, Courage desperately thinks over the cook's offer, presumably her last hope of settling down.

Kattrin decides to spare her mother the need to make a decision, packs her bundle and leaves a message. By the end of the begging song, Courage has made up her mind to decline the offer. She still goes into the presbytery with the cook for the sake of the soup.

Kattrin comes in with a bundle and deposits her mother's skirt with the cook's trousers over it on the wagon shaft.

Mother Courage stops Kattrin from running away and goes on alone with her. Courage catches Kattrin just as she is about to steal away. She has brought a dish of soup. Feeding her as one would a child, she assures her that it has never occurred to her to desert the wagon. She throws the cook's bundle and trousers out of the wagon, puts herself and Kattrin in harness and starts off with her (behind the house, to the right).

The cook goes to Utrecht. The cook sees that the women and wagon are gone. He silently picks up his bundle and starts on his way, right rear, to settle down in Utrecht.

The cook

In this scene the cook must not under any circumstances be represented as brutal. The tavern he has inherited is too small to keep three people, and the customers cannot be expected to put up with the sight of the disfigured Kattrin. That's all there is to it. Courage does not find his arguments unreasonable. Weigel showed plainly that Courage thought the proposition over—she thinks every proposition over. This she did by looking over toward the wagon during the first stanza of the begging song with an expression compounded of indecision, fear and pity.

[. . .]

A detail

In this scene, in which her arguments are rather thin, Courage spoke to her daughter as one speaks to a person who is hard of hearing. Her loud, slow delivery also gives the impression that she is speaking in the name of the cook as well, and in this does not feel at all sure of herself.

Kattrin's demonstration

In laying out the trousers and skirt Kattrin tries to leave her mother a message explaining why she has gone away. But Hurwicz also indicated a note of resentment by glancing at the presbytery where her mother and the cook were presumably eating soup, then looking at her composition and stifling an uncanny, malignant giggle by raising her hand to her mouth before sneaking away.

A detail

While saying the words "Don't go thinking I've given him the gate on your account," Courage put a spoonful of soup into Kattrin's mouth.
[. . .]

The cook starts for Utrecht

Scenes of this kind must be fully acted out: Courage and Kattrin harness themselves to the wagon, push it back a few feet so as to be able to circle the presbytery, and then move off to the right. The cook comes out, still chewing on a piece of bread, sees his belongings, picks them up and goes off to the rear with long steps. We see him disappear. Thus the parting of the ways is made visible.

Scene 10

Still on the road

Mother and daughter hear someone in a peasant house singing the "Song of Home."

The song in the Munich production

A fine variation used in the Munich production: the song was sung with unfeeling, provocative self-assurance. The arrogant pride of possession expressed in the singing turned the listeners on the road into damned souls.

Expression not wanted

The two women enter, pulling the wagon. They hear the voice from the peasant house, stop, listen, and start off again. What goes on in their minds should not be shown; the audience can imagine.

A detail

In one of the later performances Weigel, when starting off again, tossed her head and shook it like a tired draft horse getting back to work. It is doubtful whether this gesture can be imitated.

Scene 11

Mute Kattrin saves the city of Halle

A surprise attack is planned on the city of Halle; soldiers force a young peasant to show them the way. The peasant and his wife tell Kattrin to join them in praying for the city. Kattrin climbs up on the barn roof and beats the drum to awaken the city. Neither the offer to spare her mother in the city nor the threat to smash the wagon can make her stop drumming. Kattrin's death.

Over-all arrangement

A surprise attack is planned on the city of Halle; soldiers force a young peasant to show them the way. A lieutenant and two soldiers come to a farm at night. They drag the peasants, still half asleep, out of the house and Kattrin out of her wagon. By threatening to kill the peasants' only ox they force the young peasant to serve as their guide. (They lead him to the rear; the party go out right.)

The peasant and his wife tell Kattrin to join them in praying for the city. The peasant moves a ladder over to the barn (right), climbs up and sees that the woods are swarming with armed men. He comes down, he and his wife talk it over and decide not to endanger themselves by trying to warn the city. The peasant woman goes over to Kattrin (right front) and tells her to pray God to help the city. The three of them kneel down and pray.

Kattrin climbs up on the barn roof and beats the drum to awaken the city. From the peasant woman's prayer Kattrin learns that the children in Halle are in danger. Stealthily she takes the drum from the wagon, the same drum she had brought back when she was disfigured. With it she climbs up on the barn roof. She starts drumming. The peasants try in vain to make her stop.

Neither the offer to spare her mother in the city nor the threat to smash the wagon can make her stop drumming. At the sound of the drum the lieutenant and the soldiers come back with the young peasant. The soldiers take up a position by the wagon and the lieutenant threatens the peasants with his sword. First one of the soldiers, then the lieutenant moves to the center to make promises to Kattrin. The peasant goes over to a log (left front) and chops at it with an ax to drown out the sound of the drum. Kattrin is victorious in the noise contest, the lieutenant starts to go into the house to set it on fire, the peasant woman indicates the wagon. One of the soldiers kicks the young peasant and forces him to batter the wagon with a plank, the other soldier is sent off for a musket. He sets up the musket, the lieutenant orders him to fire.

Kattrin's death. Kattrin falls forward, the drumsticks in her drooping hands stike one full beat followed by a feeble beat; for a moment the lieutenant is triumphant, then the cannon of Halle respond, taking up the rhythm of Kattrin's drumbeats.

Bad comedians always laugh
Bad tragedians always weep

In sad scenes just as much as in comic ones precision must be combined with ease; the hand that guides the arrangement must be both firm and relaxed. The actors take their positions and form their groups in very much the same way as the marbles tossed into a wooden bowl in certain roulette-like children's games fall into hollows, with the difference that in the games it is not decided in advance which marbles will fall into which hollows, whereas in theatrical arrangements there only seems to be no advance decision. And indeed the reason for the stiffness or heaviness that is so characteristic of sad scenes in the German theater is that in tragedy the human body is unjustifiably neglected and so seems to be afflicted with muscular cramp. Which is deplorable.

Kattrin's two fears

Kattrin's muteness does not save her. The war gives her a drum. With this unsold drum she must climb up on the barn roof, and save the children of Halle.

Conventional heroism must be avoided. Kattrin is ridden by two fears: her fear for the city of Halle and her fear for herself.

"The dramatic scene"

Audiences were especially stirred by the drum scene. Some explained this by saying that it is the most dramatic scene in the play and that the public likes its theater dramatic rather than epic. In reality the epic theater, while capable of portraying other things than stirring incidents, clashes, conspiracies, psychological torments and so on, is also capable of portraying these. Spectators may identify themselves with Kattrin in this scene; empathy may give them the happy feeling that they too possess such strength. But they are not likely to have experienced such empathy throughout the play—in the first scenes, for example.

Alienation

If the scene is to be saved from a wild excitement amid which everything worth noticing is lost, close attention must be given to alienation.

For example: if the conversation of the peasants is swallowed up by a general hubbub, the audience will be in danger of being "carried away"; then they will fail to take note how the peasants justify their failure to act, how they fortify each other in the belief that there is nothing they can do, so that the only remaining possibility of "action" becomes prayer.

In view of this, the actors in rehearsal were made to add "said the man" or "said the woman" after each speech. For example:

" 'The sentry will see them in time,' said the woman."
" 'They must have killed the sentry,' said the man."
" 'If there were more of us,' said the woman."
" 'All by ourselves up here with a cripple,' said the man."
" 'We can't do a thing. Do you think . . .' said the woman."
" 'Not a thing,' said the man," and so on.

Kattrin's drumming

Kattrin keeps watching what is going on down below. Consequently her drumming breaks off after the following sentences.

"Jesus, what's she doing?"
"I'll cut you to pieces."
"We've got a friendly proposition."
"No wonder with your mug!"
"We'll have to set the house on fire."

Detail in tempestuous scenes

Such scenes as the one where the peasant tries to drown the noise of Kattrin's drumming by chopping wood must be fully acted out. As she drums, Kattrin must look down at the peasant and accept the challenge. In tempestuous scenes the director needs a certain amount of stubbornnesss to make miming of this sort last long enough.

A detail

Hurwicz showed increasing exhaustion while drumming.

The ritual character of despair

The lamentations of the peasant woman, whose son the soldiers have taken away and whose farm they threaten when Kattrin starts her drumming to wake the townspeople, must have a certain routine quality about it; it must suggest a "set behavior pattern." The war has been going on too long. Begging, lamenting, and informing have frozen into fixed forms: those are the things you do when the soldiery arrive.

It is worth foregoing the "immediate impression" of a particular, seemingly unique episode of horror so as to penetrate a deeper stratum of horror and to show how repeated, constantly recurring misfortune has driven people to ritualize their gestures of self-defense—though of course these ritual gestures can never free them from the reality of fear, which on the stage must permeate the ritual.

[. . .]

Scene 12

Mother Courage moves on

The peasants have to convince Courage that Kattrin is dead. The lullaby for Kattrin. Mother Courage pays for Kattrin's burial and receives the condolences of the peasants. Alone, Mother Courage harnesses herself to the empty wagon; still hoping to get back into business, she follows the ragged army.

Over-all arrangement

The peasants have to convince Courage that Kattrin is dead. The wagon is standing on the empty stage. Mother Courage is sitting with the dead Kattrin's head in her lap. The peasants are standing in a hostile knot at the dead girl's feet. Courage speaks as if her daughter were only sleeping, deliberately disregarding the reproaches of the peasants who are saying that she is to blame for Kattrin's death.

The lullaby for Kattrin. The mother's face is bent low over her daughter's face. Her song fails to pacify the peasants.

Mother Courage pays for Kattrin's burial and receives the condolences of the peasants. When she realizes that her last child is dead, she rises painfully to her feet and hobbles around the corpse (on the right) and along the footlights to behind the wagon. She comes back with a sheet of canvas. The peasants ask her if she has no one else; she answers over her shoulder: "Yes, there's one of them left. Eilif." And with her back to the audience she lays the canvas over the body. Then at the head end of the body she pulls it up over the face and stands behind the body, facing the audience. The peasant and his son give her their hands and bow ceremoniously before carrying the body away (to the right). The woman also gives Courage her hand, goes to the right and stops again in indecision. The women exchange a few words, then the peasant woman goes away.

Alone, Mother Courage harnesses herself to her empty wagon; still hoping to get back into business, she follows the ragged army. Slowly the old woman goes to the wagon, unrolls the cord which Kattrin had until then been pulling, takes a stick, examines it, pulls the loop of the second cord through, wedges the stick under her arm and moves off. The last stanza of the "Mother Courage Song" has begun when she was bending down over the shaft. The revolving stage begins to turn and Mother Courage circles the stage once. The curtain falls as she turns right rear for the second time.

The peasants

The peasants' attitude toward Courage is hostile. She has caused them great difficulties and they will have her on their hands if she cannot catch up with the departing army. As they see it, she is to blame for what has happened. Besides, she is an unsedentary element, and now in wartime belongs with the incendiaries, cutthroats and looters who follow in the wake of armies. In condoling with her by giving her their hands, they are only doing what is customary.

The bow

During the whole scene Weigel showed an almost bestial stupor. All the more beautiful was her deep bow when the body was carried away.

The lullaby

The lullaby must be sung without any sentimentality or desire to provoke sentimentality. Otherwise its significance is lost. The idea underlying this song is murderous: this mother's child must fare better than other children of other mothers. By slight emphasis on the "you," Weigel portrayed Courage's treacherous hope of bringing her child, and perhaps hers alone, through the war. To this child who had lacked even the most ordinary things, she promised the most extraordinary.

Paying for the burial

Even in paying for the burial, Weigel gave one last hint of Courage's character. She fished a few coins out of her leather bag, put one back and gave the peasants the rest. This did not in the least detract from the overpowering effect of desolation.

The last stanza

The last stanza of the "Mother Courage Song" was struck up by the musicians in the box while Courage was slowly harnessing herself to the wagon. It gives powerful expression to her still unshattered hope of getting her cut from the war. It gains in power if the illusion that the song is being sung by marching armies in the distance is dropped.
[. . .]

Timing

At the end as at the beginning the wagon must be seen rolling along. Of course the audience would understand if it were simply pulled away. When it goes on rolling there is a moment of irritation ("this has been going on long enough"). But when it goes on still longer, a deeper understanding sets in.

The pulling of the wagon in the last scene

For scene 12 the peasants' house and the barn with roof (from scene 11) were removed from the stage; only the wagon and Kattrin's body remained. The word "Saxony" in big letters is hoisted into the flies when the music starts. Thus the wagon is hauled off a completely empty stage recalling scene 1. Mother Courage described a complete circle with it on the revolving stage, passing the footlights for the last time. As usual, the stage was brightly lit.

Realistic discoveries

In giving the peasants the money for Kattrin's burial, Weigel quite mechanically puts back one of the coins she has taken out of her purse. What does this gesture accomplish? It shows that in all her grief the business woman has not wholly forgotten how to reckon—money is hard to come by. This little gesture has the power and suddenness of a discovery—a discovery concerning human nature, which is molded by conditions. To dig out the truth from the rubble of the self-evident, to link the particular strikingly with the universal, to capture the particular that characterizes a general process, that is the art of the realist.

A change in the text

After "I'll manage, there isn't much in it," Courage added, first in the Munich, then in the Berlin production: "I've got to get back into business."

Mother Courage learns nothing

In the last scene Weigel's Courage seemed to be eighty years old. And she understands nothing. She reacts only to remarks connected with the war, such as that she mustn't be left behind, and takes no notice when the peasants brutally accuse her of being to blame for Kattrin's death.

In 1938, when the play was written, Courage's inability to learn from the unprofitable character of the war was a prophecy. At the time of the 1948 Berlin production the wish was expressed that at least in the play Courage would understand.

In order that the realism of this play should benefit the spectator, that is, in order that the spectator should learn something, the theater must work out a way of playing it which does not lead to audience identification with the principal character (heroine).

To judge by press reviews and statements of spectators, the original production in Zurich, for example, though artistically on a high level, merely pictured war as a natural catastrophe and ineluctable fate, confirming the belief of the petit-bourgeois members of the audience in their own indestructibility and power to survive. But even for the equally petit-bourgeois Mother Courage the decision whether or not to join in was left open throughout the play. It follows that the production must have represented Courage's business activity, her desire to get her cut and her willingness to take risks, as perfectly natural and "eternally human" phenomena, so that there was no way out. Today the petit bourgeois can no longer in fact keep out of the war, as Courage could have done. And probably no performance of the play can give a petit bourgeois anything more than a real horror of war and a certain insight into the fact that the big business deals that constitute war are not made by the little people. A play is more instructive than reality, because in it the war situation is set up experimentally for the purpose of giving insight; that is, the spectator assumes the attitude of a student—provided the production is right. The proletarians in the audience, the members of a class which really can take action against war and eliminate it, must be given an insight—

which of course is possible only if the play is performed in the right way—into the connection between war and commerce: the proletarian as a class can do away with war by doing away with capitalism. Here, of course, a good deal depends on the growth of self-awareness among the proletariat, a process that is going on both inside and outside the theater.

The epic element

As for the epic element in the Deutsches Theater production, indications of it could be seen in the arrangement, in the delineation of the characters, in the accurate execution of detail, and in the spirited rhythm of the entire performance. Moreover, the contradictions that pervade the play were not taken over ready-made, but worked out, and the parts, visible as such, fitted well into the whole. Nonetheless, the central aim of the epic theater was not achieved. Much was shown, but the element of showing was absent. Only in a few rehearsals devoted to recasting was it brought out clearly. Here the actors "demonstrated," that is, they showed the new members of the cast certain positions and tones, and the whole took on the wonderfully relaxed, effortless, and unobtrusive quality that stimulates the spectator to think and feel for himself.

No one missed this fundamental epic element; and that is probably why the actors did not dare to provide it.

Concerning these notes

It is to be hoped that the present notes, indicating a few of the ideas and devices of various kinds that are necessary for the performance of a play, will not make an impression of misplaced seriousness. It is difficult in writing about these things to convey the carefree lightness that is essential to the theater. Even in their instructive aspect, the arts belong to the realm of entertainment.

[From *Mutter Courage und ihre Kinder. Text/Aufführung/Anmerkungen.* Henschel-Verlag, East Berlin, 1956.]

Two Ways of Playing Mother Courage

When the title role is played in the usual way, so as to communicate empathy, the spectator (according to numerous witnesses)
experiences an extraordinary pleasure: the indestructible vitality of this woman beset by the hardships of war leaves him with
a sense of triumph. Mother Courage's active participation in the
war is not taken seriously; the war is a source, perhaps her only
source, of livelihood. Apart from this element of participation,
in spite of it, the effect is very much as in *Schweyk*, where—in
a comic perspective, to be sure—the audience triumphs with
Schweyk over the plans of the belligerent powers to sacrifice
him. But in the case of Mother Courage such an effect has far
less social value, precisely because her participation, however
indirect it may seem, is not taken into consideration. The effect
is indeed negative. Courage is represented chiefly as a mother,
and like Niobe she is unable to protect her children against fate
—in this case, war. At most, her merchant's trade and the way
she plies it give her a "realistic, un-ideal" quality; they do not
prevent the war from being seen as fate. It remains, of course,
wholly evil, but after all she comes through it alive, though
deformed. By contrast Weigel, employing a technique which
prevents complete empathy, treated the merchant's trade not as
a natural but as a historical one—that is, belonging to a historical, *transient* period—and war as the best time for it. Here too
the war was a self-evident source of livelihood, but this spring
from which Mother Courage drank death was a polluted one.
The merchant-mother became a great living contradiction, and
it was this contradiction which utterly disfigured and deformed
her. In the battlefield scene, which is cut in most productions,
she was really a hyena; she parted with the shirts because she
saw her daughter's hatred and feared violence; she cursed at the
soldier with the coat and pounced on him like a tigress. When
her daughter was disfigured, she cursed the war with the same
profound sincerity that characterized her praise of it in the
scene immediately following. Thus she played the contra-

dictions in all their irreconcilable sharpness. Her daughter's rebellion against her (when the city of Halle is saved) stunned her completely and taught her nothing. The tragedy of Mother Courage and of her life, which the audience was made to feel deeply, lay in a terrible contradiction which destroyed a human being, a contradiction which has been transcended, but only by society itself in long and terrible struggles. What made this way of playing the part morally superior was that human beings— even the strongest of them—were shown to be destructible.

[Written 1951. From GW *Schriften zum Theater*, p. 895. First published in *Theaterarbeit*, 1952.]

[Misfortune in itself is a poor teacher]

The audience gave off the acrid smell of clothing that had not been properly cleaned, but this did not detract from the festive atmosphere. Those who had come to see the play had come from ruins and would be going back to ruins. There was more light on the stage than on any square or in any house.

The wise old stage manager from the days of Max Reinhardt had received me like a king, but what gave the production its hard realism was a bitter experience shared by all. The dressmakers in the workshops realized that the costumes had to be richer at the beginning of the play than at the end. The stage hands knew how the canvas over Mother Courage's wagon had to be: white and new at the beginning, then dirty and patched, then somewhat cleaner, but never again really white, and at the end a rag.

Weigel's way of playing Mother Courage was hard and angry; that is, her Mother Courage was not angry; she herself, the actress, was angry. She showed a merchant, a strong crafty woman who loses her children to the war one after another and still goes on believing in the profit to be derived from war.

A number of people remarked at the time that Mother Courage learns nothing from her misery, that even at the end she does not *understand*. Few realized that just this was the bitterest and most meaningful lesson of the play.

Undoubtedly the play was a great success; that is, it made a big impression. People pointed out Weigel on the street and said: "Mother Courage!" But I do not believe, and I did not believe at the time, that the people of Berlin—or of any other city where the play was shown—understood the play. They were all convinced that they had learned something from the war; what they failed to grasp was that, in the playwright's view, Mother Courage was to have learned nothing from her war. They did not see what the playwright was driving at: that war teaches people nothing.

Misfortune in itself is a poor teacher. Its pupils learn hunger and thirst, but seldom hunger for truth or thirst for knowledge. Suffering does not transform a sick man into a physician. Neither what he sees from a distance nor what he sees face to face is enough to turn an eyewitness into an expert.

The audiences of 1949 and the ensuing years did not see Mother Courage's crimes, her participation, her desire to share in the profits of the war business; they saw only her failure, her sufferings. And that was their view of Hitler's war in which they had participated: it had been a bad war and now they were suffering. In short, it was exactly as the playwright had prophesied. The war would bring them suffering, and the inability to learn from it.

The production of *Mother Courage and Her Children* is now in its sixth year. It is certainly a brilliant production, with great actors. Undoubtedly something has changed. The play is no longer a play that came too late, that is, *after* a war. Today a new war is threatening with all its horrors. No one speaks of it, but everyone knows. The masses are not in favor of war. But life is so full of hardships. Mightn't war do away with these? Didn't people make a very good living in the last war, at any rate till just before the end? And aren't there such things as successful wars?

I am curious to know how many of those who see *Mother Courage and Her Children* today understand its warning.

[Written 1954. From GW *Schriften zum Theater*, p. 1147.]

Notes on *Mother Courage and Her Children*

Mother Courage and Her Children was first performed in Zurich during the Second World War, with the extraordinary Therese Giehse in the title role. Despite the antifascist and pacifist orientation of the Zurich Schauspielhaus company, which at that time consisted largely of German refugees, the production made it possible for the bourgeois press to speak of the "Niobe tragedy" and of the "heart-rending vitality of this mother animal." Warned, the author made a few changes for the Berlin production. The original text follows.

Scene 1, p. 142

MOTHER COURAGE   ... Be careful, all of you, you'll need to be. And now we'll climb up and drive on.

THE SERGEANT   I'm not feeling so good.

THE RECRUITER   Maybe you caught cold when you took your helmet off in the wind.

(*The sergeant grabs the helmet*)

MOTHER COURAGE   And now give me back my papers. Somebody else might ask for them, and there I'd be without any papers. (*She puts them away in the tin box*)

THE RECRUITER (*to Eilif*)   At least you could take a look at the boots. And then we'll have a drink, just you and me. I'll show you I've got the money, come behind the wagon. (*They go behind the wagon*)

THE SERGEANT   I don't get it. I always stay in the rear. There's no safer place for a sergeant. You can send the men up forward to win glory. You've spoiled my dinner. It won't go down, I know it. Not a bite.

MOTHER COURAGE (*going toward him*)   Don't take it to heart. Don't let it spoil your appetite. Just keep behind the lines. Here, take a drink of schnapps, man. And no hard feelings. (*She reaches into the wagon and hands him a drink*)

THE RECRUITER (*has taken Eilif's arm and is pulling him away toward the rear*)   One way or another, you're sunk. You've pulled a cross, so what? A bonus of ten guilders, and you'll

be a brave man and you'll fight for the king, and the women will tear each other's hair out over you. And you can clout me one on the kisser for insulting you. (*Both go out*)
(*Mute Kattrin has seen the abduction and emits raucous sounds*)

MOTHER COURAGE Just a minute, Kattrin, just a minute. The sergeant's not feeling so good, he's superstitious. I hadn't thought of that. And now we'll be going. Where's Eilif got to?

SWISS CHEESE He must have gone with the recruiter. He was talking with him the whole time.

Scene 5, p. 174

MOTHER COURAGE (*to the others*) What's that? You can't pay? No money, no schnapps. Plenty of victory marches for the Lord, but no pay for the men.

THE SOLDIER (*threatening*) I want schnapps. I came too late for the looting. They only gave us permission to loot the city for an hour. The general says he's not a monster. The mayor must have paid him, that's what I hear.

THE CHAPLAIN (*staggers in*) There's still some wounded in the house. The peasant and his family. Help me, somebody. I need linen.
(*The second soldier goes out with him*)

MOTHER COURAGE I haven't got any. The Regiment's bought up all my bandages. You think I'm going to rip up my officers' shirts for the likes of them?

THE CHAPLAIN (*calling back*) I need linen, I tell you.

MOTHER COURAGE (*rummaging around in her wagon*) Nothing doing. They won't pay, they got nothing to pay with.

THE CHAPLAIN (*bending over a woman whom he has carried out*) Why did you stay here in all that gunfire?

THE PEASANT WOMAN (*feebly*) Farm.

MOTHER COURAGE You won't catch them leaving their property. My beautiful shirts. Tomorrow the officers will be coming over, and I won't have a thing. (*She throws down one, which Kattrin takes to the peasant woman*) Why should I part with my belongings? I didn't start the war.

THE FIRST SOLDIER They're Protestants. Why do they have to be Protestants?

MOTHER COURAGE   Who cares about their religion? They've lost their farm.

THE SECOND SOLDIER   They're no Protestants. They're Catholics like us.

THE FIRST SOLDIER   How do we know who we're shooting at?

A PEASANT (*whom the chaplain brings in*)   My arm is broken.

(*The anguished cry of a baby is heard from the house*)

THE CHAPLAIN   Don't move.

MOTHER COURAGE   Bring the baby out.

(*Kattrin runs into the house*)

MOTHER COURAGE (*ripping up shirts*)   Half a guilder apiece. I'm ruined. Don't move her when you dress the wound. Maybe it's her back. (*To Kattrin, who emerges from the ruins with a baby and goes about cradling it in her arms*) Oh, so you've found another baby to carry around? Give that baby back to its mother this minute, or it'll take me all day to get it away from you. Do you hear me? (*Kattrin pays no attention to her*) Your victory's costing me a pretty penny. There, that's enough, chaplain. Don't run hog-wild with my linen. I won't stand for it.

THE CHAPLAIN   I need more, the blood's coming through.

MOTHER COURAGE (*looking down at Kattrin*)   There she sits, happy in all this misery; give it back this minute, the mother's coming to. (*While Kattrin at last reluctantly brings the baby to the peasant woman, she rips up another shirt*) I'm not giving anything, you can't make me, I've got to think of myself. (*To the second soldier*) Don't stand there gaping, go back and tell them to stop that music, I can see right here that they've won a victory. Take a drink of schnapps, chaplain, don't argue, I've got trouble enough. (*She has to come down from the wagon to snatch her daughter away from the first soldier, who is drunk*) You beast, haven't you had enough victories for today? Stop. You're not running out on me, you've got to pay first. (*To the peasant*) Your baby's all right. Put (*Pointing to the woman*) something under her. (*To the first soldier*) Then leave your coat here, it's stolen anyway. (*The first soldier totters away. Mother Courage goes on ripping up shirts*)

THE CHAPLAIN   There's still somebody in there.

MOTHER COURAGE   Don't worry, I'll rip them all up.

Scene 7, p. 185
Highway. The chaplain, Mother Courage and Kattrin are pulling the
wagon. It is dirty and bedraggled, but new wares are hanging on it.
MOTHER COURAGE (*sings*)

Some people think they'd like to ride out
The war, leave danger to the brave
And dig themselves a cozy hideout—
They'll dig themselves an early grave.
I've seen them running from the thunder
To find a refuge from the war—
But once they're resting six feet under
They wonder what they hurried for.

(*She plays the refrain "The Spring is Come" on her Jew's harp*)

Scene 12, p. 209
PEASANTS   You'll have to be going, woman. There's only one
    more regiment to come. You can't go alone.
MOTHER COURAGE   She's still breathing. Maybe I can get her
    to sleep.

The revolutionary impetus of the Reformation had been destroyed by the Peasant Wars, the greatest disaster in German
history. What remained was business and cynicism. Like her
friends and customers and almost everyone else, Mother Courage—I say this as a help to producers of the play—is aware of
the purely mercantile character of war, and that is precisely
what attracts her. She believes in the war to the very end. It
doesn't so much as dawn on her that only the powerful can hope
to benefit by war. Those who suppose that the victims of catas-
trophes will learn a lesson from them are mistaken. As long as
the masses are the *object* of politics, they cannot look upon what
happens to them as an experiment, but only as a fate; they learn
no more from a catastrophe than a guinea pig learns about
biology. It is not the playwright's business to make Mother

Courage see clearly in the end—she sees certain things toward the middle of the play, at the end of scene 6, and then loses sight of them—what matters to the playwright is that the audience should see.

[From GW *Stücke*, pp. 1439 ff.]

Editorial Note

The first typescript of *Mother Courage*, in Brecht's own typing with its characteristic absence of capital letters, was made in 1939, though there is also what may be a slightly earlier draft of the first few pages in verse. Amended by Brecht and by his collaborator Margarete Steffin, who died in 1941, it was then duplicated for the Zurich production and again in 1946 by the Kurt Reiss agency in Basel. This seems to have been the text which Brecht circulated to some of his friends, and of which one scene was accordingly published in the Moscow *Internationale Literatur* before the première, while a copy served as the basis for H.R. Hays's first American translation. Brecht made a few further additions and alterations to the 1946 version, which was once again duplicated for the Deutsches Theater production of 1949. Brecht's own copies of this Deutsches Theater script bear yet more notes and small amendments, as well as cuts which were disregarded in the published version. This appeared as *Versuche 9* in 1949, continuing the gray paperbound series of Brecht's writings which had been interrupted in 1933.

The main shifts of emphasis in the play were indicated by Brecht in his own notes which followed the first publication of the play in the *Versuche* (1949) and have been reprinted in subsequent editions (pp. 390–394 above). The final versions of these passages, with the exception of the last (which concludes the play) are to be found in the additions to the Deutsches Theater typescript. In the case of the last scene, the major change took place subsequently, between the *Versuche* edition of 1949 and the reprint of 1950. It consisted in the insertion of the stage directions showing Mother Courage first covering her daughter's body, then handing over money to the peasants who carry it away, and of the last sentence "I've got to get back in business."

In previous versions, too, she was made to join in the refrain of the final song. Now, presumably, she was too old and exhausted to do more than pull her wagon.

These changes were, as Brecht said, calculated to bring out Courage's short-sighted concentration on business and alienate the audience's sympathies. Thus in scene 1 she now became distracted by the chance of selling a belt buckle; in scene 5 she no longer helped the others to make bandages of her expensive shirts; while in scene 7 she was shown prospering (her lines up to "The stay-at-homes are the first to get it" were new, while the scene title "Mother Courage at the height of her business career" and the silver necklace of the stage direction were added after the 1949 edition). Besides these, however, Brecht made earlier alterations to two of the main characters—the cook and the camp prostitute Yvette—and to virtually all the songs, whose independent role in the play became considerably strengthened as a result. Scene 8 seems to have called for re-peated amendment, thanks partly to Brecht's uncertainty about the Yvette–cook relationship, which in turn depended on the choice of song for scene 3, where it is first expressed. Another confusion which has perhaps left its mark on the final text concerns religion: the first typescript gave the chaplain the Catholic title of "Kaplan" throughout, putting Courage ini-tially in the Catholic camp, which the Lutherans then overran in scene 3. Though Brecht corrected this on the script, to con-form with the rest of the story, the religious antagonism emerges none too clearly even in the final version.

Brecht's first typescript also numbered the scenes rather dif-ferently, so as to run from 1 to 11, omitting the present scenes 7 and 10. He altered this to make 9 scenes, a division which he retained in the 1946 script, writing the original scene titles, to correspond with it, very nearly in their present form. "The Story" (pp. 331 ff. above) refers to this numbering, as also does a note attached to the typescript:

The minor parts can easily be divided among a small number of actors. For instance the sergeant in scene 1 can also play the wounded peasant in scene 5 and the young man in scene 7 [8]; the general in scene 2 can be the clerk in scene 4 and the old peasant in scene 9 [11], and so on. Moreover the soldier in scene 3, the young soldier in scene 4 and the lieutenant in scene 9 [11] can be performed by the same actor without alteration of makeup.

Settings and costumes
High road with a Swedish city in the background/Inside the general's tent/Camp/Outside an officer's tent/In a bombarded village/In a canteen tent during rain/In the woods outside a city/Outside a rectory in the winter/Near a thatched peasant dwelling.

The chief item of scenery consists in Courage's wagon, from which one must be able to deduce her current financial situation. The brief scenes on the high road which are appended to scenes 6 and 8 [now scenes 7 and 10] can be played in front of the curtain.

So far as the costumes are concerned, care must be taken to avoid the brand-new elegance common in historical plays. They must show the poverty involved in a long war.

The following scene-by-scene résumé of the changes follows the same numbering, the present scene numbers being given in square brackets.

1. [*1*]

In Brecht's first typescript the family arrive to the sound of a piano-accordion, not a Jew's harp, and there are some minor differences in the Mother Courage song.

2. [*2*]

The cook's original name "Feilinger" is amended to "Lamb" on the first typescript. The general's reference to the king and Eilif's reply were added to this; the general's following "You're something like him already" was an afterthought added on the Deutsches Theater script (according to Manfred Wekwerth it was meant to refer to the enthusiasm with which Eilif drank). Eilif's *"doing a war dance with his sabre"* was penned by Brecht on the 1946 script.

The song itself is taken over from Brecht's first collection of

poems, *Die Hauspostille* (1927), and derives originally from the
verse at the end of Kipling's short story *Love o' Women*.

3. [3]

The three sub-scenes (divided by the passage of time) are numbered 3, 3a and 3b, of which only the first has a title. Yvette
originally was Jessie Potter, amended on the first typescript to
Jeannette Pottier; she had become Yvette by 1946. The scene
started with Mother Courage's remark to Swiss Cheese "Here's
your underdrawers," everything to do with the ordnance officer
being added to the first typescript (p. 151).

   Instead of the "Song of Fraternization," Jessie *"sings the song
of Surabaya-Johnny"* (from *Happy End*), immediately after the
words "Then I'll talk about it, because it makes me feel better,"
Courage having just said "Just don't start in on your Johnny."
The text of this song is not reproduced in the typescript, but a
first version of Johnny's description is inserted, with Jeannette
"growing up on Batavia" and the man being a "ship's cook,
blond, a Swede, but skinny." In pen, Batavia is changed to
Flanders, ship's cook to army cook and Swede to Dutchman. A
"Song of Pipe-and-Drum Henny" is added, which is a slightly
adapted version of "Surabaya-Johnny" in three verses (the refrain appears only in the 1946 script). In the text of this song,
which still fits the Weill music, Burma is amended to Utrecht
and the fish market (in "You were something to do with the fish
market / And nothing to do with the army") to a tulip market.
Besides the beginning ("When I was only sixteen") the second
quatrain of the second verse was absorbed in the "Song of
Fraternization," which is substituted in Brecht's amended copy
of the 1946 script. This also adds that the Cook was called "Pipe-
Henny" because he never took his pipe out of his mouth when
he was doing it.

   Some light on the camp prostitute's varying ages is cast by her
ensuing remark about her failure to run him to earth. In the first
typescript it happened "twenty years ago," in the 1946 and
Deutsches Theater scripts "ten years ago," before being reduced to the present "five" some time between 1949 and 1953.

The chaplain's "Song of the Hours" occurs for the first time in the Deutsches Theater script, where it consists of seven verses only and is sung before the curtain to introduce sub-scene 3b. In Mother Courage's subsequent speech on corruptibility (p. 168) there is a section which was cut in this script but is of interest for its anticipation of *The Caucasian Chalk Circle:*

I used to know a judge in Franconia who was so out for money, even small sums from poor people, that he was universally regarded as a good man right up into Saxony, and that's some way. People talked about him as if he were a saint, he'd listen to everybody, he was tough about the amount—wouldn't let anyone say they were penniless if they had anything—widow or profiteer, he treated them all alike, all of them had to give.

4. [4]

The young soldier was originally complaining about the delay in getting his base pay. Brecht's amendments to his typescript introduced the idea of a special reward, as well as giving Mother Courage more to say. The song was called "The Song of Waiting" in this typescript and was amended at every stage, first and foremost by adding the (spoken) parentheses.

5. [5]

See p. 391 above. The cry "Pshagreff!"—Polish Psia Krew (blood of a dog)—near the end was simply "Stop!" until after the 1949 edition.

6. [6]

This scene appeared in the Moscow monthly *Internationale Literatur* (then edited by J. R. Becher), No. 12, 1940. Courage's speech beginning "Money first!" was very much longer there, as also in the first two scripts. The drunken soldier and his song were additions to the first typescript; Courage's suggestion that he may have been responsible for the attack on Kattrin being an addition to the 1946 script. In *Internationale Literatur* and prior to the Deutsches Theater version Kattrin accepts the red shoes at the end of the scene and "sets about her work; she has calmed down."

6a. [7]

See p. 393 above.

7. [8]

This scene (Eilif's death) is the most heavily amended, partly in order to get the confrontation of the cook and Yvette straight. Originally, on the first typescript, she denounces him as "That's Surabaya-Johnny," which prompts Courage to hum the refrain of the song. Courage previously has a song of her own, following the chaplain's "Off war, you mean. Aha!" (p. 190), which she introduces by the lines:

If the Emperor's on top now, what with the King of Sweden being dead, all it'll mean is that the taxes go to the Emperor. Ever seen a water wheel? Mills have them. I'm going to sing you a song about one of those water wheels, a parable featuring the great. (*She sings the Song of the Water Wheel*)
—a song to Eisler's music which is to be found in Brecht's *The Roundheads and Peakheads*. It was omitted from the 1946 script.

8. [9]

The fourth (St. Martin) verse of the "Solomon Song" (itself of course partly taken over from the *Threepenny Opera*) made its appearance in the 1946 script. The cook's tavern was originally in Uppsala, amended when he became a Dutchman.

8a. [10]

The scene was originally un-numbered. The title was added between the 1949 and 1953 *Versuche* editions.

9. [*11*]

The date of the title was at first March 1635 and the threatened town Havelberg. The only change of any substance took place after the peasant's "We could get one [pine tree] and knock her down . . . ," where in all three scripts the soldiers proceeded to fetch one and actually tried to dislodge Kattrin with it. This was deleted on Brecht's Deutsches Theater script, which incidentally bears marks showing exactly where the drumbeats should fall.

9a. [*12*]

See p. 393, 395. On the first typescript lines 5–7 of the song originally read
    He gets his uniform and rations
    The regiment gives him his pay.
    The rest defeats our comprehension
    Tomorrow is another day.
before Brecht amended them to read as now.

APPENDIX

Galileo

BY **BERTOLT BRECHT**

Translated by Charles Laughton

It is my opinion that the earth is very noble and admirable
by reason of so many and so different alterations and generations which are incessantly made therein.

—GALILEO GALILEI

CHARACTERS

GALILEO GALILEI

ANDREA SARTI (*two actors: boy and man*)

MRS. SARTI

LUDOVICO MARSILI

PRIULI, THE CURATOR

SAGREDO, *Galileo's friend*

VIRGINIA GALILEI

TWO SENATORS

MATTI, *an iron founder*

PHILOSOPHER (*later, Rector of the University*)

ELDERLY LADY

YOUNG LADY

FEDERZONI, *assistant to Galileo*

MATHEMATICIAN

LORD CHAMBERLAIN

FAT PRELATE

TWO SCHOLARS

TWO MONKS

INFURIATED MONK

OLD CARDINAL

ATTENDANT MONK

CHRISTOPHER CLAVIUS

LITTLE MONK

TWO SECRETARIES

CARDINAL BELLARMIN

CARDINAL BARBERINI

CARDINAL INQUISITOR

YOUNG GIRL

HER FRIEND

GIUSEPPE

STREET SINGER

HIS WIFE

REVELLER

A LOUD VOICE

INFORMER

TOWN CRIER

OFFICIAL

PEASANT

CUSTOMS OFFICER

BOY

SENATORS, OFFICIALS, PROFESSORS, LADIES, GUESTS, CHILDREN

There are two wordless roles: The DOGE *in Scene Two and* PRINCE COSMO DI MEDICI *in Scene Four. The ballad of Scene Nine is filled out by a pantomime: among the individuals in the pantomimic crowd are three extras (including the* "KING OF HUNGARY"), COBBLER'S BOY, THREE CHILDREN, PEASANT WOMAN, MONK, RICH COUPLE, DWARF, BEGGAR, *and* GIRL.

Scene One

*In the year sixteen hundred and nine
Science' light began to shine.
At Padua City, in a modest house
Galileo Galilei set out to prove
The sun is still, the earth is on the move.*

*Galileo's scantily furnished study. Morning. Galileo is washing himself.
A bare-footed boy, Andrea, son of his housekeeper, Mrs. Sarti, enters
with a big astronomical model.*

GALILEO Where did you get that thing?

ANDREA The coachman brought it.

GALILEO Who sent it?

ANDREA It said "From the Court of Naples" on the box.

GALILEO I don't want their stupid presents. Illuminated manuscripts, a statue of Hercules the size of an elephant—they
never send money.

ANDREA But isn't this an astronomical instrument, Mr. Galilei?

GALILEO That is an antique too. An expensive toy.

ANDREA What's it for?

GALILEO It's a map of the sky according to the wise men of
ancient Greece. Bosh! We'll try and sell it to the university.
They still teach it there.

ANDREA How does it work, Mr. Galilei?

GALILEO It's complicated.

ANDREA   I think I could understand it.

GALILEO (*interested*)   Maybe. Let's begin at the beginning. Description!

ANDREA   There are metal rings, a lot of them.

GALILEO   How many?

ANDREA   Eight.

GALILEO   Correct. And?

ANDREA   There are words painted on the bands.

GALILEO   What words?

ANDREA   The names of stars.

GALILEO   Such as?

ANDREA   Here is a band with the sun on it and on the inside band is the moon.

GALILEO   Those metal bands represent crystal globes, eight of them.

ANDREA   Crystal?

GALILEO   Like huge soap bubbles one inside the other and the stars are supposed to be tacked on to them. Spin the band with the sun on it. (*Andrea does*) You see the fixed ball in the middle?

ANDREA   Yes.

GALILEO   That's the earth. For two thousand years man has chosen to believe that the sun and all the host of stars revolve about him. Well. The Pope, the Cardinals, the princes, the scholars, captains, merchants, housewives, have pictured themselves squatting in the middle of an affair like that.

ANDREA   Locked up inside?

GALILEO (*triumphant*)   Ah!

ANDREA   It's like a cage.

GALILEO   So you sensed that. (*Against the model*) I like to think the ships began it.

ANDREA   Why?

GALILEO   They used to hug the coasts and then all of a sudden they left the coasts and spread over the oceans. A new age was coming. I was on to it years ago. I was a young man, in Siena. There was a group of masons arguing. They had to raise a block of granite. It was hot. To help matters, one of them wanted to try a new arrangement of ropes. After five minutes' discussion, out went a method which had been employed for a thousand years. The millenium of faith is ended, said I, this is the millenium of doubt. And we are pulling out of that contraption. The sayings of the wise men won't wash any-more. Everybody, at last, is getting nosey. I predict that in our time astronomy will become the gossip of the market place and the sons of fishwives will pack the schools.

ANDREA   You're off again, Mr. Galilei. Give me the towel. (*He wipes some soap from Galileo's back*)

GALILEO   By that time, with any luck, they will be learning that the earth rolls round the sun, and that their mothers, the captains, the scholars, the princes and the Pope are rolling with it.

ANDREA   That turning-round-business is no good. I can see with my own eyes that the sun comes up in one place in the morning and goes down in a different place in the evening. It doesn't stand still, I can see it move.

GALILEO   You see nothing, all you do is gawk. Gawking is not seeing. (*He puts the iron washstand in the middle of the room*) Now: that's the sun. Sit down. (*Andrea sits on a chair. Galileo stands behind him*) Where is the sun, on your right or on your left?

ANDREA   Left.

GALILEO   And how will it get to the right?

ANDREA   By your putting it there, of course.

GALILEO   Of course? (*He picks Andrea up, chair and all, and carries him round to the other side of the washstand*) Now where is the sun?

ANDREA   On the right.

GALILEO   And did it move?

ANDREA   I did.

GALILEO   Wrong. Stupid! The chair moved.

ANDREA   But I was on it.

GALILEO   Of course. The chair is the earth, and you're sitting on it.

(*Mrs. Sarti, who has come in with a glass of milk and a roll, has been watching*)

MRS. SARTI   What are you doing with my son, Mr. Galilei?

ANDREA   Now, mother, you don't understand.

MRS. SARTI   You understand, don't you? Last night he tried to tell me that the earth goes round the sun. You'll soon have him saying that two times two is five.

GALILEO (*eating his breakfast*)   Apparently we are on the threshold of a new era, Mrs. Sarti.

MRS. SARTI   Well, I hope we can pay the milkman in this new era. A young gentleman is here to take private lessons and he is well-dressed and don't you frighten him away like you did the others. Wasting your time with Andrea! (*To Andrea*) How many times have I told you not to wheedle free lessons out of Mr. Galilei? (*Mrs. Sarti goes*)

GALILEO   So you thought enough of the turning-round-business to tell your mother about it.

ANDREA   Just to surprise her.

GALILEO   Andrea, I wouldn't talk about our ideas outside.

ANDREA   Why not?

GALILEO   Certain of the authorities won't like it.

ANDREA   Why not, if it's the truth?

GALILEO (*laughs*)   Because we are like the worms who are little and have dim eyes and can hardly see the stars at all, and the new astronomy is a framework of guesses or very little more —yet.

(*Mrs. Sarti shows in Ludovico Marsili, a presentable young man*)

GALILEO   This house is like a marketplace. (*Pointing to the model*) Move that out of the way! Put it down there! (*Ludovico does*)

LUDOVICO   Good morning, sir. My name is Ludovico Marsili.

GALILEO (*reading a letter of recommendation he has brought*)   You came by way of Holland and your family lives in the Campagna? Private lessons, thirty scudi a month.

LUDOVICO   That's all right, of course, sir.

GALILEO   What is your subject?

LUDOVICO   Horses.

GALILEO   Aha.

LUDOVICO   I don't understand science, sir.

GALILEO   Aha.

LUDOVICO   They showed me an instrument like that in Amsterdam. You'll pardon me, sir, but it didn't make sense to me at all.

GALILEO   It's out of date now.

(*Andrea goes*)

LUDOVICO   You'll have to be patient with me, sir. Nothing in science makes sense to me.

GALILEO   Aha.

LUDOVICO   I saw a brand new instrument in Amsterdam. A tube affair. "See things five times as large as life!" It had two lenses, one at each end, one lens bulged and the other was like that. (*Gesture*) Any normal person would think that different lenses cancel each other out. They didn't! I just stood and looked a fool.

GALILEO   I don't quite follow you. What does one see enlarged?

LUDOVICO   Church steeples, pigeons, boats. Anything at a distance.

GALILEO   Did you yourself—see things enlarged?

LUDOVICO   Yes, sir.

GALILEO   And the tube had two lenses? Was it like this? (*He has been making a sketch*)
(*Ludovico nods*)

GALILEO   A recent invention?

LUDOVICO   It must be. They only started peddling it on the streets a few days before I left Holland.

GALILEO (*starts to scribble calculations on the sketch; almost friendly*) Why do you bother your head with science? Why don't you just breed horses?
(*Enter Mrs. Sarti. Galileo doesn't see her. She listens to the following*)

LUDOVICO   My mother is set on the idea that science is necessary nowadays for conversation.

GALILEO   Aha. You'll find Latin or philosophy easier. (*Mrs. Sarti catches his eye*) I'll see you on Tuesday afternoon.

LUDOVICO   I shall look forward to it, sir.

GALILEO   Good morning. (*He goes to the window and shouts into the street*) Andrea! Hey, Redhead, Redhead!

MRS. SARTI   The curator of the museum is here to see you.

GALILEO   Don't look at me like that. I took him, didn't I?

MRS. SARTI   I caught your eye in time.

GALILEO   Show the curator in.
(*She goes. He scribbles something on a new sheet of paper. The Curator comes in*)

CURATOR   Good morning, Mr. Galilei.

GALILEO   Lend me a scudo. (*He takes it and goes to the window, wrapping the coin in the paper on which he has been scribbling*) Redhead, run to the spectacle-maker and bring me two lenses; here are the measurements. (*He throws the paper out of the window. During the following scene Galileo studies his sketch of the lenses*)

CURATOR   Mr. Galilei, I have come to return your petition for an honorarium. Unfortunately I am unable to recommend your request.

GALILEO   My good sir, how can I make ends meet on five hundred scudi?

CURATOR   What about your private students?

GALILEO   If I spend all my time with students, when am I to study? My particular science is on the threshold of important discoveries. (*He throws a manuscript on the table*) Here are my findings on the laws of falling bodies. That should be worth 200 scudi.

CURATOR   I am sure that any paper of yours is of infinite worth, Mr. Galilei. . . .

GALILEO   I was limiting it to 200 scudi.

CURATOR (*cool*)   Mr. Galilei, if you want money and leisure, go to Florence. I have no doubt Prince Cosmo de Medici will be glad to subsidize you, but eventually you will be forbidden to think—in the name of the Inquisition. (*Galileo says nothing*) Now let us not make a mountain out of a molehill. You are happy here in the Republic of Venice but you need money. Well, that's human, Mr. Galilei, may I suggest a simple solution? You remember that chart you made for the army to extract cube roots without any knowledge of mathematics? Now that was practical!

GALILEO   Bosh!

CURATOR   Don't say bosh about something that astounded the Chamber of Commerce. Our city elders are businessmen. Why don't you invent something useful that will bring them a little profit?

GALILEO (*playing with the sketch of the lenses; suddenly*)   I see. Mr. Priuli, I may have something for you.

CURATOR   You don't say so.

GALILEO   It's not quite there yet, but . . .

CURATOR   You've never let me down yet, Galilei.

GALILEO   You are always an inspiration to me, Priuli.

CURATOR   You are a great man: a discontented man, but I've always said you are a great man.

GALILEO (*tartly*)   My discontent, Priuli, is for the most part with myself. I am forty-six years of age and have achieved nothing which satisfies me.

CURATOR   I won't disturb you any further.

GALILEO   Thank you. Good morning.

CURATOR   Good morning. And thank you.

(*He goes. Galileo sighs. Andrea returns, bringing lenses*)

ANDREA   One scudo was not enough. I had to leave my cap with him before he'd let me take them away.

GALILEO   We'll get it back some day. Give them to me. (*He takes the lenses over to the window, holding them in the relation they would have in a telescope*)

ANDREA   What are those for?

GALILEO   Something for the senate. With any luck, they will rake in 200 scudi. Take a look!

ANDREA   My, things look close! I can read the copper letters on the bell in the Campanile. And the washerwomen by the river, I can see their washboards!

GALILEO   Get out of the way. (*Looking through the lenses himself*) Aha!

Scene Two

No one's virtue is complete:
Great Galileo liked to eat.
You will not resent, we hope,
The truth about his telescope.

The great arsenal of Venice, overlooking the harbor full of ships. Senators and Officials on one side, Galileo, his daughter Virginia and his friend Sagredo, on the other side. They are dressed in formal, festive clothes. Virginia is fourteen and charming. She carries a velvet cushion on which lies a brand new telescope. Behind Galileo are some Artisans from the arsenal. There are onlookers, Ludovico amongst them.

CURATOR (*announcing*)   Senators, Artisans of the Great Arsenal of Venice; Mr. Galileo Galilei, professor of mathematics at your University of Padua.
(*Galileo steps forward and starts to speak*)
GALILEO   Members of the High Senate! Gentlemen: I have great pleasure, as director of this institute, in presenting for your approval and acceptance an entirely new instrument originating from this our great arsenal of the Republic of Venice. As professor of mathematics at your University of Padua, your obedient servant has always counted it his privilege to offer you such discoveries and inventions as might prove lucrative to the manufacturers and merchants of our Venetian Republic. Thus, in all humility, I tender you this, my optical tube, or telescope, constructed, I assure you, on the most scientific and Christian principles, the product of seventeen years patient research at your University of Padua.
(*Galileo steps back. The senators applaud*)
SAGREDO (*aside to Galileo*)   Now you will be able to pay your bills.
GALILEO   Yes. It will make money for them. But you realize that it is more than a money-making gadget? — I turned it on the moon last night . . .

CURATOR (*in his best chamber-of-commerce manner*) Gentlemen: Our Republic is to be congratulated not only because this new acquisition will be one more feather in the cap of Venetian culture . . . (*Polite applause*) . . . not only because our own Mr. Galilei has generously handed this fresh product of his teeming brain entirely over to you, allowing you to manufacture as many of these highly saleable articles as you please. . . . (*Considerable applause*) But Gentlemen of the Senate, has it occurred to you that—with the help of this remarkable new instrument—the battlefleet of the enemy will be visible to us a full two hours before we are visible to him? (*Tremendous applause*)

GALILEO (*aside to Sagredo*) We have been held up three generations for lack of a thing like this. I want to go home.

SAGREDO What about the moon?

GALILEO Well, for one thing, it doesn't give off its own light.

CURATOR (*continuing his oration*) And now, Your Excellency, and Members of the Senate, Mr. Galilei entreats you to accept the instrument from the hands of his charming daughter Virginia.

(*Polite applause. He beckons to Virginia who steps forward and presents the telescope to the Doge*)

CURATOR (*during this*) Mr. Galilei gives his invention entirely into your hands, Gentlemen, enjoining you to construct as many of these instruments as you may please.

(*More applause. The Senators gather round the telescope, examining it, and looking through it*)

GALILEO (*aside to Sagredo*) Do you know what the Milky Way is made of?

SAGREDO No.

GALILEO I do.

CURATOR (*interrupting*) Congratulations, Mr. Galilei. Your extra five hundred scudi a year are safe.

GALILEO Pardon? What? Of course, the five hundred scudi! Yes!

(*A prosperous man is standing beside the Curator*)

CURATOR Mr. Galilei, Mr. Matti of Florence.

MATTI You're opening new fields, Mr. Galilei. We could do with you at Florence.

CURATOR Now, Mr. Matti, leave something to us poor Venetians.

MATTI   It is a pity that a great republic has to seek an excuse to pay its great men their right and proper dues.

CURATOR   Even a great man has to have an incentive. (*He joins the Senators at the telescope*)

MATTI   I am an iron founder.

GALILEO   Iron founder!

MATTI   With factories at Pisa and Florence. I wanted to talk to you about a machine you designed for a friend of mine in Padua.

GALILEO   I'll put you on to someone to copy it for you, I am not going to have the time.—How are things in Florence? (*They wander away*)

FIRST SENATOR (*peering*)   Extraordinary! They're having their lunch on that frigate. Lobsters! I'm hungry! (*Laughter*)

SECOND SENATOR   Oh, good heavens, look at her! I must tell my wife to stop bathing on the roof. When can I buy one of these things? (*Laughter. Virginia has spotted Ludovico among the onlookers and drags him to Galileo*)

VIRGINIA (*to Ludovico*)   Did I do it nicely?

LUDOVICO   I thought so.

VIRGINIA   Here's Ludovico to congratulate you, father.

LUDOVICO (*embarrassed*)   Congratulations, sir.

GALILEO   I improved it.

LUDOVICO   Yes, sir. I am beginning to understand science. (*Galileo is surrounded*)

VIRGINIA   Isn't father a great man?

LUDOVICO   Yes.

VIRGINIA   Isn't that new thing father made pretty?

LUDOVICO   Yes, a pretty red. Where I saw it first it was covered in green.

VIRGINIA   What was?

LUDOVICO   Never mind. (*A short pause*) Have you ever been to Holland? (*They go. All Venice is congratulating Galileo, who wants to go home*)

Scene Three

January ten, sixteen ten:
Galileo Galilei abolishes heaven.

Galileo's study at Padua. It is night. Galileo and Sagredo at a telescope.

SAGREDO (*softly*)   The edge of the crescent is jagged. All along the dark part, near the shiny crescent, bright particles of light keep coming up, one after the other and growing larger and merging with the bright crescent.

GALILEO   How do you explain those spots of light?

SAGREDO   It can't be true . . .

GALILEO   It *is* true: they are high mountains.

SAGREDO   On a star?

GALILEO   Yes. The shining particles are mountain peaks catching the first rays of the rising sun while the slopes of the mountains are still dark, and what you see is the sunlight moving down from the peaks into the valleys.

SAGREDO   But this gives the lie to all the astronomy that's been taught for the last two thousand years.

GALILEO   Yes. What you are seeing now has been seen by no other man beside myself.

SAGREDO   But the moon can't be an earth with mountains and valleys like our own any more than the earth can be a star.

GALILEO   The moon *is* an earth with mountains and valleys,— and the earth *is* a star. As the moon appears to us, so we appear to the moon. From the moon, the earth looks something like a crescent, sometimes like a half-globe, sometimes a full-globe, and sometimes it is not visible at all.

SAGREDO   Galileo, this is frightening.

(*An urgent knocking on the door*)

GALILEO   I've discovered something else, something even more astonishing.

(*More knocking. Galileo opens the door and the Curator comes in*)

CURATOR   There it is—your "miraculous optical tube." Do you know that this invention he so picturesquely termed "the fruit of seventeen years research" will be on sale tomorrow for two scudi apiece at every street corner in Venice? A shipload of them has just arrived from Holland.

SAGREDO   Oh, dear!

(*Galileo turns his back and adjusts the telescope*)

CURATOR   When I think of the poor gentlemen of the senate who believed they were getting an invention they could monopolize for their own profit. . . . Why, when they took their first look through the glass, it was only by the merest chance that they didn't see a peddler, seven times enlarged, selling tubes exactly like it at the corner of the street.

SAGREDO   Mr. Priuli, with the help of this instrument, Mr. Galilei has made discoveries that will revolutionize our concept of the universe.

CURATOR   Mr. Galilei provided the city with a first rate water pump and the irrigation works he designed function splendidly. How was I to expect this?

GALILEO (*still at the telescope*)   Not so fast, Priuli. I may be on the track of a very large gadget. Certain of the stars appear to have regular movements. If there were a clock in the sky, it could be seen from anywhere. That might be useful for your shipowners.

CURATOR   I won't listen to you. I listened to you before, and as a reward for my friendship you have made me the laughing-stock of the town. You can laugh—you got your money. But let me tell you this: you've destroyed my faith in a lot of things, Mr. Galilei. I'm disgusted with the world. That's all I have to say. (*He storms out*)

GALILEO (*embarrassed*)   Businessmen bore me, they suffer so. Did you see the frightened look in his eyes when he caught sight of a world not created solely for the purpose of doing business?

SAGREDO   Did you know that telescopes had been made in Holland?

GALILEO   I'd heard about it. But the one I made for the Senators was twice as good as any Dutchman's. Besides, I needed the money. How can I work, with the tax collector on the doorstep? And my poor daughter will never acquire a husband unless she has a dowry, she's not too bright. And I like to buy books—all kinds of books. Why not? And what about my appetite? I don't think well unless I eat well. Can I help it if I get my best ideas over a good meal and a bottle of wine? They don't pay me as much as they pay the butcher's boy. If only I could have five years to do nothing but research! Come on. I am going to show you something else.

SAGREDO   I don't know that I want to look again.

GALILEO   This is one of the brighter nebulae of the Milky Way. What do you see?

SAGREDO   But it's made up of stars—countless stars.

GALILEO   Countless worlds.

SAGREDO (*hesitating*)   What about the theory that the earth revolves round the sun? Have you run across anything about that?

GALILEO   No. But I noticed something on Tuesday that might prove a step towards even that. Where's Jupiter? There are four lesser stars near Jupiter. I happened on them on Monday but didn't take any particular note of their position. On Tuesday I looked again. I could have sworn they had moved. They have changed again. Tell me what you see.

SAGREDO   I only see three.

GALILEO   Where's the fourth? Let's get the charts and settle down to work.

(*They work and the lights dim. The lights go up again. It is near dawn*)

GALILEO   The only place the fourth can be is round at the back of the larger star where we cannot see it. This means there are small stars revolving around a big star. Where are the crystal shells now that the stars are supposed to be fixed to?

SAGREDO   Jupiter can't be attached to anything: there are other stars revolving round it.

GALILEO   There is no support in the heavens. (*Sagredo laughs awkwardly*) Don't stand there looking at me as if it weren't true.

SAGREDO   I suppose it is true. I'm afraid.

GALILEO   Why?

SAGREDO   What do you think is going to happen to you for saying that there is another sun around which other earths

revolve? And that there are only stars and no difference between earth and heaven? Where is God then?

GALILEO   What do you mean?

SAGREDO   God? Where is God?

GALILEO (*angrily*)   Not there! Any more than he'd be here—if
creatures from the moon came down to look for him!

SAGREDO   Then where is He?

GALILEO   I'm not a theologian: I'm a mathematician.

SAGREDO   You are a human being! (*Almost shouting*) Where is
God in your system of the universe?

GALILEO   Within ourselves. Or—nowhere.

SAGREDO   Ten years ago a man was burned at the stake for
saying that.

GALILEO   Giordano Bruno was an idiot: he spoke too soon. He
would never have been condemned if he could have backed
up what he said with proof.

SAGREDO (*incredulously*)   Do you really believe proof will make
any difference?

GALILEO   I believe in the human race. The only people that
can't be reasoned with are the dead. Human beings are intelligent.

SAGREDO   Intelligent—or merely shrewd?

GALILEO   I know they call a donkey a horse when they want to
sell it, and a horse a donkey when they want to buy it. But
is that the whole story? Aren't they susceptible to truth as
well? (*He fishes a small pebble out of his pocket*) If anybody were
to drop a stone . . . (*Drops the pebble*) . . . and tell them that it
didn't fall, do you think they would keep quiet? The evidence
of your own eyes is a very seductive thing. Sooner or later
everybody must succumb to it.

SAGREDO   Galileo, I am helpless when you talk.

(*A church bell has been ringing for some time, calling people to mass.
Enter Virginia, muffled up for mass, carrying a candle, protected
from the wind by a globe*)

VIRGINIA   Oh, father, you promised to go to bed tonight, and it's
five o'clock again.

GALILEO   Why are you up at this hour?

VIRGINIA   I'm going to mass with Mrs. Sarti. Ludovico is going
too. How was the night, father?

GALILEO   Bright.

VIRGINIA   What did you find through the tube?

GALILEO   Only some little specks by the side of a star. I must draw attention to them somehow. I think I'll name them after the Prince of Florence. Why not call them the Medicean planets? By the way, we may move to Florence. I've written to His Highness, asking if he can use me as Court Mathematician.

VIRGINIA   Oh, father, we'll be at the court!

SAGREDO   (*amazed*)   Galileo!

GALILEO   My dear Sagredo, I must have leisure. My only worry is that His Highness after all may not take me. I'm not accustomed to writing formal letters to great personages. Here, do you think this is the right sort of thing?

SAGREDO   (*reads and quotes*)   "Whose sole desire is to reside in Your Highness' presence—the rising sun of our great age." Cosmo di Medici is a boy of nine.

GALILEO   The only way a man like me can land a good job is by crawling on his stomach. Your father, my dear, is going to take his share of the pleasures of life in exchange for all his hard work, and about time too. I have no patience, Sagredo, with a man who doesn't use his brains to fill his belly. Run along to mass now.

(*Virginia goes*)

SAGREDO   Galileo, do not go to Florence.

GALILEO   Why not?

SAGREDO   The monks are in power there.

GALILEO   Going to mass is a small price to pay for a full belly. And there are many famous scholars at the court of Florence.

SAGREDO   Court monkeys.

GALILEO   I shall enjoy taking them by the scruff of the neck and making them look through the telescope.

SAGREDO   Galileo, you are traveling the road to disaster. You are suspicious and skeptical in science, but in politics you are as naive as your daughter! How can people in power leave a man at large who tells the truth, even if it be the truth about the distant stars? Can you see the Pope scribbling a note in his diary: "10th of January, 1610, Heaven abolished?" A moment ago, when you were at the telescope, I saw you tied to the stake, and when you said you believed in proof, I smelt burning flesh!

GALILEO   I am going to Florence.

(*Before the next scene a curtain with the following legend on it is lowered*)
By setting the name of Medici in the sky, I am bestowing immortality upon the stars. I commend myself to you as your most faithful and devoted servant, whose sole desire is to reside in Your Highness' presence, the rising sun of our great age.

—GALILEO GALILEI

Scene Four

Galileo's house at Florence. Well-appointed. Galileo is demonstrating his telescope to Prince Cosmo di Medici, a boy of nine, accompanied by his Lord Chamberlain, Ladies and Gentlemen of the Court and an assortment of university Professors. With Galileo are Andrea and Federzoni, the new assistant (an old man). Mrs. Sarti stands by. Before the scene opens the voice of the Philosopher can be heard.

VOICE OF THE PHILOSOPHER   Quaedam miracula universi. Orbes mystice canorae, arcus crystallini, circulatio corporum coelestium. Cyclorum epicyclorumque intoxicatio, integritas tabulae chordarum et architectura elata globorum coelestium.

GALILEO   Shall we speak in everyday language? My colleague Mr. Federzoni does not understand Latin.

PHILOSOPHER   Is it necessary that he should?

GALILEO   Yes.

PHILOSOPHER   Forgive me. I thought he was your mechanic.

ANDREA   Mr. Federzoni is a mechanic and a scholar.

PHILOSOPHER   Thank you, young man. If Mr. Federzoni insists . . .

GALILEO   I insist.

PHILOSOPHER   It will not be as clear, but it's your house. Your Highness . . . (*The Prince is ineffectually trying to establish contact with Andrea*) I was about to recall to Mr. Galilei some of the wonders of the universe as they are set down for us in the Divine Classics. (*The Ladies "ah"*) Remind him of the "mystically musical spheres, the crystal arches, the circulation of the heavenly bodies—"

ELDERLY LADY   Perfect poise!

PHILOSOPHER   "—the intoxication of the cycles and epicycles, the integrity of the tables of chords and the enraptured architecture of the celestial globes."

ELDERLY LADY   What diction!

PHILOSOPHER   May I pose the question: Why should we go out of our way to look for things that can only strike a discord in this ineffable harmony?

(*The Ladies applaud*)

FEDERZONI   Take a look through here—you'll be interested.

ANDREA   Sit down here, please.

(*The Professors laugh*)

MATHEMATICIAN   Mr. Galilei, nobody doubts that your brain child—or is it your adopted brain child?—is brilliantly contrived.

GALILEO   Your Highness, one can see the four stars as large as life, you know.

(*The Prince looks to the Elderly Lady for guidance*)

MATHEMATICIAN   Ah. But has it occurred to you that an eyeglass through which one sees such phenomena might not be a too reliable eyeglass?

GALILEO   How is that?

MATHEMATICIAN   If one could be sure you would keep your temper, Mr. Galilei, I could suggest that what one sees in the eyeglass and what is in the heavens are two entirely different things.

GALILEO (*quietly*)   You are suggesting fraud?

MATHEMATICIAN   No! How could I, in the presence of His Highness?

ELDERLY LADY   The gentlemen are just wondering if Your Highness' stars are really, really there!

(*Pause*)

YOUNG LADY (*trying to be helpful*)   Can one see the claws on the Great Bear?

GALILEO   And everything on Taurus the Bull.

FEDERZONI   Are you going to look through it or not?

MATHEMATICIAN   With the greatest of pleasure.

(*Pause. Nobody goes near the telescope. All of a sudden the boy Andrea turns and marches pale and erect past them through the whole length of the room. The Guests follow with their eyes*)

MRS. SARTI (*as he passes her*)   What is the matter with you?

ANDREA (*shocked*)   They are wicked.

PHILOSOPHER   Your Highness, it is a delicate matter and I had no intention of bringing it up, but Mr. Galilei was about to demonstrate the impossible. His new stars would have broken the outer crystal sphere—which we know of on the authority of Aristotle. I am sorry.

MATHEMATICIAN   The last word.

FEDERZONI   He had no telescope.

MATHEMATICIAN   Quite.

GALILEO (*keeping his temper*)   "Truth is the daughter of Time, not of Authority." Gentlemen, the sum of our knowledge is pitiful. It has been my singular good fortune to find a new instrument which brings a small patch of the universe a little bit closer. It is at your disposal.

PHILOSOPHER   Where is all this leading?

GALILEO   Are we, as scholars, concerned with where the truth might lead us?

PHILOSOPHER   Mr. Galilei, the truth might lead us anywhere!

GALILEO   I can only beg you to look through my eyeglass.

MATHEMATICIAN (*wild*)   If I understand Mr. Galilei correctly, he is asking us to discard the teachings of two thousand years.

GALILEO   For two thousand years we have been looking at the sky and didn't see the four moons of Jupiter, and there they were all the time. Why defend shaken teachings? You should be doing the shaking. (*The Prince is sleepy*) Your Highness! My work in the Great Arsenal of Venice brought me in daily contact with sailors, carpenters, and so on. These men are unread. They depend on the evidence of their senses. But they taught me many new ways of doing things. The question is whether these gentlemen here want to be found out as fools by men who might not have had the advantages of a classical education but who are not afraid to use their eyes. I tell you that our dockyards are stirring with that same high curiosity which was the true glory of Ancient Greece.

(*Pause*)

PHILOSOPHER   I have no doubt Mr. Galilei's theories will arouse the enthusiasm of the dockyards.

CHAMBERLAIN   Your Highness, I find to my amazement that this highly informative discussion has exceeded the time we had allowed for it. May I remind Your Highness that the State Ball begins in three-quarters of an hour?

(*The Court bows low*)

ELDERLY LADY   We would really have liked to look through your eyeglass, Mr. Galilei, wouldn't we, Your Highness?

(*The Prince bows politely and is led to the door. Galileo follows the Prince, Chamberlain and Ladies towards the exit. The Professors remain at the telescope*)

GALILEO (*almost servile*)   All anybody has to do is look through the telescope, Your Highness.

(*Mrs. Sarti takes a plate with candies to the Prince as he is walking out*)

MRS SARTI   A piece of homemade candy, Your Highness?

ELDERLY LADY   Not now. Thank you. It is too soon before His Highness' supper.

PHILOSOPHER   Wouldn't I like to take that thing to pieces.

MATHEMATICIAN   Ingenious contraption. It must be quite difficult to keep clean. (*He rubs the lens with his handkerchief and looks at the handkerchief*)

FEDERZONI   We did not paint the Medicean stars on the lens.

ELDERLY LADY (*to the Prince, who has whispered something to her*)   No, no, no, there is nothing the matter with your stars!

CHAMBERLAIN (*across the stage to Galileo*)   His Highness will of course seek the opinion of the greatest living authority: Christopher Clavius, Chief Astronomer to the Papal College in Rome.

Scene Five

Things take indeed a wondrous turn
When learned men do stoop to learn.
Clavius, we are pleased to say,
Upheld Galileo Galilei.

A burst of laughter is heard and the curtains reveal a hall in the
Collegium Romanum. High Churchmen, monks and Scholars standing
about talking and laughing. Galileo by himself in a corner.

FAT PRELATE (*shaking with laughter*)   Hopeless! Hopeless! Hopeless! Will you tell me something people won't believe?

A SCHOLAR   Yes, that you don't love your stomach!

FAT PRELATE   They'd believe that. They only do not believe
what's good for them. They doubt the devil, but fill them up
with some fiddle-de-dee about the earth rolling like a marble
in the gutter and they swallow it hook, line, and sinker.
Sancta simplicitas!

(*He laughs until the tears run down his cheeks. The others laugh with*
him. A group has formed whose members boisterously begin to pretend
they are standing on a rolling globe)

A MONK   It's rolling fast, I'm dizzy. May I hold on to you,
Professor? (*He sways dizzily and clings to one of the scholars for*
support)

THE SCHOLAR   Old Mother Earth's been at the bottle again.
Whoa!

MONK   Hey! Hey! We're slipping off! Help!

SECOND SCHOLAR   Look! There's Venus! Hold me, lads. Whee!

SECOND MONK   Don't, don't hurl us off on to the moon. There
are nasty sharp mountain peaks on the moon, brethren!

VARIOUSLY   Hold tight! Hold tight! Don't look down! Hold
tight! It'll make you giddy!

FAT PRELATE   And we cannot have giddy people in Holy Rome.
(*They rock with laughter. An infuriated Monk comes out from a large*

door at the rear holding a Bible in his hand and pointing out a page with his finger)

INFURIATED MONK   What does the Bible say—"Sun, stand thou still on Gideon and thou, moon, in the valley of Ajalon." Can the sun come to a standstill if it doesn't ever move? Does the Bible lie?

FAT PRELATE   How did Christopher Clavius, the greatest astronomer we have, get mixed up in an investigation of this kind?

INFURIATED MONK   He's in there with his eye glued to that diabolical instrument.

FAT PRELATE (*to Galileo, who has been playing with his pebble and has dropped it*)   Mr. Galilei, something dropped down.

GALILEO   Monsignor, are you sure it didn't drop up?

INFURIATED MONK   As astronomers we are aware that there are phenomena which are beyond us, but man can't expect to understand everything!

(*Enter a very old Cardinal leaning on a Monk for support. Others move aside*)

OLD CARDINAL   Aren't they out yet? Can't they reach a decision on that paltry matter? Christopher Clavius ought to know his astronomy after all these years. I am informed that Mr. Galilei transfers mankind from the center of the universe to somewhere on the outskirts. Mr. Galilei is therefore an enemy of mankind and must be dealt with as such. Is it conceivable that God would trust this most precious fruit of His labor to a minor frolicking star? Would He have sent His Son to such a place? How can there be people with such twisted minds that they believe what they're told by the slave of a multiplication table?

FAT PRELATE (*quietly to Cardinal*)   The gentleman is over there.

OLD CARDINAL   So you are the man. You know my eyes are not what they were, but I can see you bear a striking resemblance to the man we burned. What was his name?

MONK   Your Eminence must avoid excitement, the doctor said . . .

OLD CARDINAL (*disregarding him*)   So you have degraded the earth despite the fact that you live by her and receive everything from her. I won't have it! I won't have it! I won't be a nobody on an inconsequential star briefly twirling hither and thither. I tread the earth, and the earth is firm beneath my feet, and there is no motion to the earth, and the earth is the center of all things, and I am the center of the earth, and the eye of the creator is upon me. About me revolve, affixed to their crystal shells, the lesser lights of the stars and the great light of the sun, created to give light upon me that God might see me— Man, God's greatest effort, the center of creation. "In the image of God created He him." Immortal . . . (*His strength fails him and he catches for the Monk for support*)

MONK   You musn't overtax your strength, Your Eminence.

(*At this moment the door at the rear opens and Christopher Clavius enters followed by his Astronomers. He strides hastily across the hall, looking neither to right nor left. As he goes by we hear him say—*)

CLAVIUS   He is right.

(*Deadly silence. All turn to Galileo*)

OLD CARDINAL   What is it? Have they reached a decision?

(*No one speaks*)

MONK   It is time that Your Eminence went home.

(*The hall is emptying fast. One little Monk who had entered with Clavius speaks to Galileo*)

LITTLE MONK   Mr. Galilei, I heard Father Clavius say: "Now it's for the theologians to set the heavens right again." You have won.

(*Before the next scene a curtain with the following legend on it is lowered*)

. . . . . . As these new astronomical charts enable us to determine longitudes at sea and so make it possible to reach the new continents by the shortest routes, we would beseech Your Excellency to aid us in reaching Mr. Galilei, mathematician to the Court of Florence, who is now in Rome . . . . . .

> —From a letter written by a member of the Genoa Chamber of Commerce and Navigation to the Papal Legation.

Scene Six

When Galileo was in Rome
A Cardinal asked him to his home
He wined and dined him as his guest
And only made one small request.

Cardinal Bellarmin's house in Rome. Music is heard and the chatter of many guests. Two Secretaries are at the rear of the stage at a desk. Galileo, his daughter Virginia, now 21, and Ludovico Marsili, who has become her fiancé, are just arriving. A few Guests, standing near the entrance with masks in their hands, nudge each other and are suddenly silent. Galileo looks at them. They applaud him politely and bow.

VIRGINIA O father! I'm so happy. I won't dance with anyone but you, Ludovico.

GALILEO *(to a Secretary)* I was to wait here for His Eminence.

FIRST SECRETARY His Eminence will be with you in a few minutes.

VIRGINIA Do I look proper?

LUDOVICO You are showing some lace.

(Galileo puts his arms around their shoulders)

GALILEO *(quoting mischievously)*
Fret not, daughter, if perchance
You attract a wanton glance.
The eyes that catch a trembling lace
Will guess the heartbeat's quickened pace.
Lovely woman still may be
Careless with felicity.

VIRGINIA *(to Galileo)* Feel my heart.

GALILEO *(to Ludovico)* It's thumping.

VIRGINIA I hope I always say the right thing.

LUDOVICO She's afraid she's going to let us down.

VIRGINIA Oh, I want to look beautiful.

GALILEO   You'd better. If you don't they'll start saying all over again that the earth doesn't turn.

LUDOVICO (*laughing*)   It *doesn't* turn, sir.

(*Galileo laughs*)

GALILEO   Go and enjoy yourselves. (*He speaks to one of the Secretaries*) A large fête?

FIRST SECRETARY   Two hundred and fifty guests, Mr. Galilei. We have represented here this evening most of the great families of Italy, the Orsinis, the Villanis, the Nuccolis, the Soldanieris, the Canes, the Lecchis, the Estensis, the Colombinis, the . . .

(*Virginia comes running back*)

VIRGINIA   Oh father, I didn't tell you: you're famous.

GALILEO   Why?

VIRGINIA   The hairdresser in the Via Vittorio kept four other ladies waiting and took me first. (*Exit*)

GALILEO (*at the stairway, leaning over the well*)   Rome!

(*Enter Cardinal Bellarmin, wearing the mask of a lamb, and Cardinal Barberini, wearing the mask of a dove*)

SECRETARIES   Their Eminences, Cardinals Bellarmin and Barberini.

(*The Cardinals lower their masks*)

GALILEO (*to Bellarmin*)   Your Eminence.

BELLARMIN   Mr. Galilei, Cardinal Barberini.

GALILEO   Your Eminence.

BARBERINI   So you are the father of that lovely child!

BELLARMIN   Who is inordinately proud of being her father's daughter.

(*They laugh*)

BARBERINI (*points his finger at Galileo*)   "The sun riseth and setteth and returneth to its place," saith the Bible. What saith Galilei?

GALILEO   Appearances are notoriously deceptive, Your Eminence. Once when I was so high, I was standing on a ship that was pulling away from the shore and I shouted, "The shore is moving!" I know now that it was the ship which was moving.

BARBERINI (*laughs*)   You can't catch that man. I tell you, Bellarmin, his moons around Jupiter are hard nuts to crack. Unfortunately for me I happened to glance at a few papers on astronomy once. It is harder to get rid of than the itch.

BELLARMIN.   Let's move with the times. If it makes navigation easier for sailors to use new charts based on a new hypothesis let them have them. We only have to scotch doctrines that contradict Holy Writ.

(*He leans over the balustrade of the well and acknowledges various Guests*)

BARBERINI   But Bellarmin, you haven't caught on to this fellow. The scriptures don't satisfy him. Copernicus does.

GALILEO   Copernicus? "He that withholdeth corn the people shall curse him." Book of Proverbs.

BARBERINI   "A prudent man concealeth knowledge." Also Book of Proverbs.

GALILEO   "Where no oxen are, the stable is clean, but much increase is by the strength of the ox."

BARBERINI   "He that ruleth his spirit is better than he that taketh a city."

GALILEO   "But a broken spirit drieth up the bones." (*Pause*) "Doth not wisdom cry?"

BARBERINI   "Can one walk on hot coals and his feet not be scorched?" — Welcome to Rome, Friend Galileo. You recall the legend of our city's origin? Two small boys found sustenance and refuge with a she-wolf and from that day we have paid the price for the she-wolf's milk. But the place is not bad. We have everything for your pleasure—from a scholarly dispute with Bellarmin to ladies of high degree. Look at that woman flaunting herself. No? He wants a weighty discussion! All right! (*To Galileo*) You people speak in terms of circles and ellipses and regular velocities—simple movements that the human mind can grasp—very convenient—but suppose Almighty God had taken it into his head to make the stars move like that . . . (*He describes an irregular motion with his fingers through the air*) . . . then where would you be?

GALILEO   My good man—the Almighty would have endowed us with brains like that . . . (*Repeats the movement*) . . . so that we could grasp the movements . . . (*Repeats the movement*) . . . like that. I believe in the brain.

BARBERINI   I consider the brain inadequate. He doesn't answer.

He is too polite to tell me he considers *my* brain inadequate. What is one to do with him? Butter wouldn't melt in his mouth. All he wants to do is to prove that God made a few boners in astronomy. God didn't study his astronomy hard enough before he composed Holy Writ. (*To the Secretaries*) Don't take anything down. This is a scientific discussion among friends.

BELLARMIN (*to Galileo*) Does it not appear more probable—even to you—that the Creator knows more about his work than the created?

GALILEO In his blindness man is liable to misread not only the sky but also the Bible.

BELLARMIN The interpretation of the Bible is a matter for the ministers of God. (*Galileo remains silent*) At last you are quiet. (*He gestures to the Secretaries. They start writing*) Tonight the Holy Office has decided that the theory according to which the earth goes around the sun is foolish, absurd, and a heresy. I am charged, Mr. Galilei, with cautioning you to abandon these teachings. (*To the First Secretary*) Would you repeat that?

FIRST SECRETARY (*reading*) "His Eminence, Cardinal Bellarmin, to the aforesaid Galilei: The Holy Office has resolved that the theory according to which the earth goes around the sun is foolish, absurd, and a heresy. I am charged, Mr. Galilei, with cautioning you to abandon these teachings."

GALILEO (*rocking on his base*) But the facts!

BARBERINI (*consoling*) Your findings have been ratified by the Papal Observatory, Galilei. That should be most flattering to you . . .

BELLARMIN (*cutting in*) The Holy Office formulated the decree without going into details.

GALILEO (*to Barberini*) Do you realize, the future of all scientific research is . . .

BELLARMIN (*cutting in*) Completely assured, Mr. Galilei. It is not given to man to know the truth: it is granted to him to seek after the truth. Science is the legitimate and beloved daughter of the Church. She must have confidence in the Church.

GALILEO (*infuriated*) I would not try confidence by whistling her too often.

BARBERINI (*quickly*) Be careful what you're doing—you'll be throwing out the baby with the bath water, friend Galilei. (*Serious*) We need you more than you need us.

BELLARMIN Well, it is time we introduced our distinguished friend to our guests. The whole country talks of him!

BARBERINI Let us replace our masks, Bellarmin. Poor Galilei hasn't got one.

(*He laughs. They take Galileo out*)

FIRST SECRETARY Did you get his last sentence?

SECOND SECRETARY Yes. Do you have what he said about believing in the brain?

(*Another cardinal—the Inquisitor—enters*)

INQUISITOR Did the conference take place?

(*The First Secretary hands him the papers and the Inquisitor dismisses the Secretaries. They go. The Inquisitor sits down and starts to read the transcription. Two or three Young Ladies skitter across the stage; they see the Inquisitor and curtsy as they go*)

YOUNG GIRL Who was that?

HER FRIEND The Cardinal Inquisitor.

(*They giggle and go. Enter Virginia. She curtsies as she goes. The Inquisitor stops her*)

INQUISITOR Good evening, my child. Beautiful night. May I congratulate you on your betrothal? Your young man comes from a fine family. Are you staying with us here in Rome?

VIRGINIA Not now, Your Eminence. I must go home to prepare for the wedding.

INQUISITOR Ah. You are accompanying your father to Florence. That should please him. Science must be cold comfort in a home. Your youth and warmth will keep him down to earth. It is easy to get lost up there. (*He gestures to the sky*)

VIRGINIA He doesn't talk to me about the stars, Your Eminence.

INQUISITOR No. (*He laughs*) They don't eat fish in the fisherman's house. I can tell you something about astronomy. My child, it seems that God has blessed our modern astronomers with imaginations. It is quite alarming! Do you know that the earth—which we old fogies supposed to be so large—has shrunk to something no bigger than a walnut, and the new universe has grown so vast that prelates—and even cardinals

—look like ants. Why, God Almighty might lose sight of a Pope! I wonder if I know your Father Confessor.

VIRGINIA   Father Christopherus, from Saint Ursula's at Florence, Your Eminence.

INQUISITOR   My dear child, you father will need you. Not so much now perhaps, but one of these days. You are pure, and there is strength in purity. Greatness is sometimes, indeed often, too heavy a burden for those to whom God has granted it. What man is so great that he has no place in a prayer? But I am keeping you, my dear. Your fiancé will be jealous of me, and I am afraid your father will never forgive me for holding forth on astronomy. Go to your dancing and remember me to Father Christopherus.

(*Virginia kisses his ring and runs off. The Inquisitor resumes his reading*)

Scene Seven

Galileo, feeling grim,
A young monk came to visit him.
The monk was born of common folk.
It was of science that they spoke.

Garden of the Florentine Ambassador in Rome. Distant hum of a great city. Galileo and the Little Monk of Scene Five are talking.

GALILEO   Let's hear it. That robe you're wearing gives you the right to say whatever you want to say. Let's hear it.

LITTLE MONK   I have studied physics, Mr. Galilei.

GALILEO   That might help us if it enabled you to admit that two and two are four.

LITTLE MONK   Mr. Galilei, I have spent four sleepless nights trying to reconcile the decree that I have read with the moons of Jupiter that I have seen. This morning I decided to come to see you after I had said Mass.

GALILEO   To tell me that Jupiter has no moons?

LITTLE MONK   No, I found out that I think the decree a wise decree. It has shocked me into realizing that free research has its dangers. I have had to decide to give up astronomy. However, I felt the impulse to confide in you some of the motives which have impelled even a passionate physicist to abandon his work.

GALILEO   Your motives are familiar to me.

LITTLE MONK   You mean, of course, the special powers invested in certain commissions of the Holy Office? But there is something else. I would like to talk to you about my family. I do not come from the great city. My parents are peasants in the Campagna, who know about the cultivation of the olive tree, and not much about anything else. Too often these days when I am trying to concentrate on tracking down the moons of Jupiter, I see my parents. I see them sitting by the fire with my sister, eating their curded cheese. I see the beams of the ceiling above them, which the smoke of centuries has blackened, and I can see the veins stand out on their toil-worn hands, and the little spoons in their hands. They scrape a living, and underlying their poverty there is a sort of order. There are routines. The routine of scrubbing the floors, the routine of the seasons in the olive orchard, the routine of paying taxes. The troubles that come to them are recurrent troubles. My father did not get his poor bent back all at once, but little by little, year by year, in the olive orchard; just as year after year, with unfailing regularity, childbirth has made my mother more and more sexless. They draw the strength they need to sweat with their loaded baskets up the stony paths, to bear children, even to eat, from the sight of the trees greening each year anew, from the reproachful face of the soil, which is never satisfied, and from the little church and Bible texts they hear there on Sunday. They have been told that God relies upon them and that the pageant of the world has been written around them that they may be tested in the important or unimportant parts handed out to them. How could they take it, were I to tell them that they are on a lump of stone ceaselessly spinning in empty space, circling around a second-rate star? What, then, would be the use of their

patience, their acceptance of misery? What comfort, then, the
Holy Scriptures, which have mercifully explained their cru-
cifixion? The Holy Scriptures would then be proved full of
mistakes. No, I see them begin to look frightened. I see them
slowly put their spoons down on the table. They would feel
cheated. "There is no eye watching over us, after all," they
would say. "We have to start out on our own, at our time of
life. Nobody has planned a part for us beyond this wretched
one on a worthless star. There is no meaning in our misery.
Hunger is just not having eaten. It is no test of strength.
Effort is just stooping and carrying. It is not a virtue." Can
you understand that I read into the decree of the Holy Office
a noble motherly pity and a great goodness of the soul?

GALILEO (*embarrassed*)   Hm, well at least you have found out that
it is not a question of the satellites of Jupiter, but of the
peasants of the Campagna! And don't try to break me down
by the halo of beauty that radiates from old age. How does a
pearl develop in an oyster? A jagged grain of sand makes its
way into the oyster's shell and makes its life unbearable. The
oyster exudes slime to cover the grain of sand and the slime
eventually hardens into a pearl. The oyster nearly dies in the
process. To hell with the pearl, give me the healthy oyster!
And virtues are not exclusive to misery. If your parents were
prosperous and happy, they might develop the virtues of
happiness and prosperity. Today the virtues of exhaustion
are caused by the exhausted land. For that my new water
pumps could work more wonders than their ridiculous superhuman efforts. Be fruitful and multiply: for war will cut
down the population, and our fields are barren! (*A pause*) Shall
I lie to your people?

LITTLE MONK   We must be silent from the highest of motives:
the inward peace of less fortunate souls.

GALILEO   My dear man, as a bonus for not meddling with your
parents' peace, the authorities are tendering me, on a silver
platter, persecution-free, my share of the fat sweated from
your parents, who, as you know, were made in God's image.
Should I condone this decree, my motives might not be disin-
terested: easy life, no persecution and so on.

LITTLE MONK   Mr. Galilei, I am a priest.

GALILEO   You are also a physicist. How can new machinery be evolved to domesticate the river water if we physicists are forbidden to study, discuss, and pool our findings about the greatest machinery of all, the machinery of the heavenly bodies? Can I reconcile my findings on the paths of falling bodies with the current belief in the tracks of witches on broom sticks? (*A pause*) I am sorry—I shouldn't have said that.

LITTLE MONK   You don't think that the truth, if it is the truth, would make its way without us?

GALILEO   No! No! No! As much of the truth gets through as we push through. You talk about the Campagna peasants as if they were the moss on their huts. Naturally, if they don't get a move on and learn to think for themselves, the most efficient of irrigation systems cannot help them. I can see their divine patience, but where is their divine fury?

LITTLE MONK (*helpless*)   They are old!

(*Galileo stands for a moment, beaten; he cannot meet the little monk's eyes. He takes a manuscript from the table and throws it violently on the ground*)

LITTLE MONK   What is that?

GALILEO   Here is writ what draws the ocean when it ebbs and flows. Let it lie there. Thou shalt not read. (*Little Monk has picked up the manuscript*) Already! An apple of the tree of knowledge, he can't wait, he wolfs it down. He will rot in hell for all eternity. Look at him, where are his manners?—Sometimes I think I would let them imprison me in a place a thousand feet beneath the earth where no light could reach me, if in exchange I could find out what stuff that is: "Light." The bad thing is that, when I find something, I have to boast about it like a lover or a drunkard or a traitor. That is a hopeless vice and leads to the abyss. I wonder how long I shall be content to discuss it with my dog!

LITTLE MONK (*immersed in the manuscript*)   I don't understand this sentence.

GALILEO   I'll explain it to you, I'll explain it to you.

(*They are sitting on the floor*)

Scene Eight

Eight long years with tongue in cheek
Of what he knew he did not speak.
Then temptation grew too great
And Galileo challenged fate.

Galileo's house in Florence again. Galileo is supervising his Assistants Andrea, Federzoni, and the Little Monk who are about to prepare an experiment. Mrs. Sarti and Virginia are at a long table sewing bridal linen. There is a new telescope, larger than the old one. At the moment it is covered with a cloth.

ANDREA (*looking up a schedule*) Thursday. Afternoon. Floating bodies again. Ice, bowl of water, scales, and it says here an iron needle. Aristotle.

VIRGINIA Ludovico likes to entertain. We must take care to be neat. His mother notices every stitch. She doesn't approve of father's books.

MRS. SARTI That's all a thing of the past. He hasn't published a book for years.

VIRGINIA That's true. Oh Sarti, it's fun sewing a trousseau.

MRS. SARTI Virginia, I want to talk to you. You are very young, and you have no mother, and your father is putting those pieces of ice in water, and marriage is too serious a business to go into blind. Now you should go to see a real astronomer from the university and have him cast your horoscope so you know where you stand. (*Virginia giggles*) What's the matter?

VIRGINIA I've been already.

MRS. SARTI Tell Sarti.

VIRGINIA I have to be careful for three months now because the sun is in Capricorn, but after that I get a favorable ascendant, and I can undertake a journey if I am careful of Uranus, as I'm a Scorpion.

MRS. SARTI What about Ludovico?

VIRGINIA He's a Leo, the astronomer said. Leos are sensual. (*Giggles*)

(*There is a knock at the door, it opens. Enter the Rector of the University, the philosopher of Scene Four, bringing a book*)

RECTOR (*to Virginia*)   This is about the burning issue of the moment. He may want to glance over it. My faculty would appreciate his comments. No, don't disturb him now, my dear. Every minute one takes of your father's time is stolen from Italy. (*He goes*)

VIRGINIA   Federzoni! The rector of the university brought this. (*Federzoni takes it*)

GALILEO   What's it about?

FEDERZONI (*spelling*)   De maculis in sole.

ANDREA   Oh, it's on the sun spots! (*Andrea comes one side, and the Little Monk the other, to look at the book*)

ANDREA   A new one! (*Federzoni resentfully puts the book into their hands and continues with the preparation of the experiment*)

ANDREA   Listen to this dedication. (*Quotes*) "To the greatest living authority on physics, Galileo Galilei."—I read Fabricius' paper the other day. Fabricius says the spots are clusters of planets between us and the sun.

LITTLE MONK   Doubtful.

GALILEO (*noncommittal*)   Yes?

ANDREA   Paris and Prague hold that they are vapors from the sun. Federzoni doubts that.

FERDERZONI   Me? You leave me out. I said "hm," that was all. And don't discuss new things before me. I can't read the material, it's in Latin. (*He drops the scales and stands trembling with fury*) Tell me, can I doubt anything? (*Galileo walks over and picks up the scales silently. Pause*)

LITTLE MONK   There is happiness in doubting, I wonder why.

ANDREA   Aren't we going to take this up?

GALILEO   At the moment we are investigating floating bodies.

ANDREA   Mother has baskets full of letters from all over Europe asking his opinion.

FEDERZONI   The question is whether you can afford to remain silent.

GALILEO   I cannot afford to be smoked on a wood fire like a ham.

ANDREA (*surprised*)   Ah. You think the sun spots may have something to do with that again? (*Galileo does not answer*)

ANDREA   Well, we stick to fiddling about with bits of ice in water. They can't hurt you.

GALILEO   Correct.—Our thesis!

ANDREA   All things that are lighter than water float, and all things that are heavier sink.

GALILEO   Aristotle says—

LITTLE MONK   (*reading out of a book, translating*) "A broad and flat disk of ice, although heavier than water, still floats, because it is unable to divide the water."

GALILEO   Well, now I push the ice below the surface. I take away the pressure of my hands. What happens?
(*Pause*)

LITTLE MONK   It rises to the surface.

GALILEO   Correct. It seems to be able to divide the water as it's coming up, doesn't it?

LITTLE MONK   Could it be lighter than water after all?

GALILEO   Aha!

ANDREA   Then all things that are lighter than water float, and all things that are heavier sink. Q. e. d.

GALILEO   Not at all. Hand me that iron needle. Heavier than water? (*They all nod*) A piece of paper. (*He places the needle on a piece of paper and floats it on the surface of the water. Pause*) Do not be hasty with your conclusion. (*Pause*) What happens?

FEDERZONI   The paper has sunk, the needle is floating.

VIRGINIA   What's the matter?

MRS. SARTI   Every time I hear them laugh it sends shivers down my spine.
(*There is a knocking at the outer door*)

MRS. SARTI   Who's that at the door?
(*Enter Ludovico. Virginia runs to him. They embrace. Ludovico is followed by a servant with baggage*)

MRS. SARTI   Well!

VIRGINIA   Oh! Why didn't you write that you were coming?

LUDOVICO   I decided on the spur of the moment. I was over inspecting our vineyards at Bucciole. I couldn't keep away.

GALILEO   Who's that?

LITTLE MONK   Miss Virginia's intended. What's the matter with your eyes?

GALILEO (*blinking*)   Oh yes, it's Ludovico, so it is. Well! Sarti, get

a jug of that Sicilian wine, the old kind. We celebrate.
(*Everybody sits down. Mrs. Sarti has left, followed by Ludovico's Servant.*)

GALILEO   Well, Ludovico, old man. How are the horses?

LUDOVICO   The horses are fine.

GALILEO   Fine.

LUDOVICO   But those vineyards need a firm hand. (*To Virginia*) You look pale. Country life will suit you. Mother's planning on September.

VIRGINIA   I suppose I oughtn't, but stay here, I've got something to show you.

LUDOVICO   What?

VIRGINIA   Never mind. I won't be ten minutes. (*She runs out*)

LUDOVICO   How's life these days, sir?

GALILEO   Dull.—How was the journey?

LUDOVICO   Dull.—Before I forget, mother sends her congratulations on your admirable tact over the latest rumblings of science.

GALILEO   Thank her from me.

LUDOVICO   Christopher Clavius had all Rome on its ears. He said he was afraid that the turning around business might crop up again on account of these spots on the sun.

ANDREA   Clavius is on the same track! (*To Ludovico*) My mother's baskets are full of letters from all over Europe asking Mr. Galilei's opinion.

GALILEO   I am engaged in investigating the habits of floating bodies. Any harm in that?
(*Mrs. Sarti re-enters, followed by the Servant. They bring wine and glasses on a tray*)

GALILEO (*hands out the wine*)   What news from the Holy City, apart from the prospect of my sins?

LUDOVICO   The Holy Father is on his death bed. Hadn't you heard?

LITTLE MONK   My goodness! What about the succession?

LUDOVICO   All the talk is of Barberini.

GALILEO   Barberini?

ANDREA   Mr. Galilei knows Barberini.

LITTLE MONK   Cardinal Barberini is a mathematician.

FEDERZONI   A scientist in the chair of Peter!
(*Pause*)

GALILEO (*cheering up enormously*)   This means change. We might
live to see the day, Federzoni, when we don't have to whisper
that two and two are four. (*To Ludovico*) I like this wine. Don't
you, Ludovico?

LUDOVICO   I like it.

GALILEO   I know the hill where it is grown. The slope is steep
and stony, the grape almost blue. I am fond of this wine.

LUDOVICO   Yes, sir.

GALILEO   There are shadows in this wine. It is almost sweet but
just stops short.—Andrea, clear that stuff away, ice, bowl and
needle.—I cherish the consolations of the flesh. I have no
patience with cowards who call them weaknesses. I say there
is a certain achievement in enjoying things.

(*The Pupils get up and go to the experiment table*)

LITTLE MONK   What are we to do?

FEDERZONI   He is starting on the sun.

(*They begin with clearing up*)

ANDREA (*singing in a low voice*)
    The Bible proves the earth stands still,
    The Pope, he swears with tears:
    The earth stands still. To prove it so
    He takes it by the ears.

LUDOVICO   What's the excitement?

MRS. SARTI   You're not going to start those hellish goings-on
again, Mr. Galilei?

ANDREA
    And gentlefolk, they say so too.
    Each learned doctor proves,
    (If you grease his palm): The earth stands still.
    And yet—and yet it moves.

GALILEO   Barberini is in the ascendant, so your mother is uneasy, and you're sent to investigate me. Correct me if I am
wrong, Ludovico. Clavius is right: these spots on the sun
interest me.

ANDREA   We might find out that the sun also revolves. How
would you like that, Ludovico?

GALILEO   Do you like my wine, Ludovico?

LUDOVICO   I told you I did, sir.

GALILEO   You really like it?

LUDOVICO   I like it.

GALILEO   Tell me, Ludovico, would you consider going so far as to accept a man's wine or his daughter without insisting that he drop his profession? I have no wish to intrude, but have the moons of Jupiter affected Virginia's bottom?

MRS. SARTI   That isn't funny, it's just vulgar. I am going for Virginia.

LUDOVICO (*keeps her back*)   Marriages in families such as mine are not arranged on a basis of sexual attraction alone.

GALILEO   Did they keep you back from marrying my daughter for eight years because I was on probation?

LUDOVICO   My future wife must take her place in the family pew.

GALILEO   You mean, if the daughter of a bad man sat in your family pew, your peasants might stop paying the rent?

LUDOVICO   In a sort of way.

GALILEO   When I was your age, the only person I allowed to rap me on the knuckles was my girl.

LUDOVICO   My mother was assured that you had undertaken not to get mixed up in this turning around business again, sir.

GALILEO   We had a conservative Pope then.

MRS. SARTI   Had! His Holiness is not dead yet!

GALILEO (*with relish*)   Pretty nearly.

MRS. SARTI   That man will weigh a chip of ice fifty times, but when it comes to something that's convenient, he believes it blindly. "Is His Holiness dead?" — "Pretty nearly!"

LUDOVICO   You will find, sir, if His Holiness passes away, the new Pope, whoever he turns out to be, will respect the convictions held by the solid families of the country.

GALILEO (*to Andrea*)   That remains to be seen. — Andrea, get out the screen. We'll throw the image of the sun on our screen to save our eyes.

LITTLE MONK   I thought you'd been working at it. Do you know when I guessed it? When you didn't recognize Mr. Marsili.

MRS. SARTI   If my son has to go to hell for sticking to you, that's my affair, but you have no right to trample on your daughter's happiness.

LUDOVICO (*to his Servant*)   Giuseppe, take my baggage back to the coach, will you?

MRS. SARTI   This will kill her. (*She runs out, still clutching the jug*)

LUDOVICO (*politely*)   Mr. Galilei, if we Marsilis were to countenance teachings frowned on by the church, it would unsettle
our peasants. Bear in mind: these poor people in their brute
state get everything upside down. They are nothing but animals. They will never comprehend the finer points of astronomy. Why, two months ago a rumor went around, an
apple had been found on a pear tree, and they left their work
in the fields to discuss it.

GALILEO (*interested*)   Did they?

LUDOVICO   I have seen the day when my poor mother has had
to have a dog whipped before their eyes to remind them to
keep their place. Oh, you may have seen the waving corn
from the window of your comfortable coach. You have, no
doubt, nibbled our olives, and absentmindedly eaten our
cheese, but you can have no idea how much responsibility
that sort of thing entails.

GALILEO   Young man, I do not eat my cheese absentmindedly.
(*To Andrea*) Are we ready?

ANDREA   Yes, sir.

GALILEO (*leaves Ludovico and adjusts the mirror*)   You would not
confine your whippings to dogs to remind your peasants to
keep their places, would you, Marsili?

LUDOVICO (*after a pause*)   Mr. Galilei, you have a wonderful
brain, it's a pity.

LITTLE MONK (*astonished*)   He threatened you.

GALILEO   Yes. And he threatened you too. We might unsettle
his peasants. Your sister, Fulganzio, who works the lever of
the olive press, might laugh out loud if she heard the sun is
not a gilded coat of arms but a lever too. The earth turns
because the sun turns it.

ANDREA   That could interest his steward too and even his
money lender—and the seaport towns. . . .

FEDERZONI   None of them speak Latin.

GALILEO   I might write in plain language. The work we do is
exacting. Who would go through the strain for less than the
population at large!

LUDOVICO   I see you have made your decision. It was inevitable.
You will always be a slave of your passions. Excuse me to
Virginia, I think it's as well I don't see her now.

GALILEO   The dowry is at your disposal at any time.

LUDOVICO   Good afternoon. (*He goes followed by the Servant*)

ANDREA   Exit Ludovico. To hell with all Marsilis, Villanis, Orsinis, Canes, Nuccolis, Soldanieris. . . .

FEDERZONI   . . . who ordered the earth stand still because their castles might be shaken loose if it revolves . . .

LITTLE MONK   . . . and who only kiss the Pope's feet as long as he uses them to trample on the people. God made the physical world, God made the human brain. God will allow physics.

ANDREA   They will try to stop us.

GALILEO   Thus we enter the observation of these spots on the sun in which we are interested, at our own risk, not counting on protection from a problematical new Pope . . .

ANDREA   . . . but with great likelihood of dispelling Fabricius' vapors, and the shadows of Paris and Prague, and of establishing the rotation of the sun . . .

GALILEO   . . . and with *some* likelihood of establishing the rotation of the sun. My intention is not to prove that I was right but to find out *whether* I was right. "Abandon hope all ye who enter—an observation." Before assuming these phenomena are spots, which would suit us, let us first set about proving that they are not—fried fish. We crawl by inches. What we find today we will wipe from the blackboard tomorrow and reject it—unless it shows up again the day after tomorrow. And if we find anything which would suit us, that thing we will eye with particular distrust. In fact, we will approach this observing of the sun with the implacable determination to prove that the earth stands still and only if hopelessly defeated in this pious undertaking can we allow ourselves to wonder if we may not have been right all the time: the earth revolves. Take the cloth off the telescope and turn it on the sun.

(*Quietly they start work. When the corruscating image of the sun is focused on the screen, Virginia enters hurriedly, her wedding dress on, her hair disheveled, Mrs. Sarti with her, carrying her wedding veil. The two women realize what has happened. Virginia faints. Andrea, Little Monk and Galileo rush to her. Federzoni continues working*)

Scene Nine

On April Fool's Day, thirty two,
Of science there was much ado.
People had learned from Galilei:
They used his teaching in their way.

Around the corner from the market place a Street Singer and his Wife, who is costumed to represent the earth in a skeleton globe made of thin bands of brass, are holding the attention of a sprinkling of representative citizens, some in masquerade who were on their way to see the carnival procession. From the market place the noise of an impatient crowd.

BALLAD SINGER (*accompanied by his Wife on the guitar*)
When the Almighty made the universe
He made the earth and then he made the sun.
Then round the earth he bade the sun to turn—
That's in the Bible, Genesis, Chapter One.
And from that time all beings here below
Were in obedient circles meant to go:
    Around the pope the cardinals
    Around the cardinals the bishops
    Around the bishops the secretaries
    Around the secretaries the aldermen
    Around the aldermen the craftsmen
    Around the craftsmen the servants
    Around the servants the dogs, the chickens, and the beg-
      gars.
    (*A conspicuous reveller—henceforth called the Spinner—has slowly caught on and is exhibiting his idea of spinning around. He does not lose dignity, he faints with mock grace*)
BALLAD SINGER
Up stood the learned Galileo
Glanced briefly at the sun
And said: "Almighty God was wrong

In Genesis, Chapter One!"
 Now that was rash, my friends, it is no matter small
 For heresy will spread today like foul diseases.
 Change Holy Writ, forsooth? What will be left at all?
 Why: each of us would say and do just what he pleases!
(Three wretched Extras, employed by the chamber of commerce, enter.
Two of them, in ragged costumes, moodily bear a litter with a mock
throne. The third sits on the throne. He wears sacking, a false beard,
a prop crown, he carries a prop orb and sceptre, and around his chest
the inscription "The King of Hungary." The litter has a card with
"No. 4" written on it. The litter bearers dump him down and listen
to the Ballad Singer)

BALLAD SINGER

Good people, what will come to pass
If Galileo's teachings spread?
No altar boy will serve the mass
No servant girl will make the bed.
 Now that is grave, my friends, it is no matter small:
 For independent spirit spreads like foul diseases!
 (Yet life is sweet and man is weak and after all—
 How nice it is, for a little change, to do just as one pleases!)
(The Ballad Singer takes over the guitar. His Wife dances around
him, illustrating the motion of the earth. A Cobbler's Boy with a pair
of resplendent lacquered boots hung over his shoulder has been jumping
up and down in mock excitement. There are three more children,
dressed as grownups among the spectators, two together and a single
one with mother. The Cobbler's Boy takes the three Children in hand,
forms a chain and leads it, moving to the music, in and out among
the spectators, "whipping" the chain so that the last child bumps into
people. On the way past a Peasant Woman, he steals an egg from her
basket. She gestures to him to return it. As he passes her again he
quietly breaks the egg over her head. The King of Hungary ceremoni-
ously hands his orb to one of his bearers, marches down with mock
dignity, and chastises the Cobbler's Boy. The parents remove the three
Children. The unseemliness subsides)

BALLAD SINGER

The carpenters take wood and build
Their houses—not the church's pews.
And members of the cobblers' guild

Now boldly walk the streets—in shoes.
The tenant kicks the noble lord
Quite off the land he owned—like that!
The milk his wife once gave the priest
Now makes (at last!) her children fat.
  Ts, ts, ts, ts, my friends, this is no matter small
  For independent spirit spreads like foul diseases
  People must keep their place, some down and some on top!
  (Though it is nice, for a little change, to do just as one
  pleases!)
(*The Cobbler's Boy has put on the lacquered boots he was carrying.
He struts off. The Ballad Singer takes over the guitar again. His Wife
dances around him in increased tempo. A Monk has been standing
near a rich Couple, who are in subdued costly clothes, without masks:
shocked at the song, he now leaves. A Dwarf in the costume of an
astronomer turns his telescope on the departing Monk, thus drawing
attention to the rich Couple. In imitation of the Cobbler's Boy, the
Spinner forms a chain of grownups. They move to the music, in and
out, and between the rich Couple. The Spinner changes the Gentleman's bonnet for the ragged hat of a Beggar. The Gentleman decides
to take this in good part, and a Girl is emboldened to take his dagger.
The Gentleman is miffed, throws the Beggar's hat back. The Beggar
discards the Gentleman's bonnet and drops it on the ground. The King
of Hungary has walked from his throne, taken an egg from the
Peasant Woman, and paid for it. He now ceremoniously breaks it
over the Gentleman's head as he is bending down to pick up his bonnet.
The Gentleman conducts the Lady away from the scene. The King of
Hungary, about to resume his throne, finds one of the Children sitting
on it. The Gentleman returns to retrieve his dagger. Merriment. The
Ballad Singer wanders off. This is part of his routine. His Wife sings
to the Spinner*)*
WIFE
Now speaking for myself I feel
That I could also do with a change.
You know, for me . . . (*Turning to a reveller*) . . . *you* have appeal
Maybe tonight we could arrange . . .
(*The Dwarf-Astronomer has been amusing the people by focusing his
telescope on her legs. The Ballad Singer has returned*)

BALLAD SINGER
No, no, no, no, no, stop, Galileo, stop!
For independent spirit spreads like foul diseases
People must keep their place, some down and some on top!
(Though it is nice, for a little change, to do just as one pleases!)
(*The Spectators stand embarrassed. A Girl laughs loudly*)
BALLAD SINGER AND HIS WIFE
Good people who have trouble here below
In serving cruel lords and gentle Jesus
Who bids you turn the other cheek just so . . . (*With mimicry*)
While they prepare to strike the second blow:
Obedience will never cure your woe
So each of you wake up and do just as he pleases!
(*The Ballad Singer and his Wife hurriedly start to try to sell pamphlets to the spectators*)
BALLAD SINGER   Read all about the earth going round the sun, two centesimi only. As proved by the great Galileo. Two centesimi only. Written by a local scholar. Understandable to one and all. Buy one for your friends, your children and your aunty Rosa, two centesimi only. Abbreviated but complete. Fully illustrated with pictures of the planets, including Venus, two centesimi only.
(*During the speech of the Ballad Singer we hear the carnival procession approaching followed by laughter. A Reveller rushes in*)
REVELLER   The procession!
(*The litter bearers speedily joggle out the King of Hungary. The Spectators turn and look at the first float of the procession, which now makes its appearance. It bears a gigantic figure of Galileo, holding in one hand an open Bible with the pages crossed out. The other hand points to the Bible, and the head mechanically turns from side to side as if to say "No! No!"*)
A LOUD VOICE   Galileo, the Bible killer!
(*The laughter from the market place becomes uproarious. The Monk comes flying from the market place followed by delighted Children*)

Scene Ten

The depths are hot, the heights are chill
The streets are loud, the court is still.

Ante-Chamber and staircase in the Medicean palace in Florence.
Galileo, with a book under his arm, waits with his Daughter to be
admitted to the presence of the Prince.

VIRGINIA   They are a long time.

GALILEO   Yes.

VIRGINIA   Who is that funny looking man? (*She indicates the In-*
former who has entered casually and seated himself in the background,
taking no apparent notice of Galileo)

GALILEO   I don't know.

VIRGINIA   It's not the first time I have seen him around. He
gives me the creeps.

GALILEO   Nonsense. We're in Florence, not among robbers in
the mountains of Corsica.

VIRGINIA   Here comes the Rector.

(*The Rector comes down the stairs*)

GALILEO   Gaffone is a bore. He attaches himself to you.

(*The Rector passes, scarcely nodding*)

GALILEO   My eyes are bad today. Did he acknowledge us?

VIRGINIA   Barely. (*Pause*) What's in your book? Will they say it's
heretical?

GALILEO   You hang around church too much. And getting up
at dawn and scurrying to mass is ruining your skin. You pray
for me, don't you?

(*A Man comes down the stairs*)

VIRGINIA   Here's Mr. Matti. You designed a machine for his
Iron Foundries.

MATTI   How were the squabs, Mr. Galilei? (*Low*) My brother
and I had a good laugh the other day. He picked up a racy
pamphlet against the Bible somewhere. It quoted you.

GALILEO   The squabs, Matti, were wonderful, thank you again. Pamphlets I know nothing about. The Bible and Homer are my favorite reading.

MATTI   No necessity to be cautious with me, Mr. Galilei. I am on your side. I am not a man who knows about the motions of the stars, but you have championed the freedom to teach new things. Take that mechanical cultivator they have in Germany which you described to me. I can tell you, it will never be used in this country. The same circles that are hampering you now will forbid the physicians at Bologna to cut up corpses for research. Do you know, they have such things as money markets in Amsterdam and in London? Schools for business, too. Regular papers with news. Here we are not even free to make money. I have a stake in your career. They are against iron foundries because they say the gathering of so many workers in one place fosters immorality! If they ever try anything, Mr. Galilei, remember you have friends in all walks of life including an iron founder. Good luck to you. (*He goes*)

GALILEO   Good man, but need he be so affectionate in public? His voice carries. They will always claim me as their spiritual leader particularly in places where it doesn't help me at all. I have written a book about the mechanics of the firmament, that is all. What they do or don't do with it is not my concern.

VIRGINIA (*loud*)   If people only knew how you disagreed with those goings-on all over the country last All Fools day.

GALILEO   Yes. Offer honey to a bear, and lose your arm if the beast is hungry.

VIRGINIA (*low*)   Did the prince ask you to come here today?

GALILEO   I sent word I was coming. He will want the book, he has paid for it. My health hasn't been any too good lately. I may accept Sagredo's invitation to stay with him in Padua for a few weeks.

VIRGINIA   You couldn't manage without your books.

GALILEO   Sagredo has an excellent library.

VIRGINIA   We haven't had this month's salary yet—

GALILEO   Yes. (*The Cardinal Inquisitor passes down the staircase. He bows deeply in answer to Galileo's bow*) What is he doing in Florence? If they try to do anything to me, the new Pope will meet them with an iron NO. And the Prince is my pupil, he would never have me extradited.

VIRGINIA   Psst. The Lord Chamberlain.

(*The Lord Chamberlain comes down the stairs*)

LORD CHAMBERLAIN   His Highness had hoped to find time for you, Mr. Galilei. Unfortunately, he has to leave immediately to judge the parade at the Riding Academy. On what business did you wish to see His Highness?

GALILEO   I wanted to present my book to His Highness.

LORD CHAMBERLAIN   How are your eyes today?

GALILEO   So, so. With His Highness' permission, I am dedicating the book . . .

LORD CHAMBERLAIN   Your eyes are a matter of great concern to His Highness. Could it be that you have been looking too long and too often through your marvelous tube? (*He leaves without accepting the book*)

VIRGINIA (*greatly agitated*)   Father, I am afraid.

GALILEO   He didn't take the book, did he? (*Low and resolute*) Keep a straight face. We are not going home, but to the house of the lens-grinder. There is a coach and horses in his backyard. Keep your eyes to the front, don't look back at that man. (*They start. The Lord Chamberlain comes back*)

LORD CHAMBERLAIN   Oh, Mr. Galilei, His Highness has just charged me to inform you that the Florentine Court is no longer in a position to oppose the request of the Holy Inquisition to interrogate you in Rome.

Scene Eleven

The Pope

A chamber in the Vatican. The Pope, Urban VIII—formerly Cardinal Barberini—is giving audience to the Cardinal Inquisitor. The trampling and shuffling of many feet is heard throughout the scene from the adjoining corridors. During the scene the Pope is being robed for the conclave he is about to attend: at the beginning of the scene he is plainly Barberini, but as the scene proceeds he is more and more obscured by grandiose vestments.

POPE   No! No! No!

INQUISITOR (*referring to the owners of the shuffling feet*)   Doctors of all chairs from the universities, representatives of the special orders of the Church, representatives of the clergy as a whole who have come believing with child-like faith in the word of God as set forth in the Scriptures, who have come to hear Your Holiness confirm their faith: and Your Holiness is really going to tell them that the Bible can no longer be regarded as the alphabet of truth?

POPE   I will not set myself up against the multiplication table. No!

INQUISITOR   Ah, that is what these people say, that it is the multiplication table. Their cry is, "The figures compel us," but where do these figures come from? Plainly they come from doubt. These men doubt everything. Can society stand on doubt and not on faith? "Thou art my master, but I doubt whether it is for the best." "This is my neighbor's house and my neighbor's wife, but why shouldn't they belong to me?" After the plague, after the new war, after the unparalleled disaster of the Reformation, your dwindling flock look to their shepherd, and now the mathematicians turn their tubes on the sky and announce to the world that you have not the best advice about the heavens either—up to now your only uncontested sphere of influence. This Galilei started meddling in machines at an early age. Now that men in ships are venturing on the great oceans—I am not against that of course—they are putting their faith in a brass bowl they call a compass and not in Almighty God.

POPE   This man is the greatest physicist of our time. He is the light of Italy, and not just any muddle-head.

INQUISITOR   Would we have had to arrest him otherwise? This bad man knows what he is doing, not writing his books in Latin, but in the jargon of the market place.

POPE (*occupied with the shuffling feet*)   That was not in the best of taste. (*A pause*) These shuffling feet are making me nervous.

INQUISITOR   May they be more telling than my words, Your Holiness. Shall all these go from you with doubt in their hearts?

POPE   This man has friends. What about Versailles? What about the Viennese court? They will call Holy Church a cesspool for defunct ideas. Keep your hands off him.

INQUISITOR   In practice it will never get far. He is a man of the flesh. He would soften at once.

POPE   He has more enjoyment in him than any man I ever saw. He loves eating and drinking and thinking. To excess. He indulges in thinking-bouts! He cannot say no to an old wine or a new thought. (*Furious*) I do not want a condemnation of physical facts. I do not want to hear battle cries: Church, church, church! Reason, reason, reason! (*Pause*) These shuffling feet are intolerable. Has the whole world come to my door?

INQUISITOR   Not the whole world, Your Holiness. A select gathering of the faithful.

(*Pause*)

POPE   (*exhausted*)   It is clearly understood: he is not to be tortured. (*Pause*) At the very most, he may be shown the instruments.

INQUISITOR   That will be adequate, Your Holiness. Mr. Galilei understands machinery.

(*The eyes of Barberini look helplessly at the Cardinal Inquisitor from under the completely assembled panoply of Pope Urban VIII*)

Scene Twelve

June twenty second, sixteen thirty three,
A momentous date for you and me.
Of all the days that was the one
An age of reason could have begun.

Again the garden of the Florentine Ambassador at Rome, where Galileo's assistants wait the news of the trial. The Little Monk and Federzoni are attempting to concentrate on a game of chess. Virginia kneels in a corner, praying and counting her beads.

LITTLE MONK The Pope didn't even grant him an audience.

FEDERZONI No more scientific discussions.

ANDREA The "Discorsi" will never be finished. The sum of his findings. They will kill him.

FEDERZONI (*stealing a glance at him*) Do you really think so?

ANDREA He will never recant.

(*Silence*)

LITTLE MONK You know when you lie awake at night how your mind fastens on to something irrelevant. Last night I kept thinking: if only they would let him take his little stone in with him, the appeal-to-reason-pebble that he always carried in his pocket.

FEDERZONI In the room *they'll* take him to, he won't have a pocket.

ANDREA But he will not recant.

LITTLE MONK How can they beat the truth out of a man who gave his sight in order to see?

FEDERZONI Maybe they can't.

(*Silence*)

ANDREA (*speaking about Virginia*) She is praying that he will recant.

FEDERZONI   Leave her alone. She doesn't know whether she's on her head or on her heels since they got hold of her. They brought her Father Confessor from Florence.
(*The Informer of Scene Ten enters*)
INFORMER   Mr. Galilei will be here soon. He may need a bed.
FEDERZONI   Have they let him out?
INFORMER   Mr. Galilei is expected to recant at five o'clock. The big bell of Saint Marcus will be rung and the complete text of his recantation publicly announced.
ANDREA   I don't believe it.
INFORMER   Mr. Galilei will be brought to the garden gate at the back of the house, to avoid the crowds collecting in the streets. (*He goes*)
(*Silence*)
ANDREA   The moon is an earth because the light of the moon is not her own. Jupiter is a fixed star, and four moons turn around Jupiter, therefore we are not shut in by crystal shells. The sun is the pivot of our world, therefore the earth is not the center. The earth moves, spinning about the sun. And he showed us. You can't make a man unsee what he has seen.
(*Silence*)
FEDERZONI   Five o'clock is one minute.
(*Virginia prays louder*)
ANDREA   Listen all of you, they are murdering the truth.
(*He stops up his ears with his fingers. The two other pupils do the same. Federzoni goes over the Little Monk, and all of them stand absolutely still in cramped positions. Nothing happens. No bell sounds. After a silence, filled with the murmur of Virginia's prayers, Federzoni runs to the wall to look at the clock. He turns around, his expression changed. He shakes his head. They drop their hands*)
FEDERZONI   No. No bell. It is three minutes after.
LITTLE MONK   He hasn't.
ANDREA   He held true. It is all right, it is all right.
LITTLE MONK   He did not recant.
FEDERZONI   No.
(*They embrace each other, they are delirious with joy*)
ANDREA   So force cannot accomplish everything. What has been seen can't be unseen. Man is constant in the face of death.

FEDERZONI   June 22, 1633: dawn of the age of reason. I wouldn't have wanted to go on living if he had recanted.

LITTLE MONK   I didn't say anything, but I was in agony. Oh, ye of little faith!

ANDREA   I was sure.

FEDERZONI   It would have turned our morning to night.

ANDREA   It would have been as if the mountain had turned to water.

LITTLE MONK (*kneeling down, crying*)   Oh God, I thank Thee.

ANDREA   Beaten humanity can lift its head. A man has stood up and said "no."

(*At this moment the bell of Saint Marcus begins to toll. They stand like statues. Virginia stands up*)

VIRGINIA   The bell of Saint Marcus. He is not damned.

(*From the street one hears the Town Crier reading Galileo's recantation*)

TOWN CRIER   I, Galileo Galilei, Teacher of Mathematics and Physics, do hereby publicly renounce my teaching that the earth moves. I foreswear this teaching with a sincere heart and unfeigned faith and detest and curse this and all other errors and heresies repugnant to the Holy Scriptures.

(*The lights dim; when they come up again the bell of Saint Marcus is petering out. Virginia has gone but the Scholars are still there waiting*)

ANDREA (*loud*)   The mountain did turn to water.

(*Galileo has entered quietly and unnoticed. He is changed, almost unrecognizable. He has heard Andrea. He waits some seconds by the door for somebody to greet him. Nobody does. They retreat from him. He goes slowly and, because of his bad sight, uncertainly, to the front of the stage where he finds a chair, and sits down*)

ANDREA   I can't look at him. Tell him to go away.

FEDERZONI   Steady.

ANDREA (*hysterically*)   He saved his big gut.

FEDERZONI   Get him a glass of water.

(*The Little Monk fetches a glass of water for Andrea. Nobody acknowledges the presence of Galileo, who sits silently on his chair listening to the voice of the Town Crier, now in another street*)

ANDREA   I can walk. Just help me a bit.

(*They help him to the door*)

ANDREA (*in the door*)   "Unhappy is the land that breeds no hero."
GALILEO   No, Andrea: "Unhappy is the land that needs a hero."

(Before the next scene a curtain with the following legend on it is lowered)

You can plainly see that if a horse were to fall from a height of three or four feet, it could break its bones, whereas a dog would not suffer injury. The same applies to a cat from a height of as much as eight or ten feet, to a grasshopper from the top of a tower, and to an ant falling down from the moon. Nature could not allow a horse to become as big as twenty horses nor a giant as big as ten men, unless she were to change the proportions of all its members, particularly the bones. Thus the common assumption that great and small structures are equally tough is obviously wrong.

—From the "Discorsi"

Scene Thirteen

1633–1642.
Galileo Galilei remains a prisoner
of the Inquisition until his death.

A country house near Florence. A large room simply furnished. There is a huge table, a leather chair, a globe of the world on a stand, and a narrow bed. A portion of the adjoining anteroom is visible, and the front door which opens into it. An Official of the Inquisition sits on guard in the anteroom. In the large room, Galileo is quietly experimenting with a bent wooden rail and a small ball of wood. He is still vigorous but almost blind. After a while there is a knocking at the outside door. The Official opens it to a peasant who brings a plucked goose. Virginia comes from the kitchen. She is past forty.

PEASANT (*handing the goose to Virginia*) I was told to deliver this here.
VIRGINIA I didn't order a goose.
PEASANT I was told to say it's from someone who was passing through.
  (*Virginia takes the goose, surprised. The Official takes it from her and examines it suspiciously. Then, reassured, he hands it back to her. The Peasant goes. Virginia brings the goose in to Galileo*)
VIRGINIA Somebody who was passing through sent you something.
GALILEO What is it?
VIRGINIA Can't you see it?
GALILEO No. (*He walks over*) A goose. Any name?
VIRGINIA No.
GALILEO (*weighing the goose*) Solid.
VIRGINIA (*cautiously*) Will you eat the liver, if I have it cooked with a little apple?

GALILEO I had my dinner. Are you under orders to finish me off with food?

VIRGINIA It's not rich. And what is wrong with your eyes again? You should be able to see it.

GALILEO You were standing in the light.

VIRGINIA I was not.—You haven't been writing again?

GALILEO (*sneering*) What do you think?

(*Virginia takes the goose out into the anteroom and speaks to the Official*)

VIRGINIA You had better ask Monsignor Carpula to send the doctor. Father couldn't see this goose across the room.— Don't look at me like that. He has not been writing. He dictates everything to me, as you know.

OFFICIAL Yes?

VIRGINIA He abides by the rules. My father's repentance is sincere. I keep an eye on him. (*She hands him the goose*) Tell the cook to fry the liver with an apple and an onion. (*She goes back into the large room*) And you have no business to be doing that with those eyes of yours, father.

GALILEO You may read me some Horace.

VIRGINIA We should go on with your weekly letter to the Archbishop. Monsignor Carpula to whom we owe so much was all smiles the other day because the Archbishop had expressed his pleasure at your collaboration.

GALILEO Where were we?

VIRGINIA (*sits down to take his dictation*) Paragraph four.

GALILEO Read what you have.

VIRGINIA "The position of the Church in the matter of the unrest at Genoa. I agree with Cardinal Spoletti in the matter of the unrest among the Venetian ropemakers . . ."

GALILEO Yes. (*Dictates*) I agree with Cardinal Spoletti in the matter of the unrest among the Venetian ropemakers: it is better to distribute good nourishing food in the name of charity than to pay them more for their bellropes. It being surely better to strengthen their faith than to encourage their acquisitiveness. St. Paul says: Charity never faileth. — How is that?

VIRGINIA It's beautiful, father.

GALILEO It couldn't be taken as irony?

VIRGINIA   No. The Archbishop will like it. It's so practical.

GALILEO   I trust your judgment. Read it over slowly.

VIRGINIA   "The position of the Church in the matter of the unrest . . ."

(There is a knocking at the outside door. Virginia goes into the anteroom. The Official opens the door. It is Andrea)

ANDREA   Good evening. I am sorry to call so late, I'm on my way to Holland. I was asked to look him up. Can I go in?

VIRGINIA   I don't know whether he will see you. You never came.

ANDREA   Ask him.

(Galileo recognizes the voice. He sits motionless. Virginia comes in to Galileo)

GALILEO   Is that Andrea?

VIRGINIA   Yes. *(Pause)* I will send him away.

GALILEO   Show him in.

(Virginia shows Andrea in. Virginia sits, Andrea remains standing)

ANDREA *(cool)*   Have you been keeping well, Mr. Galilei?

GALILEO   Sit down. What are you doing these days? What are you working on? I heard it was something about hydraulics in Milan.

ANDREA   As he knew I was passing through, Fabricius of Amsterdam asked me to visit you and inquire about your health. *(Pause)*

GALILEO   I am very well.

ANDREA *(formally)*   I am glad I can report you are in good health.

GALILEO   Fabricius will be glad to hear it. And you might inform him that, on account of the depth of my repentance, I live in comparative comfort.

ANDREA   Yes, we understand that the church is more than pleased with you. Your complete acceptance has had its effect. Not one paper expounding a new thesis has made its appearance in Italy since your submission. *(Pause)*

GALILEO   Unfortunately there are countries not under the wing of the church. Would you not say the erroneous condemned theories are still taught—there?

ANDREA *(relentless)*   Things are almost at a standstill.

GALILEO   Are they? (*Pause*) Nothing from Descartes in Paris?

ANDREA   Yes. On receiving the news of your recantation, he shelved his treatise on the nature of light.

GALILEO   I sometimes worry about my assistants whom I led into error. Have they benefited by my example?

ANDREA   In order to work I have to go to Holland.

GALILEO   Yes.

ANDREA   Federzoni is grinding lenses again, back in some shop.

GALILEO   He can't read the books.

ANDREA   Fulganzio, our little monk, has abandoned research and is resting in peace in the church.

GALILEO   So. (*Pause*) My superiors are looking forward to my spiritual recovery. I am progressing as well as can be expected.

VIRGINIA   You are doing well, father.

GALILEO   Virginia, leave the room.

(*Virginia rises uncertainly and goes out*)

VIRGINIA (*to the Official*)   He was his pupil, so now he is his enemy.—Help me in the kitchen.

(*She leaves the anteroom with the Official*)

ANDREA   May I go now, sir?

GALILEO   I do not know why you came, Sarti. To unsettle me? I have to be prudent.

ANDREA   I'll be on my way.

GALILEO   As it is, I have relapses. I completed the "Discorsi."

ANDREA   You completed what?

GALILEO   My "Discorsi."

ANDREA   How?

GALILEO   I am allowed pen and paper. My superiors are intelligent men. They know the habits of a lifetime cannot be broken abruptly. But they protect me from any unpleasant consequences: they lock my pages away as I dictate them. And I should know better than to risk my comfort. I wrote the "Discorsi" out again during the night. The manuscript is in the globe. My vanity has up to now prevented me from destroying it. If you consider taking it, you will shoulder the entire risk. You will say it was pirated from the original in the hands of the Holy Office.

(*Andrea, as in a trance, has gone to the globe. He lifts the upper half and gets the book. He turns the pages as if wanting to devour them. In the background the opening sentences of the "Discorsi" appear:* MY PURPOSE IS TO SET FORTH A VERY NEW SCIENCE DEALING WITH A VERY ANCIENT SUBJECT—MOTION. . . . AND I HAVE DISCOVERED BY EXPERIMENT SOME PROPERTIES OF IT WHICH ARE WORTH KNOWING. . . .)

GALILEO   I had to employ my time somehow.

(*The text disappears*)

ANDREA   Two new sciences! This will be the foundation stone of a new physics.

GALILEO   Yes. Put it under your coat.

ANDREA   And we thought you had deserted. (*In a low voice*) Mr. Galilei, how can I begin to express my shame. Mine has been the loudest voice against you.

GALILEO   That would seem to have been proper. I taught you science and I decried the truth.

ANDREA   Did you? I think not. Everything is changed!

GALILEO   What is changed?

ANDREA   You shielded the truth from the oppressor. Now I see! In your dealings with the Inquisition you used the same superb common sense you brought to physics.

GALILEO   Oh!

ANDREA   We lost our heads. With the crowd at the street corners we said: "He will die, he will never surrender!" You came back: "I surrendered but I am alive." We cried: "Your hands are stained!" You say: "Better stained than empty."

GALILEO   "Better stained than empty."—It sounds realistic. Sounds like me.

ANDREA   And I of all people should have known. I was twelve when you sold another man's telescope to the Venetian Senate, and saw you put it to immortal use. Your friends were baffled when you bowed to the Prince of Florence: Science gained a wider audience. You always laughed at heroics. "People who suffer bore me," you said. "Misfortunes are due mainly to miscalculations." And: "If there are obstacles, the shortest line between two points may be the crooked line."

GALILEO   It makes a picture.

ANDREA   And when you stooped to recant in 1633, I should have understood that you were again about your business.

GALILEO   My business being?

ANDREA   Science. The study of the properties of motion, mother of the machines which will themselves change the ugly face of the earth.

GALILEO   Aha!

ANDREA   You gained time to write a book that only you could write. Had you burned at the stake in a blaze of glory they would have won.

GALILEO   They have won. And there is no such thing as a scientific work that only one man can write.

ANDREA   Then why did you recant, tell me that!

GALILEO   I recanted because I was afraid of physical pain.

ANDREA   No!

GALILEO   They showed me the instruments.

ANDREA   It was not a plan?

GALILEO   It was not.

(*Pause*)

ANDREA   But you have contributed. Science has only one commandment: contribution. And you have contributed more than any man for a hundred years.

GALILEO   Have I? Then welcome to my gutter, dear colleague in science and brother in treason: I sold out, you are a buyer. The first sight of the book! His mouth watered and his scoldings were drowned. Blessed be our bargaining, whitewashing, deathfearing community!

ANDREA   The fear of death is human.

GALILEO   Even the church will teach you that to be weak is not human. It is just evil.

ANDREA   The church, yes! But science is not concerned with our weaknesses.

GALILEO   No? My dear Sarti, in spite of my present convictions, I may be able to give you a few pointers as to the concerns of your chosen profession.

(*Enter Virginia with a platter*)

In my spare time, I happen to have gone over this case. I have spare time.—Even a man who sells wool, however good he is at buying wool cheap and selling it dear, must be concerned with the standing of the wool trade. The practice of science would seem to call for valor. She trades in knowledge, which is the product of doubt. And this new art of doubt has enchanted the public. The plight of the multitude is old as the rocks, and is believed to be basic as the rocks. But now they have learned to doubt. They snatched the telescopes out of our hands and had them trained on their tormentors: prince, official, public moralist. The mechanism of the heavens was clearer, the mechanism of their courts was still murky. The battle to measure the heavens is won by doubt; by credulity the Roman housewife's battle for milk will always be lost. Word is passed down that this is of no concern to the scientist who is told he will only release such of his findings as do not disturb the peace, that is, the peace of mind of the well-to-do. Threats and bribes fill the air. Can the scientist hold out on the numbers?—For what reason do you labor? I take it the intent of science is to ease human existence. If you give way to coercion, science can be crippled, and your new machines may simply suggest new drudgeries. Should you then, in time, discover all there is to be discovered, your progress must then become a progress away from the bulk of humanity. The gulf might even grow so wide that the sound of your cheering at some new achievement would be echoed by a universal howl of horror.—As a scientist I had an almost unique opportunity. In my day astronomy emerged into the market place. At that particular time, had one man put up a fight, it could have had wide repercussions. I have come to believe that I was never in real danger; for some years I was as strong as the authorities, and I surrendered my knowledge to the powers that be, to use it, no, not *use* it, *abuse* it, as it suits their ends. I have betrayed my profession. Any man who does what I have done must not be tolerated in the ranks of science.

(*Virginia, who has stood motionless, puts the platter on the table*)

VIRGINIA   You are accepted in the ranks of the faithful, father.

GALILEO (*sees her*)   Correct. (*He goes over to the table*) I have to eat now.

VIRGINIA   We lock up at eight.

ANDREA   I am glad I came. (*He extends his hand. Galileo ignores it and goes over to his meal*)

GALILEO (*examining the plate; to Andrea*) Somebody who knows me sent me a goose. I still enjoy eating.

ANDREA And your opinion is now that the "new age" was an illusion?

GALILEO Well.—This age of ours turned out to be a whore, spattered with blood. Maybe, new ages look like blood-spattered whores. Take care of yourself.

ANDREA Yes. (*Unable to go*) With reference to your evaluation of the author in question—I do not know the answer. But I cannot think that your savage analysis is the last word.

GALILEO Thank you, sir.

(*Official knocks at the door*)

VIRGINIA (*showing Andrea out*) I don't like visitors from the past, they excite him.

(*She lets him out. The Official closes the iron door. Virginia returns*)

GALILEO (*eating*) Did you try and think who sent the goose?

VIRGINIA Not Andrea.

GALILEO Maybe not. I gave Redhead his first lesson; when he held out his hand, I had to remind myself he is teaching now. —How is the sky tonight?

VIRGINIA (*at the window*) Bright.

(*Galileo continues eating*)

Scene Fourteen

The great book o'er the border went
And, good folk, that was the end.
But we hope you'll keep in mind
You and I were left behind.

Before a little Italian customs house early in the morning. Andrea sits upon one of his traveling trunks at the barrier and reads Galileo's book. The window of a small house is still lit, and a big grotesque shadow, like an old witch and her cauldron, falls upon the house wall beyond. Barefoot children in rags see it and point to the little house.

CHILDREN (*singing*)
  One, two, three, four, five, six,
  Old Marina is a witch.
  At night, on a broomstick she sits
  And on the church steeple she spits.

CUSTOMS OFFICER (*to Andrea*) Why are you making this journey?

ANDREA I am a scholar.

CUSTOMS OFFICER (*to his Clerk*) Put down under "reason for leaving the country": Scholar. (*He points to the baggage*) Books! Anything dangerous in these books?

ANDREA What is dangerous?

CUSTOMS OFFICER Religion. Politics.

ANDREA These are nothing but mathematical formulas.

CUSTOMS OFFICER What's that?

ANDREA Figures.

CUSTOMS OFFICER Oh, figures. No harm in figures. Just wait a minute, sir, we will soon have your papers stamped. (*He exits with Clerk*)

(*Meanwhile, a little council of war among the Children has taken place. Andrea quietly watches. One of the Boys, pushed forward by the others, creeps up to the little house from which the shadow comes, and takes the jug of milk on the doorstep*)

ANDREA (*quietly*)   What are you doing with that milk?

BOY (*stopping in mid-movement*)   She is a witch.

(*The other Children run away behind the Custom House. One of them shouts*) "Run, Paolo!"

ANDREA   Hmm!—And because she is a witch she mustn't have milk. Is that the idea?

BOY   Yes.

ANDREA   And how do you know she is a witch?

BOY (*points to shadow on house wall*)   Look!

ANDREA   Oh! I see.

BOY   And she rides on a broomstick at night—and she bewitches the coachman's horses. My cousin Luigi looked through the hole in the stable roof, that the snow storm made, and heard the horses coughing something terrible.

ANDREA   Oh!—How big was the hole in the stable roof?

BOY   Luigi didn't tell. Why?

ANDREA   I was asking because maybe the horses got sick because it was cold in the stable. You had better ask Luigi how big that hole is.

BOY   You are not going to say Old Marina isn't a witch, because you can't.

ANDREA   No, I can't say she isn't a witch. I haven't looked into it. A man can't know about a thing he hasn't looked into, or can he?

BOY   No!—But THAT! (*He points to the shadow*) She is stirring hell-broth.

ANDREA   Let's see. Do you want to take a look? I can lift you up.

BOY   You lift me to the window, mister! (*He takes a sling shot out of his pocket*) I can really bash her from there.

ANDREA   Hadn't we better make sure she is a witch before we shoot? I'll hold that.

(*The Boy puts the milk jug down and follows him reluctantly to the window. Andrea lifts the boy up so that he can look in*)

ANDREA   What do you see?

BOY (*slowly*)   Just an old girl cooking porridge.

ANDREA   Oh! Nothing to it then. Now look at her shadow, Paolo.

(*The Boy looks over his shoulder and back and compares the reality and the shadow*)

BOY   The big thing is a soup ladle.

ANDREA   Ah! A ladle! You see, I would have taken it for a broomstick, but I haven't looked into the matter as you have, Paolo. Here is your sling.

CUSTOMS OFFICER (*returning with the Clerk and handing Andrea his papers*)   All present and correct. Good luck, sir.

(*Andrea goes, reading Galileo's book. The Clerk starts to bring his baggage after him. The barrier rises. Andrea passes through, still reading the book. The Boy kicks over the milk jug*)

BOY (*shouting after Andrea*)   She *is* a witch! She *is* a witch!

ANDREA   You saw with your own eyes: think it over!

(*The Boy joins the others. They sing*)

One, two, three, four, five, six,
Old Marina is a witch.
At night, on a broomstick she sits
And on the church steeple she spits.

(*The Customs Officers laugh. Andrea goes*)